THE POLITICS OF THE AMERICAN CIVIL LIBERTIES UNION

THE POLITICS OF
THE AMERICAN
CIVIL LIBERTIES UNION

WILLIAM A. DONOHUE

With a Foreword by

Aaron Wildavsky

Transaction Books
New Brunswick (U.S.A.) and Oxford (U.K.)

Second printing 1985

Copyright © 1985 by Transaction, Inc.
New Brunswick, New Jersey 08903

Library of Congress Catalog Number: 84-16235
ISBN: 0-88738-021-2 (cloth), 0-87855-983-3 (paper)
Printed in the United States of America

Library of Congress Cataloging in Publication Data

Donohue, William A., 1947-
    The politics of the American Civil Liberties Union.

    Includes index.
    1. American Civil Liberties Union. I. Title.
JC599.U5D66 1985   323.4'06'073   84-16235
ISBN 0-88738-021-2
ISBN 0-87855-983-3 (pbk.)

For my mother
Anna Marie Donohue
and to the memory of my grandparents
Patrick and Abbie Flynn

Contents

Foreword: The Reverse Sequence in Civil Liberties

Aaron Wildavsky

For a number of years I belonged to the American Civil Liberties Union. To me this membership was part of a commitment to perfecting American democracy. I became a political scientist for the same reason. The two commitments—American patriotism and democratic values—went together. By improving the one, the procedures for participation in political life through protection of individual liberty, the other, the United States as a force for freedom at home and in the world, would also be enhanced. The combination of a strong national defense, social welfare programs, and civil liberties, as exemplified in the 1940s and 1950s by the New York State Liberal party (in whose youth division I was active) seemed mutually reinforcing. But that combination, however comforting it seemed in the Eisenhower years, was not to last long.

In the early 1960s, while teaching politics at Oberlin College in Ohio, I served for a couple of years on the executive committee of the local ACLU. It was not easy, given our interest in procedures per se, to find violations of proper practice in a liberal college town. By moving a few miles away, however, we could come up with a couple of cases of unreasonable search or a few days of possibly unlawful detention. In retrospect, it was an innocent time and I know now, from having read William A. Donohue's *The Politics of the American Civil Liberties Union*, that it was, for me at least, a time of naiveté as well.

The ACLU was never what I thought it was, an organization standing up for people whose civil liberties were threatened by the passions of the time. The ACLU has always been what Donohue says it is: an organization committed to a shifting agenda of substantive policy change as dictated by the political perspectives of its most active members.

Nor was the ACLU what its "purist" members thought, to refer back to its name, a union of people concerned primarily with civil liberties. Whether it was support for unions in the 1920s and 1930s, or the New

Deal-Fair Deal social welfare agenda of the 1940s and 1950s, or its devotion to equal outcomes since the 1960s, the ACLU has viewed civil liberties, so Donohue shows, as instrumental to other purposes.

Starting somewhere in the mid-1960s, it became apparent to me that I was out of sympathy with the ACLU. Either it had changed, as I then thought, or I had changed, or both, as reflecting on *The Politics of the ACLU* has led me to believe. Naturally, saddened by the loss of a sympathetic association, even, to an extent, a source of identity, I wondered what had happened to it or to me. For this reason, facing up to this unwanted rite of passage, I read Donohue's manuscript with interest and recommended it to Transaction Books when it appeared too controversial for other publishers.

The book has substantial merits. The greatest among these, in my opinion, is its ethnography, what Clifford Geertz calls "thick description," of ACLU's history. Donohue's account is believable. There is enough there, including extensive interviews and documentary sources hitherto not used, to give one a feeling for the texture of organizational life. Donohue has chosen to take on the ACLU on its own terms. He is, in his way, as engaged as are the leaders of the ACLU. This combative stance serves the spirit of the enterprise, meeting as it does the ACLU on its own battlefield of the substance of issues such as affirmative action, church-state relations, and the rival rights of criminals and their victims. Well met, fairly fought, and may the best civil libertarian win!

There are also weaknesses inherent in these strengths. Though the admixture of strong personal judgment with the historian's craft of reconstruction has its charm—a fighter's book about a feisty organization—it may put off people who identify with the ACLU and who, as they consider renewing their commitment, need to know a lot more about the past and current history of the ACLU than has been known until now. That rejection would be a pity because the book does contain enough evidence to support diverse interpretations. Had Donohue refused to soil himself by wrestling in the muck of contemporary disputes about such contentious matters as abortion, and poverty as a denial of civil liberty, he might have seemed more objective, if at the cost of cowardice. The path Donohue has taken, however, has led him away from the study of the ACLU as only one of a species of the larger genus of organizations ordinarily called interest groups.

To say that organizations must adapt to a changing environment is a cliché. The ACLU is anomalous only in that it is such a classic example of the very spirit—absorption into the dominant values of the time—that the naive like myself once thought it was supposed to counter in favor of eternal verities.

When a group organizes to make demands on government to support the group's economic self-interest, no one is surprised that organizational doctrines change as a means of securing the substantive end of increasing its income. That large oil companies should favor market forces when these produce high prices, and governmental allocation when gluts produce low prices, raises few eyebrows. For organizations devoted to the betterment of humankind, like the March of Dimes, to seek new diseases to conquer after polio declined, has been a subject of mild amusement. For the ACLU to reorient its position on fundamental issues radically decade by decade, so that there is little relationship between what it said fifty years ago and what it says today is more surprising. Yet this, Donohue demonstrates, is exactly what has happened. Quotas, anathema in the past, now have become desirable as a form of positive discrimination. (Who remembers when the ACLU taught that the Constitution was color blind?) Balancing competing values, order in society with the rights of the accused, has given way to attacks upon authority. ("Lawlessness," the ACLU now says, ". . . is a direct consequence of the failure of the community.") In briefest compass, the ACLU, once devoted to achieving individual freedom from government restraint, has become converted to advocating governmental compulsion to achieve equality of condition. From defense of individual differences against government, ACLU has moved to diminish differences among people—White and Black, rich and poor, young and old, authority and citizen, parent and child, the list grows all the time. How did this happen?

Just as the ACLU identified itself with industrial unionization in earlier times, it has in recent years become part of the civil rights movement, the women's movement, the movement against "ageism," and other "isms" devoted to diminishing inequalities in American life. There has been no conspiracy. No one pushed me out or put the present participants in. Two things happened concurrently: activists in these other movements moved into the ACLU, and people discomforted by this trend toward support of equal results moved out. The process is self-reinforcing. New policies attract more like-minded adherents. No one has to tell the ACLU membership what to do. They can guess what equality of condition requires, and trial and error tells them what catches on with the people who flock to their cause.

At another time, ACLU's support of the right of Nazis to march in Skokie might have decimated its ranks, compelling it to alter course. And the episode did hurt; for a time membership declined substantially. But Skokie, in my estimation, also served to clear the decks of those who were attached to the deprived of the past, like Jews, and to reattach those who could identify with the wave of the future deprived. No more than Israel is considered part of the world's deprived by the Socialist International (therefore belonging to the protected species of the Third World) can a case be made that equality of condition is served by helping Jews. After all, if some groups are underrepresented on university faculties, who exactly is it that is overrepresented?

I have asked myself whether it was the decertification of Jews (or even Jewish professors) as a deprived minority that turned me off ACLU. I think not. My position and that of my friends was and is secure. My children are far from academia and my feelings changed long before "affirmative action" came on the scene.

I felt that the ACLU had turned against the United States not only as it was but as I wanted it to be. My gut feeling was that when "the system" was turned over to those who had been left out, it would no longer be worth having. There was something, some sea change in values and practices, behind these personal regrets, but at the time I was unable to objectify my reactions by placing them within a larger context. Here and now I shall try.

The Original Sequence

Americans are able to agree about the desirablity of equality because they mean different things by it. Equality before the law (or equal rights) signifies that people in similar positions will have similar legal standing, so that administrative and judicial decisions would be uniform and predictable. Equality of opportunity signifies the ability to enter contests of various kinds and to keep the proceeds, providing only that one does not prevent others from trying. Equality of condition (or outcome, or result) means that the resources possessed by individuals and groups in society should be roughly equivalent. Rights, opportunity, and outcomes are worlds apart, so distant in practice that it has proved expedient to deny the full extent of these differences.

The much remarked un-, or better still, a-ideological character of American political history may be attributed to the denial of these differences. Rather than to admit that more of one meant less of another, it has been the special bent of American political thought to claim just the opposite: more of one kind of equality would also lead to more of another. Equality before the law, secured by such devices as extension of the franchise and a Bill of Rights providing procedural guarantees, would help secure opportunity to participate in political and economic life. And genuine equality of opportunity, by preventing government from introducing unnatural inequalities into American life, would produce as much equality of condition as is compatible with the innate or behavioral differences among people or as is necessary to preserve republican government.

American exceptionalism is not just the absence of hereditary hierarchies, though that was (and is still) important. What was truly distinctive, in that it was not found elsewhere, was the belief that equality of opportunity, properly pursued, would lead inexorably to equality of condition. Believing people to have moderately equivalent skills, observing that social and economic conditions were far more egalitarian than in Europe, early Americans thought that competition would increase or maintain whatever equality there was; inequality could not come out of competition, unless, as the Jacksonians feared, government introduced banks, charters, franchises, and other privileges not equally available to all citizens.

Observe the initial sequence of relationships among ideas about equality. They run from equality before the law, to equality of opportunity, and only then to equality of results. Of course, the prospects for republican government were related to the relative equality of condition fostered by American circumstances. The United States was blessed. In order, as the Declaration put it, to secure these blessings for posterity, this God-given equality was not to be decreased by the kind of distant central executive against which the colonies had so recently rebelled.

Insofar as inequality of condition resulted from differences in the faculty of individuals (but only to this extent and no further), this was tolerable, expected, natural, if not entirely desirable. In no way did the varying aptitudes for acquiring property (then considered an attribute or extension of the individual person) seem to threaten self-government. The battles of the party-of-the-country against the party-of-the-king in England were appropriated by the American branch of the British Whig opposition. Without an American equivalent of the king's men in parliament—the hated placemen put there by royal patronage, including the venal sale of offices—neither the English monarch nor his American successors could maintain their preponderance of power. Once these special privileges (the antifederalists especially feared holders of national debt) were removed, equality before the law would help secure the equality of opportunity that kept sufficient equality of condition so that republican government could thrive.

As soon as it is understood that the historic source of inequality was found in central governments ruled by strong central executives, there need be no puzzle over the lack of a socialist party in the United States. The stronger the central government—in this time-bound equation, good at least until the Civil War—the weaker are individual liberties. After the Revolution was won and its posterity assured by Jacksonian democracy, the United States of America and its Constitution became the exemplar of good, i.e. reasonably egalitarian, social relations. The flag (and hence the social relations for which it stood) was worth defending. Satisfaction with the circumstances of American life reinforced the original sequence. Inequality of condition could be bracketed off, stipulated to be acceptable, provided only that legal and political equality were achieved. In this way a separated and protected preserve for civil liberties could be carved out. Of course there was nothing like universal agreement on civil liberties. But those who thought of themselves as civil libertarians could reflect a simultaneous satisfaction with conditions in general and dissatisfaction with flat-out violations of legal and political rights.

The Reverse Sequence

The original sequence, in which equality before the law helps secure equality of opportunity and both, taken together, prevent such gross disparities of condition as to render republican government suspect, is based on assumptions subject to the ravages of time. The rise of corporate capitalism after the Civil War strained the social fabric. Yet populists could not quite bring themselves to turn against their Jeffersonian and Jacksonian forebears by embracing big government as the antidote to big corporations. Eventually populists merged into the Progressive movement, which sought regulation to restore the conditions of competition that would return the equality of opportunity essential to reducing the inequalities fostered by giant capital. It took the Great Depression and the civil rights movement to raise (and, for some, to answer affirmatively) the question of whether the orignal sequence needed reversal.

It is the *reverse sequence* (to use a dramatic term from a quite different field) that characterized the ACLU world view. Increasingly, unceasingly, equality of condition was viewed as a precondition of equality of opportunity.[1] For without equality of resources, it was argued, competition for the good things of life was prejudged in favor of those who had more and against those who had less. To do better, one had to be preendowed with the results of already having done better. Hence positive discrimination. What is more, without this substantive equality, the lack of equal opportunity would mean a denial of equality before the law. The opportunities that equal rights had been thought essential to maintain (for those who had them) or achieve (for those who did not) instead became the prerequisite. Civil liberties had been stood on their heads. The causes—equal rights and equal opportunity—had become the consequences of equal results. What had been widely agreed—the indispensability of equal rights as a precondition of equal opportunity—was replaced in importance by what had been problematic—securing equal outcomes.

To this very day the profound consequences of adopting the reverse sequence remain with those who regard themselves as civil libertarians. The spoken premise had been that people who disagreed about policy outcomes could still agree on process and procedure. The American political system, it was widely held, was legitimated by agreement that its processes accorded with equality before the law, which nurtured equality of political opportunity. Even if mass attitudes did not always favor the Bill of Rights, elites, despite policy differences, would rally around these procedural guarantees. Exceptions, such as denial of the franchise to Black people, were numbered among faults to be corrected; such was the exception, not the rule. Had this not been so, it would not have been possible to distinguish civil libertarians from other people who differed about the role of government or the kinds of policies it should pursue. The reverse sequence not only sought to diminish differences among Americans in general but also obliterated the rationale for distinguishing a particular kind of American, a civil libertarian, from any other political actor.

Now we knew from casual observation, as William Donohue shows in detail, that most members of the ACLU were political liberals as well. In the era after World War II, this meant that they (I would then have said "we") favored governmental action to improve the economic conditions of poor people and the political opportunities of racial minorities. Insofar as the reverse sequence meant adopting the liberal welfare program, it may have discomforted economic conservatives but not those who agreed with the substance. (This was a mistake, but it is not easy for people to see a threat behind those who agree with them on policy.) If the ACLU were becoming more liberal, or so I thought in the early sixties, it must be because liberals cared more than conservatives about the people being hurt.

Another consequence of adopting the reverse sequence that emerged in the 1970s was harder to deny. The very government that was urged to achieve greater equality of results was also, by virtue of being in authority, responsible for keeping the deprived down. What else but "the system," i.e. established authority, denied poor people, racial minorities, and women the equal rights and opportunity that could be enjoyed only by first achieving equality of condition? The disposition to blame the system led to an antiauthority position. This explains why, amidst an epidemic of strong-arm crime, the ACLU fought to make arrest, detention, and conviction more difficult.

At one and the same time, therefore, the ACLU, responding to the reverse sequence, favored stronger governmental action to reduce inequality while simultaneously attacking government's authority. A long-overdue appreciation of this no-win situation—government in the United States damned if it did and damned if it didn't—led to my unwillingness to renew membership.

I do not mean to say that those who were out of sympathy did not change at all while the ACLU did all the changing. We have less reason to cry foul than I once thought. For one thing, those who joined the organization in the 1950s became active in an aberrant period. The patriotism fostered by the war against fascism created common ground that gave way when the enemy stood for something other than gross racial, religious, political, and economic inequality. During the conservative Eisenhower era, widespread antipathy to communism and the Communist party made it unsafe to leap to their defense. Faced with a bipartisan consensus on security matters, the ACLU ducked difficult issues, not least by bargaining with J. Edgar Hoover, head of the Federal Bureau of Investigation. Of this the membership knew nothing. What it did know was that in those days the ACLU concentrated almost entirely on procedural rights. Criticism and patriotism still seemed compatible. Donohue's history reveals that the times both before and after this period—when, by default, means were more important than ends— were decades in which the reverse—policy ends mattered more than pro- cedural means—was more nearly true.

The period from the mid-1960s to the mid-1980s should also show us purist civil libertarians that we shared more commitments to the substance of policy than we had once imagined. The author of this volume, for instance, seems to me committed, in part at least, to a hierarchical con- ception of moral and political life. His values go beyond the equality of opportunity he wants to defend. Social differences become defensible as they protect moral differences. Hence Donohue's dismay at the casual dis- missal of family solidarity so as to protect the unborn that is manifest in ACLU positions. His Father's house has many mansions and Donohue wants to balance values among the occupants so that traditional morality, rooted in social differences, can coexist with the permissive society, rooted in diminishing moral distinctions. This balancing act is inappropriate, evil even, if the distinctions one wishes to uphold are deemed to be part and parcel of a pattern of cumulative inequalities that effectively voids pro- cedural rights.

Those of us who felt aggrieved at having our ACLU taken from us were too self-satisfied by far. Because we did believe in the pure civil liberties project and those who displaced us did not, we identified ourselves as the long-suffering adherents of the original creed. So far as it went, that was true enough. But we did not understand at that time (certainly I did not) that the initial sequence reflected a set of preferences about how American society should be organized. We were (and are) no more neutral in our views than curent ACLU adherents; the difference (and it is profound) is that what they take for granted—the desirability of equal results, even at some sacrifice of equal rights—is problematic for us and what we assume—

the desirability of equal rights and opportunity, even if inequalities do not thereby decline—has become problematic for them. The separating out of legal rights from the maelstrom of social life, which makes us true-blue civil libertarians in our eyes, makes us in their eyes apologists for unconscionable inequalities. And that (leaving out the "unconscionable") is what is in dispute.

Guilty as charged! Some of us, like William Donohue, discover that we approve of many aspects of traditional morality and, therefore, of the social hierarchy from which it stems. Acceptance of a modicum of hierarchy, moreover, includes respect for authority as well as other forms of inequality. Others among us 1940s and 1950s civil libertarians, less well represented in this book, discovered that if we wanted the creativity and spontaneity of market forces, we had to accept the inequality (as well as the vulgarity) that went with it. Had we believed that the combination of hierarchy and market relationships that constitute whatever established authority remains in American life was vicious, leading to cumulative inequalities threatening American democracy, along with its civil liberties, we, too, might have considered equality before the law as an epiphenomenon and equality of condition as all that was worth fighting for.

When the ACLU accepted the reverse sequence (sometime in the late 1960s or mid-1970s) it also rejected the insulation of law and opportunity from condition. From then on equality of condition was primary and equality before the law, secondary.

The ACLU has become an adjunct of movements to attack existing authority in the name of equality. If these movements weaken, the ACLU, if its past is any guide to its future, will abandon the reverse sequence and retreat to delineating a privileged position for legal rights. Should these egalitarian movements grow stronger, ACLU may well become absorbed into them, making manifest what is now latent, namely, its service as their legal arm. Whatever happens, the experience of the ACLU, so vibrantly portrayed in this book, will have taught us something about the conditions for treating civil liberties as an end in itself.

One such condition occurs when civil libertarians are numerous enough to band together, but still so weak as a group as to require tolerance from dominant social forces. Rather than fight losing battles over the substance of policy, this civil liberties group seeks to operate itself and its issues from substantive outcomes. The stance is tactical; emphasis on procedures because the group is sure to lose on policy. Once the group is strong enough to enter contests over policy, civil liberties become the means to more important ends. Those who disagree on substance leave the organization; gradually, the ends sought overwhelm the former expedient concentration on means, and the initial sequence gives way to the reverse sequence.

Are there, then, no social conditions that would sustain disagreement over substance in the midst of agreement over procedures? Yes, but these conditions are delicate in that they require a certain kind of balance among forces. There must be people favoring hierarchy, for without hierarchy there is no place for legal rights, universalistic rules, adjudication of who has the right to do what, or predictable responses from government. And to some degree there must be market forces. Without them there would be no one who believed in competition for its own sake. And without people to safegaurd the right to switch support, there could be no change in political office. Egalitarians are needed, also, to keep differences—including those between authority and citizen—from growing too large. Otherwise, hierarchies might seek to throttle competition and capitalists to control markets, making it difficult for newcomers to enter. Should any of these social orders grow too powerful (the threat of which Aristotle was well aware of), procedural rights would be nullified. Hierarchy might deny alternation in office and the criticism that goes with it; market forces might cumulate inequalities; and an egalitarian social order might deny liberties on the grounds they would interfere with equality. What the proper balance should be has, to be sure, eluded all of us. No doubt those who promote the reverse sequence would argue there is so little equality of condition that American society could stand for a lot more before it became unbalanced. No doubt others will say that the pendulum has swung too far toward seeking equal conditions. I believe that the reverse sequence, by making civil liberties hostage to prior conditions, will weaken liberty without achieving equality.

To see why this is so, that is, why equal conditions drive out equal rights, rather than fully achieving them, as is commonly asserted, consider the coercive qualities required to maintain the reverse sequence. How can it be guaranteed that no citizen or group will acquire an unfair (in contemporary discourse, read "unequal") command over resources? Acknowledging that perfect equality of condition is unobtainable and may even be undesirable, attempting to attain it nevertheless justifies regulation of virtually every aspect of life that tends toward substantive inequality, i.e. most everything. So long as every deviation from equal conditions is regarded as unfair, undemocratic and, therefore, illegitimate, governmental intervention in the interstices of social life is mandated. In so sweeping a conception of democracy, equality before the law, except for instantaneous votes at the moment of achieving equality of resources, is a fatal impediment.

A different view of democracy, not heard from much in recent times, is that people get together to find common grounds on which to secure the blessings of liberty. The initial sequence, the procedural rights they can agree on, matters mightily precisely because they do not agree on substantive ends. They expect to come in with different degrees of interest and information; they expect to be unequal in some respects because they want to be taken as they are; and they expect that established positions will give way only slowly because these should have an advantage, since this resistance to change will dampen their proclivity to do whatever they decide to do. By foreclosing the end, or, rather, by making the end of equal condition the only legitimate beginning of political life, there is no room for a democracy of learning what to prefer but only a democracy of enforcing prior preferences. And that, ironically, renders civil liberties useless because there are no preferences to be changed. The reverse sequence and the original sequence are antithetic to each other; if you have one, despite what the song says, you can't have the other.

Note

1. Driving home the proposition that the most widely espoused principles—equality before the law and equality of opportunity—had been denied to Black citizens, i.e. that the powers that be had not followed their own announced beliefs, the civil rights movement legitimated much that it touched, including a focus on group as distinguished from individual rights. When a number of its leaders came to believe that equal opportunity would, in their circumstances, lead inexorably to inequality of results, they began to seek policies enforcing equality of condition on a group basis. Their position deserves elucidation. Under their formulation, equal opportunity may promote inequality of outcomes for individuals but not for groups. Their objective is not to alter the range of inequality of results among individuals, they say, but to assure that the same distribution of inequality of results obtains across all relevant groups—whatever that range may be. Therefore, to them, a rough group parity of outcomes is a reasonable measure of the actual degree of equality of opportunity that exists. Thus they argue that no group as such (because it is *that* group) should be denied significant shares of equal opportunity, measured by equal outcomes compared to other groups. Whether those who hold these views, once group differences narrowed, would accept unequal outcomes for individuals within them, I cannot say. For others, of course, the present range of unequal outcomes (among both groups and individuals) is too high, and their goal is to greatly narrow the range. It is this view, embodied in the reverse sequence, that I believe currently characterizes ACLU action.

Abbreviations

AR   Annual Report
Bd. Min. Board Minutes
PG   Policy Guide

Interviews

Roger Baldwin, 2 June 1978, New York.
Aryeh Neier, 19 June 1978, New York.
Alan Reitman, 20 June 1978, New York.

Acknowledgments

My interest in the ACLU began in earnest in the summer of 1976. Initially, my research focused on the events that contributed to a change in Union policy. This effort culminated in my New York University doctoral dissertation and laid the foundation for this book. Convinced of the affinity between ACLU thought and liberalism, I began to look for new evidence on the Union while pursuing an investigation of the transformation of liberalism in the twentieth century. What follows is the result of that undertaking.

There are many people who, in one way or another, made this work possible. At New York University, I had the good fortune of securing three distinguished sociologists to serve on my dissertation committee: Dennis H. Wrong, Edwin Schur, and Edward W. Lehman. I knew then that I had a very helpful committee. I know now, from talking to many young Ph.D's, how lucky I was to work with such a dedicated group.

In the fall of 1982, I received a letter from Irving Kristol commenting on the first chapter of my book. His words of encouragement gave me the impetus to continue despite his admonition that publishing a polemic on the ACLU would be difficult. He proved to be correct. Were it not for Aaron Wildavsky, this book might not have been published. He believed in my work and directed me to Transaction. Unlike every other publisher I had dealt with, Irving Louis Horowitz responded promptly and affirmatively. I cannot thank him enough for his consistent support and advice. Many thanks also to Scott B. Bramson and to Dalia Buzin of Transaction.

Alan Reitman, associate director of the ACLU, provided me with a copy of the Union's annual reports, gave me access to its archives (including the FBI files on the Union), and granted me an opportunity to interview him. Obviously, I could not have done the required research for this book without his assistance. I very much appreciate his cooperation. Barbara Eichman was extremely helpful in giving me the chance to read the minutes of the Union's board of directors. My research on liberalism was facilitated by the work of the library staff at La Roche College. I am especially indebted to Sr. Georgine Sieber, the world's greatest librarian. Ruth Lide's typing of the manuscript and her thoughtful suggestions made my job easier.

My wife, Valerie, was unyielding in her belief that this book would eventually succeed. However much it has is due in no small way to her contribution. Without the backing of my mother, Anna Donohue, none of what I have accomplished would have been possible. Tara, my sister, deserves a special thanks for helping me to see just how porous many of today's fashionable ideas really are. The steady support of Bob and Althea Fowlie and Tom and Linda Boyle is much appreciated. And to my friends who offered their good will and inspiration, I am most grateful. In particular, I would like to thank Mike Mansfield, Dave Duffy, Herb Fleming, Kevin McDonald, Mike Vota, Chuck Mansfield, Amos Eslieb, Gary Field, M.J. Hannush, Grant Dinsmore, Dave Borrebach, Diane Adams, and Pat Mansfield.

1

Introduction: Liberalism and the ACLU

The Making of a Reputation

Americans have always been preoccupied with freedom. In literature and in the law, in clubs and in conversations, they have shown themselves to be more consumed with the subject of freedom than any other people in the world. Americans are not alone in prizing freedom but they are singularly renowned for their stubborn fixation on the value of liberty. Freedom for them is not simply an idea—it is a belief. Like any other value, it does not exist in isolation; when joined with equality, individualism, democracy, and rule of law under a constitution, we have what Samuel P. Huntington calls the values of the American Creed.[1]

The American Creed is not a carefully drawn ideology; rather, it constitutes "a complex and amorphous amalgam of goals and values."[2] Its function, according to Huntington, is to act as a basis of national identity.[3] The Americans are different, in this respect, from the British and the French: they have no "Creed" as such. They have divergent political ideologies but no central set of ideas and principles that are held by most countrymen.[4] The sources of the American Creed and the liberal-bourgeois values they entail are well known. The very absence of feudalism, argued Louis Hartz, implied the natural development of liberalism.[5] Without the burden of feudal tenures and inherited privilege, the future of the United States was primed for an experiment in liberty. The bountiful land and waterways that so impressed Tocqueville, the prospects for individual mobility, the formal limitations on church and state, all of these factors contributed to the growth of an open society.

Behaviorally, the American people have never been able to attain their ideals. This is not surprising. The commanding nature of American ideals insures against their total realization; the size of the gap between ideals and institutions in any country is determined by the nobility of its ideals. "In

1

no other country in the Western world," noted Clinton Rossiter, "has this gap been so wide as in the United States."[6] The disharmonic polity that Huntington sees as the logical outcome of such a chasm,[7] is the price that a nation pays for pursuing freedom. It also gives testimony to the fact that democracy is a process that never ends.

The American Civil Liberties Union epitomizes the struggle to make the American Creed a reality. It is motivated by a spirit that incorporates the ideals of liberty, equality, individualism, democracy, and constitutionalism. With characteristic American impatience, the Union rushes to bridge the gap between ideals and institutions. Although there are many other organizations that contribute to the making of American democracy, in the field of civil liberties[8] the ACLU has no rival. The National Emergency Civil Liberties Committee and the National Lawyers Guild can hardly claim to equal the influence of the ACLU. Even ACLU critic William F. Buckley, Jr., acknowledges that the Union is the most prestigious organization of its kind in the world.[9]

To be sure, the direction of freedom in the United States would be somewhat different had it not been for the efforts of the ACLU. Since 1920, it has fought tens of thousands of cases in the state and federal courts. Responsible for many landmark victories in the Supreme Court, it typically appears as a friend of the court. Nationwide, the work is done by some 5,000 volunteer lawyers and some 10,000 persons who serve on the committees and boards of the ACLU's 400 local chapters, 50 state and regional affiliates, and the national organization, and by the 350 persons who serve on the staffs of the various parts of the organization. With over 250,000 members, the Union participates in approximately 6,000 court cases a year.

Former Chief Justice of the United States Earl Warren spoke for many when he said of the ACLU that "it is difficult to appreciate how far our freedoms might have eroded had it not been for the Union's valiant representation in the courts of the constitutional rights of people of all persuasions."[10] It is doubtful whether Warren would have made the same statement regarding the National Emergency Civil Liberties Committee or the National Lawyers Guild. Both of these organizations are rightfully perceived as special-interest groups, selectively choosing their cases from a radical agenda; the National Lawyers Guild, in particular, has long been the favorite choice of leftist groups. As a result, neither organization has been able to muster the following that the ACLU commands.

The Union breaks ranks with these organizations primarily because it is seen as a politically disinterested force. Indeed, the strength of the ACLU is directly tied to its nonpartisan image. From its inception, the Union has maintained that it "makes no distinction as to whose liberties it defends."[11]

It lays claim to the same neutral position in virtually every one of its advertisements and brochures. Its sole raison d'être is the defense of the Bill of Rights for every American, regardless of ideological bent, race, sex, or class. Its impartiality is underscored by its policy commitment against the endorsement of or opposition to any candidate for elective or appointive office. "Nor does the Union criticize public officials," the policy states, "except when they follow a course of action in violation of civil liberties."[12] "Nor have we tried to influence the political process," adds John H.F. Shattuck, former director of the national office of the ACLU in Washington, D.C.[13] In short, the ACLU admits to no political orientation, either in its motives or decisions.

The ACLU has long argued that there is no correlation between the clients it defends and its own political preferences. If it defends the constitutional rights of the Ku Klux Klan or the American Communist party, it does so not because it endorses their beliefs or behavior but because the rights of such extremists are often undermined by the authorities. If it more frequently defends the rights of labor, minorities, and women, it does so because their rights are more frequently abused than those of other segments of the population. That does not make the Union a "liberal" organization. It defends the rights of business people, too. That does not make it a "conservative" organization. "The Bill of Rights is the ACLU's only client." Now it may be that those who are associated with the Union embrace liberal ideas, but that does not necessarily make the organization liberal. Jay A. Miller, executive director of the ACLU Illinois division, does not deny that its membership is predominantly liberal: "I'm sure that most people in the ACLU would consider themselves probably liberal."[14] But it is also true that people of all political persuasions are members of the Union.[15] More important, the Union clearly disavows that the private political beliefs of its staff filter into and color its decisions: "It's not a liberal or radical or even progressive organization," say Miller.[16]

Despite the Union's disclaimers, it has often been criticized as a politically motivated organization. The National Emergency Civil Liberties Committee, founded in 1951, charged that the ACLU was timid in its defense of Communists during the McCarthy era.[17] The National Lawyers Guild complained vigorously when the Union defended the Klan in the late seventies.[18] At the same time, the Union came under heavy fire from the Jewish Defense League for its defense of Nazis in Skokie, Illinois.[19] But most of the criticism has come from conservative quarters assailing the Union for being too radical.[20] The American Legion and numerous religious and civic groups, as well as many local newspapers, have branded the ACLU as a leftist organization. Congressional committees, such as the House Un-American Activities Committee, suspected the ACLU as a

Communist front. The FBI investigated its operations for decades, hoping to uncover subversive tactics. Openly denounced as a Communist institution by "patriotic" officials, the Union has often been put on the defensive. In the 1960s, even some of those who had hitherto been uncritical of the Union charged that it had become politicized by involving itself in issues that were outside its chartered domain and smacked of a liberal bias. In the 1980s, Edwin Meese, counselor to President Reagan, stunned the Union with a speech before the California Peace Officers Association labeling the ACLU as a "criminals' lobby."[21]

Those who have made in-depth studies of the ACLU are convinced that it has shown no political bias whatsoever. Charles Lam Markmann, author of the sole history of the ACLU, concluded his work with this comment: "What has largely contributed to the esteem that the Union has gained from both government and the enlightened public is its utter lack of partisanship and its concentration on principle."[22] Barton Bean, who wrote a doctoral dissertation on the Union, came to the identical conclusion: "It is non-partisan, having neither political affiliation nor corporate sympathy with the beliefs of those whose rights it upholds."[23] Bean does admit, however, that the ACLU is "made up mostly of partisans," i.e. partisans of left-of-center politics.[24] Nonetheless, he is certain that the personal beliefs of its staff do no affect its neutrality.[25] This position is also shared by Donald Johnson, author of a study on the ACLU's formative years: "To speak of . . . the ACLU as 'radical' . . . would be misleading. The ACLU's leaders certainly had their own political views in private, but the organization has never publicly defended any doctrine other than its own credo of unlimited free speech, free press and free assembly."[26] According to Bean, those who have accused the Union of being politically tainted have made charges that "cannot be sustained."[27] "The most violent and detailed attacks by both its friends and enemies," writes Bean, "have never shown more than a momentary wavering quickly corrected, or a minor error made in the heat of battle by all-too-human agents."[28] In summary, Bean proclaims the ACLU a "success," mainly due to "the fact that it is and has been a group of unusual human beings."[29]

The Myth of Nonpartisanship

As we have seen, the ACLU's claim to neutrality has been supported by students of its history. This book contends that such a judgment is largely undeserved. On trial is the Union's "utter lack of partisanship." The evidence amassed here indicates that the ACLU is no more free from partisanship than the Republican and Democratic parties. Quite simply, the ACLU has a politics, and that politics is liberalism. From its first annual report to its most recent legal brief, the voice of the ACLU has been the voice of liberalism. More than any other organization, including the avowedly liberal Americans for Democratic Action, the ACLU has shown itself to embody the ethos of liberalism. Indeed, the ACLU represents American liberalism par excellence. It is not a radical organization, although radicals have been active in its ranks. It is not a special-interest group like the National Lawyers Guild. It is not a lobbying group for criminals. It is not a front for the Communist party. Never was. But it is a decidedly liberal organization. Always has been.

It is neither the ACLU's clients nor its proclaimed goal that make it a politically driven organization. A glance at the Union's history offers support to the proposition that its clients are drawn from across the political spectrum. It is generally true that the ACLU "makes no distinction as to whose liberties it defends"; important departures from this principle can be found but the overall record is admirable. The ACLU's neutral image is similarly untarnished by accounts that point to its stated goal and conclude that it is a liberal organization. By definition, any organization that makes the defense of the Bill of Rights its goal is a liberal organization. Individual rights form the core of liberalism. This is why longtime Union activist and writer Alan Westin has identified the ACLU as a liberal organization.[30] Scholar William Gerber, in his book *American Liberalism*, also lists the ACLU as a liberal group.[31] And the *New York Times* counts the Union as liberal.[32] Such labels are intended to provide us with a descriptive taxonomy of the organization's function; they are not meant to imply impartiality.

The charge being made here is different. It is the decisions that the ACLU renders that make it a politically partisan organization. Wedded to liberalism, the ACLU cannot help but expose its values whenever it takes a stand on a civil liberties issue; everything from its lobbying efforts to its policy decisions is reflective of its value priorities. Those values—egalitarianism, rationalism, secularism, optimism, and antitraditionalism—are what motivates the ACLU. It is precisely because its behavior is so closely patterned on its values that the ACLU can be regarded as the quintessential embodiment of American liberalism.

The ACLU and the Moral Majority have two things in common: both pretend to be nonpartisan and both are wrong.[33] Jerry Falwell's group is a right-wing organization clearly trying to mobilize people on behalf of conservative values. The ACLU, although it can claim a nonpartisan record on the selection of its clients, can do no better than the Moral Majority in hiding its political values. It is no exaggeration to say that social reform, in a liberal direction, is the sine qua non of the ACLU. Its record, far from showing a "momentary wavering" from impartiality, is replete with attempts to reform American society according to the wisdom of liberalism. The truth of the matter is that the ACLU has always been a highly politicized organization.

The ACLU does not screen its cases the way the Consumers Union screens automobiles and appliances. It cannot. Most legal decisions involve a conflict of values. No one can pretend to be neutral; the law is not neutral. Legal decisions must be made and they will ultimately reflect the values of the decision-makers. It is unrealistic to expect that any person—never mind an organization—can successfully sever private political beliefs from his or her decisions on legal matters; they will appear, regardless of whether they are consciously intended. Consider the Supreme Court. When we say that the Warren Court was liberal and the Burger Court is conservative, we are saying that on the basis of the overall record of the court, Justice Burger presides over a group that exhibits values different from those of its predecessor. This is why we thoroughly investigate the political leanings of each nominated justice before confirmation is given. No one is satisfied to learn that serving on the Supreme Court is a "liberal" function; we want to know the politics of each candidate. Similarly, we should know the politics of those who seek to influence the court.

It is true that the ACLU does not endorse candidates for political office. But that has not precluded it from writing speeches for politicians whom it likes.[34] And no amount of rationalizing can justify John Shattuck's claim that the Union does not try to influence the political process. Bean estimated that "between a quarter and a third of the activities of the ACLU have been in the broad field of political pressure, in the manner called, for want of a better term, lobbying."[35] That was thirty years ago. Even Shattuck concedes that political pressuring has increased: "We have a non-tax-deductible arm, the ACLU Foundation, which does our lobbying with the legislature. The Washington office is concerned with that. But that has become a much bigger and more important part of the ACLU than it used to be."[36] And what are we to make of the ACLU's custom of annually issuing "score cards" on the members of a state legislature?[37] Or of its practice of sponsoring a politician's appeal requesting contributions for a cause for which the politician is fighting?[38] Are these not examples, however discreet, of trying to influence the political process?

The Meaning of Liberalism

It has often been said that the terms *liberal* and *conservative* have lost their meaning. But not everyone agrees. "Continuing ambiguities notwithstanding, the words liberal and conservative are indispensable; they tell us more about an individual's political philosophy than do the party labels

Democrat and Republican."[39] This is the position of Robert Nisbet. It is also the position that informs this book. Just how indispensable the terms are, however, is contingent on the clarity of their usage. In this vein, Sidney Hook's advice is instructive: "We should insist that when these words [*liberal* and *conservative*] are used, their meaning should be spelled out. And we should hold their users to consistent usage."[40] As a former student of Professor Hook's, I take his dictum seriously.

The word *liberal* means free; freedom from restraint.* Historically, it has been associated with emancipation. John Dewey noted that at one time *liberty* meant liberation from chattel slavery. At another time it meant freedom from serfdom. In the late seventeenth and early eighteenth century it was identified with liberation from despotic rule. Capitalists a century later used the term to describe freedom from restrictive laws that stymied economic growth. In the twentieth century we have come to think of *liberal* as liberation from material want.[41] No doubt many Americans today have come to think of *liberal* in Rousseauistic terms: freedom from social convention. All of these examples illustrate negative freedom, i.e. freedom from restraint.

Liberalism is the philosophy that gives expression to the meaning of liberal. It may be defined as a doctrine that holds that every individual should have the right to realize his or her potential. That, at least, is the one continuous thread joining together classical and contemporary liberalism. The classical liberalism of the nineteenth century affirmed, as Dennis Wrong notes, "the widest possible extension of individual freedom from institutional authorities."[42] Individual liberty was equated with negative freedom. That every individual had the right to realize his or her potential meant freedom from artificial barriers to mobility; custom, tradition, and inherited status would no longer be decisive. Liberalism of the late nineteenth and early twentieth century argued that all individuals should have the *equal* right to realize their potentials. No longer satisfied by removing social impediments, liberals now sought to reconstruct social institutions so as to provide for equal opportunity. In the 1960s, liberalism changed again. This time the credo read every individual *has the right to be equal regardless of personal potential*. Ergo, all, or nearly all, inequality is illegitimate. The solution: social equality should be imposed from above. The state would do what all previous efforts could not: order equality into existence.

Ever since liberalism became identified as a political philosophy in the

---

*The terms *liberty* and *freedom*, while not strictly synonymous, will be used interchangeably so as to avoid unnecessary confusion.

first half of the nineteenth century, the English and the Americans have steadily redefined its meaning. Although continuity does exist, the revisions have been impressive. Liberalism has been associated with notions of equality and distributive justice as well as meritocracy and hierarchy. It has been antistatist and prostatist. It has preached restraint and the abandonment of it. It has been seen as militaristic and pacifistic. Such a term provides liabilities but not, as Hartz said, "insuperable barriers."[43]

Classical liberals were resolute in their defense of individual rights. They did not all arrive at such a position, however, from the same reasoning. Locke insisted that all men had natural rights that government could not enjoin. Bentham rejected this notion as ludicrous, positing instead that individual liberty was right because it served the greatest good for the greatest number of people. What all classical liberals did agree on was the nature of society. Society was seen as self-regulating, needing no supervisory directives from above. Isolated individuals, independent of the strictures that constitute group and class membership, would cumulatively and coincidentially serve the public interest.

More than any other liberal of the classical age, the one who has exerted the most enduring influence is John Stuart Mill. His position on freedom of speech and action has been adopted by many contemporary liberals, including the directors of the ACLU. In essence, Mill argued that every individual should have the right to do exactly as she or he pleases, just so long as the rights of others are not directly interfered with. This is the "one very simple principle" that Mill sought to advance. Innocuous on its face, this principle has anything but simple ramifications for society. Its profundity can be grasped only if we recognize that Mill was not promoting utilitarian doctrine; his objective was to elevate this principle to an absolute status.

Freedom of thought, speech, and action; these were the fundamental liberties that concerned Mill. Without them no society could be regarded as free. They were to be enjoyed absolutely; government had no legitimate right to intervene in the affairs of humans unless their actions proved to be injurious to the physical safety of others. What people said, no matter how immoral or socially reckless it may be, was no concern of the law. Speech lay in that sphere of society that is outside the bounds of the state. Only when speech could directly be linked to physical harm could the authorities inject themselves. Anticipating the Supreme Court's *Schenck* decision of 1919, Mill saw that freedom of speech could be abused by those who would incite a mob to assault someone; such speech would then lose its immunity. But unless speech constituted what Justice Holmes would later declare to be a clear and present danger, it was impermissible to invoke the law. "If all mankind minus one were of one opinion," proclaimed Mill, "and only one person were of the contrary opinion, mankind would be no more justified in silencing that one person, than he, if he had the power would be justified in silencing mankind."[44] Mill found it easy to say this because he adamantly rejected the contention that there may be some truths that are unassailable. It was incumbent on society to allow all speech to be heard, for it could not hope to progress unless it did. Humans are not infallible; they can never be certain in their beliefs. What we regard as untrue and evil today, others might find wise and profitable tomorrow. Accepting this logic, it becomes absolutely necessary to defend the speech of everyone, no matter how odious and corrupting it may be. Society can never be sure of the veracity of its values.

It is not his writings on freedom of speech that Mill is most remembered for but his position on freedom of action. Gertrude Himmelfarb, in her brilliant analysis of *On Liberty*, explains that the Founding Fathers were less absolutist in their convictions on freedom of action than they were in appreciating freedom of speech.[45] Not so for Mill. "Where Mill went beyond the *Zeitgeist*," Himmelfarb notes, ". . . was in extending the principle of freedom to the entire range of opinion and, more radically, to the entire range of action. It was the latter especially that was Mill's claim to novelty and boldness."[46] Most liberals, including the Founding Fathers, considered self-restraint to be axiomatic in any discussion on freedom of action; it was seen as a virtue. Without moderation and sobriety, individuals would jeopardize their free status.[47] By contrast, Mill was too busy exalting the individual to worry about self-discipline. In fact self-discipline is not only unrelated to freedom, it is in conflict with it. Mill lists liberty and discipline as one of the "standing antagonisms of practical life."[48] The message is clear: to be free is to be liberated from internal, as well as external, constraint.

The free society will allow us to commit any act we want "so long as it is at [our] own risk and peril."[49] We may decide to pollute our morals or plunder our talents and resources; we need not answer to society for such acts of depravity. When the sole victim of a morally destitute act is the actor, the act is considered "self-regarding" and is consequently removed from the legal concerns of the community. We may counsel or castigate, beckon or banish the actor, but we may not stop the actor from depleting his or her moral stock. Self-regarding acts, being self-limiting, are never within the purview of the state or society no matter how morally bankrupt they may be.[50] The term *duty to oneself*, meaning self-respect or self-development, has no social meaning: we cannot be held accountable to our fellow human beings because the good of all is not affected.[51] It is for these reasons that Himmelfarb branded Mill's essay "a form of moral laissez-faireism," lacking in distinctions between good and bad.[52]

From Classical to Contemporary Liberalism

In the latter part of the nineteenth century, liberalism underwent a transformation. The new liberalism was, as Edward Shils notes, collectivistic instead of autonomist.[53] Collectivistic liberalism was born out of a desire to rescue the individual from the excesses of autonomistic liberalism. To be sure, liberalism proved to be victorious in denying inherited privilege its stationary role and contributed significantly to an open society. And although status by ascription was dealt a severe blow, once individuals were emancipated from traditional constraints, they generated new inequalities based on achievement. The fruits of capitalism left society marked by newly drawn lines of stratification. Less rigid than the estate system, the class society was nonetheless restrictive of equal opportunity. Poverty and misery—the common condition of humankind throughout history—were now seen as social problems, i.e. as something that could be rectified. Their resolution required a potent tonic; the state, of course, was seen as the right stimulant.

Once liberalism overcame its bias against the state, there was no looking back. Liberals pressed for societywide institutional reforms—all in the name of the individual. It did not take long before the confusion between liberalism and socialism began. In fact J. A. Hobson, the English intellectual, as well as new liberal L. T. Hobhouse, referred to liberalism as "practicable socialism."[54] Michael Freeden spots the similarity: "On some issues it was actually difficult to pinpoint distinctions between Hobson and the Fabians as to what the state was to undertake."[55] That the new collectivistic liberals could be associated with the likes of Sidney and Beatrice Webb goes to show how far liberalism has traveled since its autonomistic beginnings. It was not only in England that the affinity between liberalism and socialism could be noted. Shils maintains that the relationship has been even stronger in the United States, owing partly to the absence of a large socialist party. Those who might otherwise have joined a socialist organization have gravitated toward liberal associations. "They joined with the humanitarian social reformers, with the improvers of government machinery, and with 'civil libertarians' to form a coalition such as has not quite existed elsewhere. . . . This coalition had been in process of formation since late in the nineteenth century but it became animated in the 1920s."[56] Shils chose the right decade to mark the coalition of liberal forces: the ACLU was a product of the twenties.

Just how far the liberalism of the twentieth century departs from the classical tradition is debatable. Freeden thinks the separation has been exaggerated: "If the question is posed as one of liberal continuity versus a break in the liberal tradition, the reply must decidedly be in favor of continuity."⁵⁷ Robert Nisbet emphasizes that "nothing is more evident than the transformation during this century of the meaning of liberalism in America."⁵⁸ Yet Nisbet concedes that the break between the two liberalisms was not a clean one; he cites Herbert Spencer as a source of both strands.⁵⁹ What connects the two liberalisms has been observed by Kenneth Minogue: "The unity which allows us to discuss liberalism over the last few centuries as a single and continuing entity is intellectual; we are confronted with a single tradition of thought, whose method is intermittently empirical, whose reality is found in the concept of the individual, and whose ethics are consistently utilitarian."⁶⁰ Shils sees some different parallels: both are against tradition and favor rationalism; they are concerned with the entire society; they are tolerant of diverse beliefs; they are indifferent and secularist in their attitude toward religion; they favor equal opportunity and equality before the law; they accept pluralism and prize individual autonomy.⁶¹ But for all their commonality, autonomistic and collectivistic liberalism have points of departure that cannot be dismissed as mere differences in style. When collectivistic liberalism can be confused with socialism or radicalism, there is something fundamentally different about this brand of liberalism that separates it from its autonomistic predecessor. The work of John Dewey clearly illustrates the newness of collectivistic liberalism.

Dewey contended that "the ends which liberalism has always professed can be attained only as control of the means of the production and distribution is taken out of the hands of the individuals who exercise powers created socially for narrow individual interest."⁶² Social control of the economy was what Dewey advocated. As Edmund Wilson once noted, social control was a code word for socialism that liberals used in the thirties: "We have always talked about the desirability of a planned society—the phrase 'social control' has been our blessed Mesopotamian word. But if this means anything, does it not mean socialism? And should we not do well to make this perfectly plain?"⁶³ Small wonder that collectivistic liberalism has often been mistaken for old-fashioned socialism. Both adhere strictly to the "common good." As Hobhouse said, "The good of each is, on the principle of the common good, matter of concern to all."⁶⁴ Such conceptions of society have no place for self-regarding acts; it is incomprehensible to believe that individual acts could have only individual consequences.⁶⁵ To ensure freedom, better allow social control to become mobilized whenever the common good is threatened.

Liberals failed to achieve their noble goals because they used the wrong method. Dewey knew how to correct the situation: "The ends can now be achieved *only* by reversal of the means to which early liberalism was committed."⁶⁶ The early liberalism had succeeded in displacing monopoly privilege but it still left the individual prey to unfair advantage. To restore Jeffersonian democracy, Dewey pleaded, we must realize that unrestricted individualism is destructive of freedom.[67] Hobhouse concurred: "It is at least the first step in freedom to be emancipated from the arbitrary power of the individual, even if we only exchange it for the uniform and impartial control of the law."[68] Hobhouse was incessant in his call for restraint over the individual: "The liberty of each then must, on the principle of the common good, be limited by the rights of all."[69] From freedom of contract[70] to the rights of conscientious objectors,[71] the common good was held to be paramount. Even civil liberties fell under the common good. Dewey concluded that "the justification for the various civil liberties is the contribution they make to the welfare of the community."[72] All of these components made up what Dewey himself called "collectivistic liberalism."[73]

In the 1960s, liberalism entered its third phase: at long last it had been fully radicalized. As Shils notes, radicalism was always the new liberalism's next of kin:

> It [radicalism] is in fact only an extension, to the point of corruption, of the principles contained in liberalism. . . . Contrary to the beliefs of radicals that their program is disjunctively different from that of collectivistic liberalism, there has been a movement toward a close approximation between them. A process of transformation has swept collectivistic liberalism towards radicalism.[74]

Five elements constitute current liberal thought: "a demand for far-reaching freedom of expression and opinion, particularly of opinion critical of authority and of established institutional arrangements"; a demand for "participatory democracy"; a call for freedom of "affective expression"; a fondness for centralized government and the "common welfare"; and, last, "a belief in the urgency of realizing these ends and in the wickedness of those who disagree with this from other than a radical standpoint."[75] As we shall see, Shils might have been thinking about the ACLU when he wrote this.

The Mind-Set of the ACLU

The ACLU has selectively drawn on features of both autonomistic and collectivistic liberalism. So has liberalism in its latest, most radicalized form. The five elements of contemporary liberalism that Shils has identified are exemplified by the ACLU of the 1980s. Borrowing a leaf from Mill, the Union's position on free speech is the broadest, most absolute interpretation ever advanced by serious students of the First Amendment. Supportive of participatory democracy, the Union's concept of fairness in organizational decision-making is receptive to the idea of quotas; all segments of the population should have an equal voice. Freedom of affective expression is seen by the ACLU as important a part of free speech as political discourse; it refuses to draw distinctions. As with collectivistic liberals, the Union looks favorably on using government to further social reforms; when it comes to social justice and egalitarian ends, the ACLU has no problem in supporting big government. Last, the ACLU has often dismissed those who disagree with its positions as being either ignorant of the Constitution or working to undermine civil liberties. All of these features will become evident as the succeeding chapters unfold.

The ACLU is actually a cross between Gay Talese and John Kenneth Galbraith. It voices Talese's sentiments on moral issues, believing that the state should respect "self-regarding acts." On issues of social and economic concern, it is, with Galbraith, prostatist. Perhaps the ACLU is an approximation of what Robert Lekachman calls "libertarian socialism."[76] In any event, it is the Union's *Weltanschauung* or world view—more than anything else—that makes it a truly liberal organization. It fully embraces all the values, beliefs, and sentiments that are constitutive of liberalism: egalitarianism, optimism, rationalism, antitraditionalism, and secularism. These are the values through which the ACLU sees the world. By acting on these values, the ACLU evinces its liberal heritage and carries forth the predominant (some would say the only)[77] intellectual tradition in the United States. Representative of that tradition, the Union is an organization that transcribes liberalism from thought to action; it gives existential meaning to the idea of liberalism.

The mind-set of the ACLU liberals is optimistic about the chances of making society more equal. The conditions that give rise to inequality are seen, for the most part, as stemming from societal creations. That is good news for the liberals because now they believe that they can proceed to alter the conditions and thereby construct equality. Human beings are seen as plastic, malleable objects, capable of being reshaped by their environment. The history of humankind may be colored with inequality and deprivation but there is no need to despair: Humankind is always eligible for remaking, and it is the faith of every liberal that the right blueprint will yet be found. Such optimism is derived from the belief that human beings are essentially good. Reinhold Niebuhr (a liberal whom Arthur Schlesinger is fond of quoting as proof that liberals do not necessarily believe in the goodness of man)[78] explicitly said that the heart of liberalism was "faith in man's essential goodness" which can be attained when man "returns to nature" or "becomes rational."[79] For further proof, I offer Ramsey Clark. No one will doubt that Clark is, in every respect, a model of liberal thought. What makes him such a splendid example of liberal thought is his position as chairman of the ACLU's National Advisory Council—a position he has held since 1970. These are his words: "Freedom is right because people are inherently good. We have not met an enemy that is us. There is no enemy, the bad man, the sinister force that we use to deny freedom. . . . The recognition of our common humanity, the equal worth of each person, the love of people is the source of freedom."[80]

Is there any liberal who could improve on this?

Above all, the liberal mind-set is rational. Richard Chase, writing in *Partisan Review* in 1949, identified the essence of liberalism:

> The practical instruments of modern liberalism are democratic, libertarian politics and the doctrine that the human reason, in its secular function, is capable of establishing the social conditions of freedom. I take this to be fundamental truth for our time, and think that no declared liberal can be taken seriously who does not base his liberalism upon this truth.[81]

It would not be easy to find a better description of the mentality of the ACLU than this. Throughout its policies governing the social order, the ACLU weaves a rationalistic leitmotif, forever expecting that the social conditions of freedom can be consciously constructed and processed. The natural nemesis of such a perspective is tradition. To the liberal, tradition and authority are generally seen as obstacles to the rational reform of society. The hierarchal social arrangements of the past were based on irrational, and therefore unacceptable, criteria. True freedom, then, implied rational conduct. "Rational behavior," writes Minogue, "excludes habitual action, impulsive action, or acts done in slavish imitation of ossified traditions."[82]

The fifth characteristic of the ACLU's mind-set is its secular, non-religious character. From the Union's perspective, separation between church and state means erecting an iron curtain between the two institutions. It is skeptical, if not distrustful, of the ambitions of the clergy. Freedom is won by relegating religion to a purely private sphere remote from the body politic. In fact, the establishment of a free society is predicated on the idea that religion must be surgically removed from culture. Freedom to worship must be protected but a free people will guard against the untoward consequences that religious influence might bring. Therefore, a cultural vivisection is in order: remove religion and immunize society (via the legislature and judiciary) against its reoccurrence.

Organizational Change in Four Eras of Vigilance

The ACLU is not simply an aggregate of individuals who share a concern for civil liberties: it is an organization. As such, it can be studied as much for what it is as for what it does. Because it is an organization, the ACLU does not have anywhere near complete mastery of its fate. Like any other organization, it must negotiate with its environment to be successful. Environmental constraints coupled with the structural limitations of the organization itself, have the effect of drawing boundary lines around decision-making. The ACLU does not act at will; it acts according to the strictures of its environment.[83] This is not to say, however, that the Union is a passive entity; it acts on and modifies its environment with as much energy as it can muster.[84] It is truly a dynamic organization.

All organizations have goals—both stated and unstated. The formal, stated goal of the ACLU has always been the defense of the Bill of Rights. Its unstated, or operative, goal(s) is not so easily discernible. It can be ascertained only through a careful examination of the policy positions of the national Board of Directors. Once this is done, we are in a much better position to judge what the ACLU really does. According to Charles Perrow, operative goals "tell us what the organization actually is trying to do, regardless of what the official goals say are the aims."[85] Another sociologist, Amitai Etzioni, has maintained that although stated goals can serve as a clue to actual goals, they cannot be uncritically accepted because organizations tend to hold "public" goals for front purposes.[86] There is no reason to believe that the ACLU is, in this respect, atypical. It, too, has charted a course that is not identical to its announced ends. In this context, it is worth repeating that social reform, in a liberal direction, is the sine qua non of the ACLU. That is what its operative goal was from the very beginning and that is what it is today.

There have always been at least two major factions within the ACLU: purists and instrumentalists.[87] The purists maintain a "strict constructionist" interpretation of the Bill of Rights; civil liberties are seen as an end in themselves. Instrumentalists see the Bill of Rights as an instrument to be used in service toward a "socially desirable" end. Although each faction can accurately claim to have exerted the predominant influence at one time or other, the evidence suggests that the instrumentalists have been the most successful at steering the Union's course. The eclipse of one faction by the other turns on the issues and the decade in which they surfaced. In the Union's case, it is important to note that it has witnessed four eras of development: the era of emergence (1920s and 1930s); the era of expedience (1940s and 1950s); the era of expansion (1960s and 1970s); and the fourth era (1980s and 1990s), which it now appears can best be described as the era of endurance.

The era of emergence opens with the founding of the ACLU by Roger Nash Baldwin in 1920. More than any other individual, Roger Baldwin made the ACLU what it is today. Born to wealth in the Boston suburb of Wellesley on 21 January 1884, young Roger received his earliest ideological influence from his aunt Ruth. She was a founder of the National Urban League and a member of the Socialist party.[88] Baldwin later had an opportunity to strengthen his political views at Harvard, where he received both an A.B. and an M.A.[89] Upon graduation, Baldwin traveled to St. Louis, where he had a chance to practice his beliefs, working amongst the poor in a settlement house while teaching sociology at Washington University. Successful at both jobs, it was the former that earned him a national reputation. As chief probation officer of the Juvenile Court, he was in a position to gain the insight he needed to coauthor *Juvenile Courts and Probation*, which was the standard text in the field for many years. From 1910 to 1917, he was also secretary of the reform Civic League of St. Louis, a post that proved to be a turning point for him. Baldwin once said that he got his "first impulse to civil liberties" when the police denied Margaret Sanger, the birth-control advocate, the right to hold a meeting in a private hall.[90] When the United States entered World War I in 1917, he went to New York, where he became involved in the antiwar movement. Three years later, he founded the ACLU. He remained loyal to his organization until the end: he died at age ninety-seven on 26 August 1981, in Ridgewood, New Jersey. Just eight months earlier, on his birthday, President Carter had awarded him the Medal of Freedom, the nation's highest civilian honor.[91]

During the 1920s, the ACLU confined itself mostly to First Amendment issues. Its most notable case came in 1925 when the Union defended John Scopes in the so-called Monkey Trial. But most of its energy was spent defending the rights of labor, not schoolteachers. The Union wanted to do more, but, like any other organization, it had to work within its resources. By the end of the twenties, however, Baldwin proposed that the Union should broaden its scope by tackling issues that went beyond the traditional concerns of freedom of speech, press, and assembly. In a letter to the members of the National Committee dated 7 February 1929, Baldwin outlined his ideas. The ACLU was, in his estimation, "a highly centralized organization operating from New York on cases arising all over the country."[92] To decentralize and broaden the program, "new" activities were charted that would engender organizational change:

1. Aid to Negroes in their fight for civil rights.
2. Aid to aliens discriminated against in their public relations and in proceedings for naturalization and deportation.
3. Opposition to the efforts to break down the constitutional guarantees of defendants in criminal cases—including a fight against the third degree and allied police practices.
4. Opposition to unlawful searches and seizures, now common in Prohibition and other cases.
5. Discrimination in all public institutions against persons because of race or religion.

6. Opposition to the censorship of books, plays, radio, talking movies.
7. Aid in the campaign against compulsory military training.
8. Aid in the present campaign for the rights of American Indians.
9. Opposition to the use of military or naval forces of the United States to control weaker nations—as a violation of their civil liberties.
10. Publicity and protest by Americans against repression in other countries, where American interests are involved.[93]

Baldwin's decision to expand appears to have been motivated strictly out of concern to "enlarge the membership to reach every group interested in any aspect of civil liberty."[94] He knew that the Union's effectiveness would turn in large part on its ability to increase its program and hence its membership. After almost ten years, the record showed that it had grown at a disturbingly slow pace. Moreover, with only 2,400 regular contributors, the total contributions amounted to only $5,100.[95] Given the sizable agenda before the Union, this was next to nothing.

The state of the economy in the 1930s affected both the condition of civil liberties and the ACLU. Organizationally, during the depth of the depression in 1932, the Union's operating fund dropped 20 percent from the previous fiscal year; the special funds dropped even more. Total income from all sources between 1 February 1931 and 31 January 1933 dropped from $46,700 to $27,000. The number of contributions slipped from 3,600 in the year ending 31 January 1932 to 2,900 the following year; membership fell from 3,200 to 2,500.[96] The Union made a modest recovery by the end of the decade: in 1940, membership stood at 4,732; total receipts, however, rose to only $29,500.[97] Internally, there was one major change during the decade: by resolution, the membership of the National Committee was completely separated from that of the Board of Directors. This decision in the spring of 1939 limited policy decision-making to members of the board.[98] Interpreted as a political maneuver by some, the decision did have the effect of concentrating power in the hands of fewer members.

According to the Union, as the economy changed, so did the conditions of civil liberties. When the depression began, the Union noted that the "great increase in repression was due to the fear of unrest and disorder during the economic depression."[99] When the recovery was apparent in 1935-36, the improving economy was cited as a factor that helped to ameliorate the state of civil liberties.[100] The Union tackled a variety of issues in the early thirties, ranging from censorship to the release of "political prisoners";[101] however, the rights of labor were once again paramount.

The ACLU's second era (1940s and 1950s) deserves to be called the era of expediency because it was at that time that the Union displaced its commitment to civil liberties and chose instead to follow an expedient course. Quite literally, it was fighting for its survival. Internal dissension and a hostile external environment wracked the Union with conflict the likes of which it had never witnessed before. Incendiary topics, such as the right of a Communist to be a member of the Board of Directors of the ACLU, made certain that the organization would be scarred no matter what decision it made. The civil liberties issues at home that arose from U.S. engagement in World War II also kept the Union busy. And, of course, McCarthyism in the fifties provided the Union with a test it had to face. What it did to save itself during this chapter of American history tells us as much about the workings of the ACLU as it does about the political and social environment that existed at that time.

Although subject to extraordinary pressures, the ACLU managed to do more than survive—it grew. Membership during the 1940s almost doubled, rising from 4,732 to 9,355, but financially the Union progressed more slowly.[102] It was not until the fifties that marked progress could be seen: membership nearly quadrupled, due, in part, to the efforts of the new executive director, Patrick Murphy Malin. Baldwin had retired from that post (though not, of course, from the Union), and Malin spotted an opportunity and seized it. Twelve new branches brought the number of affiliates to twenty-eight.[103] The expansion was the result of a determined effort to increase the resources of the Union. For example, in 1953, the Union complained that it was being pressed to do "too much with too little." More important, dissatisfaction was expressed over its image: "The ACLU must not be an esoteric cult worshiping itself."[104] Baldwin himself admitted to unwisely curtailing growth: "I was probably wrong in holding down the expansion and budget of the Union."[105]

Another organizational innovation that the ACLU experienced in the fifties was the creation in November 1952 of an office in Washington, D.C. It was not just another branch with a routine schedule but had several particular functions: to establish contact with legislative and executive staffs that were working on civil liberties problems; to arrange for the appearance of ACLU spokesmen before congressional committees; and to conduct an ongoing study of the informal pressure groups that operated in the capitol.[106] All of this activity was a response to the increasing complexity of civil liberties matters. Litigation was no longer the sole means by which civil liberties problems were handled. The Union had to extend its operations if its efforts were to be successful. However, the Union continued to act independently; it restated its policy to refuse to join with other organizations in sponsoring briefs *amicus*.[107]

The ACLU's third era, the era of expansion (1960s and 1970s), was led by John de J. Pemberton, Jr., in the sixties and Aryeh Neier in the seventies. In many ways the most interesting era in its history, the ACLU flowered as it never had before. The war in Vietnam was matched in intensity at home as several segments of the population squared off against one another in a battle over values and rights. The war on poverty, as well as the entire Great Society program, brought new issues before civil libertarians. The increasing size of government, the demands of national security, and the concomitant need for privacy were only some of the items that crowded the calendar of the ACLU. No matter how hard it tried, it could not keep pace with the onslaught of new events. No one else could either.

At the beginning of the sixties, the ACLU had a total membership of 49,000; at the end of the decade, 140,000.[108] With more than $2,000,000 in contributions at the close of the decade,[109] the Union was active in establishing affiliates from Alaska to Florida.[110] In the early sixties, it formed the Vigilance Fund to receive all unrestricted bequests and major gifts made in memory or in honor of a named person.[111] Other new programs, such as "Operation Southern Justice," were begun in the 1960s to combat racial injustice.[112]

In the first three years of the 1970s, the ACLU underwent the fastest increase in membership it ever recorded in such a time span: it climbed 96 percent to 275,000.[113] There were four principal reasons for the forward surge in the late sixties and early seventies: internal changes within the Union's hierarchy; demographic change; the organized quest for equality on the part of minorities and women; and government lawlessness. The most significant internal change came in 1970 when the Board of Directors chose Aryeh Neier as the fourth executive director. Under Neier's aggressive leadership, the Union moved beyond its traditional domain by tackling issues that had previously been considered outside its scope. Demographic changes, particularly the large number of young people in the population—the "baby-boom" cohort—had the effect of creating new recruits and issues for the ACLU. Typically the most idealistic segment of the population, young people were active in the sixties in the antidraft and antiwar movements as well as the civil rights movement. The Watergate scandal also did much to bolster the ACLU's membership; the Union's role in calling for President Nixon's impeachment attracted new supporters.

At the start of the seventies, it appeared as though the ACLU's golden decade had finally arrived; everything was going its way. Buoyed by ballooning resources, the Union broadened its horizons by expanding its nonlitigation activities; it became a legislative action organization in Congress and in state and local legislatures.[114] Then in the midseventies, it received an unexpected lift from "the establishment": the Ford, Rockefeller, and Carnegie foundations all made generous grants.[115] But the optimism proved to be short-lived. Much of the progress that had been made was rent by the events in Skokie, Illinois, in 1977. American Nazis, assisted by the ACLU, were planning to march in the Jewish community of Skokie. This incident pitted one civil libertarian against the other, extracting arguments of reason and emotion from both sides. When it was over, the Union had made many enemies and few friends. But it survived nonetheless and regrouped with as much verve as one could expect.

From the perspective of the ACLU, it seems fair to say that the 1980s (and by inference the 1990s) will be remembered as the era of endurance. The election of Ronald Reagan, the rise of the New Right, and the public's desire for stability and direction have sent the liberal community into a tailspin. Even on the intellectual front, liberals have to face a challenge: the neoconservatives have emerged and are armed with contrary ideas. Men and women such as Irving Kristol, Norman Podhoretz, Midge Decter, and Jeane Kirkpatrick have attacked liberalism from all sides. *Public Interest, Commentary, American Spectator, Policy Review*, and the many publications of the American Enterprise Institute are just some of the organs in which neoconservative thought can be found. Committed to the tenets of liberalism before it became radicalized, the neoconservatives have targeted the ACLU as an organization that they "can do without."[116] Whether the ACLU will be able to meet this test of endurance depends partially on the efforts of its fifth executive director, Ira Glasser, who has held the top position since 1978. Glasser's true test is not likely to come from the New Right; extremists do not have a very impressive track record in the United States. The "thunder on the right" that the Union will not be able to avoid, however, comes from its neoconservative critics, many of whom are prepared to meet the ACLU face to face in the courts.

A Note on ACLU Policy

Throughout all of the chapters, coverage is given primarily to the policy decisions of the Union's national Board of Directors. Occasionally, reference will be made to the behavior of its affiliates. The national office, located in New York City, grants considerable autonomy to its affiliates throughout the country. Until 1950, policy decisions were made almost exclusively by the Board of Directors (and before 1929, by the Executive Committee). The board itself was "personally involved in almost every decision affecting the operation of the Union."[117] In 1950 it decided to become a "grass-roots" organization and the policy-making process became more intricate.[118] The ACLU did not have a policy guide of any sort until 1966, an important milestone in the growth of the Union.[119] The policy guides state the decisions of the national board on various civil liberties issues as a reference for its affiliates. In no way are the policy guides expected to be a "set of rigid commandments handed down by the Board."[120]

The constitution of the ACLU states that the national Board of Directors shall be composed of (a) one director elected by each affiliate, (b) thirty-six directors, who shall be elected at large, and (c) the chairman of the National Advisory Council *ex officio*. The board meets four times a year to decide policy.[121] Since 1950 it has received input from standing committees; if the committee recommendation is approved, it becomes policy for everyone.[122] The board makes every effort not to isolate itself from the rank and file; the Biennial Conferences are particularly helpful in this regard.

Although most members of the ACLU share a liberal bias, it should not be assumed that sharp disagreements over policies are uncommon. Liberals, as well as conservatives, have an identifiable mind-set, but that does not mean that unanimity is easily achieved on every issue. There is considerable room for argument within liberal and conservative circles alike. We see this diversity in action within the ACLU when there is disagreement between the national board and one of the affiliates. Generally, the national board will yield to an affiliate when a dispute arises over policy. In serious cases, the board will assert itself; it may, for example, decide to take a case that an affiliate has chosen to reject. Occasionally, discord extends to a confrontation between affiliates; this may occur when there is confusion as to whose rights have been violated in a particular case. Much more common is the struggle that ensues within the national board when new policies are being considered. Like the Supreme Court, the board decides by majority vote. And, as with the court, it is on the final outcomes that judgments must be made regarding its record. It is with this understanding that the following judgments on the ACLU's record are made.

Notes

1. Samuel P. Huntington, *American Politics: The Politics of Disharmony* (Cambridge: Harvard University Press, 1981), p. 14.
2. Ibid., p. 15.
3. Ibid., p. 23.
4. Ibid., p. 25.
5. Louis Hartz, *The Liberal Tradition in America* (New York: Harcourt, Brace and World, 1955), p. 21.
6. Clinton Rossiter, *Conservatism in America,* 2d ed. rev. (New York: Random House, 1962), p. 78.
7. Huntington, *American Politics,* pp. 12, 39.
8. Civil liberties are the rights of individuals as defined by the Bill of Rights. *Civil rights* refers to equal treatment before the law regardless of group membership.
9. "'I Fear the Attrition of the Law's Prestige': A Conversation with William F. Buckley, Jr.," *Civil Liberties Review,* March/April 1978, p. 47.

10. AR '77, front cover.
11. AR 1, pp. 7-8.
12. '81 PG, #524.
13. Interview with John H. F. Shattuck, "The Defense of Liberty," *Center Magazine*, November/December 1979, p. 43.
14. David Smothers, "ACLU Struggles Against Conversative Times," *Pittsburgh Press,* 9 August 1980, p. B-1.
15. Interview with Roger N. Baldwin, June 1978, at his home in New York City.
16. Smothers, "ACLU Struggles Against Conservative Times," p. B-1.
17. Corliss Lamont, *Yes to Life: Memoirs of Corliss Lamont* (New York: Horizon Press, 1981), ch. 12.
18. J. Anthony Lukas, "The ACLU Against Itself," *New York Times Magazine,* 9 July 1978, pp. 10-11.
19. Ibid., p. 10.
20. The Union has made numerous references to such charges in its annual reports, newsletters, and public statements since 1920. See also Charles Lam Markmann, *The Noblest Cry* (New York: St. Martin's Press, 1965), pp. 428-29.
21. "Offensive/Defensive," *New York Times,* 19 May 1981, p. A14.
22. Markmann, *The Noblest Cry,* p. 428.
23. Barton Bean, "Pressure for Freedom: The American Civil Liberties Union," Ph.D. diss., Cornell University, 1955, p. i.
24. Ibid., p. 316.
25. Ibid., pp. 279-81; 288-89.
26. Donald Johnson, *The Challenge to American Freedoms* (Lexington: University of Kentucky Press, 1963), p. vi.
27. Bean, "Pressure for Freedom," p. 289.
28. Ibid., p. 378.
29. Ibid., p. 390.
30. Alan F. Westin, "Our Freedom—And the Rights of Communists: A Reply to Irving Kristol," *Commentary,* July 1952, p. 35.
31. William Gerber, *American Liberalism* (Boston: Twayne Publishers, 1975), p. 123.
32. Bernard Weinraub, "Liberal Groups Are Joining Forces to Defend Their Goals and Gains," *New York Times,* 9 March 1981, p. B6.
33. Moral Majority advertisement, *New York Times,* 23 March 1981, p. B11.
34. Bean, "Pressure for Freedom," p. 355.
35. Ibid., p. 349.
36. Interview with John H. F. Shattuck, p. 44.
37. "New York Liberties Union Lauds Legislature," *New York Times,* 4 October 1981, p. 53.
38. In fall 1982, just prior to the November elections, the ACLU paid for a letter to be sent to its members requesting contributions to finance its effort to enforce the Voting Rights Act. The letter was written and signed by Lucius Holloway, councilman from Dawson, Georgia. This is only one of several ways the ACLU has used to convey its sympathies for a particular political figure.
39. Robert Nisbet, in symposium "What Is a Liberal—Who Is Conservative," *Commentary,* September 1976, p. 84.
40. Sidney Hook, ibid., p. 70.
41. John Dewey, *Liberalism and Social Action* (New York: Capricorn Books, 1935), p. 48.

42. Dennis Wrong, in symposium "What Is a Liberal—Who Is Conservative," *Commentary,* September 1976, p. 111.
43. Hartz, *Liberal Tradition in America,* p. 4.
44. John Stuart Mill, "On Liberty," in *The Philosophy of John Stuart Mill,* ed. Marshall Cohen (New York: Modern Library, 1961), p. 204.
45. Gertrude Himmelfarb, *On Liberty and Liberalism: The Case of John Stuart Mill* (New York: Knopf, 1974), pp. 71-72.
46. Ibid., p. 299.
47. Ibid., pp. 72-73, 283.
48. Mill, "On Liberty," p. 240.
49. Ibid., p. 249.
50. Ibid., pp. 275-76.
51. Ibid.
52. Himmelfarb, *On Liberty and Liberalism,* p. 285.
53. Edward Shils, "The Antinomies of Liberalism," in *The Relevance of Liberalism,* ed. Zbigniew Brzezinski (Boulder, Colo.: Westview Press, 1978). This essay by Shils is the most useful one of its kind in understanding the transformation of liberalism.
54. Michael Freeden, *The New Liberalism* (Oxford: Clarendon Press, 1978), pp. 22-23.
55. Ibid., p. 71.
56. Shils, "Antinomies of Liberalism," pp. 142-44.
57. Freeden, *New Liberalism,* p. 22.
58. Nisbet, in "What Is a Liberal—Who Is a Conservative," p. 85.
59. Nisbet, *The History of the Idea of Progress* (New York: Basic Books, 1980), p. 235.
60. Kenneth Minogue, *The Liberal Mind* (London: Methuen, 1963), p. 14.
61. Shils, "Antinomies of Liberalism," p. 138.
62. John Dewey, "The Meaning of Liberalism," *Social Frontier,* December 1935, p. 75.
63. Edmund Wilson, "An Appeal to Progressives," *New Republic,* 14 January 1931, p. 237.
64. L. T. Hobhouse, *The Elements of Social Justice* (London: Allen and Unwin, 1922), p. 61.
65. Ibid., pp. 60-61.
66. Dewey, *Liberalism and Social Action,* p. 54.
67. John Dewey, "Liberalism and Equality," *Social Frontier,* January 1936, pp. 105-6.
68. Hobhouse, *Elements of Social Justice,* p. 58.
69. Ibid., p. 62.
70. Ibid., pp. 74-75.
71. Ibid., pp. 83-84.
72. John Dewey, "Liberalism and Civil Liberties," *Social Frontier,* February 1936, p. 137.
73. Dewey, *Liberalism and Social Action,* p. 20.
74. Shils, "Antinomies of Liberalism," p. 160.
75. Ibid., p. 140.
76. Robert Lekachman, *Greed Is Not Enough* (New York: Pantheon, 1982), p. 208.
77. Lionel Trilling, *The Liberal Imagination* (New York: Viking Press, 1950), p. ix. More recently, Peter Berger has argued that contemporary conservatism is

unmistakenly liberal in inspiration. See Peter Steinfels, *The Neo-Conservatives* (New York: Simon and Schuster, 1979), ch. 1. For a different view see George H. Nash, *The Conservative Intellectual Tradition in America* (New York: Basic Books, 1976).

78. In 1956 and 1980, Schlesinger wrote articles on contemporary liberalism in the *New York Times Magazine.* On both occasions he cited the Niebuhr example. See his "Conservative vs. Liberal—A Debate," 4 March 1956, pp. 11, 58, and "Is Liberalism Dead?" 30 March 1980, p. 70.
79. Quoted in Gerber, *American Liberalism,* p. 85.
80. Clark's admission is in the foreword to Alan Reitman, *The Pulse of Freedom* (New York: W. W. Norton, 1975), p. xvi.
81. Richard Chase, "Liberalism and Literature," *Partisan Review,* June 1949, p. 649.
82. Minogue, *Liberal Mind,* p. 25.
83. The study of the interaction between an organization and its environment is known as an open-systems approach. This is the model that is adopted here. It is especially suited for studying organizational change. See James D. Thompson, *Organizations in Action* (New York: McGraw-Hill, 1967), for a good account of this approach. For an organizational account of the ACLU, see my dissertation, "Organizational Change Within the American Civil Liberties Union," New York University, 1980.
84. For a good account of how organizations affect their environment, see Gerald Zaltman, Robert Duncan, and Jonny Holbek, *Innovations and Organizations* (New York: John Wiley and Sons, 1973).
85. Charles Perrow, "An Analysis of Goals in Complex Organizations," *American Sociological Review* 26 (December 1961):855.
86. Amitai Etzioni, *A Comparative Analysis of Complex Organizations,* rev. ed. (New York: Free Press, 1961), p. 104.
87. These terms have been used by Alan Reitman of the ACLU. See his chapter "Past, Present and Future," in his edited work, *The Pulse of Freedom.*
88. See the splendid biography of Baldwin by Peggy Lamson, *Roger Baldwin: Founder of the American Civil Liberties Union* (Boston: Houghton Mifflin, 1976), p. 9.
89. Ibid., p. 18.
90. "Roger Baldwin, 97, Is Dead: Crusader for Civil Rights Founded the ACLU," *New York Times,* 27 August 1981, p. D18.
91. Ibid.
92. Letter by Baldwin to the members of the National Committee, 7 February 1929, p. 1. The letter is contained in the minutes of the early Board meetings.
93. Ibid., p. 2.
94. Ibid., p. 1.
95. AR 9, pp. 44, 46.
96. AR 12, p. 58.
97. AR 18, pp. 52-53.
98. AR 17, p. 54.
99. AR 10, p. 3.
100. AR 15, p. 8.
101. AR 12, p. 29.
102. AR 18, p. 53; AR 28, pp. 82-83.
103. This includes the Northern California branch, which maintained separate membership. AR 28, p. 82; AR 36, p. 76.

104. AR 29, pp. 11-13.
105. Lamson, *Baldwin,* p. 267.
106. AR 30, p. 116.
107. AR 28, p. 79.
108. AR 36, p. 76; AR 43, p. 32.
109. AR 43, p. 32.
110. Ibid., p. 29 and AR 24, p. 145.
111. AR 39, p. 98.
112. AR 43, p. 24.
113. AR 43, p. 32; AR '72-'73, p. 3.
114. AR '72-'73, p. 3.
115. Bd. Min., 6/21-22/75, p. 7.
116. The editors of *Esquire* listed the ACLU as one of the organizations that "Neocons Can Do Without" on 13 February 1979, p. 31.
117. Alan Reitman, "Introduction," '76 PG, p. 2.
118. Ibid.
119. Reitman, "Introduction," '81 PG, p. ii.
120. Ibid.
121. '81 PG, #501.
122. '76 PG, pp. 2-3.

2

Civil Liberties, Equality, and Social Justice

The Political Origins of the ACLU

Reform is an American tradition. There is hardly an American institution that has not, at one time or another, come under serious examination, questioning, and criticism. Just how much change such efforts have brought is open to debate, but what no one questions is the American resolve to engage in the enterprise of reform. Tocqueville noticed this over 150 years ago: "It is hard to explain the place filled by political concerns in the life of an American. To take a hand in the government of society and to talk about it is his most important business, and so to say, the only pleasure he knows."[1] While this is no doubt an overstatement, it does draw our attention to the dynamic nature of the American temperament.

The politics of reform has been associated with the politics of liberalism. This is particularly true of twentieth-century liberalism. Indeed, the twentieth century was born in an era of reform—the Progressive era. It was the liberals of that era who pushed for reform and established equality and social justice as national goals.[2] These goals would remain in force throughout the twentieth century, as liberals targeted a series of issues that merited a response. The issues they seized upon—war, the draft, government regulation of big business, poverty, welfare, tax reform, voting reform, crime, the environment, job safety, health, and the rights of Blacks, women, workers, and consumers—are the issues of the Progressive era as well as the issues of the 1960s.

It was during the Progressive era that liberalism initially moved left, absorbing the spirit, if not the agenda, of its radical allies. The policies of Theodore Roosevelt and the ideas of Herbert Croly became the pillar of the new liberalism. Both men asserted what all liberals came to accept, namely, that Jeffersonian ideals could best be achieved by adopting Hamiltonian means. "Reform is both meaningless and powerless," wrote Croly, "unless the Jeffersonian principle of non-interference is abandoned."[3] The price to be paid for unnecessarily restraining the role of the federal government was greater inequalities and attendant social problems. The free market, Croly contended, led to the absence of freedom: "Americans have always associated individual freedom with the unlimited popular enjoyment of all available economic opportunities. Yet it would be far more true to say that popular enjoyment of practically unrestrained economic opportunities is precisely the condition which makes for individual bondage."[4] This rejection of laissez-faire did not lead liberals to follow the European model of forming a new labor party. Perhaps it was the Burkean strain in American liberalism[5] that accounted for the unwillingness of most liberals to pursue the ambitions of Eugene V. Debs. At any rate, it was the goal of Croly, founder of the *New Republic*, and his colleagues Walter Weyl and Walter Lippmann, to strengthen liberalism while finding a substitute for socialism.[6]

Historian Charles Forcey has labeled the years during and after World War I as the "crossroads of liberalism."[7] It was then that liberals braced for the challenge of war in Europe and the conflict between classes at home. Capitalism was under strong attack from many quarters, propelling liberal intellectuals to mobilize their resources in an attempt to address the social and economic divisions that existed. Liberals and Progressives were now one and the same,[8] aligning themselves with the labor movement. Seeking social melioration, liberalism became "goodwill turned doctrinaire."[9] Modern liberals, writes Kenneth Minogue, are a group that "consists of those who consider themselves morally bound to become involved in any suffering situation of which they are aware."[10] Such a description is an apt portrait of liberals at the time of World War I.

When the war broke out in Europe some members of the liberal community in the United States quickly organized a collective response. Imbued with a sense of urgency, a distinguished group of men and women, most of whom were social workers, religious leaders, and intellectuals, gathered together for the purpose of opposing the war and the preparedness movement at home. Paul Kellogg, editor of *Survey*, an influential magazine for social workers; Jane Addams, founder of Chicago's Hull House; and Lillian Wald, director of the Henry Street Settlement House in New York City, began the antimilitarist campaign in the fall of 1914. They summoned a "who's who" of liberals, all dedicated to pressure President Wilson "to advance the cause of world federation." Their efforts gave birth to the American Union Against Militarism (AUAM) in 1915.

In the spring of 1917, Roger Baldwin joined the AUAM national directing committee. The young social worker was given this opportunity by Wald and Oswald Garrison Villard, editor of the *Nation*, when one of the members, socialist Crystal Eastman, took ill. Possessing more energy and leadership than any of his colleagues, Baldwin was largely responsible for more than doubling the size of the AUAM within his first six months of service.[11] Once the United States entered the war, he turned his attention to the problems of war resisters; he formed the Bureau for Conscientious Objectors as an arm of the AUAM. With all this, he even found time to join the People's Council, another antiwar group composed mostly of socialists.[12]

Problems arose within the AUAM when Wald, Kellogg, and others were urging the Wilson administration to make a negotiated peace while Baldwin was simultaneously attacking the authorities for their prosecution of war resisters. Wald, in fact, threatened to resign unless Baldwin tempered his criticisms. The Board of Directors of the AUAM backed Baldwin but suggested that a less inflammatory name for his Bureau for Conscientious Objectors be adopted. The name "Civil Liberties Bureau" was chosen but it failed to persuade the skeptics. After the *New York Times* denounced the new organization for hindering the work of the AUAM, Wald again threatened resignation. The issue was resolved when the bureau formally split with the AUAM and became the National Civil Liberties Bureau (NCLB). Baldwin, now delighted, took charge of the new organization on 1 October, 1917.[13]

Most of the leaders of the NCLB were radicals[14] who derived their ideological inspiration from the Progressives.[15] Many of them, including Baldwin, were even more radical than most Progressives, drawing their ideas from socialist and anarchist writers.[16] Baldwin, for example, leaned heavily on Kropotkin, the Russian anarchist, and was, in many ways, more unyielding in his beliefs than most others in the NCLB. What most joined members of the NCLB together, however, was a strong animus against capitalism. Donald Johnson has observed the same characteristic of the NCLB staff: "There was always an undercurrent of anti-industrialism, of opposition to big business, in the thinking of Baldwin and other civil libertarians."[17] Opposed to both capitalism and the war,[18] Baldwin and the NCLB continued to defend war resisters and the members of the International Workers of the World, the so-called Wobblies. Baldwin, in fact, had been a member of the IWW.[19] As a result of the NCLB's defending those who had been convicted under the Espionage Act of 1917, the FBI raided the New York offices of the NCLB in the late summer of 1918.[20] This was part of the notorious Palmer raids conducted under the aegis of Attorney General A. Mitchell Palmer.[21]

In September 1918, Baldwin pled guilty to refusing the draft and was sentenced to one year in jail. He wrote a letter to his local draft board explaining his reasoning: "My opposition is not only to direct military service, but to any service whatever designed to help the war. I am further-more opposed to the principle of conscription in time of war or peace, for any purpose whatsoever. I will decline to perform any service under com-pulsion, regardless of its character."[22]

When Baldwin left prison in 1919, he announced his primary objective: "I am going to do what a so-called intellectual can do in the labor move-ment and aid in the struggle of the workers to control society in the inter-ests of the mass."[23] Johnson's comment on this statement of Baldwin's is telling: "These are the words of men who believe that the struggle for civil liberties is essentially a struggle against the evils of industrial capitalism."[24] The freed Baldwin returned to the NCLB and actually partook, however briefly, in "workers'" jobs: he carried bricks on a construction job, laid rails with a railroad section gang, and shoveled coal in a lead smelter. He even participated in the great national steel strike in 1919.[25] Convinced that the workers were the key to social change, he sought to instruct his allies at the NCLB that the defense of civil liberties for labor was a realistic way to advance their political beliefs.

One gets a feel for Baldwin's leftist proclivities at this time by reading the correspondence he had with his friends. In a letter to Joseph Cannon, Baldwin opened with "Dear Brother Cannon."[26] Similarly, those who wrote to him frequently began by stating their solidarity; Fred Biedenkapp, trea-surer of the Workers Defense Union, thanked Baldwin for his NCLB con-tribution by addressing him as "Dear Comrade."[27] Baldwin's close friend Emma Goldman provides us with an even more graphic picture of the cast of mind of radicals at this time. Upon her deportation from the United States in December 1919, she and her associate, Alexander Berkman, spoke for many radicals when they issued their pamphlet "Last Message to the People of America":

> Liberty is dead, and white terror on top dominates the country. Free speech is a thing of the past. Revolution is stalking across Europe. Its spectre is threat-ening America. Disquieting signs multiply daily. A new discontent, boding ill and full of terrible possibilities, is manifest in every walk of life. The war has satisfied no one. Only too obviously the glorious promises failed of fulfilment [sic]. Excepting the great financial interests and some smaller war profiteers, the American people at large are aching with a poignant disappointment. Some vaguely, other [sic] more consciously and clearly, but almost all feel themselves in some way victimized.[28]

When the war ended, many at the NCLB were concerned that the bu-reau's image had become too easily associated with pacifists, conscientious objectors, and opponents of the war.[29] It was fitting that the most powerful figure in the NCLB, director Baldwin, would lead the way. In December

1919, he sent a memo to his colleagues urging a reorganization of the NCLB. His thinking reveals the real intention of the "civil libertarians" and the nascent ACLU:

> The Bureau was organized to deal with war-time problems. Because of the sharp division of opinion it was practicable to secure the support and interests only of those who opposed the war or who supported it with reservations. That issue being now past, a new line-up is necessary if the Bureau is to serve the cause of freedom in the industrial struggle. The Bureau is bound to serve partisan causes though standing on a general principle. *The cause we now serve is labor. We are frankly partisans of labor in the present struggle. It would be absurd to expect opponents of the cause of labor to join with us in the application of the general principle.*[30] [Emphasis added.]

Specifically, Baldwin recommended that the NCLB organize the steel workers in western Pennsylvania, provoking them to challenge public officials: "We have got [to] take the risks of conflict with the authorities and even of mob violence. We can do nothing effective by sitting safely in New York. The business of the office here should be merely to back up those in the field."[31] These do not sound like the words of someone who is exclusively dedicated to the Bill of Rights. Nor do they sound like the words of a "pacifist."

One month later, on 20 January, 1920, the American Civil Liberties Union was born. Three groups of people were sought by Baldwin to serve in the ACLU: "1) those directly engaged in the labor struggle . . . , 2) those who by their writing and speaking are close to labor problems, and 3) those who stand on general principles for freedom of expression"[32] (the great catchall category, as Peggy Lamson has noted). According to Barton Bean, Baldwin's stance represented his "apparent need to express his nearness to the organized radical movement" and "his emphasis on social ends rather than on the process of freedom."[33] More recently, one of the Union's senior officials, John Shattuck, stated that "Baldwin saw the ACLU not as a collection of lawyers but as a collection of activists."[34] Activists, it might be said, in service to labor and in opposition to capitalism.

When the ACLU was founded, it had two directing committees. The large National Executive Committee was composed of "labor leaders, labor sympathizers and 'unattached liberals'"; the Directing Committee consisted of National Committee members who lived in New York.[35] The National Executive Committee, later renamed the Board of Directors,[36] had sixty-four members in 1920, all of them "showcase personalities, good for letterheads,"[37] as Baldwin later described them. Dr. Harry F. Ward, professor at the Union Theological Seminary, was chairman. Serving as vice-chairmen were Duncan McDonald, president of the United Mine Workers in Chicago, and Jeannette Rankin, the only member of Congress to vote against both world wars. Baldwin shared the directorship with Albert De-Silver, a respected lawyer who died in an accident at the age of thirty-six. Other notables included L. Hollingsworth Wood, Norman Thomas, Crystal Eastman, John Lovejoy Elliott, John Haynes Holmes, Agnes Brown Leach, Judah Magnes, Helen Phelps Stokes, Walter Nelles, Joseph Cannon, John Codman, Elizabeth Gurley Flynn, William Z. Foster, Felix Frankfurter, Arthur Garfield Hays, James Weldon Johnson, Helen Keller, Robert Lovett, Scott Nearing, John Nevin Sayre, and Oswald Garrison Villard.[38]

Roger Baldwin was a busy man in 1920, founding not only the ACLU but three other organizations as well. All of them were started to serve partisan politics—the cause of the Left. The Mutual Aid Society was formed to assist radicals who needed help getting jobs, loans, counsel, bail, etc. Those who serviced such clients were, as Baldwin once described them, "leftist intellectuals, trade unionists, the radical fringe. The Mutual Aid Society was used exclusively for people on the left and people in the labor movement."[39] The International Committee for Political Prisoners (ICPP) was set up by Baldwin after his companion Emma Goldman was deported, along with thousands of other radicals. The purpose of this organization was to raise money for the deported aliens and to contact agencies in foreign countries that could aid them. Baldwin's depiction of the ICPP and his reply to Peggy Lamson's question is a frank admission of the circles he traveled in: "We set up a network of correspondents in the various countries, and we had contacts with the Communist movement and with the Socialist International in New York plus a very strong committee." "The usual ACLU People?" "Yes, a lot of the same crowd."[40] Baldwin's fourth organization of 1920 was the American Fund for Public Service. It was established after Baldwin learned that a Boston radical had inherited millions of dollars—money that the young man could not, in good conscience, spend on himself. Baldwin found a way for him to spend his money with pride: give it to radical causes. On the board of this new adventure were Baldwin's regulars: "We had a liberal leftist board of my usual colleagues," the founder of the ACLU once explained. Evidently, business acumen was not one of the virtues of this group: the millions were gone in twelve years.[41]

Baldwin's activities and associations in 1920 were so thoroughly politicized as to preclude the establishment of a "nonpartisan" ACLU. Indeed, his statement that "we are frankly partisans of labor" indicates the lack of neutrality that the Union represented. As we have seen, those who were drawn to the ACLU came, intentionally, from the ranks of the Left. It is therefore not surprising to learn that no industrialist ever sat on the National Executive Committee. This fact prompted Donald Johnson to re-mark that "the ACLU's approach to civil liberties appears to have been quite definitely one-sided."[42] Johnson's phrase "appears to have been quite definitely" is indicative of his unwillingness to conclude firmly that the early ACLU was not a "nonpartisan" organization. After presenting evidence to the contrary, Johnson is still driven to defend the "objectivity" of the civil libertarians:

> All of this might seem to indicate that the NCLB-ACLU was not actually civil libertarian; that it was a special interest group, devoted perhaps not only to the cause of labor, but to the elimination of the capitalist system. This kind of an interpretation, however, would be completely misleading and would distort the real significance of the civil liberties movement.[43]

Is it "completely misleading" to argue that the NCLB-ACLU was more interested in advancing the agenda of the Left than it was in protecting the First Amendments rights of, say, Catholics? The evidence would not suggest so. Consider Baldwin's reply to Lamson when he was asked why there were so few Jews on the first ACLU Board. "Because the Jews behaved badly, that's why not." When pressed to be explicit, Baldwin countered, "I mean they were all for the war," and added, "And what's more they were not pro-labor either."[44] Being prolabor was without question the ideological litmus test for sitting on the ACLU's board.

During the first ten days of May 1920, E. M. Humphreys, under the supervision of Rexford Tugwell, conducted a civil liberties survey for the Union in Philadelphia. Twenty-three persons were questioned, offering their name, address, occupation and interests. Interestingly, twenty listed themselves as liberal, socialist, Communist, or radical; the other three were Democrats.[45] These were the kinds of persons whom the ACLU trusted for advice. It was so well known that the Union was identified with partisan politics that few persons, either in or outside the organization, even bothered to question it. One person who did was board member John Codman. Remembered by Baldwin as an "untouchable, above reproach,"[46] Codman began to raise serious questions about the ACLU's leftist approach within a month after its founding.

Codman's inquiries concerning ACLU activities led Elizabeth Gurley Flynn, one of the Union's most active radicals, to counsel Baldwin about the reliability of Codman. She informed Baldwin that Codman had been a guard in the Boston police strike, indicating his lack of sympathy to labor. On 28 February, Baldwin wrote to a Mrs. Anna Davis, asking her to confirm Flynn's charge. He wrote that Flynn had told him about Codman's having been a guard in the strike and his having "justified before the

League of Democratic Control his activism as a defender of law and order against the striking policemen." The critical reason for Baldwin's concern, however, was the ACLU's image amongst its principal clients: "Miss Flynn points out that this will prejudice our appeal to the labor groups because Mr. Codman's record seems to be somewhat known among them."[47]

After Codman wrote Baldwin asking about the political status of the ACLU, Baldwin retaliated with an inquiry of his own as to whether Codman had actually been a guard in the police strike: "The attitude of the labor folks is apparently that any person performing such service is opposed to the interests of organized labor." Codman responded that he had, in fact, been a guard in the strike, explaining that "I would have done this no matter where my sympathies lay. After the strike took place the city needed help maintaining law and order and it was the duty of every man to do what he could to assist." He concluded his letter of 8 March with a statement of principle:

> Finally I would say that my interest in the American Civil Liberties Union is entirely in the interest of maintaining civil rights guaranteed by the Constitution. I am no more interested in these rights for the laboring men than I am for anybody else and I do not like the idea of the American Civil Liberties Union becoming a partisan of labor, and I hope it is not the intentions of the Union to do so.

Upon receipt of Codman's letter, Baldwin replied that partaking as a guard in the strike "has nothing to do with civil liberties and has no connection with the work of our organization. But I suppose that serving largely the interests of labor in the struggle for free speech and free press we are bound to have such inquiries about our attitude on the labor struggle itself."[48]

In the fall of 1920, Herbert Croly wrote a provocative article for the *New Republic*, "The Eclipse of Progressivism." He declared that the present government was "sick" and incapable of rectifying the divisions that capitalism had created:

> Class cleavage born of one-class domination itself poisons the democratic government which should be able to cure its own maladies. Political democracy must call to its assistance social and industrial democracy in order to regain its health. Those progressives who refuse a radical diagnosis of the sickness of political democracy will cease to be progressives.[49]

Croly was convinced that the "capitalist class" had thwarted the ideals of democracy. After citing a few examples, he reflected:

> These instances convinced me of the futility of expecting the American government to heal the class cleavage through the action exclusively of the

existing machinery of political self-government. American law and practice place economic and social power preponderantly in the hands of one class. The class exploits the organization and shibboleths of democracy. . . . Its ownership of the press enables it to foster the stigma of disloyalty upon wage earners who are threatening in the interest of their own independence the existing control of industry. . . .[50]

What is most interesting about Croly's tirade is the fact that the ACLU took the identical position in its first annual report. Even the jargon is the same:

Behind this machinery [of suppression] stand the property interests of the country, so completely in control of our political life as to establish what is in effect a class government,—a government by and for business. Political democracy as conceived by many of America's greatest leaders, does not exist, except in a few communities. This condition is not yet understood by the public at large. They are drugged by propaganda and blinded by a press necessarily subservient to property interests. Dazed by the kaleidoscopic changes of the last few years, the rank and file citizens accept the dictatorship of property in the name of patriotism.[51]

The parallels between the thinking of the *New Republic* and the ACLU are striking but hardly surprising, given their political leanings. Both called for liberalism to be more aggressive[52] and to look toward the working class as a means for change.[53] Freedom, for the ACLU, was predicated on economic power: "We realize that these standards of civil liberty cannot be attained as abstract principles or as constitutional guarantees. Economic or political power is necessary to assert and maintain all 'rights.'"[54] Freedom would be won through "the union of organized labor, the farmers, radical and liberal movements."[55]

When I interviewed Baldwin in his home in New York City in 1978, I asked him about the ACLU's first annual report. I told him that statements such as "there is a dictatorship of the propertied class in America" sounded like an orthodox Marxist position. His reply was enlightening, but did not directly answer my question:

Well, you don't have to be a Marxist to describe the differences between the employing class and the working class. They are opposed to each other. The working class is trying to get as much out of the employer and the capitalist as he can, and the capitalist is trying to pay the lowest wages that he can. You don't need Karl Marx to explain that to you. That's a natural hostility—class hostility—between two groups of people who are diametrically opposed. Now, Marx may have described it, but you don't need to be a Marxist to describe a perfectly obvious fact of life.[56]

Baldwin is correct: one does not have to be a Marxist to accept Marxian logic. But it is also true that one need not be sympathetic to Marxism to be a civil libertarian.

Throughout the 1920s the ACLU saw itself as a part of the "center of resistance" that had emerged to counter the forces of repression. Other organizations that constituted the "center of resistance" included, according to the Union, the United Mine Workers, the IWW, the Amalgamated Clothing Workers, and the Communist party.[57] Such a coalition was not enough to satisfy the ACLU: "A militant, central bureau in the labor movement for legal aid, defense strategy, information, and propaganda is an obvious need."[58] The abridgment of civil liberties affecting workers had become so extensive during the decade that the ACLU could claim that "the whole fight has been transferred to the field of conflict of organized capital and organized labor. . . ."[59]

Even if the ACLU had not been an organization whose cause was labor and had been instead the nonpartisan group that it advertised itself to be, it would have found itself defending the rights of labor more than any other segment of the population, save perhaps Blacks; the rights of labor in the 1920s were summarily violated by the authorities in many parts of the country. In California, Upton Sinclair, an original member of the ACLU, was arrested after he tried to read the Bill of Rights and the Constitution to a group of strikers.[60] Meetings of the Workers party were broken up in many places, from McKeesport, Pennsylvania, to Centralia, Washington.[61] The worst abuses of the decade occurred in New Jersey, western Pennsylvania, and West Virginia. In 1924, in Paterson, New Jersey, the ACLU came to the aid of the Associated Silk Workers, whose 6,000 members went out on strike. The Union and the strikers sought to hold a rally after the police chief had closed down meetings of the strikers. The police moved in and arrested several persons, including Baldwin. Baldwin was indicted by a grand jury for breaking a 1796 law barring unlawful assembly. His conviction was reversed by the New Jersey Supreme Court, which voided the antiquated statute.[62] A similar law was tested two years later in Passaic when Norman Thomas was arrested for speaking against the "riot law." Successful again, the ACLU was instrumental in the decision to issue an injunction preventing the authorities from interfering with peaceful assembly.[63]

In what seemed to be an eternal struggle, the ACLU was frequently assisting the rights of mine workers and steel workers in Logan, West Virginia, and in Pittsburgh. In 1924, the Union concluded that "violations of civil rights are probably more common in West Virginia than in any other part of the United States."[64] In Logan County, for example, mine operators paid armed guards and deputized them as sheriffs in an attempt to harass their employees.[65] By the end of the decade, the condition of labor had deteriorated so far in Pennsylvania that the Union exclaimed, "More violations of civil rights occur in Pennsylvania than in all the other states combined."[66] The situation was so bad in the western part of the state that the faculty at the University of Pittsburgh founded a branch of the ACLU to defend the rights of local industrial workers.[67] It is not surprising, then, that in the Union's last report of the 1920s, it found that four out of every five cases that were brought to its attention involved industrial conflict.[68]

Given the extent of the repression that labor suffered in the 1920s, it would be plausible to conclude, as Johnson, Bean, and others have, that the ACLU was not a partisan of labor: If it defended labor more than any other segment of the population, it is because the rights of labor were more often abused. Tempting as this deduction is, it does not square with the evidence. The ACLU was prolabor because the personal politics of the founding members was left of center. Baldwin, as we have seen, did not even try to hide his political convictions. And neither did most of his colleagues. The only reason that Codman was upset about the politicization of the ACLU was because he thought, mistakenly, that he had joined a nonpartisan organization. The others were never upset; they knew what they had joined: an organization dedicated to the ends of social justice and equality, not civil liberties. Even Samuel Gompers, the head of the Amercian Federation of Labor, knew that the ACLU was interested in achieving goals that transcended its free speech efforts on the part of workers. He openly accused the ACLU and Baldwin's American Fund for Public Service of aiding and abetting revolutionary movements.[69]

The politics of the civil libertarians in the 1920s has been observed by Edward Shils: "The chief protégés of the civil libertarians tended to be radicals of socialistic inclinations."[70] Their real intent, he adds, was less than pure: "They were also usually friendly towards civil liberties because it was the critics of existing social conditions whose civil liberties were being restricted."[71] Lest one think that Shils's criticism of civil libertarians does not hold for the ACLU because the rights of the Ku Klux Klan were also defended, it would be instructive to consider Johnson's remark: "To be sure, the Union did not go out of its way to defend the Klan in the twenties; the civil liberties movement was too close to the days of its origin, too immersed in a struggle for liberals and the left, to worry about the difficulties of the right-wing."[72] The ACLU was so immersed in the platform of the Left that it even ignored the wholesale deprivation of basic civil liberties that the Volstead Act created. Imagine, an organization that vaunts its image as a protector of civil liberties does not raise its voice in protest to Prohibition! Bean absolves the Union by stating that it merely constituted one of several "errors of omission."[73] Baldwin was more candid: "We thought the Volstead Act was none of our business since it didn't touch on democratic liberties. We were wrong. We should have read the bill of rights."[74] Another explanation is afforded by Paul Murphy: "The ACLU's interests were so clearly political-economic, and so geared to the rights of anti-militarists, labor, and radicals, that it was only as the decade progressed that the body began concerning itself with other kinds of challenges."[75] As the record will show, the politically charged ACLU of the 1920s never broke stride in the 1930s either.

Civil Liberties during the Depression

When Herbert Croly published his classic work *The Promise of American Life* in 1909, he believed, as most liberals did, that capitalism was capable of being salvaged, provided that certain restraints on industry were levied by the government. When the depression hit, liberals lost their faith. Edmund Wilson said it best: "The benevolent and intelligent capitalism on which liberals have always counted has not merely materialized to the extent of metamorphosing itself into socialism—it has not even been able to prevent a national disaster of proportion which neither capitalists nor liberals foresaw and which they both profess themselves unable to explain."[76] The millions who were unemployed were surely a factor that contributed to the loss of faith in capitalism, but not the primary reason. Paul Hollander has contended that two themes were apparent in the thinking of Western intellectuals: social justice and, above all, "the striving for 'wholeness,' the sense of identity and community, meaning and purpose in life."[77] It is this lack of purpose that bothered liberals most about capitalism. When the market crashed, intellectuals like Wilson exposed their real hostility toward capitalism: "Money-making and the kind of advantages which a money-making society provides for money to buy are not enough to satisfy humanity—neither is a social system like our own where everyone is out for himself and the devil take the hindmost, with no common purpose and little common culture to give life stability and sense."[78]

The depression radicalized liberals more than any other event in the first part of the twentieth century. Those who were leaning toward socialism were now pushed into the sphere of Marxism. In writing about his days as a young New York intellectual in the 1930s, William Barrett recalled the scene: "The Great Depression hung over our heads, and socialism seemed the simple and inevitable answer."[79] To be an intellectual was to be a Marxist: "In our environment then it was taken as a matter of course that any young man of reasonable intelligence and good will would be Marxist."[80] Perhaps it was for this reason that when a major ACLU post was available in Boston and Philadelphia during the depression Baldwin requested the services of Alfred Baker Lewis, state secretary of the Socialist party of Massachusetts.[81] Fielding socialists to campaign for civil liberties simply made good sense in the 1930s; conservatives were not to be trusted.

In the Union's first annual report of the 1930s, it noted that the "great increase in repression was due to the fear of unrest and disorder during the economic depression."[82] Midway through the decade, the tone became shrill:

> The depression continues of course to create an atmosphere in which resort to gag measures is only too quick. The determination of employers to keep the labor movement in check, and passionate opposition to Communism (but to Fascism only in words) conspire to provoke attack upon all symptoms of working-class militancy, and all heresy to capitalism.[83]

To be sure, there was much to be disturbed about. Mayor Frank Hague of Jersey City declared, "I am the law," and proceeded to deny civil liberties to anyone he disliked.[84] Such occurrences were not infrequent. Although the struggle for freedom was waged on many fronts, the ACLU remained resolute in its conviction that "the struggle between capital and labor is the most vital application of the principle of civil liberty."[85] Despite such statements, and despite the opportunity that the depression afforded, the Union did not move into the arena of economic rights. On the contrary, it broke its relationship with the International Labor Defense precisely because that organization often insisted upon stressing in court the class and economic issues involved in "civil liberties" cases. "Lawyers," said the Union, "find it confusing under a joint arrangement to take directions from two sources."[86]

Just nine months before the election of Franklin Delano Roosevelt, Edmund Wilson proclaimed that personal liberty was "not today worth a cent as soon as you step out of your owning-class orbit."[87] In a vindictive article in the *New Republic*, Wilson charged that liberals such as Stuart Chase, Walter Lippmann, and Charles Beard had been duped: They failed to realize that capitalism was not capable of reforming itself.[88] John Dewey expressed a similar position: "If radicalism be defined as perception of need for radical change, then today any liberalism which is not also radicalism is irrelevant and doomed."[89] The message was clear: a liberalism that did not move left was bankrupt. It was futile, according to Wilson, to pin one's hopes on the possible election of Roosevelt; the capitalists would coopt any plan to change the status quo.[90]

It was not apparent when Roosevelt was elected that future historians would declare "he *was* liberalism."[91] Baldwin certainly did not foresee what Roosevelt's legacy would be. On the eve of the election, Baldwin announced that "whoever is elected on November 8th will not make much difference to the cause of civil liberty."[92] So pessimistic was Baldwin, that even when several ACLU members were recruited to work for the new president, it did not affect his outlook. Within a few weeks after Roosevelt's election, Baldwin remarked, "We are . . . embarrassed by the number of friends of Civil Liberty in public office in Washington and in the states because it is so difficult to quarrel with friends."[93] Baldwin's tone softened, somewhat, after he observed the first months of Roosevelt's tenure: "Since the advent of a new administration a changed and far more liberal attitude is apparent on the part of several departments of the government and of the President."[94] The people were now "under a rapidly developing regime of state capitalism."[95] The Union remarked that this was a unique event: "That this unprecedented increase in state power has not been accompanied by suppression, as in other countries, is due primarily to the fact that there is no real opposition to suppress."[96]

In June 1934 the ACLU issued an annual report entitled "Liberty Under the New Deal." The New Deal received an unfavorable report card from the Union. Industrial conflicts, it noted, had soared to new heights: "Troops have been called out against strikers in six states. Police, gunmen, sheriffs, injunctions, all have been invoked in the effort to crush labor organizations. Scores of strikers have been killed or wounded. Hundreds have been jailed on the flimsiest pretexts."[97] Against this background, the Roosevelt administration did not fare well. The New Deal policies did not modify the conditions of repression. Specifically, the ACLU charged that "government mediation has usually been at the expense of labor. Where the rights to organize have been won, the record clearly shows it is due on the whole to the determination of the workers not to governmental intervention."[98] As the Union saw it, this situation was not coincidental but, rather, a well-designed consequence of the administration's goals. The present role of the administration in the affairs of labor "could easily have been forecast by those who understand that its main purpose is the preservation of the existing economic system."[99] Then, in one of its boldest admissions, the Union asserted: "The administration is frankly an ally of business."[100] The ACLU even went as far as to charge that the New Deal devised a discriminatory wage standard in the South "obviously based on keeping Negroes in their place."[101] Events had become so bad under Roosevelt that for the first time in the Union's history, most of its work centered on Washington, as opposed to local governments.[102]

From the start, the ACLU had been downright distrustful of government. Its position was not, however, identical to that of the classical liberals, who saw government intervention as an unwarranted intrusion into the natural forces that directed social and economic life. The Union disliked government because it viewed government as an arm of the plutocrats. It had not been persuaded by the collectivistic liberals who maintained that government control could be used as an agent of reform. In this respect, the ACLU, as late as the 1930s, was closer to the radical camp than it was to liberalism. And it is for this reason that the Union did not initially welcome Roosevelt's policies affecting labor.

On 19 June 1933, the National Industrial Recovery Act (NIRA) was enacted. The administration had taken a bold move, attempting to regulate business and commerce. Minimum wages and maximum hours had been set and, more important, labor's right to organize and bargain collectively had been instituted. The ACLU, as well as the *New Republic* and the *Nation*, looked askance at the NIRA, hoping it would succeed but doubting that it would. Communists entertained no such skepticism: they denounced the Roosevelt "ploy."[103] It would not be long before the ACLU also opposed the scheme.

Whenever a conflict ensued between workers in the American Federation of Labor or the United Mine Workers (UMW), the ACLU was quick to align itself with the more radical elements. It did not support Gompers or John L. Lewis, viewing them as autocratic and conservative leaders. Consistent with this tendency, the ACLU, soon after the passage of the NIRA, became embroiled in the UMW struggle for power, siding with the dissidents. The "Progressive Miners" openly challenged the authority of Lewis, seeking autonomous representation. What Baldwin and his staff feared most was the effect that the NIRA would have on the insurgents. If the relationship between capital and labor was to become institutionalized, it would surely be at the expense of the radicals within the unions. Committed to the transformation of society, Baldwin, of course, believed it necessary to condemn vigorously any governmental plan that would enervate that process. He complained to the Labor Advisory Board of the National Recovery Administration (NRA), requesting that the Progressive Miners be protected in their right to choose their own representation. When he failed to secure the sympathies of that board, Baldwin steered the ACLU to the left, embracing the policy of the Communists.[104]

Baldwin's intransigence did not go unchallenged by other ACLU members. Morris Hillquit, socialist, labor activist, and an original member of the Union, argued that "it is not the function of the American Civil Liberties Union to meddle in internal problems and policies of organized labor."[105] For Hillquit, the ACLU was acting like "a bunch of 'intellectual busybodies,'" dividing further the rank and file of labor.[106] Similar sentiments were voiced by Joseph Schlossberg, the general secretary-treasurer of the Amalgamated Clothing Workers of America: "It is my conviction that the Civil Liberties Union should steer clear from matters pertaining to the relations between trade unions and employers."[107] Baldwin remained un-shaken, and clearly moved away from his original position of skepticism regarding the NIRA. Cletus Daniel explains why: "This change in disposition was due, in part, to the fact that there had been a strong lobby within the board of directors from the first to align the organization with those radical groups, including the Communists, who had taken the position that the New Deal ought to be opposed because it represented a last-ditch effort to prevent capitalism's well-deserved demise."[108] Daniel credits Harry F. Ward, Corliss Lamont, William B. Spofford, and Communist Robert W. Dunn with leading the left-wing segment of the ACLU's staff.[109]

In September 1933 Baldwin convened a meeting with the most extreme detractors of the New Deal. Communists and radical socialists joined with the ACLU to draft a statement to Roosevelt demanding that minority representation in the unions be recognized. In a series of highly charged statements, the coalition of radicals sought to alter substantially Roosevelt's program for labor. Predictably, Roosevelt did not want to associate himself with the radical fringe lest he alienate the great body of mainstream labor leaders.[110]

The turmoil continued when Senator Robert Wagner introduced the Labor Disputes Act on 1 March 1934. Wagner attempted to strengthen the NRA (National Recovery Administration) by investing broad powers in the National Labor Board (NLB), granting it the right to force employers to abide by its decisions as well as the right to curtail the company union. The act received the support of the NLB staff, the AFL, and the Socialist party; the Communist party and business groups opposed it, as did the ACLU. More than any other person, Mary Van Kleeck, who had been assigned by Baldwin to chair the ACLU's Subcommittee on Labor Policy, was instrumental in aligning the Union with the far Left. Van Kleeck's ideology was indistinguishable from that of the communists, replete with diatribes against capitalism and praise for the Soviet experiment. She informed Wagner that his proposal was suggestive of "the machinery of the Fascist state," and proceeded to persuade him of the futility of his good intentions. With the ACLU solidly in opposition to Wagner's initiative, along with extremists from both the Right and the Left, the Act was scrapped in favor of a substitute that was even less pleasing to the opposition.[111]

Baldwin wasted no time in convening another meeting of radicals to discuss new strategies. He was prepared to reject any federal regulation affecting labor relations, a position he shared with the Communist party. When Van Kleeck balked at Baldwin's invitation to head the ACLU contingent at the meeting, the job fell to Francis J. Gorman of the United Textile Workers. Much more moderate than Van Kleeck, Gorman did not accept the reasoning of Baldwin and other leftists on the ACLU's board that reform was an outdated strategy for coping with the engines of capitalism. As a result, the Union modified its tone somewhat, while remaining unalterably opposed to government control of labor relations.[112] Still distrustful of Roosevelt, the Union exclaimed that after the November elections, the administration had turned "to the right."[113]

The National Labor Relations Act (NLRA), which would later become known as the Wagner Act, was introduced in the Senate on 21 February 1935. The ACLU opposed it even before it was formally introduced. Baldwin contacted two liberal labor relations professors from Columbia University and three persons who accepted the Communist party line to lobby Wagner in the hope that he would accept their uncompromising position. Wagner, naturally, saw no reason to change the bill; he had, in fact, received the support of virtually the entire liberal community. Only Communists, the ACLU, and a few others would not endorse the bill. On 7 April 1935, the ACLU made its decision public, stating that it would not be taken in, as the liberals already had been, by the "delusion" that the bill would actually help labor.[114]

Once the Board of Directors rendered its opposition to the Wagner Act, it came under heavy criticism from labor supporters as well as from many persons in its own ranks. Regarded by most labor union officials as a front for the Communist party, and perceived as an unreliable voice on labor matters by a growing number of local affiliates, Baldwin knew that the board had better heed the signals lest it risk alienating the only friends it had. As pressure mounted, the board was forced to participate in an exercise of civil liberties: its decision was submitted to a referendum, allowing the members of the National Committee and the local affiliates to vote. Baldwin's effort to persuade his members was a colossal failure; virtually no one outside the board wanted to oppose the Wagner Act. The Southern California affiliate even sought to disassociate itself entirely from the parent body. [115]

On 27 May 1935, the board gave up; it changed its decision on the Wagner Act from a negative to a "no position." It was a Hobson's choice and Baldwin knew it. He remained, for a while, unyielding in his own views. After Roosevelt signed the Wagner Act into law on 5 July 1935, Baldwin was approached by many of his more moderate associates outside the ACLU; they implored him to move to the center and endorse the act as a reasonable attempt to assist labor. Once Baldwin changed his mind, it was not long before the board switched positions again. By 1936 the ACLU had become rabid supporters of the National Labor Relations Act.[116] Jerold S. Auerbach has noted the significance of this reversal: "This *volte-face* terminated negative libertarianism. Once the federal government held out the promise of safeguarding workers' rights, libertarian antipathy toward federal power receded and the American Civil Liberties Union relaxed its hostility toward the state."[117] In truth, the ACLU was never a committed libertarian organization. It opposed government because it saw the state as the arm of "the propertied class." Once the "libertarians" were convinced that the government could be used as a force for "progress," they effortlessly joined the ranks of collectivistic liberals.

In the latter part of the 1930s, the New Deal administration was never again labeled as "turning to the right." In 1936 the ACLU stated that the incumbents in the White House rarely gave aid or comfort to repression even though their opposition to it was slight. The upswing in the economy was also credited to FDR. And the Federal Relief Administration was applauded for its role in collective bargaining.[118] Again in the following year, the New Deal was cited as encouraging the freedom of organized labor to exercise its rights.[119] The Supreme Court's decision to uphold the legality of the NLRA's regulation of collective bargaining was hailed as having a far-reaching effect on civil rights.[120] In 1938 the NRLA was coined "a civil liberties document."[121] The ACLU was so committed to the Wagner Act that when two newspapers resisted a subpoena by the board of the labor coordinating body, the Union made a very un-civil libertarian remark by accusing the news media of raising "the familiar cry of freedom of the press."[122]

There are four major reasons that the ACLU belatedly became a defender of the Wagner Act. First, Baldwin and his colleagues eventually realized that their dogmatic opposition to it had the effect of isolating them from their principal constituents, namely, labor. If the Union was to be an effective voice for equality and social justice, pragmatic politics needed to be exercised before it was too late. Second, the ACLU was impressed with the sudden conversion of support for the act that the Communist party underwent once it realized that a united Left was an indispensable weapon against fascism. The official line of the party in the United States changed once it received its directives from Moscow. Daniel expresses this point cogently:

> That the change in the ACLU's attitude toward the Wagner Act coincided with the Communist Party's adoption of its new united front strategy does not, of course, prove a causal relationship; however, had the Communists maintained their policy of bitter opposition to federal regulation of labor relations it is difficult to imagine that those members who had so faithfully adhered to the party's positions on the Wagner bill would have become such ardent supporters of the Wagner Act within only months of its passage. Certainly there is no evidence to suggest that the board's left-wing faction was any less sympathetic to the Communist line in 1936 than it had been a year earlier.[123]

The third reason that the ACLU changed positions was Baldwin's admiration for Roosevelt's domestic policies: "As soon as Frank Roosevelt began to talk in terms of distributing power and money to the forgotten man and we began to have a social security system, why I changed my views, of course."[124] The fourth, and most important reason for the switch in policy, was Baldwin's dominance of the ACLU. For Daniel, "It is impossible to avoid the conclusion that the ACLU's vacillatory reaction to the Wagner Act was uniquely a function of the migratory politics of Roger Baldwin."[125] Arthur Garfield Hays, ACLU counsel and friend of Baldwin, once said that "the American Civil Liberties Union *is* Roger Baldwin." The label stuck and was picked up by many others. Is this an exaggeration? Bean concluded that "there is much truth in it."[126] When Lamson asked Baldwin to comment on this statement, he said it was "ridiculous."[127] However, later in her discussion with him, he admitted that "generally speaking it was a one-man show. In the years I was there nobody else made any decisions."[128] When I met with Baldwin, I asked him to comment on his admission.

R.B.: No, no, I never said that. No, no, no!

W.D.: Well, it is in her book.

R.B.: No, no, that's not in her book.

W.D.: I have the book right here, Mr. Baldwin.

R.B.: Well, I'm sure, but she didn't say that. [Sarcastically] Nobody else made any decisions. I was always under control of the Board which met every single week, and I did nothing without the Board's okay— nothing.[129]

One thing is certain: no one else in the ACLU approached his power and influence.

Throughout the 1930s, the Union issued several other policies designed to augment the power of labor and thwart the influence of employers. It declared that the protection of property rights, a Lockean imperative, was not a civil liberties issue because it "has nothing to do with the maintenance of democratic processes."[130] It opposed efforts that sought to incorporate trade unions, bills that made public accounting of funds mandatory, and efforts that sought to circumvent the right to strike and the freedom to conduct sit-down strikes.[131] On the issue of the closed shop, the ACLU also affirmed its support for unions: It held that a closed-shop contract between a union and employer did not violate the rights of workers who did not want to join a union.[132] The following exchange I had with Baldwin explains the ACLU's rationale:

> W.D.: If the ACLU is concerned with the rights of individuals, why doesn't it support right-to-work laws?
>
> R.B.: Because it supports unions.
>
> W.D.: Well, why wouldn't it support my right, for example, not to join a union? Why should I be coerced to join a union?
>
> R.B.: We do have a provision which many unions have, and I think that probably answers the question: that you don't have to join a union if you pay union dues.
>
> W.D.: Well, why should I have to pay union dues?
>
> R.B.: Well, the theory of that is that you get the benefits even without joining, and, therefore, you should pay for the benefits.

At this point I offered a few personal examples of how I fared as a union worker. Baldwin then defended the union shop, wherein an individual must join a union after a certain period of employment. The discussion continued:

> W.D.: But where is the freedom of the individual here? Doesn't the individual have the right to join or not join an association?
>
> R.B.: We have taken the position and this is a position that is sustained by the courts, that collective bargaining, that's collective action by workers, is a right—is a right that will be sustained by the courts. Now, as a civil liberties organization, we sustain that collective right. You don't have to work in a union industry. You can go into some other kind of an industry. You have a choice of jobs. After all, only about a quarter of the workers in the United States are organized, three quarters of them are not, and they are not controlled. But, if where you want to join a union or an industry in which the union has a monopoly and a closed shop contract, then *you are out of luck if you maintain your individual rights. You can't maintain them in that kind of industry, with that kind of contract. You can go someplace else.* [Emphasis added.]
>
> W.D.: That seems almost like it could be a Hobson's choice at some point, if that's the only job that I'm prepared for—the only skill I have. I mean you can go someplace else, that's—
>
> R.B.: That's what happened. In the building trades, for instance, they limit the number of apprentices and they limit the number of people who can join. The building trades have been notorious for that in order to maintain a monopoly of wages.[133]

Baldwin's comments are interesting because they highlight the prounion sentiments of the ACLU. That Baldwin could flatly declare that the reason that the Union did not support right-to-work laws was because it "supports unions" is demonstrative of the true priorities of the ACLU. Furthermore, his statement that "you are out of luck if you maintain your individual rights" when attempting not to join a union is indicative of the ease with which individual rights (the alleged heart of civil liberties) are jettisoned once they conflict with the ACLU's primary goal of social reform.

From its inception in 1920 the ACLU had defended Communists and fascists, labor agitators and Klansmen, but never once—not for eighteen years—did it defend the free speech rights of capitalists to oppose unions. And even then, in 1938, the ACLU could not painlessly bring itself to defend First Amendment rights for capitalists. The mere suggestion of such a fundamental civil liberties principle was greeted as heresy by many members of the ACLU's "nonpartisan" staff. The issue involved the Union's intervention in a dispute between the Ford Motor Company and the National Labor Relations Board (NLRB) over the right of the employers to wage a fight against the United Automobile Workers of America (UAW). At the outset of 1938 the NLRB found the Ford Motor Company guilty of "unfair labor practices" under the Wagner Act. The evidence, according to the ACLU was clear: the Company had organized vigilante groups, hired thugs to assault union members and sympathizers, formed a company union, fired those who had joined or assisted the UAW, and distributed antiunion literature to employees. It was this last charge that troubled some ACLU members: Do employers have the right to free speech? The NLRB did not find the question difficult. It ordered the company to cease and desist from "circulating, distributing or otherwise disseminating amongst its employees statements or propaganda disparaging or criticizing labor organizations, or advising its employees not to join such organizations."[134] The evidence that the NLRB used included "The Ford Almanac" of circa 1 April 1937, which contained an article charging that unions were a racket; a pamphlet of May 1937 entitled "Ford Gives Viewpoint on Labor"; and a set of cards labeled "Fordisms" that were distributed to workers. A typical "Fordism" read: "A monopoly of JOBS in this country is just as bad as a monopoly of BREAD."[135]

The ACLU could not remain neutral. One alternative was to defend the right of employers and thereby remain faithful to its espoused goal. But this would forsake its commitment to the rights of labor. After a bitter struggle, the Union reluctantly backed (within limits) the free speech rights of the employers. The debate became the most acute test between those who valued free speech as an end in itself and those who used it as a weapon for reform. The final decision was, according to Lamson, "one of the few occasions in labor matters in which they [the Board of Directors] defended the rights of management."[136] Indeed it was. And it was never certain that the Union would arrive at its libertarian position.

Initially, the ACLU's strong sympathy for labor triumphed over what was really a straight First Amendment case. The labor rights committee of the ACLU studied the situation and concluded that "when speech *is thus implemented by force* or by threats of discharge or violence it is not the free speech about which the ACLU is concerned."[137] Lamson characterizes the ACLU's first response as being, "clearly anti-Ford and quite understandably so, since the championship of the rights of labor had always been their primary concern."[138] Baldwin, commenting on the initial reaction, stated that when employers were asking if they too did not enjoy the right of free speech, the Union said, "No, you have no rights of free speech against unions now because the right to form a union is now a fundamental one under the National Labor Relations Act." When employers asked, "Well, can't we even talk?" most of the board members, according to Baldwin, replied, "No, you can't even talk."[139] I asked Baldwin why, if the ACLU was truly interested in defending First Amendment rights for everyone—regardless of class—did some members of the Union argue that employers had no right to free speech?

R.B.: Did some members say so?

W.D.: Yes, sir.

R.B.: That was the debate. Where do you draw the line between an employer coercing a worker not to join a union and an employer saying, "you don't need any unions in my shop because I'm going to treat you right." Where do you draw the line between the two? Some of our people said you can't say a word without coercing a union. And we said no—you've got to prove that the employer is going to do something—threaten his job—before you can stop his speech. So we said employers can say any damn thing they want to say about their unions as long as there is no coercion in it.[140]

After I asked Baldwin about the relevance of the "clear-and-present-danger" position, I tried to draw an analogy between the Ford case and the Skokie incident.

W.D.: Well, it was wrong for the Ford Motor Company to so-call "coerce" the workers by putting up their bulletin board statements that they should not join unions. Yet it is not coercion when the Nazis march in Skokie.

R.B.: The Nazis haven't any power over anyone. They are just expressing their opinions. But an employer has power.

W.D.: But doesn't an employer have the right of free speech?

R.B.: Yeah, but we never said he had the right to put any notices in his factory that "you better not join a union." All we said is that if you want to go down to the Chamber of Commerce and talk about it, you can talk about it, but don't do it around the factory.[141]

Soon after the labor committee released its report, the factional struggle began. Committee member William Fennell dissented, suggesting that the same test of coercion used by the NLRB would have to be applied to the statements of government bureaucrats, such as those in the Works Progress Administration who "coerced" relief recipients in matters of voting. Fennell's free speech cost him his membership: he was dismissed from the labor committee by Abraham Isserman. Fennell then resigned from the ACLU, protesting that this was "another liberal purge."[142] As the controversy raged, John Haynes Holmes, one of the original board members, warned that "the very life, not to say the integrity of the Union was at stake." He wrote Chairman Harry Ward that "under the impact of our real sympathy for labor's cause we are allowing ourselves to become mere advocates of the rights of labor to the denial of those rights as exercised by those who are against labor." Holmes reluctantly confessed that the Union was "using the civil liberties principle as a means of fighting labor's battles and the cause of radicalism generally." He felt that some board members (Ward et al.) wanted to manipulate civil liberties "as a means toward certain ends; namely, the advancement of labor and the revolution."[143]

It is a credit to Baldwin, who aligned himself with the Ward faction, that he resolved the matter judiciously by appeasing both sides. The Holmes group was satisfied when the board reaffirmed its principle regarding free speech: "The Civil Liberties Union is opposed to any interference with the expressions of opinion on the part of employers." Ward's followers were placated when the board announced that threats such as "We'll never recognize the United Automobile Workers Union or any other union" violated the civil liberties of the workers.[144] In a supplementary memo issued on the Ford case, the Board of Directors of the ACLU explained that it opposed prior restraint, and chastised the NLRB for not distinguishing between expressions of opinions and speech accompanied by coercion. Addressing that part of the NLRB order requiring Ford to cease and desist from expressing hostility toward the union, the board said:

> On the face of it, considered apart from the rest of the order, and the record in the case, this prohibition is an infringement of the rights of an employer to express his views, a right which the ACLU is as much obligated to defend for employers as for any other persons.
>
> But this section of the order cannot be evaluated apart from the rest of the order and cannot be understood apart from the findings of fact on which it is grounded. The order, like the body of facts which occasioned it, is an organic whole. The record shows that the anti-union propaganda of the Ford Com-

pany is not a mere expression of views, but an integral part of a unified program.

It is to be regretted in its order in the Ford Case, the NLRB did not state more fully the relation of the section prohibiting propaganda to the unlawful acts of the Company, and did not make clearer the fact that the restriction imposed upon the right of an employer to express himself to his employees concerning unions is occasioned and limited by his restriction of the right of the workers to organize.[145]

The Union's position regarding the free speech rights of employers was upheld by the Supreme Court.

Following on the heels of the Ford case were two similar episodes: Muskin Shoe Company of Westminster, Maryland, and Mock-Judson-Voehringer Company of Greensboro, North Carolina. Once again the ACLU enunciated which free speech rights employers enjoyed and which ones they did not. Interestingly, the Union finds no problem sitting in judgment on the intent of employers' speech but shudders from such an exercise when others (Nazis, for instance) are considered. This is what the board said about the companies in question:

In both cases, employer distribution of vicious anti-union literature during working hours and inside the plant was taken into account by the Board (together with many facts showing plainly unlawful employer coercion) in reaching the conclusion that the literature itself was intended to be and was coercive and that the employer had by his course of conduct interfered with his men's right of self-organization. The Civil Liberties Union is of the opinion that in neither of these cases may the employer properly claim that any right of free speech has been invaded.[146]

Amid criticism of its partisan politics, the Board of Directors, in March 1937, restated its avowed position, claiming that it had "no political or economic direction whatever," and went on to say that its defense of the Klan and William Randolph Hearst, the "archapologist for Fascism," was proof of its noncommittal stand.[147] But such disclaimers did not satisfy its critics, including the liberal Walter Lippmann:

The Union almost never goes into action when the liberties of anyone on the Right are attacked, though in fairness it should be recalled that the Union did most bravely defend some American Nazis a few years ago when they were being denied their legal prerogatives. But the directors of the Union have missed one opportunity after another to prove that they really stand for the thing they profess to stand for, that they care for civil liberty as such, as a good thing in itself and not merely because it is a convenience for communists, anarchists, socialists and labor organizers. When Senator Black was conducting his inquisition into the affairs of Mr. Hearst, the Civil Liberties

Union should have been defending Mr. Hearst, however much he may hate
the Union, however much the Union may hate Mr. Hearst. When the National Labor Relations Board recently began its amazing inquiry into the
affairs of newspapers and periodicals, the Civil Liberties Union would have
done well to manifest some concern.[148]

Throughout 1938 the ACLU came under a barrage of criticism from newspapers and magazines, all charging that it was a partisan organization.[149]
    When the ACLU is criticized for being a partisan organization, it typ-
ically responds by saying that there have always been factions within its
ranks. The purists guard civil liberties as an end in itself and show no sign
of partisanship. The instrumentalists see civil liberties as a means toward
an end; partisanship is evident in this faction. In essence, the ACLU offers
us a picture of an organization that is constantly engaged in a democratic
struggle between two contending groups. The end result, we are led to
believe, is some sort of democratic equilibrium. I asked Baldwin to comment on this split within the organization. He said the ACLU entertained
three philosophies simultaneously; capitalists, radicals, and purists each
promoted their own ideology. Capitalists felt that by using civil liberties it
was "a better help for the capitalist system than suppressing people." The
radicals employed a different means; they said, "Yeah, this is also the best
way to a revolution." And the purists proclaimed, "We just want freedom
for its own sake—it's an end in itself."[150]
    In reality, Baldwin's tripartite distinction is a ruse; purists have been few
in number, especially in the first two decades, and capitalists, as Baldwin
admitted, have not been prone to join the organization.[151] In the 1920s and
1930s the ACLU functioned almost exclusively as the legal arm of the
militant labor movement. The evidence is incontrovertible. In 1933, Baldwin conceded as much when he wrote that "civil liberties, like democracy,
are useful only as tools for social change."[152] As for the ACLU's occasional
defense of right-wing groups, one must recognize that even here its motives
were not pure; it did so not out of principle but out of concern for promoting the base from which its ideological friends could operate. These were
Baldwin's words in 1934: "If I aid the reactionaries to get free speech now
and then, if I go outside the class struggle to fight against censorship, it is
only because those liberties help to create a more hospitable atmosphere
for working class liberties."[153] The objective conditions that existed in the
1930s did entice civil libertarians to move left, but it is also true that the
instrumentalism of the ACLU was due to the ideological orientation of the
board. This point has been captured by Auerbach: "If, as the ACLU properly argued, the circumstances of industrial conflict compelled it to champion the civil liberties of workers, it is also apparent that the sympathies of
many libertarians for unionism shaped their approach to civil liberties

issues."[154] When Baldwin was asked in the 1970s to reflect on the ACLU's record during his years as director, he said, "Perhaps we were at times too pro-trade union, and we sometimes looked more pro-left or pro-Communist than the evidence justified."[155]

Labor Policies Since the 1930s

As a result of the New Deal, and the need to coordinate the large-scale administrative activities that World War II engendered, the federal government grew in size and influence in the 1940s far beyond that of any comparable period in American history. More important, it was the combined effect of the depression and the war that brought about the legitimation of big government in the eyes of the public. For liberals, the war years were generally optimistic as Keynesian economics and the rational construction of society presented new and inspiring challenges. There was talk of a "new Bill of Rights" that included economic rights as well as civil liberties. Following Alvin H. Hansen, writer and consultant to the Federal Reserve Board and the National Resources Planning Board, many liberals saw government spending, progressive taxation, and social programs as the road to economic efficiency, justice, and freedom.[156] "It seemed entirely possible," notes Shils, "to combine an omnicompetent government with public liberties without endangering the latter."[157] Aside from Sidney Hook, however, few on the Left were prepared to say that socialistic programs were meaningless without liberty.[158] For most, there was no dilemma: big government assured personal liberties.

The ACLU, of course, adopted the same position. It argued that "an appraisal of political and economic obstacles is justified in terms of what may be called 'progress.'"[159] It noted further that "progressive programs and principles" were at "the heart of any expanding economy."[160] The link between collectivistic liberalism and progress was inseparable. Those who disagreed were responsible for "creating a climate favorable to the status quo and inhospitable to any substantial challenge to it."[161] There were even a few ACLU members who did not endorse the equation between the politics of the Left and progress in civil liberties. Felix Morley of Washington, D.C., resigned from the National Committee because he believed that the Union favored undue extension of federal bureaucratic powers.[162]

According to Alonzo Hamby, the death of President Roosevelt "threw liberalism into an identity crisis."[163] Although most liberals came to accept Truman,[164] they needed more than a friend in the White House. Liberals such as Richard Chase, Lionel Trilling, and William Barrett were busy reassessing the status of liberalism and critically examining the future.[165] George H. Nash recalls the troubles that liberalism faced at this time: "In its relativistic, bend-over-backward, secular, scientific, pragmatic way, it was—said a rising chorus of critics—undermining a civilization in which it no longer believed."[166] Others, such as William Carleton, held the faith and maintained that liberalism would continue to bring about the realization of democracy, just as it had in the past.[167] Liberalism received a boost when, in 1947, Americans for Democratic Action (ADA) was founded. No friend of communism, this organization sought to unify the "vital center" of liberalism by espousing an hostility to totalitarianism along with support for social reform initiated by the government. In the words of its first national chairman, Wilson W. Wyatt, *"Liberals emphatically reject the notion that there is a fatal contradiction between planning and freedom."*[168] The government was held responsible for health, housing, education, and welfare in general.[169] In its first six-point program, the ADA also listed "protection of civil liberties from concentrated wealth and over-centralized government."[170] As John S. Rosenberg noted in 1980, the ADA has, since its founding, "provided a litmus test of liberal legitimacy."[171] The ACLU, it might be argued, has provided a litmus test of liberal sensibilities.

The ACLU's role of defending labor was greatly diminished in the 1940s because workers' rights were "now pretty firmly protected by agencies of the government."[172] Some portions of the Taft-Hartley Act of 1947 upset the Union, but no policy was passed regarding its appropriateness.[173] On the issue of whether or not public employees have the right to strike, the Union declared that "no distinction should be made between the rights of the public and private employees, save as to the right to strike in those public services whose 'discontinuance might well result in immediate catastrophe to the community,' such as the police and fire departments."[174] In a move that was characteristic of the ACLU's new image in the 1940s, the Union refused to participate in proceedings involving the Hatch Act. The Union stated that civil rights were not violated by requiring federal and state employees who receive federal funds to stay aloof from political activities.[175]

In another issue involving the political activities of labor, the Union greeted with consternation the passage of the Smith-Connally Act in June 1943. The Union supported the contention of trade unions that the act violated their political rights by prohibiting contributions to campaigns for federal office.[176] Perhaps the most interesting policy that the ACLU made in the 1940s affecting labor was its decision to pass judgment on internal union democracy. It became evident that as the labor unions gained more power, they began to abuse it with greater frequency. The annual report of July 1946 marked the first time that the Union felt obliged to intervene in the affairs of unions "to insure the right of access of employers and maintenance workers to struck plants."[177] It stated its opposition to discriminatory practices within trade unions by exclaiming that "exclusion from unions is never justified when based on race, creed or color."[178] In the years that followed, the ACLU was called upon to restate its position on internal union democracy several times.

"Complacency" is a word that has often been used to describe the 1950s. "The prevailing atmosphere was one of contentment and satisfaction," notes Samuel P. Huntington.[179] According to Granville Hicks, the source of this complacency was twofold: Intellectuals came to realize that life in the United States was preferable to life in the Soviet Union, and the social reform efforts of activists had been or were being achieved.[180] But for many intellectuals the 1950s were regarded then, as now, as an unwarranted retreat from reality. There was much unfinished business to attend to and no time for relaxation. Men like Irving Howe sought to challenge intellectuals by founding *Dissent*; political inertia was tantamount to intellectual collapse.[181] Intellectuals are bothered by periods of inaction, maintaining that such lulls are really the eye of the storm. Arthur Schlesinger, Jr., for example, continues to hold this thesis, calling the 1950s a period when "the people found themselves tired and drained."[182] Or satisfied. A more accurate picture has recently been provided by Jeffrey Hart: "I have reached the firm conclusion that when people say the 1950s were apathetic and not 'political,' they really mean that there was not much *left* politics, or rather that the *Left* had been seriously disabled."[183]

In the spring of 1953, Robert Bendiner wrote, "For liberals who want independent political action the only going concern of consequence is Americans for Democratic Action."[184] Perhaps. But there was still the ACLU. It was active, passing new policies affecting labor relations. In 1955 it reemphasized its opposition to right-to-work laws. Advocates of these laws argued that their freedom of association was violated when they were not permitted to contract individually for employment. To this the ACLU said, "The question of how much freedom of contract, or freedom from monopoly, there should be either in the labor field or in any other does not automatically produce a question of civil liberties." Freedom of access to jobs and the freedom of business contract "lie outside the scope of civil liberties."[185] On the subject of internal union democracy, the ACLU amplified its earlier commitment to defending workers who had been unfairly treated by their labor unions, this time adding that union self-regulation was needed.[186] Seven years after it issued its 1952 policy governing self-regulation, the ACLU reversed its position and called for federal legislation: "Self regulation alone cannot adequately protect the democratic rights of members within unions." The need for legislation grew out of "the failure of union constitutions to protect the First Amendment rights of freedom of speech, press and assembly. . . ."[187] Meanwhile, the Union continued to press for a "bill of rights for labor."[188]

The ACLU was not at all consistent in its labor policies during the 1950s. In 1951 it defended the right of government employees to form a union, to strike, and to establish a union shop. It later changed its mind: "Government employees, recognizing their obligation to the public service, should voluntarily relinquish any right to strike. . . . No compulsory union membership requirements should be permitted in connection with government employment."[189] These policies were emblematic of the ACLU's more conservative tone in the days of McCarthyism. Once the "scare" ended, the Union, in the late 1950s, declared that "there should be no blanket prohibition against the right to strike by government workers and that union shop agreements in government employment raise no violation of civil liberties."[190]

The 1960s and 1970s saw the ACLU become very active again, defending group rights in particular. But, owing to the secured rights of workers, the Union was noticeably inactive in the field of labor relations. In the 1960s it did not pass one new policy affecting labor. However, like good liberals, some of the affiliates joined in the support of the California grape boycott. The New York CLU even requested its members not to eat grapes.[191] The Union was somewhat more active in the 1970s. In the early 1970s the ACLU ruled against compulsory union membership, so long as the union dues were paid.[192] As Baldwin indicated, the dues were necessary because representation was being provided—like it or not. William F Buckley, Jr., did not like it and requested the ACLU to defend his right not to pay union dues to the American Federation of Radio and Television Artists. The ACLU dutifully studied the case for about a year before turning it down.[193] In essence, the ACLU said that the exercise of one's First Amendment right to free speech over the air waves was conditioned on one's payment of union dues. The furthest the Union was prepared to go in this regard was to protect one's right not to join a union and not to contribute to a political campaign.[194]

In a change in policy, the Union repealed its support for the Hatch Act. It now argued that federal employees should have the right to participate in the political campaigns of their choice.[195] But individuals had rights that organizations could not enjoy. In 1962, the board held that "expenditures by labor unions and corporations for political purposes, including the support of candidates and the expression of views on and support of legislative and social issues, are a proper exercise of the rights of free expression protected by the First Amendment."[196] Then, in 1974, the board amended its policy by stating that it supported "the prohibition of contributions to election campaigns by business corporations and associations and by labor unions from union treasury funds." Monies spent on the expression of views or support of legislative and social issues, however, was still a legitimate activity.[197] The growing power of labor unions and corporations forced the board to reconsider its policy.

In the early 1980s the ACLU condemned the J.P. Stevens Company for resisting unionization, calling on consumers, as well as all government officials, to boycott the company's goods.[198] Two of the Union's policies were amended at the beginning of the decade. It defended the right of lay teachers in parochial schools to form a union,[199] and it modified its position on union dues for all workers: "Civil liberties are served if employers and union respect claims of conscientious objection and permit employees with objections to substitute a suitable charitable contribution for the monies otherwise due to the union."[200] This policy does allow for more protection to those who wish to express their individuality, but it still confers obligations for doing so.

In the 1980s most of the ACLU's labor activities have thus far centered on the rights of farm workers. Its South Texas Project has been the most active, although suits have been brought in California, Virginia, and New Jersey as well.[201] If farm workers received the most attention, it was the striking air controllers who commanded the most publicity. The *New York Times* supported President Reagan's firing of the illegal strikers.[202] But the ACLU did not. It does not matter to the ACLU that all the air controllers had taken an oath not to strike. It does not matter that the Congress has never extended the right to strike to government employees, or that, since the 1940s, it has explicitly forbidden strikes against the federal government. It does not matter that the Supreme Court, in 1971, firmly established that such strikes were illegal. They are all wrong, according to the ACLU. Such distinctions that virtually all reasonable men have made between public and private employees are simply "unfair and irrational," according to Ira Glasser, executive director of the ACLU.[203]

Liberalism in the 1960s and 1970s

Most observers of the American scene regard the 1930s and the 1960s as the two most dynamic and radical decades of the twentieth century. If the 1930s are associated with the rights of labor, the New Deal, and big government, the 1960s are associated with the rights of Blacks, the Great Society, and even bigger government. The 1960s was the decade of sit-ins and demonstrations, civil rights and affirmative action, public interest lawyers and class-action suits, welfare and entitlements, blue-ribbon commissions and government regulations, Vietnam and conscientious objectors, draft-card burnings and flag burnings, the sex revolution and the pill, progressive education and student rights, assassinations and recriminations, the SDS and the Black Panthers, hippies and yippies, LSD and dropouts. And, above all, social justice. In the words of Irving Howe, "The 60s were political to the vary marrow and no serious person could avoid the noise, the heat, the dirt, the excitement of politics."[204]

Reflecting on the meaning of social justice, economist Friedrich Hayek has said that he is convinced "that the people who habitually employ the phrase simply do not know themselves what they mean by it and just use it as an assertion that a claim is justified without giving a reason for it."[205] It is a nebulous concept, void of any specifics, but it does, nonetheless, convey a message: Justice is a social property not reducible to individual pursuits of the common good. No matter, the activists of the 1960s invoked it frequently, often as a rationalization for liberal-Left programs. Liberal-Left objectives were basically leftist, i.e. radical. In a very real sense, the Left absorbed liberalism in the sixties, making it into a powerful ideological force. This transformation, as Shils sees it, came about as a result of a wholesale assault on liberal values: "The attack was carried out mainly by collectivistic liberals, some of whom became more radical in their censure of the limited capacities of traditional liberalism. . . . This alliance of collectivistic liberalism and radicalism cast 'elitism' and traditional liberalism in the role of the enemy."[206] At the other end of the ideological spectrum, Irving Howe unhappily agrees: "To see the Leninist-Stalinist contempt for liberal values elevated to Herbert Marcuse's haughty formulas about 'repressive tolerance,'—formulas used to rationalize the breakup of opponents' groups—made one despair of any authentic left in America."[207] To the radical liberals, it appeared, as James Neuchterlein has noted, that the entire society was decrepit and not worth saving.[208]

Samuel P. Huntington has observed that the 1960s and early 1970s were one of those periods in American history when a serious effort was made to incorporate the values of the American Creed into the fabric of society. Such periods have typically occurred in times of relative prosperity, when moral issues eclipse economic concerns.[209] They are generally associated with marked discontent, moral outrage, antipathy toward power, and extensive political participation.[210] More than any other factor, it is the gap between ideals (the American Creed) and institutions that inspires activism. This was certainly true in the sixties: "The classic values of the American Creed—equality, democracy, liberty, individual rights, the limitation of power—were rearticulated with an intensity and fervor fully equal to that of any previous outbreak of creedal passion."[211] The sociocultural dissonance was laced with a "pervasive, unrelenting questioning of an opposition to authority in almost any form."[212] Moral indignation "exhausted itself"[213] in the 1970s; economic issues again became dominant.

The 1960s caught most social critics off guard; few of them had predicted that the halcyon days of the fifties would erupt into the furor of the sixties. But at least one astute critic had seen it all coming. William Carleton stated that the next liberal movement would see the extension of voting rights and a move toward one man, one vote; mass education would become a reality; an environmental movement would be generated; social security would be widened; and government would regulate big business. He predicted this in 1948. He also foresaw the civil rights movement: "The next liberal movement in America will go much farther than ever before in protecting the legal, political, educational, and economic rights of racial minorities."[214]

A reevaluation of the role of the state in the 1960s dovetailed with the liberals' appraisal of social conditions. Leading the way was Yale lawyer Charles Reich, who would later become immortalized as the guru of America's "greening." In 1964 Reich wrote an article for his school's law journal arguing for a reassessment of the meaning of property so as to include welfare benefits.[215] He carefully documented the rise of government largess in nearly every sphere of life and showed the control that the "public interest state" had in determining the distribution of wealth. According to Reich, the public-interest state grew as a result of the abuses of private property rights by corporations; the capitalists created the need for reform. For Reich, and for many liberals, the property rights that capitalists abused were justifiably abridged by the government because all property comes from the state; property is a social construction not a Lockean natural right. Because all property is government largess, it follows that state control over property is right and proper.[216] Reich was characteristically optimistic about the future of the public-interest state: "The highly organized, scientifically planned society of the future, governed for the good of its inhabitants, promises the best life that men have ever known. In place of the misery and the injustice of the past there can be prosperity, leisure, knowledge, and rich opportunity open to all."[217] It was only a matter of time before the bureaucrats would do for us what they have never done for anyone: establish a secular heaven on earth.

John Kenneth Galbraith not only shared Reich's optimism and ideas about the state but went further than anyone else in laying down the particulars that liberalism would adopt in the 1960s and early 1970s. Dubbed the "quintessential liberal" by Robert Nisbet,[218] Galbraith boasted in 1966 that "these, without doubt, are the years of the liberal."[219] He was right. Liberalism dominated the intellectual landscape to such an extent that conservatism was regarded (and still is) as regressive and atavistic. The forces of progress were the forces of liberalism. But there was one nagging problem for Galbraith: with high production and low unemployment, it appeared as though there was nothing left for liberals to do. Galbraith would have none of it: "It cannot be the highest function of the modern liberal to work avidly to accomplish what has already been done."[220] Actually, liberals were never faced with such a prospect. As Galbraith said, "This is the age of the urban crises."[221] Poverty, it appeared, would be the most urgent concern. Galbraith's solution was straightforward: "We must also now consider measures for guaranteeing minimum levels of income for the poor."[222] He implored the ADA to follow his advice and seize on these "new" issues. It hurt Galbraith to note, however, that some of his brethren were not fond of having the government spend more of their money: "I might add that it pains me to see liberals resisting taxes, including sales taxes, which would allow of better services."[223] It has not mattered to most liberals that since Galbraith said this, taxes have soared while services have deteriorated.

The ADA listened to Galbraith, elected him its chairman, and voted for a guaranteed income for all Americans. It should be understood that liberals did not intend to help the poor so that the poor could help themselves. That was old-fashioned. The poor, according to the ADA, were to be uplifted soley through the benignancy of government. ADA member Gabe Kaimowitz of Columbia University clarified exactly what his organization meant by voting for a guaranteed income in 1968: "Now, we were *not* talking about providing an 'opportunity' for the poor to advance individually in this society. We were talking about giving the bottom money now, that money to be scraped off the top."[224] Paternalism had reached new heights and won an influential audience of opinion-makers.

By 1969 it was evident that liberalism was in trouble. *U.S. News and World Report* talked about the "plight of liberals," and questioned, "Whither the political 'liberals'?"[225] As the silent majority arrived, London journalist Andrew Knight warned that "the American liberal is now showing alarming symptoms of withdrawal."[226] Humanist Paul Kurtz found it necessary to instruct his readers on the differences between liberalism and radicalism: "We need a *radical center* prepared to defend the values of liberal democracy, reasoned dialogue and toleration. Indeed, this is the only rational option available to us today."[227] Something surely had to be done before it was too late. ACLU legal director Melvin L. Wulf spoke more candidly than most of his "nonpartisan" colleagues when he exclaimed, "We are not yet a fascist state in general."[228] Prominent liberals such as James MacGregor Burns were on the defensive.[229] By the late sixties, Burns was not the same optimist that he had been at the beginning of the decade, when he had written: "Today, on the eve of America's great choice, I believe that Kennedy in his campaign has deliberately prepared the way for the most consistently and comprehensively liberal Administration in the history of the country."[230] Kennedy did what Burns said he would. And twenty years later, Irving Howe would recall the 1960s as "The Decade That Failed."[231]

Although liberalism did run into some difficulties in the 1970s and, with the election of Ronald Reagan, in the 1980s as well, it is safe to say that it has survived quite well. The ideas of liberalism were never shaken, despite the efforts of the neoconservatives. Equality has been, and continues to be, the most salient goal of liberals. In the 1970s the "new equalitarians" appeared.[232] Men like John Rawls, Herbert Gans, Christopher Jencks, and others advanced the cause of egalitarianism beyond that of the sixties. Although Gans and Jencks are properly associated with the Left, it is undeniably true that contemporary liberalism, i.e. the radical collectivistic brand, has followed the logic of their thought. Regulate and control. Tax and spend. Rehabilitate and renew. Change and progress. Redistribute and rejoice. These are the staples of liberalism. More recently, Philip Green[233] and William Ryan[234] have demonstrated that collectivist thought is more imaginative than anyone previously believed.

The ACLU, it is fair to say, has been in the middle of liberal rumblings since the 1960s. More accurately, it has been at the forefront of liberal battles for the past few decades. There is scarcely an issue that has been of interest to the liberal community that it has not addressed. And in many cases, it was the Union that led that community. The primary reason for the Union's aggressiveness lay in the tremendous growth that it experienced, beginning in 1964. With more resources than it had ever enjoyed,[235] it was prepared to go beyond its traditional domain of First Amendment issues. Joseph Bishop, in the early 1970s, noticed that "the Union suffers from a problem created by its very success: to find new battles and victories its staff seems to think that it must push farther and farther toward, and beyond, the outer limits of freedom (not only of speech, but of action) and must, indeed, become a political pressure group."[236] When I asked Baldwin to comment on the ACLU's expansionist policies, he said: "There is an element in the ACLU that would like to expand a concept of civil liberties to include the injustices of the economic system. But I think we've got to stick to our original purposes."[237] The element that Baldwin was referring to had become the dominant faction within the ACLU in the 1960s and 1970s. Heading that faction was Aryeh Neier, the Union's fourth executive director. Neier was critical of people like Supreme Court Justice Warren Burger, who called upon law students to refrain from viewing the law as a political weapon.[238] He was also critical of people like Bishop, who drew attention to the split within the Union between the activists, or instrumentalists, and the traditionalists, or purists: "It is a rare issue these days on which a Board vote splits along 'activist-traditionalist' lines."[239] Neier was correct. By the early seventies, factionalism had all but disappeared—practically everyone on the board was an activist.

In the 1950s Bean wrote that "the ACLU has found itself, politically speaking, in the position of wishing to decrease the role of government more than of wishing to see it increased."[240] Just the opposite was true ten years later. The ACLU turned with increasing frequency toward the federal government as a force for equality and social justice. As Neier explained, however, there was one caveat: "Several recent decisions in cases brought by the ACLU have begun to articulate the principle that government may not intervene in people's lives to remedy ills when the almost certain consequence is to make matters worse."[241] What Neier had in mind was government programs that liberals did not like. He clearly did not have in mind welfare programs or, for that matter, any initiative that the liberal community sponsored. Neier's "principle" is elucidated in the Union's concept of the public interest. It has alternatively found a "public interest test" to be useful in considering questions important to liberals,[242] while denouncing this concept as "vague" and "ambiguous" when no such interests are involved.[243] Similarly, the concept of "social utility" is invoked whenever it is necessary for the ACLU to break ranks with established policy so as to affirm its support for liberal programs.[244]

The activism of the 1960s and the early 1970s reflected social unrest and helped to propel the expansionist organizational strategy of the ACLU. The most significant aspect of this strategy was the inauguration of a campaign to particularize the rights of certain groups in society. Commencing with Blacks, one group after another began pressing for civil liberties and government response to their grievances. Assisted by the ACLU, group rights were elevated beyond individual cases of injustice. The Union sought to educate the public, as well as its clientele, by issuing a series of handbooks on the rights of those groups that had surfaced to make their claims. The first series, published by Avon Books in 1972-73, covered the rights of servicemen, teachers, prisoners, mental patients, women, and students.[245] By the spring of 1979, fourteen new volumes had been issued covering the following groups: aliens, candidates and voters, gay people, government employees, hospital patients, lawyers and clients, the poor, reporters, suspects, tenants, young people, old people, veterans, and the mentally retarded.[246] When I interviewed Neier in 1978, I mentioned that noticeably absent from the ACLU's list of group concerns were the rights of policemen. He responded by saying, "I don't know if they are noticeably absent. We have a great many cases on behalf of the rights of policemen, and we have a handbook in preparation on the rights of policemen."[247] But aside from occasionally defending the right of a police officer to join the

John Birch Society, the Union has not been too busy defending the rights of police. In any event, the handbook finally did appear in the 1980s. Other handbooks that have recently appeared include the rights of former offenders, parents, the physically handicapped, racial minorities, and union members. There is also a handbook entitled "Sue Your Boss: Rights and Remedies."[248] There is no handbook available for those who might want to sue their employees.

Most of the equality issues that the ACLU has participated in since the 1960s have been social and economic concerns. It has, however, ruled on issues affecting political equality. In the sixties, it passed two policies that dealt with the franchise: apportionment and voting rights. The Union called for the apportionment of state electoral districts on the basis of population. The "equal protection of the law" clause of the Fourteenth Amendment "would appear to require that there be no classification between voters."[249] This statement by the board modified its 1959 stand, which drew a distinction between state legislative districts distributed according to popular representation and those established on the basis of geographical area. The new position, which made no such distinction, did not dilute an individual's right of franchise by permitting a small minority of the electorate to control a state Senate. On voting rights, the Union argued for the rights of eighteen-year-olds to vote: "The deep interest of young people in political issues, shown by their active participation in campaigns and demonstrations, proves that they are already an important part of the political community."[250] Ironically, since eighteen-year-olds have secured the right to vote, relatively few of them have shown much interest in doing so.

It was in the latter part of the 1970s that the ACLU became most active in political equality. By that time, freedom of privacy had become one of the Union's most guarded rights. A conflict between the desire for political equality and the protection of the privacy rights of individuals arose when the Union was considering its policy "Financial Disclosure Requirements of Government Officials."[251] The Free Speech-Association Committee opted for a presumption of privacy with respect to financial disclosure while the Privacy Committee argued for compulsory financial disclosure by employees working in positions that closely affect the public welfare and by candidates for such positions.[252] The board's official policy essentially sustained the Privacy Committee's idea by declaring that it opposed "broad, general disclosure requirements" but found acceptable stipulations that "relate to particular jobs and that require particular information." It added that this policy would be applied on a case-by-case basis.[253]

In its policy "Regulation of Lobbyists," the Union opposed the law of disclosure of names of persons who contribute $500 or more to organizations that lobby. However, it did rule that regulation of lobbyists was permissible when limited to the following: (a) the identity of lobbyists, (b) the identity of substantial contributors, (c) the primary subjects and measures to which lobbying is directed, (d) the clients for whom the lobbying is carried on, and (e) the annual aggregate of such lobbying expenditures.[254] In a related case, *Buckley v. Valeo,* the Supreme Court adopted the ACLU position that restrictions on the amount of money spent for campaign speeches and activities were direct restrictions on such speech itself and are, therefore, inconsistent with the First Amendment.[255] In what could be construed as a self-serving move, the Union supported legislation that permitted nonprofit, tax-exempt organizations "to communicate directly with Congress and state legislatures on matters related to these organizatons' interest, without jeopardizing their tax-deductible status."[256] The ACLU also argued against the Electoral College and in favor of direct election.[257]

The Rights of Minorities

In the 1960s the ACLU spent more time writing policies on, and defending the rights of, minorities than any other segment of the population. A key question that the Union confronted was whether or not the government had the right to gather information regarding an individual's race and ethnicity. The rocky course that the Union traveled on this issue is demonstrative of the general condition of liberalism in the 1960s. The ACLU opposed the collection of racial information *if* the data were to be used to discriminate against Blacks. If, however, it were to be used to promote equality, even if by discriminating against Whites, then that was okay. For example, throughout the fifties and most of the sixties, the right of the Census Bureau to acquire information regarding one's race and religion was viewed askance. Questions regarding one's race "could easily raise in the minds of many people the specter of some threatened discrimination."[258] In October 1968, the Union reversed its earlier support for freedom of privacy by citing the necessity for free inquiry and collection of information pertaining to the cause of civil rights.[259] A look at the Union's attitude toward the 1960 and 1970 census reveals the rationale for its new position.

At the time of the 1960 census, the Board of Directors opposed the Civil Rights Commission's recommendation that the Census Bureau be empowered to compile registration and voting statistics by race, color, and national origin. The board held that no one should be compelled to answer such questions. Its overriding fear was the use of such information to discriminate against minority groups.[260] But once the 1964 Civil Rights Act was passed and once affirmative action became a reality, the ACLU's utilitarianism became evident. In 1968 the board accepted the Privacy Committee's recommendation that the Census Bureau had the right to include questions regarding race; such questions should be voluntarily answered. The Union ruled that the data on one's race and ethnic group "had a clear social utility—for example, as the basis for effective programs by government, by industry, by unions, and by private voluntary organizations to combat discrimination in education, employment, and housing."[261] The Union's present position is similar, although it has determined that the government may now "mandate collection of information pertaining to race and ethnicity," but only so long as the data are kept separate from "personal identifying information such as name and address."[262]

In a related issue in the 1960s, the ACLU decided to oppose "collection and dissemination of information regarding race, except only where rigorous justification is shown for such action."[263] It said that those whose job it is to keep actuarial records containing racial information are legitimately performing their job. Similarly, questions about race on applications for social security cards are not improper. The Union's position on the collection of such information by school authorities reflects its instrumentalist bias best of all: "The Union opposes record-keeping by school authorities which indicate an individual's race, but it would accept that use of a head-count method when the statistics will be used for purposes of promoting integration or increasing educational opportunity."[264] Five years later, in 1967, the ACLU issued a revised policy. Gone were the earlier stipulations about what constituted proper and improper use of racial information. Impressed with the government's liberal track record of using racial information to advance social equality, the Union was ready to support the collection and dissemination of racial information whenever a "social utility" was being served.[265]

In both policies, the Union took to chastising the mass media for unnecessarily labeling people by race. This is what the board concluded in 1965: "For example, racial labeling in crime stories is likely to affect adversely the 'public image' of a minority group, exacerbate racial tension, and perhaps even offend the due process rights of the accused."[266] Such practices, the Union said, should be avoided because they "hurt the cause of equality."[267]

The ACLU has always been sensitive to the rights of minorities. In 1926 it protested the treatment of Blacks, Catholics, Jews, and the Japanese, Chinese, and Hindu minorities.[268] In its first annual report, it listed racial equality as one of its ten objectives.[269] And in the early 1920s it came to the assistance of Blacks in New York City who were "guilty" of dancing with White women.[270] Lynchings were summarily denounced throughout the twenties and thirties. But as much as the ACLU hated racism in its early years, it did not spend too many resources defending Blacks. After recounting numerous examples of repression in 1928, the Union admitted, "We leave out of account the violations of the rights of Negroes, who suffer more restriction than any minority in the country, but with whose trouble we do not deal. The National Association for the Advancement of Colored People tackles them."[271] Apparently the ACLU felt that the NAACP not only should defend Black rights by itself but should do so without any hint of association with the Union. As late as 1942, the Union, acting through Baldwin, found it necessary to fire a Black lawyer in Delaware simply because the ACLU did not want to be identified "with any special interest group."[272] It is interesting to note that the ACLU rarely expressed the same reservations about its partnership with united-front organizations.

In its first two decades, the most prominent case affecting Blacks that the ACLU involved itself in was the Scottsboro case. The conviction of seven Blacks in Scottsboro, Alabama, in May 1931, for allegedly raping two White women who were traveling on a freight train, received international attention. Two weeks after the purported crime, the defendants were sentenced in a courtroom surrounded by 10,000 people screaming for street justice—lynching. The Union investigated the Scottsboro case and raised funds for the defense but did not actually participate in the defense.[273] In 1932 the Supreme Court reversed the convictions on the grounds that the trial court had not provided adequate counsel.[274] But the racists did not give up, and succeeded in having the Blacks reindicted. Again the Supreme Court voided the convictions; no Blacks had been called on the jury panels that indicted and tried the accused.[275] The ACLU did join in the defense in the second trial.[276]

As with the liberal community in general, the ACLU did not become actively involved in the campaign for Black rights until the 1960s. To be sure, in the mid-1940s, the Union did, for the first time, state that race relations was the number-one civil liberties issue,[277] and it participated in an unprecedented number of cases at that time.[278] It even had input into President Truman's commission on civil rights.[279] And in the fifties, the Union supported the Montgomery bus boycott,[280] sit-ins, the Civil Rights Act of 1957,[281] and many other efforts to end discrimination.[282] But it was not until Blacks began to initiate the civil rights movement that the Union, as well as everyone else, began to mobilize a frontal assault on racism and discrimination.

Early in the 1960s the ACLU declared the civil rights crisis to be "the central civil liberties issue of our time."[283] The domestic turmoil that marked the 1960s was actually a bonanza for the slumping ACLU of the 1950s. The assassinations of John and Robert Kennedy and Martin Luther

King brought renewed attempts by the Union and other organizations to carry forward the cause of civil liberties. The murder of John F. Kennedy inspired the Union to break precedent by endorsing a judicial inquiry; the Warren Commission was necessary because of the "extraordinary circumstances of a presidential assassination."[284]

In the 1960s the ACLU brought about the conflation of civil liberties and civil rights. A new approach was emerging as the Union became convinced that the economic disadvantages of many minority groups were reinforced by their deprivation of legal rights. Therefore, the traditional approach of relying solely on volunteers had to be scrapped. The support of affirmative litigation, investigation of facts, and development of evidence became a new and costly enterprise for the Union. To meet this test, The Roger Baldwin Foundation of ACLU, Inc., was formed in the mid-sixties. This new branch of the Union would engage in litigation, research, and education. Significantly, the movement away from traditional litigation was the result of expanding resources. As the decade progressed, there were more members with more money; only an organization suffering from paralysis and inept leadership would have passed up the opportunity to expand its program.[285]

It did not satisfy the ACLU to identify itself simply as an ally of Black demands in the 1960s; it was important to understand empathically the strategy of the most radical segments of the Black population. It was commonplace in the sixties for White liberals everywhere to align themselves with the most militant of Black militants. There was hardly an action taken by Blacks—arson, looting, murder—that could not be appreciated by referencing the "environment" that "caused" the outbreak. Everyone from Leonard Bernstein to William Kunstler opined that rioting Blacks were not responsible for their behavior. The ACLU took the same position:

> The dominant forces in our community, and especially its elected officials, cannot escape responsibility for harsh events by pointing an accusing finger at the lawless acts of Negroes and their supporters. They must understand that if lawlessness occurs, it is a direct consequence of the failure of the community, and especially its white majority, to implement the laws of the land, the laws of human decency and the laws of social experience. Public officials must recognize the simple truth that men who have been brutalized by their society will not always act in a peaceful fashion; men who feel they have little at stake in their society will not always act conservatively for they have little to lose.[286]

The government was also blamed for inciting violence. When the W.E.B. DuBois Club was bombed in San Francisco and members were assaulted in Brooklyn on the same day, the Union said the events were "a direct result of government action." The government action to which the ACLU referred was the announcement by the attorney general on the day preceding the violence that he probably could not succeed in having the club register with the Subversive Activities Control Board.[287] It was this that had caused the violence! In addition, the Union blamed "the relentless verbal assault by high government officials against the Black Panthers" for "the excessive use of force by local police."[288] The head of the Illinois affiliate accused local officials for creating a "police-state atmosphere." The ACLU concurred.[289]

Much emphasis was given to discriminatory activities in the 1960s. The only problem that the ACLU had in this regard was deciding what to do about discrimination in private organizations. In 1965 it confessed that "because of the Union's devotion of considerable resources to urgent problems of racial discrimination in the public area, discrimination in private organizations is not a priority item on the Union's civil rights agenda." Tax-exempt organizations, agencies requiring public funds, and quasi-official institutions such as the American Medical Association should, however, be held accountable by the government for practicing nondiscriminatory policies.[290] The major problem with this policy, however, is that it put the ACLU in the position of seemingly opposing Black separatist organizations on college campuses. The Union's Equality Committee was sympathetic to this exception but could not arrive at a satisfactory resolution.[291] The Biennial Conference in 1968 passed a motion that called upon the board to study the question of self-determination of Blacks. Should Black students be permitted to choose separate living arrangements in publicly supported university dormitories? Could Whites insist upon the same right? These were just some of the questions with which the Union wrestled. Some members of the board wondered why a White middle-class organization like the ACLU should even consider such questions.[292] The issue was never fully resolved. Today the Union simply says that it opposes discrimination in any college associations.[293]

The question of segregated schools has been one of the most explosive social issues of the twentieth century. It would be fair to say that the position of the courts has not reflected the sentiments of the public on this issue. At odds are two fundamental rights: the right of parents freely to choose their child's school and the right of all children to equal educational opportunity. This controversy epitomizes the American dilemma and continues to be, especially with the advent of busing, a divisive issue permeated with racial overtones. Social scientists and lawyers have gotten good mileage from this issue, delivering mountains of evidence and counterevidence regarding the efficacy of busing. Busing was intended to raise the educational achievement level of Black and White students, promote self-esteem, and enhance race relations. Oftentimes the controversy is muddled even further by those who fail to prescind the difference between integration, desegregation, and busing. Still less attention has been given to the problems that emerge when busing across school lines is accomplished by busing across class lines.

The ACLU first took up the question of school segregation in the 1940s; there is no evidence that it thought separate schools based on race was a civil liberties concern before this time. The issue was first broached by the Congress in the mid-1940s when two bills were presented allowing for continuance of federal aid to state-segregated schools, with the proviso that funds be equally apportioned. The ACLU did not approve of the federal government's sanctioning racially segregated schools but, nonetheless, decided not to oppose the bills on those grounds. The Union stated that it recognized that "the federal government could not change state patterns and that any attempt to do so would not only be impracticable but if conceivably successful, would result in denying aid to all schools in states with segregation."[294] Ten years later the Union no longer thought that such attempts were impracticable. It greeted the Supreme Court's landmark *Brown v. Board of Education* decision of 1954 as the biggest success for civil liberties in recent years.[295] The Board of Directors, in a move that demonstrated its total support for the unanimous decision, urged implementation of the desegregation action by denying federal funds to uncooperative schools.[296]

In the 1960s the ACLU lambasted school officials who blamed segregation in the schools on housing patterns. "It is not enough," the Union argued, "for a school board to allege that the convenience, safety and welfare of children and their parents require attenndance [sic] at a neighborhood school."[297] The Massachusetts affiliate even supported a boycott of segregated schools. Rezoning was, for the Union, an acceptable vehicle to promote integration.[298] But it was not until 1972 that the ACLU added its support for busing as yet another instrument for overcoming patterns of segregation.[299] Those who maintained that busing infringed upon their freedom of choice and association were not taken seriously by the civil libertarians. For the ACLU, "race was the real issue," not busing; this was something that "everyone knew."[300] I asked Baldwin a few questions about this issue:

> W.D.: Well, then if you say that the fundamental civil liberty is the right to be left alone, how can the ACLU support busing?
>
> R.B.: Busing?
>
> W.D.: Because the communities want to be left alone.
>
> R.B.: Oh, you can't—if you have a general rule for the whole country that skin color is not to be considered in distinguishing the rights of cit-

izens, then you have to have busing in order to enforce a fundamental principle. You have to tell people you cannot live without recognizing that you are part of a country in which your children have to have the experience of democracy of growing up with others of different color and different background. It is the democratization of the schools.

W.D.: But doesn't that defy freedom of association and the whole concept of a pluralistic democracy?

R.B.: No, because if you did not use busing as a device for mixing children in the educational process, you go right back to segregation. Now we just simply cannot live with segregation in a democracy—segregation of anybody.[301]

In the 1970s and 1980s the ACLU has consistently opposed any measure that would either directly or indirectly retard the goal of social equality in the schools. It has opposed voucher plans, tuition tax credits, and other such freedom-of-choice proposals as inimical to integration. Milton Friedman's voucher plan is contested because it would "inevitably weaken the public school system as a whole."[302] This is a typical example of the ACLU's tendency to invoke ideological positions in a civil liberties matter. Similarly, it cannot resist passing social and psychological judgments on issues that are best left to social scientists. It insists that "the so-called freedom of choice would only reinforce the pattern of school segregation which has done such inestimable harm to all children."[303] In 1982 John Shattuck and David Landau imported more sociological wisdom on the subject: "It is beyond debate today, however, that separation of the races in public education is harmful, and experience and research have shown that desegregation is beneficial."[304] This would surely come as a surprise to David Armor, the Harvard sociologist who undertook the most comprehensive study of busing and its effects.[305] It also might come as a surprise to many middle-aged Japanese executives who attended segregated schools in their youth.

Although the ACLU never approved of discrimination in housing, it was not a top priority in its first few decades. Labor, as we have seen, commanded most of its attention. The first stirring of protest came in the 1940s when the government began to commit its resources to publicly funded housing. The Union registered its objections to restrictive housing provisions in many cities, including New York where there was an attempt to enforce a ban on housing Blacks in Stuyvesant Town.[306] This project, one of the first urban renewal initiatives in the country, was built by Metropolitan Life Insurance Company after it secured a lengthy tax abatement from the City of New York. The Union also came to the rescue of nineteen tenants when they were threatened with eviction for protesting the exclusion of Blacks.[307] In 1952 the ACLU joined a new group, the National Committee for Democratic Housing, aimed at public awareness over the issue.[308] It did so at a time when the board had just taken its first public policy position on discrimination in private housing. On 17 March 1952, the board went on record as opposing discrimination in housing on the basis of race, creed, or color. When an amendment was offered to include religious or political belief, it was narrowly defeated.[309]

The ACLU strengthened its housing policy in 1959 by adding that it opposed discrimination on the basis of political affiliation as well as race. State and local governments were called upon to prohibit discrimination in private housing, but the Union noted that the Fourteenth Amendment's provision for equal protection before the law did not require them to do so. "Private housing," the board stated, "is not within federal jurisdiction."[310] The Union further acknowledged that "groups established in good faith for non-housing purposes—e.g., religious bodies or fraternal orders—should be permitted in good faith to limit to their members the sale or rental of housing accommodations provided specifically for their members."[311] In a remark that contains racist overtones, the ACLU, in November 1960, argued that "a real-estate broker, though licensed by the state, cannot be prohibited by law from commenting on the possible deterioration of a racially integrated neighborhood."[312] This policy lasted throughout the 1960s.

In the 1970s the ACLU made a few changes in its housing policy. The racist remark was stricken entirely. Gone, too, was the exception to its policy that it allowed for "groups established in good faith for non-housing purposes"; the Privacy Committee recommended the deletion because it could not determine what "good faith" meant.[313] This provision, however, was later reinstated.[314] More important, the Union switched its position on the right of state and local governments to determine their own housing laws: "Local governments are creatures and delegates of the states. The state is constitutionally obliged to assure its citizens equal treatment—at the hands of the state and of its delegates."[315] This reductionist philosophy regarding the Fourteenth Amendment became vogue once the Warren Court gave new meaning to the amendment. Since that time, the ACLU has relentlessly insisted upon the most elastic interpretation of the Fourteenth Amendment to be found anywhere.

As old provisions were eliminated from the housing policy, new ones were added. To be sure that everyone knew just how adamantly the ACLU opposed discrimination in housing, it listed eight classifications that deserved application of its principle: race, color, sex, religion, national origin, political affiliation, alienage, and illegitimacy.[316] Gays were left out—intentionally. The issue was discussed all right, but William Van Alstyne persuasively argued that adding sexual preference to the list might put the Union in favor of pederasty;[317] it was not yet prepared to do so. The exceptions that the Union made to this policy sound remarkably like the the words of a Washington bureaucrat: "Individuals shall be exempt from this provision only in relation to their intimately shared living arrangements. Such living arrangements shall consist of the household of which the individual is actually a member, and shall not extend, for example, to two-family dwellings where separate living units are maintained."[318]

Should an organization that takes the position that the First Amendment admits of no exceptions do nothing when racists engage in blockbusting activities by making slanderous statements about Blacks? Not if it is more interested in social equality than "free speech." The Union settled the matter in 1972 when it decided to support "anti-blockbusting statutes which prohibit false or deceptive statements concerning changes in the racial, religious, or national character of a neighborhood, and/or the effect of those changes, made with the intent for commercial gain, to promote the sale of property."[319] The free speech implications of this policy are obvious. Interestingly, three years after this addition to the Union's housing policy was passed, board member Jim Lawing proposed an amendment to the policy that would have put the ACLU on record as opposing any legislative attempt to combat discrimination in housing "by any means offensive to the constitutional guarantee of free speech." When someone noted that this proposal would rescind, in effect, the board policy on antiblockbusting ordinances, the Lawing amendment was defeated.[320]

The ACLU has never liked zoning laws. Such laws have often been passed to safeguard the right of a community to determine its own life-style. The way the ACLU sees it, though, such laws are often passed to exclude undesirables. Both positions contain more than a kernel of truth. But since the ACLU understands only those rights encoded in the Bill of Rights, it almost always dismisses the right of a community to exercise self-determination. This perspective was operative in the 1970s when the issue of scatter-site housing arose. The Union was active in a number of lawsuits in the early part of the decade trying to prohibit midwestern cities and suburbs from establishing zoning restrictions that were principally aimed at keeping low-income housing units from being built in middle-class neighborhoods.[321] To the Union, such tactics were always seen as manifestations of race prejudice—not class prejudice. Yet in one Black middle-class neighborhood after another the response has been identical to that of the White middle class: low-income people should not be deposited in their neighborhood by visionary bureaucrats. The Union, quite naturally, saw scatter-site housing as a means of furthering the ends of integration and equality.[322] State officials, the ACLU contended, may not discriminate against low- or moderate-income people by passing zoning and other land-use control legislation that prevents the building of multifamily dwellings for such people in middle-class communities.[323] Mayor John Lindsay of New York accepted the Union idea but his constituents in Forest Hills and other communities were not so understanding: they organized to defeat him in future elections.

In the 1960s, just when equal opportunity was becoming a reality for an unprecendented number of Americans, liberals abandoned this approach in favor of equal results. Equal opportunity, it was argued, yielded unequal results. Of course, this had always been true but it never struck liberals as a problem until the 1960s. No longer satisfied with the idea that ascribed characteristics ought to have no role in determining one's status, liberals now sought to advance the notion that only by referencing ascribed qualities could progress toward equality be made. It was their commitment to social justice that proved to be decisive: If liberalism allowed for inequality, even if based on merit, it would defeat the ends of social justice. Nothing was more urgent than seeing to it that all segments of the population participated equally in all segments of society. It was precisely this idea that once led Bella Abzug to wonder why women were not a majority in Congress when they constituted a majority in the population.

The change in thought that dramatized the shift from an emphasis on equal opportunity to equal results was perhaps the most fundamental transformation in liberal ideology in the twentieth century. The transition was not painless. The concept of affirmative action, with its baggage of quotas, goals, and timetables, has not set well with all liberals. Some have accepted it enthusiastically, others with reservations, and some not at all. But even those who have not accepted it have, by and large, remained faithful to the new liberalism, rarely voicing a loud protest. Those who have openly challenged the new orthodoxy have been assigned the label neoconservative. People like Nathan Glazer, for example, were always associated with liberalism until they refused to follow the lead of the new liberals. Glazer, for instance, does not accept the idea that Blacks need preferential treatment to succeed. He does not believe that Blacks cannot learn unless they go to schools that are representative of their proportion in the population. He does not believe that all of those who oppose quotas and busing are racists. "And all those who believe these things," writes the Harvard sociologist, "believe that they are moral and the others who oppose them are immoral, that they defend the best traditions of the United States, whereas those who disagree with them would perpetuate discrimination, segregation, and inequality."[324]

The 1964 Civil Rights Act was the most important piece of legislation affecting minorities in the 1960s. Nothing since has approached its comprehensiveness. Hailed as an equal-opportunity measure for individuals, the law soon evolved as an equal-results applicator for groups. It was not supposed to be that way. Senator Hubert Humphrey, the majority whip, explained that "the proponents of the bill have carefully stated on numerous occasions that Title VII does not require an employer to achieve any sort of racial balance in his work force by giving preferential treatment to any individual or group."[325] He even went so far as to say that he would "start eating the pages [of the bill] one after another" if any language could be found that permitted "preferential treatment for Negroes or any other persons or groups" or "any quota system to maintain racial balance in employment."[326] Humphrey was right about the wording of the bill—it explicitly prohibited preferential treatment. But he was wrong regarding its interpretation by administrative agencies and the courts. In its wake have come goals, timetables, quotas, utilization studies, validation tests, maps, charts, graphs—and bureaucrats armed with their supplementary updates. And suits. The names of DeFunis, Bakke, Weber, and Fullilove have become part of the familiar litany of forced equality. There will be more.

In 1964 James Burnham published *Suicide of the West,* a searing indictment of liberalism. With rapier precision, Burnham outlined the characteristics and positions of liberals. He noted that liberals "reject 'quota systems,' especially systems related to race, color or religion, in admitting students to universities and professional institutions. A quota system could satisfy the ideal of arithmetic equality, but would imply qualitative discriminations."[327] Ironically, 1964 marks the first year that the ACLU endorsed quotas.[328] Prior to that time, it had shown no sympathy for quotas of any sort; liberalism had not yet been radicalized. In 1949 the Union said that it strongly disapproved of left-wing attempts to secure racial quotas for Blacks at the Lucky Stores in Los Angeles.[329] In the early 1950s the Union expounded its interpretation of the Thirteenth, Fourteenth, and Fifteenth Amendments, arguing that "it means treating everyone on the basis of individual merit and demerit, not of accidental membership in any group. It means keeping separate things separate, permitting distinction in treatment only on the basis of strictly relevant functional grounds."[330] At the end of the decade it said something that it could not say now, i.e. that "federal funds [should] be withheld from all schools and colleges which refuse, on racial grounds, to admit otherwise qualified students."[331] This one-time liberal idea (made defunct since *Bakke,* if not before) was expatiated upon by the Union at the same time that it was opposing the Census Bureau's questionnaire asking citizens to identify their race: "The basis of the Union's stand was that the vaguely-worded query will not result in reliable information while it 'raises in the minds of many of our people the specter of some threatened discrimination.'"[332] The very same question is now regarded as precise and reliable and the only specter that currently haunts the ACLU is the specter of Ronald Reagan.

The ACLU decided to support quotas before its affiliates did. At the same time that the parent organization endorsed quotas, the New York affiliate was taking a strong stand against preferential treatment of Blacks in housing and jobs: "The constitution is color blind. It does not permit discrimination in favor of, any more than discrimination against."[333] The New York CLU also condemned a suggestion made during the mayoralty campaign in 1965 that called for minority representation on the proposed police review board: "If a number of members . . . happen to be Negroes and Puerto Ricans, well and good; but we would not want to see anyone on the board who feels he must act in the interest of . . . a racial group. That would make a mockery of [any] claim to be impartial."[334] Times have really changed since then. This is what the ACLU said in 1982: "There should be more minority members in the legislatures because they provide perspective for other members, which for too long has been absent."[335] The evolution of this position can be traced to the work of the Equality Committee in 1964—a position that was seconded by the board: "The use of racial quotas as a technique for correcting serious racial discrimination in employment is a justifiable means of offsetting past wrongs by temporarily recruiting people of a group which has been discriminated against."[336] To be exact, the ACLU should have said that it did not mean to include Catholics or others who might easily claim inclusion: only non-Whites, and especially Blacks, were acceptable candidates for quotas. The Union also made public its position on "reverse discrimination" in the mid-1960s: "The exclusive recruitment of members of a minority group, a policy known as 'reverse discrimination,' is no less evil than any other kind of discrimination, and is certainly just as contrary to the spirit of civil liberties."[337]

It is evident that in the 1960s the Union had not yet arrived at a satisfactory position on preferential treatment. On the one hand, it supported Title VII of the Civil Rights Act,[338] which clearly disallowed preferential treatment of any kind. On the other hand, it supported quotas. And to complicate matters, it voiced rejection of "reverse discrimination." The Union's argument that quotas should be permitted "temporarily" is most interesting. This meretricious formula has been exposed by Sidney Hook:

> Another conscience-appeasing justification for the manifestly immoral violations of the principle of equal treatment under just law is the claim that measures adopted to implement reverse discrimination are "merely temporary" or "transitional," until such time as the necessity for it disappears, and race and sex can be disregarded in hiring and promotion practices. This is the position among others of the American Civil Liberties Union. It is obviously question-begging. When will the necessity for reverse discrimination disappear? When all minorities and women are represented in all avenues of work

in proportion to their numbers in the population? The American Civil Liberties Union would be outraged at the proposal "to suspend temporarily" a person's right to a fair trial until the crime wave subsides. Why should any morally principled clear-headed opponent of all forms of discrimination temporarily suspend the protection of equal rights under the law?[339]

After 1971, the ACLU dropped its objection to "reverse discrimination." The entire question of preferential treatment, quotas, and "reverse discrimination" came to a head at a board meeting in December 1972. Both sides lined up for a fiery debate. The following arguments were among the reasons given to support quotas:

1. "Quota" is a code word like "busing." To be against busing is to be against blacks; similarly, to be against quotas is to be against the aspirations of blacks and other minorities to achieve equality in employment. It would be disastrous for the ACLU to align itself with the anti-quota crusade.

2. Although quotas may be suspect according to civil liberties logic, it has been the experience of the civil rights struggle that statements of good intention in the abstract are not particularly effective. Only specific numbers will achieve results.

3. A demonstration of good faith is not enough because discrimination is the result of a course of conduct, not motive. Also, it is naive to expect good faith to be present among people accustomed to privilege.

4. The argument that quotas will result in the hiring of less qualified people reflects a presumption that people born white and male are inherently qualified and that blacks and females are inferior. The fact that one person is highly trained does not mean that another less-trained person is unqualified.

5. It is impossible at this time for employers to make pure and pristine judgments. The quota is the only factor that will make a difference now.

6. The white male has acquired his superior qualifications because of discrimination against other groups. The use of quotas for employment merely shifts to blacks and women the advantage that white males have been getting all along.

7. Young blacks will not be likely to participate in education or training programs unless they know that there will be jobs for them when they finish. Quotas would give them the assurance they need.

8. Nice liberal methods of correcting discrimination have been exhausted. Whites must pay the price for past injustice.

9. In the real world, without quotas there will only be lip service given to equality.

10. The only way to break the cycle of discrimination is to be arbitrary.

11. The fact that quotas may become malevolent does not mean that they are not a useful tool now.[340]

The following arguments were among those made against the use of quotas:

1. Classification by race or sex is forbidden by the Fourteenth Amendment, a principle which the ACLU has fought hard to establish in numerous litigative struggles.

2. Even where some courts have sustained percentage hiring of members of minority groups they have done so under affirmative action standards, not under a quota mandate. Why then resort to the use of quotas per se?

3. The dichotomy of victims and innocent beneficiaries . . . is too simple a formula and does not exhaust the universe of possibilities. For example, Jewish males are the victim of discrimination as Jews but as males are the beneficiaries of discrimination against women.

4. The innocent beneficiaries of discrimination cannot give back what they have inadvertently taken. Why should a whole new generation be dealt with less than fairly?

5. What justification can there be giving preference in hiring under a quota principle to a less qualified woman raised in economically and culturally *advantaged* conditions against a poor, economically depressed white?

6. The use of the term "quota" is horrifying because people have been subjected to exclusionary quotas in the past.

7. The ACLU should not be in the position of trading one injustice for another. This is another example of the "means and the ends." We should not use anti-civil libertarian methods to achieve civil libertarian goals.

8. Backlash from white males will be much worse if quotas are set now, when there are not enough jobs to go around.

9. The primary leverage of the Civil Liberties Union is in the promulgation of good thought and high principle. ACLU does not lack the moral fiber to find other means of attacking discrimination in employment than quotas.[341]

The final decision on quotas was not made until the board meeting in April 1973, four months later. The ACLU came out in favor of quotas. It suggested seven items that ought to be included in a model affirmative action program. The Equal Employment Opportunity Commission could not have done better. Among the recommendations was the following prescription: "The use of 'target' ratios and timetables as goals for periodic assessment of the success of the affirmative action program, together with clear lines of responsibility to assure that, if goals are not being met, efforts will be intensified."[342] At this time the Union did say that although it supported affirmative action, it would not countenance "hiring or entrance quotas that fix numbers or percentages of particular classes or groups."[343] That was before *Bakke.* It has since dropped this objection.[344]

The most controversial affirmative action case of the decade was the *Bakke* case. When Associate Justice Lewis Powell announced the Supreme Court's decision, he said: "Perhaps no case in my memory has had so much media coverage."[345] Allan Bakke, a White male, was successful in his suit against the Regents of the University of California. He claimed that he was a victim of discrimination because he had been denied entrance into the medical school at the University of California at Davis simply because he was White. The medical school reserved sixteen out of one hundred places for disadvantaged minorities. Bakke, whose test scores were higher than those of all the minority applicants, said he would have been accepted if the quota system had not been in effect. The Supreme Court, in a 5-4 decision, declared quotas to be illegal but held that affirmative action programs could give preferential consideration to disadvantaged groups.[346]

The ACLU was active in the *Bakke* case but not on his side. On 7 June 1977, the Union filed a friend-of-the-court brief supporting the special admission program of the University of California at Davis. Its brief asserted:

> The intensity and vigor of these discussions have heightened the ACLU's realization that the major civil liberties issue still facing the United States is the elimination, root and branch, of all vestiges of racism. No other asserted claim of right surpasses the wholly justified demand of the nation's discrete and insular minorities for access to the American mainstream from which they have so long been excluded.[347]

From the press release that the ACLU issued, it is possible to ascertain even further the Union's rationale behind its decision.

> The principle of non-discrimination requires that individuals should be treated individually in accordance with their personal merits, achievements and potential, and not on the basis of the supposed attributes of any class or caste with which they may be identified.
>
> But when discrimination—and particularly discrimination in employment and education—has been long and widely practiced against a particular class, it cannot be satisfactorily eliminated merely by the prospective adoption of neutral, "color-blind" statements for selection among the applicants for available jobs or educational programs.
>
> We believe that a nation which has engaged in centuries of subjugation, segregation and discrimination cannot take seriously those who now insist that under no circumstances should we abide selection processes in which race counts in the calculus. It is generations too late for that notion of neutrality to operate as anything but a preserver of the status quo.[348]

The Union argued before the Supreme Court that the university's special admission program "serves vital education and social policies," "promoted equality," and "is constitutional." Can there be any doubt but that the ACLU's position was strictly an instrumentalist one? A purist interpretation of the Bill of Rights would necessarily have insisted on the right of Allan Bakke not to be discriminated against because of the color of his skin. The three arguments the Union used before the high court show how determined it was to promote social equality: (1) Since the "central purpose of the Fourteenth Amendment is the *protection* of discrete and insular minorities, it would be a cruel irony for [the Supreme Court] to turn that shield into a weapon against state governmental efforts to redress cumulative racial injustices." (2) Since the special admission program was "not motivated by prejudice and yields 'no racial slur or stigma with regard to whites or any other race,'" the program again "is not inconsistent with the Fourteenth Amendment." (3) Just as the Supreme Court has held that it is permissible under the Fourteenth Amendment for government to redress "our society's longstanding disparate treatment of women," so too is it constitutionally permissible for government to adopt a program whose "only discernible purpose" is "the permissible one of redressing our society's longstanding disparate treatment of minorities."[349] In neither the press release nor the excerpts from the legal brief did the Union use the term *quotas; a certain number of persons,* and *timetables* are the preferred euphemisms.[350]

In the body of its brief, the ACLU relied on the inspiration of Harvard philosopher John Rawls. The Union observed:

> To admit Bakke to medical school in place of a member of a minority group would be in the words of Rawls, "expedient, but . . . not just" unless "the situation of persons not so fortunate is thereby improved." The University of California special admission program, on the other hand, is patently just for it works to improve the situation of the less fortunate.[351]

That the ACLU chose to cite the egalitarian Rawls instead of his colleague and libertarian nemesis, Robert Nozick, is demonstrative of the Union's true colors: social equality takes priority over individual liberty.

During my interviews with Baldwin, Reitman, and Neier, I asked each of them to comment on the *Bakke* case. Reitman offered a straight descriptive account of the proceedings; Baldwin and Neier delivered more revealing opinions. I will begin with my exchange with Neier.

> W.D.: The ACLU has justified discrimination against white men, specifically in the Bakke position, because it feels that affirmative action is necessary to eliminate all vestiges of racism. Since when has racism per se, as opposed to the particular deprivations of civil liberties which arise as a result of racism, been considered a violation of civil liberties?

A.N.: The idea of equal protection of the laws is that everyone should be in a position to count equally in our society. And we think it is legitimate for states to try to make sure that everyone counts equally.

W.D.: Isn't this a reversal of the ACLU's previous position?

A.N.: No, I don't think so.

W.D.: Regarding quotas for example? I have evidence of that, to show that, in the annual report that is the case.

A.N.: No, I don't think so. We have never said that admissions to colleges always have to be based on, say, competitive scores or anything like that. We never said anything like that.

W.D.: That's true. But you have taken a position against racial quotas in employment and—

A.N.: We have taken a position against racial quotas, but we have not specifically upheld racial quotas. We have opposed, by way of an amicus brief, an effort to strike down affirmative action programs. Those are two different things.

W.D.: Which affirmative action programs have you taken an effort to strike down?

A.N.: We entered the Bakke case with a friend of the court brief.

W.D.: In favor of the University of California?

A.N.: That's right. We oppose efforts to strike down affirmative action programs.

W.D.: You don't feel that Mr. Bakke himself, for example, is a victim of discrimination in this particular case?

A.N.: I don't think our secular brief reached the question of whether he is a victim of discrimination. The issue as posed by the Ninth Circuit decision is whether the California program of affirmative action is constitutional. We think it is.[352]

Baldwin was asked to comment on the ACLU's *Bakke* position. His reply was enlightening:

R.B.: I think the ACLU is wrong. I'm on the other side. I'm on the Bakke side. I think it was a great mistake. I think the ACLU—ACLU is false to its own principles when it supports a quota. We've always opposed quotas. Never supported quotas. But there is a very strong element in the ACLU today that is so impressed with the deprivation of opportunities for colored peoples and Hispanics and others, that they will go to almost any length to get them open admissions to colleges. It's a silly idea! We support open admissions. We shouldn't support open admissions. We should support standards of education. Instead of supporting standards, we have played favorites with people who are disadvantaged. I understand it. I'm very sympathetic with it, but it destroys another principle. And they've chosen the wrong one.

W.D.: Well, isn't this one more indication that the ACLU is becoming more involved in using civil liberties as an instrument to affect social change?

R.B.: Yes, it is. There is an element in ACLU that would like to expand a concept of civil liberties to include the injustices of the economic system. But I think we've got to stick to our original purposes.[353]

The ACLU's current affirmative action policy was formulated in 1979 and 1980. It is its most enthusiastic endorsement of affirmative action ever. All the slogans that one would expect are there: "invidious discrimination" (is there any other kind?); "compensatory justice"; "remedial education"; "goals"; "timetables"; "targets"; "ratios"; "quotas"; "eligible pool"; "societal discrimination"; "subjugation"; and "second-class status."[354] In a related policy, the Union brought its erudition to bear on hiring procedures: "To assist in the collection of statistical data essential to evaluation of affirmative action programs, the ACLU supports requiring at the interview stage the decision maker to give his or her perception of racial, ethnic or gender identification of the applicant, whether rejected or accepted."[355] This is one of the most arbitrary and capricious suggestions that the ACLU has made. The applicant is also expected to identify his or her race, ethnicity, and sex "on a separate form which notifies the applicant of the purpose of this self identification."[356] All this in the name of civil liberties.

For two decades the ACLU has been actively pursuing affirmative action—writing policies, giving speeches, testifying before Congress, bringing suits—all the while showing remarkably little sympathy for employers who contend that they have tried but failed to secure a representative number of qualified minority candidates. What is most disturbing about the ACLU's effrontery is its failure to abide by its own strictures. It has had its own internal affirmative action policy since 1970, updated periodically with the most specific requirements for hiring.[357] Yet at its June 1982 board meeting it announced that it would make an exception for itself: "The Board unanimously granted a waiver pursuant to the ACLU's affirmative action policy #530, to permit the hiring of a nonminority lawyer, to the extent that we continue to be unable to find a minority candidate."[358] Now, if the ACLU cannot find a minority lawyer in New York City, just how easy might it be for a small law firm in Des Moines? What is even more casuistic is the Union's continued claim to be the defender of individual rights. John Shattuck maintains that the ACLU "is utterly preoccupied with the rights of the individual."[359] Not with Mr. Bakke's rights, nor with those of legions of others. To top it off, Shattuck says, "The moment the ACLU starts taking general social interests into account it is going to be in trouble."[360] With whom? Labor, Blacks, women, gays?

Do colleges exist to promote academic excellence or equality? This was never a moot question until the 1960s; colleges had always been perceived as institutions of higher learning. But in the 1960s, schools from kindergarten through college underwent a transformation that made them prime candidates for social reform. Social engineers seized the schools as their laboratory for experimentation, expecting to create equality and social justice in the classroom. Using the schools to foster change is an honored American tradition, used by liberals and conservatives alike since the days of Horace Mann. Even though admission requirements in colleges are arguably no one's business but the officials who run them, the ACLU could not resist trying to affect the decision-making process. The ACLU positioned itself in favor of lowering academic standards for Blacks. It did not come right out and say that, but what other interpretation are we to draw?

> In order to achieve genuine equality of educational opportunity colleges should apply, in respect to persons who are members of disadvantaged groups and who previously have been denied opportunity for equal educational advantage, standards and methods of evaluating applicants different from those used with other applicants, as long as these standards and methods are reasonably designed to increase equality of educational opportunity. Massive compensatory programs for educationally deprived students should be simultaneously instituted.[361]

The 1970s saw the ACLU become even more race conscious. Its South Carolina affiliate sought to have the state's bar examination declared unconstitutional. The suit was filed after it was reported that Blacks did not do well on the examination; the affiliate said the test was biased against Blacks.[362] Another Union activity that sought social equality in education was its effort to have the Department of Health, Education, and Welfare (HEW) impose goals and timetables for the hiring of minority teachers by the New York City Board of Education. The Union's complaint, which was filed in 1976, was successful: HEW ordered the board to comply with its measure. Senator Daniel Patrick Moynihan, Democrat of New York, called the HEW action a "prescription for division and hostility," and likened it to the sorting out of human beings by race in Nazi Germany.[363]

Poverty and Civil Liberties

Psychologist and welfare rights activist William Ryan is convinced that "most Americans have very little—some so little they can barely stay alive."[364] He maintains that "the majority of American families are constantly vulnerable to economic disaster," and that "a *substantial majority* of American families will experience poverty at some point during a relatively short span of time."[365] He was not referring to conditions in the nineteenth century but to the situation facing most Americans in the 1980s. Although few outside the halls of academia might be persuaded to believe this, it is fair to say that Ryan speaks for many members of the professoriate in the liberal arts. The reason for this state of affairs, writes Ryan, "is plain to see: we don't throw enough dollars."[366] He has a solution, what he calls his "general recipe for achieving equality." What we need is an increase in expenditures for: housing subsidies, food stamps, school breakfast and lunch programs, mass transportation, regulatory agencies, social security, unemployment benefits, government jobs, higher education, counseling services, child welfare programs, protective programs for children and other "vulnerable members of society," mental health services, and day care services. We also need new programs. Ryan recommends: national health service, children allowances, homemaker allowances, fuel stamps, food stamps for everyone, state food stores, state theaters, and the nationalization of the communications industry, sports, and the arts.[367] All this is to be accomplished through the tax laws.[368]

Ryan believes, as do many liberals, that government expenditures on the poor are "shamelessly, cruelly stingy."[369] Yet budget observers such as Donald Lambro[370] have shown that the problem is not the amount that is being spent, it is where the money winds up that is distressing. As William Raspberry, the Washington writer, has said: "Poverty is big business, recession proof and growing." The federal contribution alone, he maintains, is "big enough to place the poverty industry in the top ten of the Fortune 500."[371] And although George Gilder[372] has provided a vigorous rebuttal to the ideas entertained by Ryan and others on the Left, the prevailing view amongst intellectuals is that poverty can be eliminated through redistribution programs. Thus, the very existence of poverty is due to the greed of the rich.

"Fairly early in the evolution of the idea of liberalism," writes Minogue, "poverty came to be seen as the major evil, and the source of most other evils."[373] In the parlance of liberals, poverty has long been seen as the "root cause" of many of our social problems, ranging from prostitution to heroin addiction. If we want to solve crime, the argument goes, we must root out poverty. Political scientist James Q. Wilson[374] and psychoanalyst Ernest van den Haag[375] have seriously impaired this popular thesis but, like their fellow conservative George Gilder, they have been less successful at convincing the liberal audience. To learn how fashionable the "poverty-breeds-social-pathology" thesis is, all one needs to do is consult any textbook on social problems or criminology. That poverty has decreased while crime has increased does not seem to matter: ideology is what matters.

In the 1950s, as unemployment increased, welfare increased; as unemployment decreased, so did welfare. That is not hard to understand. But in the 1960s, when unemployment hit 3.5 percent (virtually no unemployment), welfare soared. Moynihan was struck by the paradox: *"Across the nation it had become a general rule that as poverty declined, welfare dependency increased."*[376] The evolution of the "war on poverty," which was first announced in January 1964,[377] helps to explain the irony. New York lawyer Charles Morris put his finger on the key to understanding the course that the "war on poverty" followed:

> A turning point came with the publication of an article by [Richard] Cloward and [Frances Fox] Piven in the *Nation* on May 2, 1966, which set out for the first time a coherent strategy for the movement. They argued that the existing [welfare] system survived only by intimidating and underpaying clients. A massive campaign to enroll eligible clients and to get full benefits for those already on the rolls would cause the system's financial collapse and ensure its replacement by an equitable, federally administered program of guaranteed income maintenance. The tactics should include a mass educational campaign and public disruption of local welfare offices. The disruption, it was argued, was necessary to enhance the clients' sense of power in dealing with the system and to increase the pressure on state and local governments to pass the burden to the federal government. The article generated immense excitement among radical antipoverty workers and was a blueprint for the organizing drive in New York.[378]

As Irving Kristol has noted, "the 'welfare explosion' was the work, not of capitalism or of any other 'ism,' but of men and women like Miss Piven and Mr. Cloward—in the Welfare Rights Movement, the social work profession, the Office of Economic Opportunity, as so on."[379]

It is important to note that Piven is a member of the ACLU and was instrumental in seeing to it that some of her views regarding welfare were adopted by the Union.[380] As with many other questionable civil liberties issues, however, there was some initial resistance to the idea that the ACLU ought to enter the arena of economic rights. The subject of a guaranteed annual income was first discussed at the 1966 Biennial Conference. Those in favor of redistribution schemes argued that "meaningful participation in the democratic process is a fiction without an adequate income to fulfill a person's basic needs."[381] Those opposed warned that this issue was outside the Union's domain and would impair its effectiveness in the long run. The board did what the government often did in the 1960s when a consensus could not be reached: it appointed a committee to study the question.[382]

Two years later the Biennial Conference settled the issue: an income-maintenance program was recommended. In October 1968 Sheldon Ackley, chairman of the New York CLU, urged board members to adopt the conference's recommendations as policy. Ackley noted that the board members of his affiliate had already decided to support the 1968 Biennial Conference position. He argued that the present welfare system contained severe and pervasive deprivations of civil liberties and that these deprivations were intrinsic to the program. Therefore, he called upon his colleagues to adopt the following measures: "1) Income should be guaranteed as a matter of right and provided under conditions posing no interference with basic freedoms. 2) The level of income maintenance guaranteed must be high enough to meet basic human needs."[383] Howard Lesnick, who chaired the Law School Task Force on Entitlement to Government Benefits, went further. He urged the board to consider all the indignities and harassments that affect poor people; the areas of medical care, housing and education should be addressed. Others objected to both Ackley's and Lesnick's recommendations. It was argued that if the ACLU were to enter the field of broad economic and social rights, there would be no stopping it from trying to cure every imaginable social ill, including air and water pollution. These issues, it was maintained, were not civil liberties issues. Herbert Prashker's motion to have a committee consider the issue of income maintenance more thoroughly was carried by voice vote. The committee was also asked to give its attention to other programs of public assistance, e.g. education and medical care.[384]

In June 1973 Marvin Karpatkin spoke before the board in support of the recommendation adopted by the 1972 Biennial Conference. The recommendation read as follows:

> The American Civil Liberties Union holds that the United States Constitution and proper government policy require government at every level to assure every person in the United States an adequate standard of living.[385]

The following arguments were made in favor of the Biennial Conference recommendation:

1. The ACLU draws strength from the relevant issues with which it deals. It would grow further by dealing with the right to a decent standard of living.
2. The Biennial recommendation would give the Union a basis for participating in programs of a civil liberties nature that would help the poor, such as equal transportation facilities in ghetto areas.
3. The ACLU should have a new constituency and clientele: the poor. Poverty is per se a denial of civil liberties.

4. There cannot be a government of, by and for the people unless civil liberties include economic rights.
5. The ACLU must have some interest in the breakup of economic power. Such a breakup would help to advance civil liberties concerns.
6. As Mr. Justice Marshall wrote in his *Rodriguez* dissent, if you find a nexus between something not expressed in the Constitution and something that is, then it is a constitutional matter.[386]

The following arguments were made against the Biennial Conference recommendation:

1. Poverty *per se* is not a denial of civil liberties any more than a premature death from leukemia is a denial of civil liberties. ("How will we respond to the cerebral palsy or cancer people when they come and say you can't enjoy civil liberties if you've got cerebral palsy?") It isn't enough to base a finding of what is civil liberties on what results in a deprivation of civil liberties. Overpopulation results in deprivations of civil liberties, but freedom from overpopulation is not a civil liberty.
2. The Biennial recommendation is a Marxist proposal. If adopted, it would drive out much of the ACLU's membership.
3. It is not the ACLU's business to espouse an economic position. The Union's job is to defend civil liberties of all people. If the Union moves into the economic area, it will be competing with labor unions. If we adopt this policy, how can we not intervene on wage and price control issues. The ACLU should not be proposing transportation legislation and minimum wage legislation. This is a field for the A.D.A. or the Democratic National Committee, not the ACLU. ("If we adopt the recommendation we should change our name to ACLSIU—American Civil Liberties and Social Improvement Union.")
4. The Biennial recommendation refers to the "United States Constitution," but there is no constitutional basis for the proposal.
5. As the staff's factual background paper shows, the ACLU is already deeply involved in poverty litigation where clear civil liberties issues are present. The real question is whether adopting the Biennial position on poverty is good or bad symbolism. ("We're already into this 80% or 90% of the way. It's hard to justify going the additional 10% or 20%.")[387]

After further discussion, the board rejected the Biennial Conference recommendation by a roll-call vote of 20 for, 39 against, and one abstention. The board then rejected by a vote of 28-13 a list of entitlements that were recommended by the Equality Committee. Among the entitlements rejected were: (a) "Every person in the United States is entitled to decent, safe, and sanitary housing in an area of his or her choice, free of racial and ethnic concentration with equal provision of municipal services"; (b)

"Every person in the United States is entitled to adequate and comprehensive health care, accessible to where he or she lives"; (c) "Every person in the United States is entitled to income sufficient to achieve an adequate standard of living"; (d) "Every person who wants to work and is not barred by age or physical condition should be ensured a job commensurate with his or her abilities"; (e) "Every person should be entitled to access to child care sevices regardless of ability to pay."[388]

Many other liberal reforms, which had more to do with civil rights than civil liberties, were rejected before the board finally accepted, by a vote of 52-1, its general policy on poverty. The policy began by setting forth the ACLU's philosophy on the subject: "Poverty cannot be explained as resulting from 'natural' economic differences." The heart of the policy states that when there is "a direct and substantial connection between poverty and *particular* deprivations of civil liberties and civil rights, and ACLU will support positive governmental action to mitigate the effects of poverty so as to eliminate or curtail the particular deprivations of civil liberties and civil rights."[389] In essence, the board struck a compromise between those who wanted to involve the Union totally in the area of economic rights and those who resisted such engagement. By adopting this policy, the board opened the door for the equality activists without committing the Union fully to their position. It went far enough, however, to put the ACLU on record as departing from the Supreme Court's interpretation of poverty. The high court does not recognize poverty as a "suspect" category falling under its strict scrutiny provision. As Justice Potter Stewart once said, "Poverty, standing alone, is not a suspect classification"; it is not of the government's making.[390]

The equality activists did not yield in their desire to move the ACLU further into the arena of economic rights. In December 1977 they were successful in persuading the board to adopt the following additions to the policy on poverty:

> The ACLU and its affiliates recognize and urge that the denial of benefits necessary to the basic sustenance of life of some persons, while comparable benefits are afforded by government to others, has constitutional significance insofar as the requirements of equal protection and due process are concerned.
>
> In light of the drastic cutback in government benefit programs currently underway, as well as the inadequate legislative-judicial response to equal protection and due process issues in social welfare programs, the ACLU and its affiliates will themselves evaluate whether compelling societal reasons exist for exclusion of persons from major governmental programs involving basic necessities of life. Where the ACLU and/or its affiliate concludes that no compelling reason exists, the Union and/or affiliate will actively advocate in both court and legislature, against such exclusion.[391]

This amendment to the policy on poverty was proposed by the 1976 Biennial Conference. The following arguments were made in favor of the motion:

1. An adequate income is fundamental to the exercise of one's civil liberties. We need to combat a widespread view that the ACLU is not relevant to the concerns of the 1970s. In addition, many of the things we already do are involved with economic right.
2. The economic system determines how inequality is structured into law; the poor do not have the same access to courts or to civil liberties groups, and by our silence we would be defending the status quo.
3. We need to become aware of the increasing threats to the social compact which mount with growing inequality, and which raise questions about our relevance as an organization as long as we continue to resist activity in the economic area.[392]

The following arguments proved to be unsuccessful:

1. Each college textbook presents a different version of economics, yet we act as if the answers are very simple.
2. ACLU stands for something separate, special and different from other public interest organizations. The passage of this resolution would render us no different from a number of other social justice groups.
3. It is not summoning up a paper tiger to talk about the threat posed to ACLU's very existence by becoming involved in the economic rights area.[393]

The controversial resolution passed 37-30 with one abstention.[394]

In 1984, the egalitarians in the ACLU proved that their influence was decisive. At its January meeting, the board adopted the 1983 Biennial Conference resolution on poverty: "The body recommends that the ACLU national Board and staff make those civil liberties issues which have a particular impact on the poor a priority in their education, litigation, and legislative programs."[395] It's only a matter of time before income distribution will be seen as a civil liberties concern.

Welfare recipients received the ACLU's attention in the 1960s. The Union voiced support for the right to privacy, the right to a hearing, and the right to travel freely. It also supported the right of welfare recipients to receive free birth control information, and endorsed publicly funded voluntary sterilization programs.[396] In the 1970s the Union entered its objection to residency requirements, whether they be previous, continuing, or durational; only present residency requirements were found acceptable.[397] However, the ACLU's opposition to previous and continuing residency requirements was not absolute. It had no problem with such restrictions when applied to municipal workers: In the interest of affirmative action, the ACLU supported the right of cities to require its municipal workers to live within its borders.[398] Once again, the goal of equality proved to be paramount to the rights of the individual.

In 1979 the Union registered its disapproval of the long waits that welfare recipients had to endure before there was a hearing on their benefits. It also deplored "conduct that demeans individual dignity and degrades individual autonomy of beneficiaries, as exemplified by patronizing and hostile attitudes on the part of local welfare workers."[399] It offered no suggestions as to how to correct this condition. With regard to work requirements, the ACLU waffled. From 1964 to 1982 it took the position that such requirements were not, in principle, objectionable.[400] But in 1982 it decided to follow the thinking that had earlier been voiced by Piven and Cloward. More than a decade earlier they had stated flatly, "We are opposed to work-enforcing reforms."[401] The present ACLU policy is identical, arguing that it "opposes work requirements at government-assigned tasks as a condition of eligibility for welfare benefits or for any transfer payments designed to compensate for insufficient income."[402] Although the Union has carefully thought through the rights of welfare recipients, it has had absolutely nothing to say regarding any concomitant responsibilities that the beneficiaries might have.

Although Blacks received more attention than any other group in the 1960s and 1970s, the ACLU did pass a number of policies affecting the rights of other socially dispossessed groups. American Indians, the aged, and the physically handicapped did not go unnoticed. The Union expressed its empathy with the plight of Indians, asking that governmental decisions that might affect their lives be made in consultation with tribal leaders.[403] One case illustrates the Union's concern: the right of Navajo Indians to use peyote, a drug, in their religious ceremonies was defended in the early 1960s; the Supreme Court disagreed.[404] In 1974 the Union was more specific as to what Indian rights it supported: (1) a tribal land base and appurtenant natural resources; (2) tribal self-government; (3) retention of the cultural and religious heritage; and (4) enforcement of U.S. treaties.[405] Two years later it added that Indian hunting and fishing rights ought to be respected.[406] In 1978, respect for Indian water rights became policy.[407] With regard to the aged[408] and the physically handicapped,[409] the Union simply advocated that both groups be given equal employment opportunities.

The rights of the mentally retarded and the mentally ill have merited a considerable amount of time and energy on the part of the ACLU. From 1968 to 1982, New York lawyer Bruce Ennis did more to secure the rights of the mentally handicapped than perhaps anyone else in the country. He successfully launched a suit against Willowbrook, the infamous mental institution on Staten Island. By doing so he made many Americans aware of the fact that the institutionalized have civil liberties too.[410] His efforts convinced his colleagues at the ACLU to pass a policy regarding the rights of the mentally retarded, including the right of sexual expression.[411] In 1982 the Supreme Court, in *Youngberg v. Romeo,* essentially gave its stamp of approval to many of the rights of the mentally retarded for which the ACLU had lobbied over the past decade.[412]

The concerns surrounding the rights of the mentally ill are more varied and complex than is true for the mentally retarded if only because the mentally ill are more likely to return to the community after being institutionalized. The ACLU has been participating in this issue for approximately twenty years. The Union's current position, formulated in 1981, is precise: "Mental illness cannot *by itself* be a justifiable reason for depriving a person of liberty against his or her objection." Only where there is hard evidence of "imminent physical danger to such person or others" should involuntary commitment be allowed. The Union has enumerated fifteen procedures concerning commitment of persons to mental institutions, covering the right to counsel to the right to refuse any treatment whatsoever.[413] Ennis once again fielded this issue and became one of the leading advocates for deinstitutionalization in New York State.[414] Although the ACLU's motives were clearly benign, the unintended consequences of this policy have been less than salutary. Since 1965, two-thirds of New York State's mental patients have been discharged. "The only beneficiary of the state's effort to send mental patients back to their local communities has been the New York State treasury." This is the conclusion that New York City comptroller Harrison Goldin came to after an audit of the program.[415] No one doubts that the sudden increase in the homeless that surfaced in the 1970s is due largely to deinstitutionalization. There are approximately 36,000 homeless men and women walking the streets of New York City, and many, if not most, are there because of civil libertarian efforts.[416] Journalist Randy Young knows what happened: "Many of the street people were released from hospitals—some say 'dumped'—because of a revolution in psychiatric treatment know as de-institutionalization."[417] Led by New York attorney Robert Hayes, the rights of the homeless have won the vigilance of the courts.[418] Burt Neuborne, the ACLU's national legal director, would like to see his organization become more involved in the plight of the homeless. "People can't be allowed to freeze to death without the ACLU doing something."[419]

Women's Rights

When Elizabeth Cady Stanton and Lucretia Mott organized the Women's Rights Convention in 1848 at Seneca Falls, New York, they were primarily interested in persuading the public to recognize their demand that women ought to be granted such fundamental civil rights as the right to vote and the right to equal opportunity in employment and education. One hundred fifteen years later, Betty Friedan was charging that women had still not been emancipated, but the issues were different this time. Women had achieved the right to vote in 1920 and had made progress in employment and education, albeit slowly. Bread-and-butter issues were important in the 1960s, as they continue to be, but a significant shift in emphasis was taking place: social and psychological liberation took priority over economic concerns. In 1966, when the National Organization for Women (NOW) was founded, the new goals included "a sex-role revolution for men and women which will restructure all our institutions: childrearing, education, marriage, the family, medicine, work, politics, the economy, religion, psychological theory, human sexuality, morality and the very evolution of the race."[420] A formidable agenda to be sure. The women's movement was led, and continues to be led, by well-educated, White, upper-middle-class feminists. For Erica Jong, to be well educated is to be a feminist: "It seems to me that sooner or later, all intelligent women become feminists."[421] Ti-Grace Atkinson, a founding member of NOW, has identified exactly what a feminist is: "A feminist is a woman who directly attacks, through the sum of her actions, the most primary and physical manifestations constituting the oppression of women; the State and nationalism, the Church, the family, marriage, prostitution, rape, pornography; and a woman who rejects the value concept of power."[422]

One woman who never rejected the "value concept of power" was Eleanor Roosevelt. As James Burnham once said about the president's wife, "*Whatever* liberalism is, she was *it*."[423] Eleanor Roosevelt had long championed women's rights, seeking in her most active years, for example, to convince lawmakers that women needed special protection from hazardous and "demeaning" occupations. She was supported, as Peter Drucker notes, by liberals, progressives, socialists, and reformers "of all stripes."[424] In 1961 she chaired President Kennedy's Commission on the Status of Women, and helped to bring about a different conception of what liberation meant. It was now the considered judgment of feminists that differential legislation designed to protect women was the source of their subordinate position in society. Identical rights was now the issue. As with the women who first broached this idea in 1916, an equal rights amendment to the Constitution was seen as the best way to achieve the ends of feminism. The first such amendment was proposed in 1923 by the National Women's party.[425] Almost fifty years later, the ACLU decided to support the Equal Rights Amendment (ERA).[426]

The ACLU did not get involved in women's rights to any great extent until the 1940s; it became a national issue when a drive was restarted to push for an equal rights amendment. Its object was to remove inequalities between men and women. It failed. The Senate, in July 1946, decisively defeated it.[427] The ACLU rejoiced: it had succeeded in accomplishing its mission. The Union had been one of the many agencies in the national committee to oppose what they labeled the "Unequal Rights Amendment." Although the Union favored equal pay for equal work, it feared that the amendment would annul legislation designed to protect women's rights—the kind of legislation that Eleanor Roosevelt had worked so hard to achieve.[428] A slight loss in membership occurred as a result of the almost unanimous board policy.[429] The person who lobbied the hardest to have the ACLU reject the amendment was the "radical" Judge Dorothy Kenyon, who chaired the Union's Committee on Women's Rights.[430]

In the 1950s the ACLU took a much stronger stand against an equal rights amendment. One might have thought that had the Union's only dissatisfaction with such an amendment been its displeasure with the loss of rights that women might experience, it would have supported a bill that safeguarded existing benefits, rights, and exemptions. But it did not. It was relieved to see such a proviso attached as a rider to one of the bills,[431] but nevertheless remained hostile to the amendment. Referring to it as the "so-called 'equal rights amendment' (for women)," the ACLU opposed it because of "the danger that it would destroy the power to enact differential legislation granting equality in fact (as distinguished from mathematical identity)."[432] The amendment was opposed by most of the trade unions (both women's and men's) as well as the League of Women Voters. Even the American Association of University Women (AAUW) was opposed to the "liberating" amendment. In June 1953 the AAUW reconsidered its position and voted to sustain its long-held policy.[433]

The Equal Rights Amendment that the ACLU opposed in the 1950s was identical in language to that of the most recent effort: "Equality of rights under the law shall not be denied or abridged by the United States or by any State on account of sex." The reasons that the Union gave for opposing the amendment in the 1950s were similar to the ones expressed by the anti-ERA forces of the 1970s: "1—the language of the proposal might well freeze mathematical equality into our Constitution and stand in the way of or overrule desirable differential legislation, and 2—the scope of the Amendment, limited to rights under law, is not broad enough to warrant so fundamental a business as changing our Constitution." It then added that these objections were "substantial in the light of the history of women's position in society."[434] If someone were to have made these statements just ten years later, he or she would have incurred the venum of SCUM (Society for Cutting Up Men) and other sundry groups.

The Union's sense of history was remarkable. It referred to the discriminatory laws against women as "definitely on the way out. Only the remnants of feudalism remain." It then explained its position with surprising candor:

> But even in this bad area there is a little good. It is accepted social policy in most countries nowadays that it is better for mothers not to have to work outside the home but to be able to stay home with their children during a short part at least of their early infancy. For this purpose husbands must contribute support for both wife and children during the period in question. Hence the need of differential laws on this subject if true equality of opportunity and sound policy are to be achieved.[435]

The ACLU continued to offer new reasons why the ERA should be rejected by all civil libertarians. It held that "the greatest discriminations which women suffer from today do not derive from law at all but from custom and habit." The discriminatory policies that did exist "merely add up to bad habits with possibly a dash of fear of the strange and unpredictable thrown in. None of these discriminations are found in the statute books and few of them can be abolished by legislation." But the real clincher was this: "Even the practice of unequal pay for equal work, a world-wide phenomenon extremely interesting in its psychological motivations, is nothing but a universally bad habit."[436] Even Phyllis Schlafly never went that far!

In the 1960s the ACLU vigorously supported the rights of Blacks, Indians, Hispanics, labor, the poor, students, migrant farm workers, prisoners, the mentally ill, aliens, gays, conscientious objectors, GIs, Nazis, the Klan, Communists, and pornographers. But it fought the ERA. Nothing had arisen to change the Union's hostility to the amendment.[437] While endorsing the concept of equal pay for equal work, the Board nonetheless recommended that the Fifth and Fourteenth Amendments were "the most fitting instruments"[438] for women to pursue in their quest for equality. The ACLU argued that "no other amendment to the Constitution is necessary to secure equality for women."[439] It said that "the language of the proposed amendment is scanty, ambiguous and would therefore weaken the equality clause of the Fourteenth Amendment."[440] As far as the Union was concerned, "any ambiguity of language could be interpreted to forbid the enactment of differential social legislation necessary to achieve actual rather than mathematical identical equality."[441] It said it would, however, cooperate "to change discriminatory attitudes and practices surviving from ancient habits and customs."[442] When President Kennedy's Commission on the Status of Women asked the ACLU for input, it responded by rejecting the National Women's party's demand for the ERA. Once again, Judge Dorothy Kenyon led the way, asking the Union to "enthusiastically endorse the application of the Fourteenth Amendment to efforts to secure equal rights for women, and reject the Equal Rights Amendment now before the

Congress." Her motion was unanimously approved by the board.[443] The sixties ended with the ACLU leading the battle to defeat the ERA. On the board at that time were such leftist notables as Michael Harrington and William Kunstler. Harriet Pilpel served as one of three vice-chairmen.[444]

In 1972 the male-dominated Congress overwhelmingly passed the ERA and sent it to the state legislatures for ratification; thirty-eight states are needed before an amendment can become law. The male-dominated state legislatures responded quickly and affirmatively: thirty states voted to support the ERA in the year following the congressional vote. Women then organized to defeat the ERA and eventually proved successful, even allowing for an unprecedented extension of the time limit needed to pass an amendment. In 1974 three more states voted yes. In 1975 one more was added. Between 1976 and 1982 only one more state voted to confirm the ERA. The time limit expired on 30 June 1982.

The polls have shown that men have consistently been more supportive of the ERA than women. And even though a majority of women say they are in favor of the amendment, they have never voted that way. In 1975 the voters from New York and New Jersey were given the opportunity to vote on the ERA. It should be remembered that the representatives, mostly men, in these two states had already voted to support the ERA. When the vote was taken, the ERA was decisively defeated in both states. As Linda Greenhouse of the *New York Times* noted, it was women, not men, who were responsible for the defeat.[445] Obviously the politicians in these two liberal states heard the voices of the minority better than the majority.

No one will doubt that the condition of women was demonstrably better in 1970 than it had been in 1960, 1950, or 1940. Yet just when progress was surely being made to correct past injustices, the ACLU jumped on the bandwagon and joined the pro-ERA movement. What were recently regarded as bad habits were now seen as maliciously designed programs. What only yesterday could be seen as the "last remnants of feudalism" were now viewed as entrenched and pervasive sexist behavioral patterns. What had been labeled as ambiguous language was not branded as specific. What was once an unnecessary and dangerous remedy was now declared to be an indispensable and beneficial means to abet equality. The kind of equality that the ACLU had lobbied against—mathematical equality—was now its goal. In September 1970 the ACLU voted to support the ERA. Ironically, the person who had persistently fought the ERA for thirty years, Dorothy Kenyon, was responsible for the Union's new position. Many others had experienced rapid consciousness-raising as well: the vote was 52-1. One of the only reservations that was voiced was the proverbial bathroom issue; Norman Dorsen relieved the concern by suggesting that any difficulties could be worked out, if necessary.[446] The Union also voted later in the decade not to hold a regional or national meeting in any state that did not ratify the ERA.[447]

In 1976 Aryeh Neier, the executive director of the ACLU, stated flatly that the Union was "the legal branch of the women's movement."[448] Such statements help to confirm the thesis that the ACLU is more interested in social reform than anything else. Ever since the Union took a pro-ERA position, it has been evident that it pursues a posteriori logic with regard to women's issues, i.e. it reasons from the particular to the general. Its policy on day care is representative of such thinking. Why day care should be considered a civil liberties issue is not certain. However, it makes sense to squeeze day care into the civil liberties agenda if the primary goal is to effect equality. This is what the ACLU has done: "As an application of Union policy on equal employment for women, the ACLU endorses measures which would remove those barriers that have traditionally disadvantaged women in seeking and engaging in employment."[449] It is with this logic that the Union took a position supporting day care centers.

The issue of equality for women was raised again in 1977 when the question of women in athletics was considered. Some board members felt that separate but equal facilities for women were inherently unequal. Others argued that if all sports were integrated along sex lines, it would, in effect, deny most women the right to participate in nearly every sport because women are generally weaker than men. This was countered by the argument that sexual stereotyping from an early age was more responsible for the apparent physical inferiority of women than any congenital difference. Others declared varsity sports to be inherently evil because it was an invidious discrimination against the infirm and other less physically capable students! In the final analysis, the board held that "full participation by women in sports may require separate women's and men's teams but, in any event, requires access to compete for participation on integrated teams."[450]

The ACLU's support for preferential treatment for women and minorities in education and employment has always been based on its contention that veterans, as a group, have long been accorded preferential treatment. That veterans have earned preferential treatment over nonveterans as a result of their service to the country has not been emphasized by the Union. Veterans' rights, in the eyes of the ACLU, have not been seen as paramount, or even equal to, the rights of women. This was evident in the position that the Massachusetts CLU took regarding preferential treatment for veterans in the state's civil service job examination. The affiliate went to court to challenge preferential treatment for veterans because such treatment discriminated against women.[451] Whether the ACLU recognized the inconsistencies in its premise for preferential treatment is not known. The

Union lost the case. In the majority decision, the Supreme Court explained that "the 14th Amendment 'cannot be made a refuge from ill-advised laws.' The sub-standard edge granted to veterans by Ch. 31, sec. 23 may reflect unwise policy. The appellee, however, has simply failed to demonstrate that the law in any way reflects a purpose to discriminate on the basis of sex."[452]

In 1976 the Union adopted its first policy on "Use of Prior Sexual History in Rape Trials." In the conflict between freedom to a fair trial and freedom of privacy, the board voted to respect the former right. It did, however, offer a series of recommendations concerning such court proceedings. For example, it opposed the right of prosecutors to introduce evidence relating to the complainant's prior unchastity.[453] A year after this policy was passed, the Union changed the name of the policy to "Sexual Assault Laws." Maintaining its previous policy, the Union added to it the sex-neutral term "sexual assault" so as to include equal protection for both men and women; the new policy embraced an entire range of forcible sex acts. The board also asserted its position on spousal relationships: "Laws which prohibit prosecution when the complainant is the spouse of the defendant should be eliminated." Another new provision was the Union's suggestion that citizens would be better protected against sexual assaults if the penalties for such crimes were reduced.[454]

Abortion

On 22 January 1973, the Supreme Court legalized abortion. The restrictions it set forth in *Roe v. Wade* were few, and it is now widely interpreted as sanctioning abortion on demand. Shortly after this decision was rendered, a coalition of antiabortion forces emerged; it has proven to be one of the best-organized attempts to overturn a high court decision. Perhaps no other issue has evoked such emotion as the abortion issue. It has surely been one of the most divisive sociopolitical controversies in the twentieth century. The suddenness of the decision, coupled with its inclusiveness, took many observers of the issue by surprise. For a large part of American history, abortion had been considered a nonissue, at least as far as public policy was concerned. One student of the subject, Paul Taussig, wrote in 1936: "Ostrich-like, we have buried our heads in the sand and refused to look facts in the face."[455] The same was true thrity years later.

In 1955 Planned Parenthood put abortion on the national agenda; it convened a conference to consider the question of drafting proposals for a model abortion law. In 1962 the American Law Institute answered the need to advance a model law by drafting a statement in support of legalized abortion, when the following conditions were applicable: (a) the mother's life was in danger; (b) the child would be born with "grave physical or mental defect"; (c) pregnancy resulting from rape, incest, or "other felonious intercourse."[456] Throughout most of the 1960s advocates of abortion reform typically took the position of the American Law Institute, i.e. abortion on demand was not supported, only specific cases were deemed acceptable. In the mid-1960s abortion reform received unprecedented attention as a public policy issue. Dr. Alan Guttmacher, president of Planned Parenthood-World Population, recommended three modifications in state law. Abortion should be permitted, he maintained when (a) there is a real danger that the child will be born deformed; (b) when the mother is unwed and under the age of eighteen; and (c) when the child is unwanted and would be born into a family that is too large to allow for adequate development. At about the same time, 1,200 New York State obstetricians voted to recommend a change in the state law permitting abortion when the future health of the mother might be endangered and when her child would likely be born mentally or physically deficient.[457]

"The termination of any pregnancy," states Lee A. Dice, "must be carefully controlled by society."[458] He wrote this in 1965 in the liberal *Nation* magazine. At that time, it was the opinion of most liberals to restrict legalized abortion to carefully delineated cases of great saliency. Dice argued that among other things, the wishes of the husband must be respected. By the late 1960s this caveat had lost much of its weight in liberal circles. The movement was under way, led by feminist groups, to undo state abortion laws. Many of the arguments in favor of more liberalized abortion laws can be found in Edwin Schur's important work *Crimes Without Victims.* Schur, a lawyer and sociologist at New York University, alerted many readers to the problems that illegal abortions had raised. His discussion centered on self-induced abortions, police corruption, the unenforceability of abortion laws, the psychological consequences of illegally obtained abortions, the discriminatory effect of illegal abortions on the poor, and the stigmatization of unwed mothers.[459] All of the issues that he raised found their way into the litany of abortion reformists. In 1968 Planned Parenthood added another reason: population control.[460] Feminists also argued the point that every woman should be permitted to control her own body. In essence, sociological reasoning was favored over moral considerations for the life of the unborn. The position of John Noonan was not successful: "One person's freedom to obtain an abortion is the denial of another person's right to live."[461]

Not all liberals are in favor of abortion and not all conservatives oppose it. But it is fair to say that the proabortion and antiabortion positions are identified with the liberal and conservative communities, respectively. Most Americans have come to accept the Supreme Court's decision, but it is far from certain that a majority are in favor of abortion on demand.[462]

Civil libertarians have not been united on this issue, but again it is fair to say that most have moved into the proabortion camp. The ACLU's position on abortion is another example of the history of Americal liberalism. Throughout most of its history, abortion was a nonissue; it was not until 1967 that the Board of Directors gave it serious consideration. Prior to that time, it relied on the position taken by its Due Process Committee in the late 1950s. That position was listed as ACLU policy in the organization's first policy guide of 1966. The policy read as follows:

> The ACLU views the question of state abortion law reform as one to be dealt with by social agencies in the field. The Union's function would be the support of action by such agencies toward attempting to reform state abortion laws, should a campaign of this nature be organized. In the absence of such a campaign, the ACLU has taken no action.[463]

On 14 February 1967, the board reconsidered its policy on abortion. Edward Ennis moved that the board adopt the Due Process Committee position that the present abortion laws should be changed to allow a woman unfettered discretion to have an abortion during the first twenty weeks of pregnancy, with the consent of the husband, if any (assuming he was available).[464] Harriet Pilpel commented that this stand was not sufficiently strong. She attacked the present law in New York that gave legitimacy to abortion only "to preserve the life of the woman."[465] Her animus against state abortion laws led her to raise five objections—all of which eventually became part of ALCU policy.[466] The state laws were, according to Pilpel, unconstitutionally vague; they denied to women in the lower economic groups the equal protection of the laws guaranteed by the Fourteenth Amendment; they infringed upon the constitutional right to decide whether and when to have a child, as well as the marital right of privacy and the privacy between patient and physician; they impaired the constitutional right of physicians to practice in accordance with their professional obligations; finally, they deprived women of their lives and liberty, in the sense of deciding how their bodies are to be used, without the due process of law.[467]

Pilpel was not finished: she introduced other objections to the Due Process Committee's recommendations. She wanted to delete the requirement of the consent of the husband. Luther Evans countered by saying that the Union cannot neglect the father's right to have a child. Another member asked whether it was the intent of the amendment to express a view about the consent of the husband, or simply to leave it out of consideration, i.e. would the Union thereby oppose legislation that insists on the consent of the husband? Pilpel said the board should oppose such legislation. Her amendment passed by a vote of 11-3.[468]

Pilpel's second amendment also passed—this time by a vote of 10-4. This amendment stipulated that an abortion should be done only by a licensed physician.[469]

Pilpel's third amendment wrought dissensus. She moved that the Union support bills that would amend the law by permitting termination of a pregnancy after the twentieth week in certain circumstances. The situations that she envisioned included rape, the endangerment of the mother's life, etc. Judge Kenyon opposed the motion, claiming that the state does not have any legitimate interest in protecting the life of the unborn, even after twenty weeks of pregnancy. David Carliner requested that the Union substitute the phrase "three months" in place of the proposed twentieth-week stipulation. After Ralph Brown raised strong objections to what he considered "amateur gynecology," the Carliner amendment was accepted 8-5. The meeting ended with the passing of a motion to recommit all questions concerning policy on abortion after the first three months to the Due Process Committee.[470]

On 15 June 1967, Pilpel's five objections to state abortion laws became policy. The Union's main position was as follows: "It should not be deemed a crime for a woman to seek, and for a doctor to perform, the termination of a pregnancy in accordance with generally accepted community standards of medical practice."[471] No time limit on abortions was noted. The ACLU's policy clearly favored the woman's freedom of privacy. The unborn child's freedom to live was not even hinted at as a competing right. The right of the father of the child to have a voice in such a decision was similarly dismissed.

This position of the ACLU was essentially a negatively framed policy: it stated only that abortion should not be considered a criminal act. In December 1967 the attention of the board turned to the adoption of a more positive statement. After seeking the expert medical advice of Dr. Robert Hall, New York obstetrician and ACLU activist, Ennis urged the board to adopt the conclusion of the Ad Hoc Committee on Abortion and the Viable Fetus. That position read:

> The ACLU asserts as a civil right the right of a woman to have an abortion, and the right of a physician to perform, or refuse to perform, an abortion, without the threat of criminal sanctions.[472]

Ennis then brought up a point raised by Thomas J. Shaffer of Notre Dame Law School. Shaffer, in a letter to Alan Reitman, asserted that termination of pregnancy beyond the twelfth week was infanticide. Shaffer claimed that twelve weeks was the point of fetal viability, and the medically safe limit for performing an abortion. Ennis asked the board to dismiss this advice in view of the fact that most doctors recognize twenty weeks as the point of viability. Although the majority of the board members clearly favored Ennis's position, one member charged that it was ironic that the ACLU would vote one day to reinstate $20,000 for a campaign against capital punishment and then approve a policy that allows the killing of a fetus.[473]

The board finally adopted the proposal by the Ad Hoc Committee but not until after a slight amendment. It accepted a statement by Gene Bridges to include the following parenthetical note after "the right of a woman to have an abortion":

> (that is: to have a termination of pregnancy) during the period prior to the viability of the fetus, which the medical profession currently accepts as extending through the first twenty weeks of pregnancy.[474]

Acting on a motion by Dr. Irving Murray, the board also added (25-6) the following:

> The American Civil Liberties Union further asserts that it is a civil right for a woman to terminate pregnancy at any time: 1) if continued pregnancy endangers the mother's physical or mental health; 2) if it is likely that the child, if born, will be seriously deformed; 3) if the pregnancy is the result of rape or incest; or 4) if the mother is unmarried and under fifteen years of age.[475]

This second resolution did not last long. On 25 January 1968, a motion to strike it was successful. Executive Director Pemberton led the attack by suggesting that inferentially the second resolution supports actual infanticide because the last three of the four reasons cited for permitting postabortion terminations would not rationally occasion a termination unless the effect were to terminate the life of a viable fetus.[476]

The discussion then turned to a debate over the parenthetical statement of Bridges. Did the board not know what it had done the month before when it accepted this statement? Herbert Prashker believed that it had. Pilpel said that when the period of viability occurs was debatable. Louis Lusky agreed, and added that the question of infanticide was not the real danger: what is the problem is that the unwanted child always suffers in life. After further discussion, the board voted to accept a substitute motion of Osmond K. Fraenkel. The final policy resolution read as follows:

> The American Civil Liberties Union asserts that a woman has a right to have an abortion—that is, a termination of pregnancy prior to the viability of the fetus—and that a licensed physician has a right to perform an abortion, without the threat of criminal sanctions.[477]

When I interviewed Mr. Baldwin, we got into an extended discussion on abortion. I mentioned to him that in the early seventies, Senator Buckley of New York successfully hitched to a bill a rider that did not permit the execution of a pregnant woman who was guilty of a capital offense. What follows is a selection of our dialogue, beginning with my statement on the Buckley rider.

> W.D.: It's okay to execute the woman if she's not pregnant, but if she is pregnant they are not allowed to execute her. The reason being that the legislators feel that here is an innocent human life that will be taken if the woman is executed when she's pregnant. There is a recognition that there is life there.
>
> R.B.: Well, of course, it's a recognition that there is a life there and she has a right too—she has a right as a mother to produce that life.
>
> W.D.: She also has the right to take that life?
>
> R.B.: Who has the right to take—
>
> W.D.: The woman.
>
> R.B.: Oh, she doesn't have—yes, of course, she has. Of course, she has the right to decide whether she'll have the child or not.
>
> W.D.: To take the life?
>
> R.B.: Of course, she does. If she doesn't want the child, she doesn't have to have it.[478]

The ACLU, as well as other liberal organizations, has shown little interest in the constitutional basis of *Roe v. Wade*. Delighted with the decision, most of the arguments put forth in defense of *Roe* have been sociological in nature. But serious constitutional issues are at stake. John Hart Ely, professor of law at Harvard University and a specialist in constitutional law, has said that if he were a legislator, he would have voted for a statute very much like the decision rendered in *Roe*. But he sees no constitutional reason for the high court's decision, arguing that *Roe* "lacks even colorable support in the constitutional text, history, or any other appropriate source of constitutional doctrine."[479] As to whether fetuses have constitutional rights, Ely's response is that it is irrelevant to the case:

> For it has never been held or even asserted that the state interest needed to justify forcing a person to refrain from an activity, *whether or not that activity is constitutionally protected,* must implicate either the life or constitutional rights of another person. Dogs are not "persons in the whole sense" nor have they constitutional rights, but that does not mean the state cannot prohibit killing them: It does not even mean the state cannot prohibit killing them in the exercise of the First Amendment right of political protest. Come to think of it, draft cards aren't persons either.[480]

Ely has accused the court of playing politics with the abortion issue.[481] Even the *New Republic* appeared unsettled with the court's constitutional basis in *Roe*.[482] The ACLU, however, prefers to skirt this question by interpreting abortion as simply a women's issue. Liberal Mary Meehan has shed light on this rationale:

> It is one thing to argue that the state should be neutral on the abortion issue. It is quite another to argue, as some liberals do that abortion is a dandy method of birth control and should be financed by the state; or to say, as many do, that abortion is strictly a matter of women's rights. The second position is an example of deciding a debate by setting its terms. It is like deciding the war/peace issue by defining it as a national security issue or a defense issue. There is also a parallel between labeling those who oppose abortion the "so-called right-to-lifers" and classifying those who oppose war as members of a "cut-and-run-crowd." Terms like these do not aid rational debate. They just encourage shouting matches.[483]

The ACLU is guilty of Meehan's charge in all respects. Abortion is strictly a woman's right and those who oppose it are part of the "so-called right-to-life" movement, or better yet, the "anti-choice" crowd.[484] The Union has pushed for "free" abortions as well, i.e. the use of Medicaid payments for such services.[485] I asked Alan Reitman why the ACLU supported government expenditures for abortion. He replied:

> Since we're concerned not only with having a constitutional principle enunciated but making that principle meaningful from a civil liberties stance, that when government acts on a Supreme Court decision in such a way as to deny a certain class of citizens the right to exercise that constitutional right; i.e., poor people can't afford abortions out of their own pocket, then when the government acts to take away funding then we regard that as a matter of discrimination against a particular group under the equal protection of the laws. . . .[486]

Reitman's position reflects the thinking of most ACLU decision-makers on the subject of the Fourteenth Amendment. They view it as an amendment that is continually deserving of updating—according to the current themes of American liberalism. But other legal scholars have not been as quick to endorse this view. Harvard law professor Raoul Berger has made it clear that the framers of this amendment did not intend it to be used as an instrument for advancing social equality: "Again and again the framers stated their purpose was to prevent one law for blacks, another for whites. It was . . . not a mandate that the States must confer rights not theretofore enjoyed by any citizen."[487] The framers had limited purposes in mind when they endorsed "equal protection of the laws." They did not mean unlimited equality across the board. They did not even mean political rights. They meant to limit its application to the enumerated rights incorporated in the Civil Rights Act of 1866. "The Civil Rights Act," writes Berger, "secured to blacks the *same* rights to contract, to hold property, and to sue, as whites enjoyed, and the '*equal* benefit of all laws for *security of person and property*.'"[488] Berger adds that if the terms of the amendment are "vague," "it is because the Court made them so in order to shield the expanding free enterprise system from regulation."[489]

On the relatively few occasions that the ACLU has addressed the rights of the unborn, it has been apparent that the issue has not received the kind of careful deliberation that has been accorded to women's rights. For exam—ple, the day after the Supreme Court delivered its *Roe* decision, the Due Process Committee of the Union took up the question of the right of pregnant women to have unlimited access to narcotics. Some argued that the state has a legitimate interest in protecting the health of an unborn child. Others argued that the fetus has no rights whatsoever. Interestingly, one month later a majority supported the former position. One of the woman members of the committee accused the five men who voted for the restriction of "sexism" and noted that she and her lone female colleague strongly disagreed;[490] the board has no policy on this issue. Contrast that perspective with that of Union official John Shattuck and the uncertainty of the status of the unborn becomes evident. Although Shattuck says that the ACLU accepts the high court's decision in *Roe* as to when the unborn have rights, i.e. at "viability," he admits that even when the fetus can survive outside the womb, the decision of whether to abort or not is still a woman's prerogative: he is not opposed to abortions in the last stages of pregnancy.[491]

There are some officials in the ACLU who not only believe that the unborn lack rights but regard the unborn as "stuff"—the kind of stuff that is sold at an auction. In June 1977 the Louisiana affiliate offered an abortion at its annual fund-raising auction. The price: $30. A divorce went for $19, and legal services for driving while intoxicated netted $10.[492] The state director of the affiliate, Marlene Roeder, said she was surprised by the critical reaction to the abortion auction: "Abortions, after all, are legal and it's legitimate, in my perspective for a woman to get an abortion as it is for someone to get a divorce or to bid on a legal defense for a D.W.I. or any of the other professional services that we offer."[493]

In its passion for legalized abortions, the ACLU has violated the civil liberties of those who do not share its position. A case in point involves the efforts of Representative Henry J. Hyde. Hyde, a Democrat from Illinois, has authored a bill to restrict federal financing of abortions. When he began his efforts in the late 1970s, the Union was alarmed. One of the Union's main contentions was that the law amounted to the enactment of

Roman Catholic "dogma and doctrine" into law. (The Union never held that Martin Luther King's drive for a civil rights bill represented the heavy hand of his Protestant ministry.) To gather evidence for its case, the ACLU dispatched an agent to spy on Hyde's leisure-time activities. What the agent found was that Mr. Hyde went to church on Sundays—a Catholic church no less—where, as the report noted, "pregnant women and children" bore "gifts for life"; the same people, including Hyde, were said to have prayed and gone to Holy Communion. Other documentation that constituted a 301-page brief, included accounts of participants in right-to-life marches who carried rosaries and statues of the Virgin Mary. When Norman C. Miller broke this story in December 1978, he accused the ACLU of engaging in anti-Catholic bigotry.[494] Ira Glasser, the head of the ACLU, responded by defending the Union's policy on abortion and labeled the bigotry charge "unsophisticated"; he never addressed the spy activity.[495]

Representative Hyde was not totally surprised by the ACLU action: "I suppose the nazis did that—observed Jews going to the synagogues in Hitler's Germany—but I had hoped we would have gotten past that kind of fascist tactic."[496] The ACLU was not finished with Hyde; it wanted to read his mail. Upon request, Hyde complied, without a court order. The Union was looking for any detail it could find indicating that Hyde's support was religiously based. "Key words" such as "baby" and "human life" were recorded.[497] Hyde later found out about this tactic: "Interestingly enough, I am told the young lady of the ACLU had a big chart, and whenever some citizen would close a letter to me saying 'God Bless You,' the ACLU representative would put a little check by the word 'God,' thus indicating the evil, nefarious religious influence that was molding my approach to this subject. That was one of the more ludicrous aspects of their investigation."[498] It was also one of the most demagogic.

The 1980s

As the antiabortion forces gathered momentum in the 1980s, the ACLU struck back by working to defeat every "Human Life Bill" that was sponsored: H.R. 900, H.R. 618, S.158, S.26, S.210, and S.467. It has thus far proved to be successful. All of these bills are aimed at protecting the life of the unborn by having the law recognize the beginning of life at conception. Janet Benshoof, director of the Union's Reproduction Freedom Project, has termed these bills "frightening," and charges that they "would give the unborn more rights than the born. . . . It would subordinate women's bodies, health, work and lives to fetal survival. . . . To determine who is pregnant and needs watching, the government could conduct body searches and inspections. . . ."[499] For Benshoof, outlawing abortions would be a totalitarian maneuver, yet none of the bills extends itself to the lengths that she envisions. Other legal scholars also disagree with the wisdom of these bills, but they argue reasonably and without resort to hyperbole.[500] But for the ACLU, abortion is seen as a religiously charged issue and the question of when a human life begins is dismissed as an "inherently religious"[501] question. As the ACLU sees it, "the zealots among Reagan's allies had made the outlawing of abortion a religious crusade."[502]

At the state level, the Union has waged numerous fights against restrictions on abortion, most notably in Akron, Ohio,[503] but also in states from Massachusetts to Nevada.[504] It has also criticized the Justice Department in the Reagan administration for supporting state attempts to curtail abortion; Benshoof did not even wait for the Justice Department to issue its decision before lambasting it for "supporting infringement of the constitutional right to abortion."[505] The ACLU was most angry when the Supreme Court ruled that a state has the authority to require a doctor to inform a teenaged girl's parents before performing an abortion on her.[506] Margaret O'Brien Steinfels and Peter Steinfels have captured the riddle in the Union's thinking: "Why do liberals panic when faced with certain aspects of sexuality and social mores? Mention the word 'chastity' and they get all nervous and giggly. This, at least, has been a common response to the Reagan Administration's proposal requiring parental notification when adolescents obtain prescription contraceptives from federally funded clinics."[507]

The unborn, as noted, have no rights that the ACLU need respect. It is for this reason that the Union was quick to challenge a corporate policy aimed at protecting the life of the unborn. In 1978 American Cyanamid, at its Willow Island plant in West Virginia, instituted a policy that barred women of childbearing capacity from working in jobs that would expose them to toxic chemicals; the intent of the policy was to safeguard the health of the women's future children. The company's policy showed a lack of ingenuity; surely a less restrictive measure could have been found. But as far as the ACLU was concerned, there was nothing noble about the intent. The Union filed suit, claiming that the policy was discriminatory. No doubt it was, but the point is that the ACLU read the policy and saw sexism clear and simple. It did not, or perhaps could not, see that the policy was designed to protect the future rights of children. No conflict of rights here, for the ACLU has no sympathy for such policies and chooses to write them off by employing quotation marks to indicate its position on "fetal vulnerability."[508]

When the Equal Rights Amendment died in June 1982, Eleanor Smeal, president of the National Organization for Women, vowed, "We are no longer going to beg men for our rights."[509] The ACLU promised to redouble its efforts for another round of combat, assuring its membership that a new equal rights amendment would be introduced. The lack of an amendment, the Union said, caused "untold hardships in the daily lives of women struggling for economic survival."[510] In the meantime, the ACLU decided to wage a struggle in behalf of women as the issues arose. Two examples of this struggle involve the concept of "comparable worth" and the integration of all public schools. The concept of "comparable worth" is actually a strategy whereby all jobs are evaluated with respect to comparable difficulty or value and then are accorded comparable pay. The ACLU has been active in California lobbying for legislation that encodes this strategy.[511] Although the Supreme Court has never ruled on the application of the Civil Rights Act to comparable worth measures, it has shown signs that at least some of the justices might be receptive to the idea.[512] The integration of the public schools issue is an outgrowth of the Union's efforts to require Philadelphia's all-male Central High School to accept female students. The Union sees more at stake than just making Central a coeducational institution; economic, as well as social, equality is at issue. Central is Philadelphia's top high school, and therefore the ACLU sees it as a filter into "the power structure in the City of Philadelphia."[513] The instrumentalist approach to civil liberties proved once again to be triumphant.

The area of civil rights has occupied much of the ACLU's time in the 1980s. It rarely has anything to say about unions, that issue being largely "solved." One interesting issue that did emerge, however, was an internal affair: It was proposed by some board members that the ACLU purchase all of its goods and supplies from union labor, where available. The resolution was initially tabled and then moved off the agenda entirely. George Slaff, a long-time board member, called the decision "shocking" and a "shame." One of the reasons offered for declining to consider the issue was the high cost of union products. This was the first time in the ACLU's history that this reality became an item for opposing the services of labor unions.[514]

The war between the Reagan administration and the ACLU began shortly after the president's inauguration. It has continued and mounted as Reagan set out to do what the voters across the country asked him to do: cut back on big government. The Union has issued one statement after another criticizing the administration for dismantling the program that liberals had built. In October 1982 it released a report, the title of which gives the public the ACLU's perspective on the administration: *Civil Liberties in Reagan's America*.[515] Reagan's America—not the people's! In it, one finds such statements as "The Reagan Administration has turned its back on civil rights" and "One of the principal undercurrents in Reagan's America is a hostility toward women, which is masked as a nostalgic demand for a way of life based on 'traditional' family values."[516] The report concludes:

"This is not our America."[517] Meaning, of course, that ACLU members and ideas are not well represented on Pennsylvania Avenue.

As part of its attempt to curtail the growth of bureaucracy, the Reagan administration turned its attention to the enforcement activities of the Equal Employment Opportunity Commission (EEOC), the office of Federal Contract Compliance, and the Office for Civil Rights. The EEOC, the administration contended, has "created a new racism in America" by emphasizing affirmative action quotas.[518] To Ira Glasser at the ACLU, anyone who objects to the discretion of the enforcement agencies is against civil rights: "The truth of the matter is you can't be for civil rights and be against those remedies."[519] The Reagan administration's less than enthusiastic endorsement of the 1965 Voting Rights Act and its hostility to the Legal Services Corporation prompted the Union to charge that an "all-out war on civil rights" had been declared.[520] Many liberals, as well as conservatives, have expressed grave reservations about the documented abuses of the Legal Services Corporation by "public interest" lawyers, yet the ACLU has never voiced the slightest concern over these governmental excesses. In this regard, it stands apart from moderate liberal opinion.

When the Reagan administration began to carry out its budget cutbacks, the ACLU went into action: Alan Reitman requested the Board of Directors to investigate the relationship between the cuts and their impact on civil liberties. Law professors, economists, and social workers, including Frances Fox Piven, were summoned to address the issue. One of the subjects that Reitman was concerned about was the administration's plan to limit affirmative action to those individuals who had previously been victimized by discrimination. The Union's position is that mere membership in a particular minority group is sufficient cause for preferential treatment. The Reagan plan was regarded as "a direct attack against women and minorities."[521] Cuts in welfare programs were also cited as an area where civil liberties deprivations might occur. The relationship between fiscal policies and civil liberties was explored more thoroughly in the 1980s than in any previous decade and promises to be one of the most active arenas of ACLU participation in the future. By taking this approach, the Union will be able to collapse many more non-Bill of Rights issues into its civil libertarian portfolio and thereby make manifest its ideological predilections.

What has irked the ACLU most about the Reagan administration's initiatives is its attempt to use the legislative process as a means to undo or weaken court decisions. Charges of court-stripping have regularly been voiced by ACLU officials. Although the legal community is split on this admittedly sensitive issue, the Union's perspective is clear and straightforward: Congress and the state legislatures do not have the right to thwart the will of the judiciary. Abortion, busing, and prayer in schools are just some of the cases about which the Union has cause for concern. Four arguments have been put forth for attacking the Reagan-sanctioned movement: (a) court-stripping bills are unconstitutional; (b) the system of checks and balances is at stake; (c) the initiatives threaten the whole future of school desegregation; and (d) constitutional rights would vary from state to state.[522] The Union maintains that "forces in Reagan's America, unhappy with various court decisions, are attempting to destroy the independence of the federal judiciary."[523]

Ira Glasser contends that if the Reagan plan works, "it would make President Roosevelt's court-packing scheme—which conservatives properly opposed—look like child's play."[524] Glasser should have chosen a better example—the ACLU never once voiced a protest against the court-packing scheme. That's understandable; by 1937 the Union had become a supporter of Roosevelt's labor initiatives. But what is less defensible is the Union's present-day duplicity on court-stripping. Listen to what John Shattuck admitted in 1979:

> Just a month ago we managed to reverse a very bad Supreme Court decision on the Fourth Amendment by new legislation which protects people's bank records. The Supreme Court had held two years ago, in *United States v. Miller*, that your bank records have no privacy protection or privacy interest at all. . . . By legislation we were able to overturn that decision, and there is a new bill—the Bank Regulatory Act of 1978—which provides that any time a government agent seeks access to a bank record, the bank must give notice to the depositor.[525]

Is not *that* court-stripping? Apparently it is not the principle of court-stripping that bothers the ACLU so much, it is the object of the contemporary court-stripping activities that raises its ire.

Whether court-stripping is inherently unconstitutional is another matter altogether. C. Dickerman Williams, a noted New York lawyer and legal scholar, has identified the proper point of departure in this controversy: "The relevant language of the Constitution (Article III, Section 2) provides: 'The Supreme Court shall have appellate jurisdiction, both as to Law and Fact, with such Exceptions and under such Regulations as the Congress shall make.'"[526] As to the meaning and history of the "exceptions" clause, Williams notes: "The fact is that Congress has, since the organization of the judicial system in 1789, repeatedly limited the appellate jurisdiction of the Supreme Court in many respects. The Court had uniformly acquiesced in and upheld these exceptions to its appellate jurisdiction."[527] Williams offers several examples in evidence of his point and includes a prescient passage from the pen of Justice Oliver Wendell Holmes:

> I have not yet adequately expressed the more than anxiety I feel at the ever increasing scope given to the Fourteenth Amendment in cutting down what I

believe to be the constitutional rights of the States. As decisions now stand, I see hardly any limit but the sky to the invalidating of those rights if they happen to strike a majority of this court as for any reason undesirable. I cannot believe that the Amendment was intended to give us *carte blanche* to embody our economic or social beliefs in its prohibitions.[528]

Whether one accepts the position of the ACLU on court-stripping, or that of Williams, or Harvard's law professor Paul Bator (Congress does have legitimate power in this area),[529] may not be as important as the reason that this issue arose in the first place. Holmes anticipated its emergence when he alerted us to the specter of judicial activism; it has since become a reality. Liberals, who so often have been wont to search out "root causes," have generally been reticent on the causes of court-stripping schemes. Perhaps that is because they have been responsible for fostering judicial activism by seeing a "compelling governmental interest" in areas that no one had previously identified. Since the 1960s the courts have taken on responsibilities that theretofore had been the province of the legislature. This phenomenon has not escaped Robert Nisbet: "More and more the Supreme Court and the puissant federal judiciary which the Court ultimately dominates enter into the lives of the people, into the autonomies and privacies of the major institutions, into decision-making that takes the judiciary into every nook and corner of American life."[530] Teddy White has observed the same condition:

By the early 1970s, sometime in the Nixon Administration, it had become quite clear that for people who sought a new social or political goal, it was far more efficient to go to the courts than to go to the voters or move through Congress. . . . The courts were now spraying the United States Constitution into every nook and cranny of national life, into matters best left to state legislatures, or into trivia that in other times might have been left to city halls or town councils.[531]

The Board of Directors of the ACLU is certainly amongst the people whom White was writing about. The Union has followed the logic of Justice Thurgood Marshall in his *Rodriguez* dissent, arguing that "if you find a nexus between something not expressed in the Constitution and something that is, then it is a constitutional matter."[532] It is this kind of judicial interpretation that has not only troubled conservatives like Nisbet and centrists like White but has angered liberals too. Nicholas Von Hoffman, for example, has focused on the events leading up to the Supreme Court's abortion decision: "Civil-rights lawyers and judges had twisted traditional constitutional interpretations to circumnavigate the legislative branch of government, where public policy on this question had been decided for nearly 200 years."[533] Distressingly, Von Hoffman notes, "ACLU-ism has risked destroying its own cause by demanding the courts change the meaning and scope of fundamental rights."[534]

Thus far, the 1980s have not been very encouraging for liberals. The election of Ronald Reagan, the conservative tide in the country, and the unwillingness of many young people to commit themselves to political issues have left liberals waiting for the pendulum to swing their way. A one-time radical and now a respectable contemporary liberal, Tom Hayden (he did not change—liberalism did) delivered his assessment of the state of liberalism upon the victory of Reagan: "What the conservatives called 'bleeding heart liberalism' finally hemorrhaged and died in 1980."[535] But to the question "Is Liberalism Dead?" Arthur Schlesinger, Jr., answered a resounding "no."[536] When the same question was put to Barton J. Bernstein, Richard Gillan, and Michael Harrington, they uniformly agreed that the best hope for liberalism lay in a renewed partnership with socialism.[537] Liberalism, in order to succeed, would have to transcend itself and incorporate socialist ideas and strategies more than ever before. Whether liberalism will follow this vector is uncertain. But one thing is clear: whichever way it goes, the ACLU will be there leading the pack.

Notes

1. Alexis de Tocqueville, *Democracy in America,* ed. J.P. Mayer (Garden City, N.Y.: Doubleday, 1969), p. 243.
2. A fine discussion of American history at this time can be found in Louis L. Gould, ed., *The Progressive Era* (Syracuse: Syracuse University Press, 1974).
3. Herbert Croly, *The Promise of American Life* (New York: Macmillan, 1909), p. 152.
4. Ibid., p. 409.
5. Arnold A. Rogow, "Edmund Burke and the American Liberal Tradition," *Antioch Review*, June 1957, pp. 255-65.
6. Charles Forcey, *The Crossroads of Liberalism* (New York: Oxford University Press, 1961), p. 117.
7. Ibid., p. 306.
8. Ibid., p. 255.
9. Kenneth Minogue, *The Liberal Mind* (London: Methuen, 1963), p. 7.
10. Ibid., p. 12.
11. An excellent source on the AUAM and Baldwin's subsequent activities is the work of Donald Johnson, *The Challenge to American Freedoms* (Lexington: University of Kentucky Press, for the Mississippi Valley Historical Association, 1963).
12. Peggy Lamson, *Roger Baldwin: Founder of the American Civil Liberties Union* (Boston: Houghton Mifflin, 1976), ch. 6.
13. Ibid., pp. 72-73.
14. Johnson, *Challenge to American Freedoms,* p. v.
15. Ibid., p. 198.
16. Ibid.

17. Ibid.
18. Lamson, *Baldwin,* p. 81.
19. Barton Bean, "Pressure for Freedom: The American Civil Liberties Union," Ph.D. diss., Cornell University, 1955, p. 55.
20. Lamson, *Baldwin,* p. 82.
21. Paul Murphy, "Communities in Conflict," in *The Pulse of Freedom,* ed. Alan Reitman (New York: W. W. Norton, 1975), p. 4.
22. Quoted, Lamson, *Baldwin,* p. 86.
23. Quoted, Johnson, *Challenge to American Freedoms,* pp. 198-99.
24. Ibid., p. 199.
25. Ibid., p. 145.
26. ACLU Papers, New York Public Library, Reel 1, Vol. 120.
27. Ibid., Reel 16, Vol. 5.
28. Ibid., Reel 16, Vol. 115.
29. Johnson, *Challenge to American Freedoms,* p. 146.
30. ACLU Papers, Reel 1, Vol. 120, "Suggestions for Reorganization of the National Civil Liberties Bureau."
31. Ibid.
32. Quoted, Lamson, *Baldwin,* p. 124.
33. Bean, "Pressure for Freedom," p. 83.
34. Interview with John H. F. Shattuck, "The Defense of Liberty," *Center Magazine,* November/December 1979, p. 42.
35. Johnson, *Challenge to American Freedoms,* p. 146.
36. AR 8, p. 32.
37. Lamson, *Baldwin,* p. 126.
38. Ibid., pp. 75, 125-37; AR 1, p. 31.
39. Lamson, *Baldwin,* pp. 138-39.
40. Ibid., pp. 139-40.
41. Ibid., pp. 148-49.
42. Johnson, *Challenge to American Freedoms,* p. 199.
43. Ibid.
44. Lamson, *Baldwin,* p. 132.
45. ACLU Papers, Reel 16, Vol. 6.
46. Quoted in Lamson, *Baldwin,* p. 129.
47. ACLU Papers, Reel 1, Vol. 120.
48. Ibid.
49. Herbert Croly, "The Eclipse of Progressivism," *New Republic,* 27 October 1920, p. 212.
50. Ibid.
51. AR 1, p. 4.
52. Ibid., p. 18; and Croly, "The Eclipse of Progressivism," p. 210.
53. AR 1, p. 18; and Croly, "The Eclipse of Progressivism," p. 213.
54. AR 1, p. 18.
55. Ibid.
56. Interview with Roger Baldwin, 2 June 1978, New York.
57. AR 1, p. 7.
58. AR 2, p. 3.
59. Ibid., p. 6.
60. Murphy, "Communities in Conflict," p. 25.
61. AR 3, pp. 15-16.

62. Murphy, "Communities in Conflict," p. 27; and AR 4, pp. 25-26.
63. Murphy, "Communities in Conflict," pp. 27-28; and AR 6, pp. 17-18.
64. AR 4, p. 20.
65. Ibid.; and Murphy, "Communities in Conflict," pp. 12-15.
66. AR 8, p. 14.
67. Ibid.
68. Ibid., p. 4.
69. AR 3, p. 23.
70. Edward Shils, "The Antinomies of Liberalism," in *The Relevance of Liberalism,* ed. Zbigniew Brzezinski (Boulder, Colo.: Westview Press, 1978), p. 144.
71. Ibid., p. 143.
72. Johnson, *Challenge to American Freedoms,* pp. 201-2.
73. Bean, "Pressure for Freedom," pp. 316-17.
74. Quoted in Lamson, *Baldwin,* p. 266.
75. Murphy, "Communities in Conflict," p. 31.
76. Edmund Wilson, "An Appeal to Progressives," *New Republic,* 14 January 1931, p. 235.
77. Paul Hollander, *Political Pilgrims* (New York: Oxford University Press, 1981), p. 28
78. Wilson, "Appeal to Progressives," p. 236.
79. William Barrett, *The Truants* (Garden City, N.Y.: Doubleday, 1982), p. 22.
80. Ibid., p. 214.
81. ACLU Papers, Reel 157, Vol. 1081.
82. AR 10, p. 3.
83. AR 14, p. 9.
84. Jerold S. Auerbach, "The Depression Decade," in *The Pulse of Freedom,* ed. Alan Reitman (New York: W. W. Norton, 1975), p. 44.
85. AR 13, p. 5.
86. AR 10, p. 39.
87. Edmund Wilson, "What Do Liberals Hope For," *New Republic,* 10 February 1932, p. 347.
88. Ibid., pp. 345-48.
89. John Dewey, *Liberalism and Social Action* (New York: Capricorn Books, 1935), p. 62.
90. Wilson, "What Do Liberals Hope For," p. 348.
91. Alonzo L. Hamby, *Beyond the New Deal: Harry Truman and American Liberalism* (New York: Columbia University Press, 1973), p. xvii.
92. Quoted, Cletus E. Daniel, *The ACLU and the Wagner Act* (Ithaca, N.Y.: Cornell University, New York State School of Industrial and Labor Relations, 1980), p. 21.
93. Ibid., pp. 31-32.
94. AR 12, p. 3.
95. Ibid., p. 4.
96. Ibid.
97. AR 13, p. 3.
98. Ibid., pp. 3-4.
99. Ibid., p. 4.
100. Ibid.
101. Ibid.
102. Ibid., p. 5.

103. Daniel, *ACLU and the Wagner Act,* pp. 22-26. The Daniel volume is the best account of the ACLU's changing positions on labor policies in the 1930s. Most of my discussion on the Wagner Act is gleaned from Daniel.
104. Ibid., pp. 31-36.
105. Quoted, ibid., p. 39.
106. Ibid., p. 41.
107. Ibid., p. 42.
108. Ibid., p. 44.
109. Ibid., p. 45.
110. Ibid., p. 46-58.
111. Ibid., pp. 62-92.
112. Ibid., pp. 92-96.
113. AR 14, p. 4.
114. Daniel, *ACLU and the Wagner Act,* pp. 8, 16, 96-104.
115. Ibid., pp. 104-10.
116. Ibid., pp. 117-27.
117. Auerbach, "Depression Decade," p. 51.
118. AR 15, pp. 7-8.
119. AR 16, p.3.
120. Ibid., p. 16.
121. AR 16A, p. 25.
122. Ibid., p. 26.
123. Daniel, *ACLU and the Wagner Act,* p. 129.
124. Quoted in Lamson, *Baldwin,* pp. 193-94.
125. Daniel, *ACLU and the Wagner Act,* p. 135.
126. Bean, "Pressure for Freedom," p. 47.
127. Lamson, *Baldwin,* p. 136.
128. Ibid., p. 158.
129. Interview with Baldwin.
130. AR 16, p. 15.
131. Ibid., p. 76.
132. AR 17, p. 55.
133. Interview with Baldwin.
134. Board of Directors of the ACLU, "Memorandum on the Ford Case," March 1938, p. 1.
135. Ibid., pp. 1-2.
136. Lamson, *Baldwin,* p. 216.
137. Quoted by Auerbach, "Depression Decade," p. 58.
138. Lamson, *Baldwin,* p. 218.
139. Ibid., p. 217.
140. Interview with Baldwin.
141. Ibid.
142. Bean, "Pressure for Freedom," p. 293.
143. Quoted by Auerbach, "Depression Decade," pp. 58-59.
144. Memo on the Ford Case, p. 3.
145. "Supplementary Statement on the Ford Case," Board of Directors, ACLU, 27 June 1938, ACLU Papers, Reel 157, Vol. 1081.
146. "Employers' 'Free Speech' Not Curbed," *Civil Liberties Quarterly,* September 1938, p. 3, in ACLU Papers, Reel 157, Vol. 1081.
147. AR 16, p. 14.

148. Walter Lippmann in *South Carolina Independent,* 24 December 1937, in ACLU Papers, Reel 156, Vol. 115.
149. ACLU Papers, Reel 156, Vol. 115.
150. Interview with Baldwin.
151. Ibid.
152. Quoted by Auerbach, "Depression Decade," p. 57.
153. Baldwin, "Freedom in the U.S.A. and the U.S.S.R.," *Soviet Russia Today,* September 1934, p. 11.
154. Auerbach, "Depression Decade," p. 58.
155. Quoted in Lamson, *Baldwin,* p. 266.
156. Hamby, "Communities in Conflict," pp. 10-12, 27.
157. Shils, "Antinomies of Liberalism," p. 146.
158. Barrett, *Truants,* p. 85.
159. AR 25, p. 8.
160. AR 27, p. 3.
161. Ibid., p. 6.
162. Ibid., p. 68.
163. Hamby, *Beyond the New Deal,* p. xix.
164. Ibid., pp. 256-60.
165. See the articles by Richard Chase, Lionel Trilling, and William Barrett, "The Liberal Mind: Two Communications and a Reply," *Partisan Review,* June 1949, pp. 649-65.
166. George H. Nash, *The Conservative Intellectual Movement in America* (New York: Basic Books, 1976), p. 45.
167. William G. Carleton, "The Promise of American Liberalism," *Antioch Review,* Fall 1948, pp. 331-45.
168. Wilson W. Wyatt, "Creed for Liberals: A Ten-Point Program," *New York Times Magazine,* 22 July 1947, p. 7.
169. Ibid., pp. 7, 35.
170. "Americans for Democratic Action," *Commonweal,* 17 January 1947, p. 340.
171. John S. Rosenberg, "The A.D.A.'s Long Shadow," *Nation,* 23 February 1980, p. 209.
172. AR 23, p. 8.
173. AR 25, p. 19.
174. AR 20, p. 40.
175. AR 25, p. 44.
176. AR 22, pp. 51, 59.
177. AR 24, p. 8.
178. A.R. 21, p. 61.
179. Samuel P. Huntington, *American Politics: The Promise of Disharmony* (Cambridge: Harvard University Press, 1981), p. 169.
180. Granville Hicks, "Liberalism in the Fifties," *American Scholar,* Summer 1956, p. 284.
181. Ibid., pp. 285-87.
182. Arthur Schlesinger, Jr., "Is Liberalism Dead?" *New York Times Magazine,* 30 March 1980, p. 73.
183. Jeffrey Hart, *When the Going Was Good!* (New York: Crown Publishers, 1982), p. 7.
184. Robert Bendiner, "The Liberals' Political Road Back," *Commentary,* May 1953, pp. 431-32.

185. AR 31, p. 100.
186. AR 29, pp. 98-100.
187. AR 35, p. 60.
188. AR 30, pp. 86-87.
189. AR 29, p. 96.
190. AR 35, p. 61.
191. Joseph W. Bishop, Jr., "Politics and ACLU," *Commentary,* December 1971, p. 53.
192. '76 PG, #46.
193. Bishop, "Politics and ACLU," p. 53; William F. Buckley, Jr., "The Decline of the ACLU," *National Review,* 4 February 1972, p. 118.
194. '76 PG, #46.
195. Ibid., #36
196. '66, '67 and '71 PGs, #53.
197. '76 PG, #51.
198. '81 PG, #46.
199. Ibid.
200. Ibid., #48.
201. ACLU, *Civil Liberties in Reagan's America,* October 1982, pp. 55-57.
202. "Holding Up America," editorial, *New York Times* 4 August 1981, p. A14.
203. Stuart Taylor, Jr., "Strikers and the Law," *New York Times,* 5 August 1981, p. A14. See also ACLU, *Civil Liberties in Reagan's America,* p. 23.
204. Irving Howe, "The Decade That Failed," *New York Times Magazine,* 19 September 1982, p. 86.
205. Friedrich A. Hayek, *Law, Legislation and Liberty* (Chicago: University of Chicago Press, 1976), p. xi.
206. Shils, "Antinomies of Liberalism," p. 149.
207. Howe, "Decade That Failed," p. 83.
208. James A. Neuchterlein, "The People vs. the Interests," *Commentary,* March 1975, p. 70.
209. Huntington, *American Politics,* p. 144.
210. Ibid., pp. 86-87.
211. Ibid., p. 174.
212. Ibid., p. 168.
213. Ibid., p. 215.
214. Carleton, "Promise of American Liberalism," p. 338.
215. Charles Reich, "The New Property," *Yale Law Journal,* April 1964, pp. 733-87.
216. Ibid., pp. 778-79.
217. Ibid., p. 786.
218. Robert Nisbet, "The Quintessential Liberal," *Commentary,* September 1981, p. 61.
219. John Kenneth Galbraith, "An Agenda for American Liberals," *Commentary,* June 1966, p. 29.
220. Ibid.
221. Ibid., p. 30.
222. Ibid.
223. Ibid.
224. Gabe Kaimowitz, letter to the editor, *New Republic,* 22 June 1968, p. 33. For more on the ADA positions in 1968, see "Plight of the U.S. 'Liberals'—Signs That an Era Is Ending," *U.S. News and World Report,* 14 July 1969, pp. 38-41.

225. "Plight of the U.S. 'Liberals'—Signs That an Era Is Ending," p. 38.
226. Andrew Knight, "America's Frozen Liberals," *Progressive,* February 1969, p. 33.
227. Paul Kurtz, "The Radical Center," *Humanist,* May/June 1970, p. 7.
228. Quoted by Bishop, "Politics and ACLU," p. 50.
229. See James Q. Wilson, "Liberalism and Purpose," *Commentary,* May 1972, pp. 74-75.
230. James MacGregor Burns, "John F. Kennedy, Candidate on the Eve: Liberalism Without Tears," *New Republic,* 13 October 1960, p. 14.
231. Howe, "Decade That Failed," p. 42.
232. See Robert Nisbet, "The New Equalitarians," *Columbia Forum,* Winter 1975, pp. 2-11.
233. Philip Green, *The Pursuit of Inequality* (New York: Pantheon books, 1981).
234. William Ryan, *Equality* (New York: Pantheon Books, 1981).
235. AR 42, pp. 7-8.
236. Bishop, "Politics and ACLU," p. 58.
237. Interview with Baldwin.
238. AR '76, p. 4.
239. Aryeh Neier, letter to the editor, *Commentary,* March 1972, p. 10.
240. Bean, "Pressure for Freedom," p. 351.
241. AR '76, p. 5.
242. '81 PG, #14.
243. Ibid., #20.
244. Ibid., #62.
245. AR '72-'73, p. 4.
246. Information obtained from ACLU librarian Barbara Eichman, 1979.
247. Interview with Neier at ACLU national headquarters, New York, 19 June 1978.
248. ACLU Reading List, 1982.
249. AR 37, p. 32; '76 PG, #319.
250. AR 43, p. 7.
251. '77 PG, #37.
252. Bd. Min., 10/2-3/76, pp. 26-27.
253. '77 PG, #37.
254. '77 PG, #120.
255. AR '76, p. 13.
256. '76 PG, #114.
257. Ibid., #321.
258. '66 PG, #11.
259. Bd. Min., 10/5-6/68, pp. 5-6; '71 PG, #11.
260. AR 36, pp. 46-47.
261. Bd. Min., 10/5-6/68, pp. 5-6; '71 PG, #11; AR 43, p. 8.
262. '81 PG, #8.
263. '66 PG, #310.
264. Ibid.
265. Bd. Min., 12/2-3/67. See '76 PG, #310.
266. Ibid.; '66 PG #310.
267. AR 42, p. 33.
268. AR 5, p. 7.
269. AR 1, p. 18.

270. AR 2, p. 24.
271. AR 8, p. 4.
272. Lamson, *Baldwin,* pp. 162-63.
273. AR 11, p. 21.
274. AR 12, p. 6.
275. AR 14, p. 10.
276. AR 16, p. 30.
277. AR 22, p. 23; AR 23, p. 6; AR 25, p. 6.
278. AR 22, pp. 24-25.
279. AR 25, p. 56.
280. AR 32, p. 72.
281. AR 33, p. 24.
282. See the "Equality Before the Law" section in the annual reports of the 1950s.
283. AR 39, p. 78.
284. AR 40, p. 69.
285. AR 42, pp. 7-8.
286. AR 40, p. 89.
287. AR 42, p. 78.
288. AR 43, p. 11.
289. Bishop, "Politics and ACLU," p. 55.
290. '66 PG, #303.
291. Bd. Min., 10/5-6/68, pp. 17-20.
292. Bd. Min., 12/5-7/69, pp. 15-16.
293. '81 PG, #69.
294. AR 23, p. 24.
295. AR 30, p. 3.
296. Bd. Min., 2/20/56; AR 32, p. 74.
297. AR 39, p. 84.
298. AR 40, p. 94.
299. '76 PG, #305.
300. AR '71-'72, p. 1.
301. Interview with Baldwin.
302. '81 PG, #305.
303. Ibid.
304. John Shattuck and David Landau, "The *Brown* Decision—To the Junkpile?" *New York Times,* 14 February 1982, p. E19.
305. David Armor, "The Evidence on Busing," *Public Interest,* Summer 1972, pp. 90-126. See also the response to this article by Thomas Pettigrew et al. and Armor's reply in *Public Interest,* Winter 1973, pp. 88-134.
306. AR 27, p. 31.
307. AR 29, p. 110.
308. Ibid.
309. Bd. Min., 3/17/52, p. 2.
310. '66 PG, #301. See also AR 35, p. 74.
311. Ibid.
312. Ibid.
313. Bd. Min., 9/27-28/75, pp. 16-17.
314. '81 PG, #301.
315. '76 PG, #301.
316. Ibid.

317. Bd. Min., 9/27-28/75, p. 16.
318. '76 PG, #301.
319. Ibid.
320. Bd. Min., 9/27-28/75, p. 17
321. AR '70-'71, p. 31.
322. Ibid.
323. Ibid.; '76 PG, #301.
324. Nathan Glazer, *Affirmative Discrimination* (New York: Basic Books, 1975), p. 219.
325. Quoted, ibid., p. 45.
326. Quoted, John H. Bunzel, "Hiring and Firing by Quotas," *Wall Street Journal,* 21 January 1983, p. 14.
327. James Burnham, *Suicide of the West* (New York: Arlington House, 1964), p. 83.
328. '66 PG, #306.
329. AR 27, p. 40.
330. AR 29, p. 4.
331. AR 36, p. 46.
332. Ibid., p. 47.
333. AR 40, p. 96.
334. AR 41, p. 70.
335. ACLU, letter to the editor, *New York Times,* 24 June 1982, p. A22.
336. '66 PG, #306.
337. Ibid.
338. Ibid.
339. Sidney Hook, *Philosophy and Public Policy* (Carbondale and Edwardsville: Southern Illinois University Press, 1980), p. 143.
340. Bd. Min., 12/9-10/72, pp. 13-14.
341. Ibid., pp. 15-16.
342. '76 PG, #306.
343. Ibid.
344. '81 PG, #306.
345. "Bakke Wins, Quotas Lose," *Time,* 10 July 1978, p. 9.
346. Ibid., pp. 8-17.
347. Excerpts from the legal brief of the American Civil Liberties Union filed in *Regents of the University of California v. Allan Bakke.*
348. "ACLU Statement Supporting Affirmative Action in the *Bakke* Case," *ACLU News,* pp. 14-77.
349. Excerpts from the legal brief.
350. Ibid.; "ACLU Statement Supporting Affirmative Action in the *Bakke* Case."
351. Excerpts from the legal brief.
352. Interview with Neier.
353. Interview with Baldwin.
354. '81 PG, #306.
355. Ibid., #310.
356. Ibid.
357. Ibid., #530.
358. Bd. Min., 6/12-13/82, p. 3.
359. Interview with John Shattuck, "Defense of Liberty," p. 47.
360. Ibid.

361. '76 PG, #64.
362. AR '72-'73, pp. 22-23.
363. Ari Goldman, "Some Teachers Feel Like Pawns in Shift by Race," *New York Times,* 24 October 1977, p. 38.
364. Ryan, *Equality,* p. 37.
365. Ibid., p. 19.
366. Ibid., p. 112.
367. Ibid., pp. 194-98.
368. Ibid., p. 192.
369. Ibid., p. 112.
370. Donald Lambro, "Agencies Grow Rich on Poor, Reports Show," *Pittsburgh Press,* 19 February 1981, p. B-1.
371. William Raspberry, "Kill Poverty? Heck No! It's Big Business," *Pittsburgh Press,* 17 July 1980, p. B-2.
372. George Gilder, *Wealth and Poverty* (New York: Basic Books, 1981).
373. Minogue, *Liberal Mind,* p. 51.
374. James Q. Wilson, *Thinking About Crime* (New York: Basic Books, 1975).
375. Ernest van den Haag, *Punishing Criminals* (New York: Basic Books, 1975).
376. Daniel P. Moynihan, *The Politics of a Guaranteed Income* (New York: Vintage Books, 1973), p. 35.
377. Ibid.
378. Charles Morris, *The Cost of Good Intentions* (New York: W. W. Norton, 1980), p. 69.
379. Irving Kristol, "Welfare: The Best of Intentions, The Worst of Results," in *Social Problems: The Contemporary Debates,* 3d ed., ed. John B. Willamson, Linda Evans, and Anne Munley (Boston: Little, Brown, 1981), p. 90.
380. See the board minutes on a guaranteed income, 3-4 December 1977.
381. AR 42, p. 64.
382. Ibid.
383. Bd. Min., 10/5-6/68, p. 15.
384. Ibid., pp. 15-16; see also AR 42, pp. 63-64, and AR 43, p. 7.
385. Bd. Min., 6/16-17/73, p. 15.
386. Ibid., pp. 16-17.
387. Ibid., pp. 17-18.
388. Ibid., pp. 19-20.
389. Ibid., pp. 24-25; '76 PG, #317.
390. Linda Greenhouse, "'Minimal Scrutiny' Leads to a Foreseeable Decision," *New York Times,* 6 July 1980, p. 4E.
391. Bd. Min., 12/3-4/77, pp. 9-10.
392. Ibid., p. 10.
393. Ibid., p. 11.
394. Ibid., p. 12.
395. '84 PG, #317.
396. Ibid.
397. Ibid. #319.
398. Bd. Min., 3/5-6/77, p. 34.
399. '81 PG, #317.
400. Ibid.
401. Frances Fox Piven and Richard A. Cloward, *Regulating the Poor* (New York: Vintage Books, 1971), p. 347.

402. Bd. Min., 6/12-13/82, p. 1.
403. '66 PG, #313.
404. AR 39, p. 36.
405. '76 PG, #313.
406. '77 PG, #313.
407. '78 PG, #313.
408. '76 PG, #318.
409. '78 PG, #331.
410. Bd. Min., 1/23-24/82, Appendix C.
411. '81 PG, #242.
412. Linda Greenhouse, "Justices Rule Retarded Have Right to Training," *New York Times,* 19 June 1982, p. 30.
413. '81 PG, #240.
414. Bd. Min., 1/23-24/82, Appendix C.
415. "Careless of the Mentally Ill," editorial, *New York Times,* 24 October 1979, p. A30.
416. Judith Cummings, "Increase in Homeless People Tests U.S. Cities' Will to Cope," *New York Times,* 3 May 1982, p. A1. See also Randy Young, "The Homeless: The Shame of the City," *New York Magazine,* 21 December 1981, pp. 26-32.
417. Young, "Homeless," p. 27.
418. Ibid., p. 28; Cummings, "Increase in Homeless People," p. B13.
419. "A Conversation with Bert Neuborne," *Civil Liberties,* February 1983, p. 3.
420. Betty Friedan, "Up From the Kitchen Floor," *New York Times Magazine,* 4 March 1973, p. 30.
421. Jong's statement can be found in "A Feminist? Definition Varies With the Women," *New York Times* 8 November 1975, p. 32.
422. Atkinson's comment appears in the same article as Jong's.
423. Burnham, *Suicide of the West,* p. 29.
424. Peter Drucker, "Working Women: Unmaking of the 19th Century," *Wall Street Journal,* 6 July 1981, p. 12.
425. Jo Freeman, "The Origins of the Women's Liberation Movement," in *Changing Women in a Changing Society,* ed. Joan Huber (Chicago: University of Chicago Press, 1973), pp. 35, 40.
426. '81 PG, #314.
427. AR 25, p. 45.
428. Bd. Min., 5/14/45, p. 1; AR 23, p. 57; AR 24, p. 58.
429. AR 24, pp. 9, 58.
430. Ibid., p. 60.
431. AR 28, p. 61.
432. AR 29, p. 121.
433. Ibid., p. 122.
434. AR 31, p. 106.
435. Ibid.
436. Ibid., p. 107.
437. AR 39, p. 78. See also '66 PG, #316.
438. AR 40, pp. 87-88.
439. Ibid.
440. AR 39, p. 78.
441. '66 PG, #316.

442. Ibid.
443. Bd. Min., 4/1/63, p. 2.
444. AR 42, p. 143.
445. Linda Greenhouse, "Defeat of Equal Rights Bills Traced to Women's Vote," *New York Times,* 6 November 1975, p. 1.
446. Bd. Min., 9/26-27/70, p. 3.
447. '78 PG, #314.
448. Quoted J. Anthony Lukas, "The A.C.L.U. Against Itself," *New York Times Magazine,* 9 July 1978, p. 26.
449. '81 PG, #315.
450. Bd. Min., 9/24-25/77, pp. 9-10.
451. Linda Greenhouse, "High Court Upholds A Civil Service Edge for War Veterans," *New York Times,* 6 June 1979, p. 1.
452. Ibid., p. A16.
453. '76 PG, #229.
454. '77 PG, #229.
455. Quoted in Edwin M. Schur, *Crimes Without Victims* (Englewood Cliffs, N.J.: Prentice-Hall, 1965), p. 55.
456. Ibid., p. 57.
457. Lee R. Dice, "When Abortion Is Justified," *Nation,* 22 February 1965, pp. 189-90.
458. Ibid., p. 190.
459. Schur, *Crimes Without Victims,* pp. 11-66.
460. John T. Noonan, Jr., ed., *The Morality of Abortion* (Cambridge: Harvard University Press, 1970), p. xiv.
461. Ibid., p. xvii.
462. See the article by Peter Skerry for a good analysis of this controversy: "The Class Conflict Over Abortion," *Public Interest,* Summer 1978, pp. 69-84.
463. '66 PG, #247.
464. Bd. Min., 2/14/67, p. 3.
465. Ibid.
466. '67 PG, #247.
467. Ibid.; Bd. Min., 2/14/67, pp. 3-4.
468. Bd. Min., 2/14/67, p. 4.
469. Ibid., pp. 4-5.
470. Ibid., pp. 4-7.
471. '67 PG, #247; AR 43, p. 8.
472. Bd. Min., 12/2-3/67, pp. 19-21.
473. Ibid., pp. 21-22.
474. Ibid.
475. Ibid., p.23.
476. Bd. Min., 1/25/68, pp. 3-4.
477. Ibid., pp. 4-5.
478. Interview with Baldwin.
479. John Hart Ely, "The Wages of Crying Wolf," *Human Life Review,* Winter 1975, p. 57.
480. Ibid., p. 47.
481. John Hart Ely and Lawrence H. Tribe, "Let There Be Life," *New York Times,* 17 March 1981, p. A17.
482. "Abortion and the Law-II," editorial, *New Republic,* 22 June 1974, p. 6.

483. Mary Meehan, "A Housecleaning for American Liberals," *America*, 16 February 1974, p. 108.
484. "Reproductive Freedom," *Civil Liberties Alert*, October/ November 1982, p. 4.
485. AR '70-'71, p. 12.
486. Interview with Reitman.
487. Raoul Berger, *Government by Judiciary* (Cambridge: Harvard University Press, 1977), p. 179.
488. Ibid., pp. 169-76.
489. Ibid., pp. 167-68.
490. Ronald Bayer, "Drug stores, liquor stores and heroin: an analysis of the libertarian debate," *Contemporary Drug Problem*, Winter 1975, pp. 470-71, 478.
491. Interview with John Shattuck, "Defense of Liberty," pp. 42-43.
492. "Auction of an Abortion Criticized in Louisiana," *New York Times*, 26 June 1977, p. 26.
493. Ibid. See also William F. Buckley, Jr., "Auction Time at the ACLU," *National Review*, 22 July 1977, p. 845.
494. Norman C. Miller, "A New Anti-Catholic Bigotry," *Wall Street Journal*, 14 December 1978, p. 22.
495. Ira Glasser, letter to the editor, *Wall Street Journal*, 29 December 1978, p. 8.
496. "Hyde on 'Con-Con' and ACLU Tactics," *National Catholic Register*, 5 August 1979, p. 6f.
497. Basile Uddo, "The American Civil Liberties Union: One Step Too Far, Too Often," *America*, 19 May 1979, p. 413.
498. "Hyde on 'Con-Con' and ACLU Tactics."
499. *ACLU News*, PR 1-81, for release, 5 April 1981.
500. Rhonda Copelon, "Constitutional Analysis of S.158 (Helms-D'Amato) and H.R.900 (Hyde-Mazzoli)," *Center for Constitutional Rights*, March 1981.
501. "Reproductive Freedom and the 'Human Life Statute,'" *Bill of Rights Lobby Brief*, 21 June 1981, p. 2.
502. ACLU *Civil Liberties in Reagan's America*, p. 40.
503. Linda Greenhouse, "Abortion Restriction Cases Argued Before High Court," *New York Times*, 1 December 1982, p. 14.
504. ACLU, *Civil Liberties in Reagan's America*, p. 41.
505. Stuart Taylor, Jr., "U.S. to Support States in Regulating Abortions," *New York Times*, 29 July 1982, p. A17.
506. ACLU, *Civil Liberties in Reagan's America*, p. 42; Linda Greenhouse, "Court Backs Law to Notify Parents Before an Abortion on a Teen-ager," *New York Times*, 24 March 1981, p. A1.
507. Margaret O'Brien Steinfels and Peter Steinfels, "Of Sex and Liberals," *New York Times,* 22 April 1982, p. A31.
508. ACLU *Civil Liberties in Reagan's America*, pp. 43-44. See also Amy Mereson, "Women Workers are Sterilized or Lose Their Jobs," *Civil Liberties*, July 1982, p. 6.
509. Ann McFeatters, "Women's Rights Still Alive Despite ERA Setback," *Pittsburgh Press*, 27 June 1982, p. B-3.
510. Isabelle Katz Pinzler, "After the ERA—What Now?" *Civil Liberties*, July 1982, p. 7.
511. ACLU, *Civil Liberties in Reagan's America*, pp. 44-45.
512. Linda Greenhouse, "Justices Widen Range of Women's Pay Suits," *New York Times*, 9 June 1981, p. Al.

513. Sherry Jaffe, "Equal Rights for High School Girls," *Civil Liberties Record* (Pennsylvania), January 1983, pp. 2, 7.
514. George Slaff, "A.C.L.U. and Unions," *Nation*, 25 December 1982, p. 690.
515. ACLU, *Civil Liberties in Reagan's America*, p. 34.
516. Ibid., p. 43.
517. Ibid., p. 60.
518. Joan Lublin, "Reagan's Advisers Accuse EEOC of 'Racism,' Suggest Big Cutback," *Wall Street Journal*, 30 January 1981, sec. 2.
519. Howell Raines, "Blacks Shift to Sharper Criticism on Civil Rights," *New York Times*, 26 July 1981. p. E4.
520. "Voting Rights Bill Sweeps Congress; Administration Declares All-Out War on Civil Rights," *Civil Liberties Alert*, October/November 1982, p. 3.
521. Bd. Min., 10/10-11/81, pp. 1-2.
522. "Congress Dangerously Close to Curtailing Court Powers," *Civil Liberties Alert*, May 1982, p. 3.
523. ACLU, *Civil Liberties in Reagan's America*, p. 25.
524. Ira Glasser, "The Coming Assault on Civil Liberties," in *What Reagan Is Doing to Us*, ed. Alan Gartner, Colin Greer, and Frank Riessman (New York: Harper and Row, 1982), p. 242.
525. Interview with John Shattuck, "Defense of Liberty," p. 49.
526. C. Dickerman Williams, "Congress and the Supreme Court," *National Review*, 5 February 1982, p. 109.
527. Ibid.
528. Ibid., p. 126.
529. Stuart Taylor, Jr., "Legal Scholars Assail Legislation to Curb Power of Federal Courts," *New York Times*, 21 May 1981, p. B12.
530. Robert Nisbet, *Prejudices: A Philosophical Dictionary* (Cambridge: Harvard University Press, 1982), p. 207.
531. Theodore White, "Summing Up," *New York Times Magazine*, 25 April 1982, p. 42.
532. This position is popular amongst ACLU directors. See Bd. Min. 6/16-17/73, p. 17, for an example.
533. Nicholas Von Hoffman, "When Civil Liberties Become Liabilities," *Penthouse*, April 1982, p. 101.
534. Ibid.
535. Tom Hayden, "The Future Politics of Liberalism," *Nation*, 21 February 1981, p. 193.
536. Arthur Schlesinger, Jr., "Is Liberalism Dead?" *New York Times Magazine,* 30 March 1980, p. 42.
537. Symposium "Liberalism in America," *Center Magazine*, March/April 1981, pp. 41, 50, 54.

3

Civil Liberties, Communism, and the State

Liberalism and World War I

Liberals and conservatives both claim to reject war as an acceptable solution to world conflict. Radicals hold the same position. Yet in the course of history, support for war has come from all ideological quarters, including many "pacifist" groups. What seems to matter is not war itself, but the nature of the conflict, the goals sought, and the leadership involved. At almost every juncture in history, war has proven to be the predominant condition of at least some people somewhere on the globe. That the combatants would rather live in peace is often true but not universally so; the same can be said for citizens at home during time of war. An enigma it is not, for the pages of history reveal that war brings to many a sense of psychological release, as well as exhaustion, from the mundane and the ordinary.

The affinity that intellectuals have had with war has been observed by many, but no one has been more incisive than Robert Nisbet: "There is a natural crisis-mindedness, I think, among intellectuals generally; a fondness for the great changes and great decisions which the crisis of war makes possible."[1] In a similar vein, Arthur Schlesinger, Jr., has noted the less than coincidental relationship between periods of idealism at home and adventures overseas: "When government takes an affirmative role at home, it is likely also to take an affirmative role in the world. The great domestic reformers have also been the great foreign-policy activists—T.R., Wilson, F.D.R., Truman, Kennedy, Johnson. There is a disturbing tendency for the United States to get involved in war during activist times."[2]

The periods of activism that Schlesinger refers to are regarded as moments in the history of American liberalism. The utility of Schlesinger's explanation is that it beckons us to consider the emotive side of liberalism: the kind of idealism and high energy that liberals bring to public affairs accounts for some of their more Herculean undertakings.

Whatever association there is between liberalism and war, it surely is not ideological. The liberals' optimistic picture of humankind, as well as their favoritism for "rational" behavior, does not allow them to regard war as an inevitable or necessary condition. War is seen as an irrational exercise brought about largely by people who are not content to provide for the redress of grievances through calculated and judicious means. Above all, war is avoidable. The League of Nations, the United Nations, the idea of a world government—these are the answers that liberals give when pressed for alternatives to war. It is axiomatic to liberals that peace will be established once we recognize our common humanness and begin to cooperate in a planned fashion toward the realization of our united interests. Because humans are essentially good, the basis for institutionalizing the "family of man" is already set, awaiting our good-will and determination. Organizational problems may emerge, especially in a world federation, but cures can be found eventually; polishing our intercultural communication skills will mitigate many difficulties.

Although liberals are united in their recipe for preventing the outbreak of war, they have been unable to strike a consensus when confronted with the imminence of war. World War I provides a good illustration of this dissensus. The liberal community was split between those who preached pacifism and nonintervention and those who saw the war as an opportunity to make the world safe for democracy. To a large degree, the members of both schools of thought were imbedded in the Progressive tradition. The pacifists were led by Jane Addams, Lillian Wald, and Paul Kellogg, i.e. the leaders of the American Union Against Militarism (AUAM). The "new liberals," who claimed to represent conventional liberal thought, were drawn from the offices of the *New Republic*, namely, Herbert Croly, Walter Weyl, and Walter Lippmann. Based in New York, both factions attempted to influence the decision-making in the White House.

The AUAM, founded in 1915, was composed of experienced social reformers, most of whom had worked in settlement houses. Sympathetic to socialism, it was a distinguished blend of intellectuals: Adolph A. Berle, John Lovejoy Elliott, David Starr Johnson, Scott Nearing, Amos Pinchot, Norman Thomas, Oswald Garrison Villard, John Haynes Holmes, L. Hollingworth Wood, Rabbi Stephen Wise, Louis Lochner, Alice Lewisohn, and Max Eastman. Their objective was to mobilize reaction against the preparedness movement, which they saw as a prelude to U.S. entrance into the war. They even took issue with the militarism of the Boy Scouts. Through lobbying, publishing, and speaking engagements, they sought to dissuade the public from supporting the appeals of President Woodrow Wilson. Some members sought to "dare" the president by launching a series of lectures across the country in open defiance of his preparedness efforts.[3]

The *New Republic* liberals made no attempt to stump the country in opposition to Wilson. At first they remained, with Wilson, neutral and noncommittal. Isolationism, however, was strongly rejected, especially by Croly. As Charles Forcey described it, the *New Republic* men were not given to the pacifistic notions of the AUAM: "The sources of their new liberalism in the imperialism of Theodore Roosevelt, the dependence of their magazine upon the bounty of the Anglophile interventionist Willard Straight, and their own intimacy with the largely pro-allied educated classes of the Northeast—all made for militant internationalism rather than isolation."[4] Only Harold Stearns and Randolph Bourne on the staff of the *New Republic* were adamently opposed to American involvement; Felix Frankfurter, Learned Hand, and Alvin Johnson were solidly in the pro-Allied camp. Even the "pacifist" Norman Angell moved toward an interventionist stance. In 1915 the *New Republic* published articles by John Dewey, George Santayana, and Rebecca West, all of which "seemed clearly designed to rouse American sympathies for the Allies."[5] Economist Thorstein Veblen and historian Charles A. Beard joined the chorus in support of the Allies.[6]

The sinking of the *Lusitania* in May 1915 proved to be decisive: it put an end to the *New Republic*'s "pretence to neutrality."[7] By the end of the year, the editors had become increasingly aggressive, taking a prowar position. The president was criticized for his weak leadership as pleas were made to return to the heroics of San Juan Hill.[8] Wilson's preparedness speech was praised as a "decisive point in the history of the world,"[9] but it was still too flaccid to satisfy the new liberals, who announced that the president "was not up to his job."[10] As militant as anyone, Croly wrote that "the American nation needs the tonic of a serious moral adventure."[11] Throughout 1916 the *New Republic* declared that "the issue of military preparedness makes progressivism more urgent than ever."[12] Calls for "constructive patriotism" were designed to motivate the loyalty of workers during wartime.[13] Pacifists were either ridiculed for selling "passivism"[14] or denounced, as Jane Addams was by Dewey,[15] as an obstacle to lasting peace. But even Addams joined the ranks of her detractors in supporting Wilson's reelection.[16]

When the United States entered the war in April 1917, the new liberals were elated and took credit for Wilson's decision. Intellectuals like them, they boasted, "are the numerically insignificant class whose influence has been successfully exerted in favor of American participation."[17] The time had come, they were convinced, to shape the destiny of mankind. Helping the cause was George Creel, who chaired the Committee on Public Information. Creel's committee had been established by the president to "sell the war" to the American public. He did a fine job recruiting scholars from academia and elsewhere, all the while persuading them that they were partaking in a liberal exercise.[18] But without Wilson, the academic, it is not likely that Creel would have been so successful. In Wilson, many intellectuals saw one of their own, and could not pass up the opportunity to work as official agents of propaganda. Nisbet recalls the scene with clarity:

> The bond between Creel and Wilson was almost absolute; there is no record of Wilson's ever questioning, much less reproving, any of Creel's extraordinary invasions of civic morality. And overwhelmingly the intellectuals—novelists, poets, musical composers, dramatists, performers, clergymen, and, well toward the front, university and college professors—allowed themselves to be, nay, demanded to be, willing manipulators of the public mind. In America, not Russia or Germany, were first to be seen "artists in uniform."[19]

To be sure, not all liberals gravitated toward the war effort. Outstanding among them was Roger Baldwin. Bright, hardworking, and a born leader, Baldwin joined the local AUAM in St. Louis in 1916 while holding his job as a probation officer for the juvenile court. The following year he moved to New York, where he became instrumental in fighting the conscription bills in Congress. When the United States entered the war, he set out to establish the Bureau for Conscientious Objectors within the AUAM. Problems arose when some of the founding members of the AUAM concluded that Baldwin's aggressiveness had the effect of jeopardizing the organization's persuasiveness in Washington. After much dissension, Baldwin launched the National Civil Liberties Bureau (NCLB) as an independent organization dedicated to the rights of conscientious objectors. But it did more than simply oppose the draft and the war: it broadened its agenda to include the rights of left-wing activists who came under fire for their alleged subversive role in society. The NCLB rushed to the defense of the Wobblies, members of Industrial Workers of the World(the IWW), and declared that their intent was to "put the whole industrial system on trial."[20]

The Espionage Act of June 1917 triggered strong reaction from the AUAM staff. President Wilson thought the legislation was necessary to combat those who might thwart the war effort. The most controversial part of the act was Title XII, which gave the postmaster general the power to prohibit from the mails any literature "advocating or urging treason, insurrection, or forcible resistance to any law of the United States."[21] Postmaster General Albert S. Burleson moved without delay to order local postmasters to turn over to him any "unsealed matter, newspapers, etc., containing matter which is calculated to interfere with the success of any Federal loan . . . or to cause insubordination, disloyalty, mutiny, or refusal of duty in the military or naval service, or to obstruct the recruiting, draft or enlistment services . . . or otherwise to *embarrass* or hamper the Government in conducting the war."[22] More than a dozen publications were seized as a result of this policy, including Max Eastman's *Masses*; the *Nation*, as well as some NCLB pamphlets, came under strong criticism as well.[23]

The Sedition Act of 1918 was another attempt to proscribe disloyalty. It, too, was met by protest. Baldwin approached the president's adviser, Colonel Edward M. House, and registered his objections, but to no avail. House was sympathetic to Baldwin's appeal but could not, he believed, override the advice of Attorney General Thomas Gregory, who largely had written the bill. Meanwhile, Lillian Wald issued her own protest to the president, charging that civil liberties were being routinely violated by the Justice Department. She was not ignored but did not succeed in putting an end to repressive tactics, many of which were carried out by nongovernmental entities.[24] It was difficult to stage a rally in defense of individual liberty during wartime, and especially at a time when those who did not support the war could not win the backing of the press. The *New York Times*, for instance, lumped pacifism and pro-Germanism together, wondering "if there be any real difference between the two."[25]

NCLB publications became increasingly radical, drawing the attention of the Justice Department. Piqued at the apparent disloyalty of Baldwin's organization, the authorities began an investigation of NCLB literature. They chastised the NCLB for failing to recognize that the exigencies of war demanded a more subdued approach to civil liberties. The Justice Department sent an agent, armed with a warrant and a revolver, to survey the NCLB files. Baldwin had already resigned from his position, taking leave to fight his conscription into the army. A southern lawyer, George Gordon Battle, was recruited to deal with the agents. Well known and respected by government officials, Battle was able to temper his adversaries' attitudes sufficiently enough to avoid an indictment. The final report cleared the NCLB of any wrongdoing.[26]

When Baldwin landed in jail for refusing to comply with the draft, Albert DeSilver, a New York lawyer, took command of the NCLB. In his term of office he was presented with the job of confronting the infamous A. Mitchell Palmer, the new attorney general. Palmer and his minions conducted a series of raids and prosecutions against radicals. They targeted the Union of Russian Workers, which advocated violent revolution, along with others who merited deportation. The *The New York Times* gave its blessings to the arrests, as did J. Edgar Hoover. DeSilver protested, but in general the NCLB kept a low profile.[27] Bowing to Palmer's insistence, the Congress enacted sedition legislation during peacetime; thirty-five states passed similar bills.[28] The Supreme Court, for its part, ruled in *Schenck* that during time of war, the exercise of freedoms that posed a "clear and present danger" to the national interest could be limited. Even so, the wartime Sedition Act was repealed in 1921.[29]

The events surrounding World War I can be credited with the launching of the civil liberties movement in this country; not until then did the Bill of Rights become a public policy concern of the first order. Although many people contributed to the movement's development, the work of Zechariah Chafee and Roger Baldwin ranks foremost. Chafee, in his landmark book *Freedom of Speech*, provided more than an adumbration of civil liberties for future legal scholars—he helped to define the issues and parameters of serious debate on the subject. Baldwin, of course, had a more ambitious project in mind: he not only tried to reform the law but sought to redesign society itself. Wartime violations were one thing, but abuses of civil liberties during peacetime and the deprivation of rights that the propertyless class experienced were something else again. The founding of the American Civil Liberties Union was Baldwin's corrective: equality through liberty became the *modus operandi* of the new civil libertarians.

The 1920s and 1930s

In the ACLU's first annual report, it listed "amnesty for political prisoners" as its most urgent concern. Most of those detained by the government were members of the IWW, a group with which the Union strongly identified. Amnesty for conscientious objectors, opposition to sedition bills, and the defense of the rights of radicals in general became the causes of the newly created ACLU.[30] The Union sought to restore citizenship to all persons convicted under the Espionage Act, worked to remove the conditions attached to a number of commutations granted to radicals, and labored to undo the deportation orders that had been levied against convicted activists.[31] It challenged the conviction of Benjamin Gitlow, who had been arrested for breaking New York's criminal anarchy law. The Supreme Court upheld the constitutionality of the state law.[32] The denial of citizenship to pacifists also evoked the Union's interest and involvement. In 1926 a case had arisen concerning Mary King, an Irish Quaker, who said that she would not, if she were a man, bear arms in the event of war with Japan. The judge for the District Court in Portland, Oregon, denied her citizenship papers.[33] But it was not until 1929 that the issue became a national one. Madame Roszika Schwimmer, a renowned Hungarian pacifist, applied for U.S. citizenship but was refused when she said that she would not bear arms in war. The ACLU rallied to her defense. In Chicago, the local district court found her guilty. The Court of Appeals, however, admitted her to citizenship. The Supreme Court settled the case in 1929, denying Schwimmer's application.[34] After World War II the court overturned its decision.[35]

The ACLU's radical proclivities and hostility toward government were quite visible during its formative years. Every radical, famous and unknown, had a friend in the ACLU. So vehement was the Union in its hatred of government prosecutions that it never once sided with the position of the authorities in a showdown between the state and radicals. The government was always wrong, and radicals were always, or nearly always, innocent of any wrongdoing; on the few occasions when radicals were deemed guilty, the government was nonetheless responsible for creating an atmosphere of repression. And if there was ever any doubt regarding innocence or guilt, the Union could be counted on to defend the radicals. This becomes intelligible once we realize that for the ACLU the innocence or guilt of radicals was not its main concern; achieving the ends of radicalism through liberal means was the paramount objective. So it was that the ACLU rushed to the defense of Tom Mooney and Warren K. Billings. Both men had been sentenced to life imprisonment in 1916 for allegedly planning and executing a Preparedness Day bombing in San Francisco. In a highly controversial case, the ACLU sought to release the men on the grounds that they were innocent. In 1939, both men were set free.[36]

The ACLU'S most pronounced rendezvous with radicals during the 1920s occurred in Dedham, Massachusetts, the scene of the legendary Sacco and Vanzetti trial. Nicola Sacco and Bartolomeo Vanzetti, avowed anarchists, were accused of the murder of a paymaster at a shoe factory in South Braintree on 15 April 1920. They maintained their innocence to the end; on 23 August 1927, they died in the electric chair. To this day, many liberals remain fixed in their belief that the men were innocent. The reasons given for this view are varied but include: they were framed; the evidence was inconclusive; the evidence was circumstantial and occasionally contradictory; they were radicals; they were Italians. It has become so fashionable for liberals to proclaim Sacco and Vanzetti innocent that many young liberals, those born after World War II, think it strange that they ought to inform themselves about the facts involved in the case: the innocence of the radicals is accepted as dogma. They have learned from their mentors, like historian Eric Foner, that erroneous verdicts and prejudiced trials are not at all uncommon in the United States.[37] Given this cast of mind, it is not surprising that they tropistically lean toward the innocence of the Dedham defendants.

The ACLU's role in the Sacco-Vanzetti affair was not central, but it was not insignificant either. Fred H. Moore led the defense, assisted by an array of Italian activists. The Union, as Baldwin once recalled, helped the cause but "never had any inside authority of any kind."[38] The ACLU was active, however, in reorganizing the defense work in 1924 after the trial judge denied a new trial.[39] One of the main reasons that the ACLU did not take a more integral role in the case was due to its reputation: the Union was regarded as a radical organization and would have undoubtedly prejudiced the chances of the famed anarchists. Indeed, the Union was warned by one of its own board members, Felix Frankfurter, to stay clear of the case altogether:

> I hope very deeply you will do nothing until after the Sacco-Vanzetti case is out of the way completely: If the Civil Liberties Union and other like-minded organizations now come in, it is bound to be entangled with the efforts on behalf of Sacco and Vanzetti, and all such entanglement would hurt the cause of those men. I speak from a great deal of attention to the situation and a detailed familiarity, I believe, with the governing forces of the community.[40]

Frankfurter's plea takes on greater weight when one considers the fact that he was more responsible for mobilizing credible support for Sacco and Vanzetti than any other individual in the country.[41]

After Sacco and Vanzetti were sentenced to death on 9 April 1927, the liberal-Left community, in Europe as well as in the United States, called for an appeal. Anarchists in France pushed for a massive uprising. The Communist party in this country set up an "emergency committee" and promised to call a mass metting in Union Square (then known as "Red Square"), New York. The ACLU chose to act surreptitiously. Baldwin notified his colleagues of the strategy:

> The Civil Liberties Union has been connected with the Sacco and Vanzetti matter, but has hidden its participation under various false fronts. We are at present instigating a nation-wide movement among lawyers in various university faculties to join as signatories . . . for a review of the case de novo. This work is being done behind the name of a group of lawyers at Columbia. Karl Llewellyn is the chief promoter.[42]

Louis Joughin, one-time research director of the ACLU and coauthor of a book on Sacco and Vanzetti, said of Baldwin's message: "It [the ACLU] did itself, and the lawyers involved, no service by writing about its activity in a conspiratorial tone—with references to 'false fronts' and instigation."[43] But Baldwin was only telling the truth. ACLU participation in various front groups was not uncommon in those days.

When Sacco and Vanzetti were executed in 1927, the ACLU declared it to be "the outstanding and tragic event of the year." It was convinced that the men were prosecuted "primarily because of their radical activities."[44] Almost fifty years later, Baldwin held pretty much to the same conclusion: "Well, I don't say they were *absolutely* innocent. I just say they were never guilty beyond a reasonable doubt. . . . In the last analysis I think the outstanding issue really was that they were condemned because they were

Italians and anarchists."[45] ACLU staff member George Slaff is more certain: "Every decent unprejudiced human being who has studied the Sacco-Vanzetti case has reversed their conviction and sentence."[46] Not hardly—many have examined the evidence and are still not sure; others are convinced that Sacco, at least, was guilty. After a comprehensive review of the case, authors Louis Joughin and Edmund M. Morgan confessed that "we do not know"[47] if they were innocent, adding that "no answer can be made"[48] regarding the charges. When Francis Russell first took to questioning their innocence or guilt, he was convinced that they were innocent. That was in 1953. Intrigued by the case, Russell continued his examination of the case until finally, after years of work, he concluded that Sacco was guilty indeed; Vanzetti, however, may have been innocent. The evidence that Russell has marshaled is impressive. He covered everything from Sacco's associates and alibis to personally supervising a ballistics test. His ballistics test in 1961 confirmed the judgment of others: "Ballistics tests conducted by various experts, Goddard in 1927 and Jury and Weller in 1961, have shown beyond any visible doubt that a shell found at the scene of the crime and a bullet taken from a murdered guard's body match test shells and test bullets found in the Colt automatic found on Sacco the night of his arrest."[49] Even Fred Moore, the chief defense counsel for the anarchists, admitted that "Sacco probably and Vanzetti possibly [were] guilty." And as Russell points out, one has to wonder what motivated Sacco's son, Dante, to remain largely silent and aloof from the controversy throughout his life, despite many requests to campaign in behalf of his father's innocence.[50]

That the trial was unfair is at once the weakest and yet most commonly applied criticism. The issue of fairness, as Russell argues, was not raised until over five years after the trial itself. Even Fred Moore told the judge that regardless of the jury's verdict, no one could claim that his clients did not have a fair trial. One of his assistant counsels, Jerry McAnarney, voiced the same sentiment to the judge prior to the jury's decision: "I want to say on behalf of these men and their friends that they have had every opportunity here, every patience, every consideration."[51] But evidence carries no weight with true believers. To Katherine Anne Porter, who was present at the gates of Charlestown Prison the night the two men were executed, the Sacco and Vanzetti trial is analogous to the trial of Jesus Christ and to the Moscow trials of 1937.[52] Eric Foner eulogizes his martyrs as "dreamers of a perfect world" and laments that utopian visions no longer color the American psyche.[53] Others simply choose to associate Sacco and Vanzetti with the trappings of a capitalist state.

The ACLU's record of defending radicals of every stripe earned the enmity of many Americans, including public officials. William J. Burns, founder of the "world's greatest international detective agency," and onetime director of the Bureau of Investigation of the Department of Justice, offered these remarks before a subcommittee of the House Appropriations Committee on 1 April 1924:

> I dare say that unless the country becomes thoroughly aroused concerning the danger of this radical element in this country, we will have a very serious situation. These parlor Bolsheviks have sprung up everywhere, as evidenced by this American Civil Liberties Union of New York. They have organized a civil liberties union on the coast. Wherever we seek to suppress these radicals, a civil liberties union promptly gets busy.[54]

Four years later, a committee of the New York legislature reached the same verdict:

> The American Civil Liberties Union, in the last analysis, is a supporter of all subversive movements; its propaganda is detrimental to the interests of the State. It attempts not only to protect crime, but to encourage attacks upon our institutions in every form. . . .[Its] main work is to uphold the communists in spreading revolutionary propaganda and inciting revolutionary activities to undermine our American institutions and overthrow our Federal Government.[55]

One might argue that such comments simply reflect the Red-scare mentality of the 1920s. But another argument, equally as plausible, is that the leadership of the ACLU invited these charges. In the 1920s Robert W. Dunn, board member and founder of the New England CLU, made two pilgrimages to the Soviet Union in an attempt to provide assistance to the newly established communist state.[56] Baldwin journeyed to the Soviet state as well. In 1924 Baldwin, along with his friends in the leftist Committee for International Political Prisoners, published *Letters from Russian Prisons*, which contained letters written by political prisoners in the USSR. Although Baldwin did not approve of the holding of political prisoners, his criticism was rather limp compared to the praise he had for the "grand experiment." In the introduction of the book he wrote that

> many of the members of the Committee for Political Prisoners as individuals [and as his biographer Lamson noted, he included himself] regard the Russian Revolution as the greatest and most daring experiment yet undertaken to recreate society in terms of human values. . . . Many of them look upon Russia today as a great laboratory of social experimentation of incalculable value to the development of the world.[57]

Baldwin's enthusiasm for the Marxist experiment did not sit well with his close friend Emma Goldman. Goldman had had considerable influence on

Baldwin when he was working in St. Louis, in his pre-NCLB days. Listening to her lecture on the "class struggle" had moved the young Baldwin to assess the merits of the radical position.[58] Prior to 1920 Goldman was regarded as one of the champions of radicalism. Just before her deportation to Russia on the *Buford*, Goldman offered her appraisal of the land she was about to visit:

> The Pioneer social experiment now being tried in Russia—the greatest and most fundamental ever witnessed in all history—is the guiding star to all the oppressed and disinherited of the world. . . . It is darkest before dawn, in history as in nature. But the dawn has begun. In Russia. Its light is a promise and the hope of the world.[59]

But within the first year of her stay in the Soviet Union, Goldman had reassessed her thoughts on the wonders of applied Marxism: "The British Mission was entertained royally with theatres, operas, ballets and excursions. Luxury was heaped upon them while the people slaved and went hungry. The Soviet Government left nothing undone to create a good impression and everything of a disturbing nature was kept from the visitors."[60]

After about two years of observing Marxian praxis, Goldman called it quits. She wrote Baldwin in 1922 from Berlin about those who were "obsessed by the Bolshevik superstition."[61] Two years later she told him what she thought of those who advertised themselves as defenders of liberty:

> Tell me whether you too do not think the silence of the American liberals in the face of such horror is the most damnable thing? These people who shouted themselves hoarse for amnesty of political prisoners, how dare they keep silent now that their own "pet government" is guilty of such heinous crimes. Any publicity you can give the matter will be appreciated by the unfortunate victims of Leninism.[62]

It is important to note that this was written *before* the "Great Terror" of Joseph Stalin.

In 1923 Baldwin made his first visit to the Soviet Union. He went with a team of leftists, all involved in a project called the Kousbas Autonomous Industrial Colony. This undertaking was in response to the efforts of the Wobblies and the American Communists, who had secured land in the Siberian Urals for the purpose of developing a mechanized "autonomous" farm. Baldwin helped to raise a half-million dollars by selling shares of the land to eager, like-minded Americans. Hundreds of men, women, and children traveled to the promised land, only to suffer disillusionment and rejection in the end; they returned home once reality conquered their idealism.[63] Baldwin, however, was unfazed.

Baldwin's reputation in leftist circles enabled him to obtain permission from the Soviet authorities to make a return trip to their country in 1927. He was given the typical guided tour, with all the hospitality that is accorded to Soviet sympathizers.[64] However, something unusual happened on Baldwin's last night in Georgia: his tour guide broke down and confessed that the secret police ran the country and deliberately concealed from fellow travelers the terrible torture that took place behind closed doors. When Baldwin was asked by Peggy Lamson whether this information shook him at that time, he replied, "No. I'm afraid not. I was too prejudiced in the beginning to let signs—even clear signs like that one— count heavily in my total picture. Great upheavals like the Russian Revolution have their price, I told myself. Violent storms had to run their course."[65] He added that he had never questioned the violations of civil liberties that were an everyday occurrence under Stalin.[66]

Baldwin, the father of American civil liberties, not only failed to question the abuses of freedom in Russia but actually defended the repressive regime. In 1928 he published his glowing account of Russia in *Liberty Under the Soviets*. In it he confessed that he held a favorable bias toward the Soviet Union, as the title of his work conveys. Economic freedom, i.e. the abolition of class privilege, was more important than civil liberties. Anticipating the charge that he was engaging in duplicity, Baldwin frankly acknowledged that "repressions in western democracies are violations of professed constitutional liberties, and I condemn them as such. Repressions in Soviet Russia are weapons of struggle in a transition period to socialism."[67] Emma Goldman, by then the scourge of liberals and Communists alike for her 1923 book, *My Disillusionment with Russia*, reacted sharply but fairly in a letter to Baldwin:

> Do you really deplore the evils in Soviet Russia as I do? Do you deplore them as much and do you protest against them as much as you do against the evils in Italy and other countries under the iron whip of dictatorship? If so I have never heard about it or seen it in cold print. Oh I know that you have spoken up on occasions and have written against the abuses in Russia, but you have always done so in a very faint voice, Roger dear, and with so many apologies for the so-called good of the Soviet regime that your protest was fairly swamped, and made no impression whatever. Unless you have become an apologist for dictatorship I cannot understand how you can cry out indignantly against the horrors going on under the capitalistic regime and only whisper your protest against the crimes committed in the name of Revolution and Socialism.[68]

The depression of the 1930s did not cause American liberals to become enamored of the Soviet system, it simply hastened their attraction. The deprecation of the American society and the glorification of the Soviet Union in which so many Western intellectuals indulged in the 1930s has been comprehensively portrayed by sociologist Paul Hollander[69] and historian William O'Neill.[70] Hollander maintains that estrangement from one's own society precedes the attraction to other societies where a utopian experience seems certain. So it is that intellectuals are pulled toward admiration for the Soviet or Chinese or Cuban societies once alienation with the United States takes hold. The pattern is not inevitable, but historically it appears to have worked that way. Surely the depression was cause for alarm, but it by no means necessitated intellectuals to take up the cause of communism. Yet many did. Edmund Wilson did, and so did many of his colleagues at the *New Republic*. In an emotionally charged article for the liberal tabloid in 1931, Wilson implored his readers to examine the "apparent success" of the Soviet Five-Year Plan. Liberals, he said, did not take Marx's prophecy seriously enough. It was up to them to "take Communism away from the Communists." "What we need in this country," he wrote, "is a genuine opposition, and it is a long time since the liberals have been one. A genuine opposition must, it seems to me, openly confess that the Declaration of Independence and the Constitution are due to be supplanted by some new manifestoes and some new bills of rights."[71] Economic rights, by which Wilson meant the abolition of classes, must take precedence over civil liberties. With this, Roger Baldwin had no quarrel.

Just how many liberals had been taken in by the Communist line is hard to judge, but no one denies that it was more than a handful. It was in New York, more than Washington, where the Communists scored their biggest success.[72] The term "Liblab" was commonly invoked in those days in New York to describe, as William Barrett recalls it, "the kneejerk Liberal who was a patsy for pro-Soviet propaganda."[73] It was these "patsies" with whom the Communists worked, creating united fronts to foster their goals. Many years later the ADA would say of this period: "It is difficult to understand or remember the extent of the perversion of American liberalism by a handful of skillful and articulate Communists who sought a united front."[74] Some of those who ventured to the Soviet Union, however, rebelled against communism once they got a taste of real-life Marxism. Among the notables were Eugene Lyons, Malcolm Muggeridge, Max Eastman, Freda Utley, and William Henry Chamberlain.[75] And of course, Emma Goldman. Others who contributed to the protestation against the Soviet Union included socialists Sidney Hook and his mentor, John Dewey. Hook broke with the liberal-Left orthodoxy early in the 1930s,[76] and has remained one of the United States' most perceptive critics of Soviet communism. Dewey led a commission of inquiry at the time of the Moscow trials in 1937 in an attempt to uncover the truth, but the liberal-Left did not want to hear the awful truth and roundly condemned him for his effort. He was accused of slandering the name of Joseph Stalin and standing in the way of progress.[77] The most vicious denunciations came from Lillian Hellman.[78]

The ACLU continued to have a cordial relationship with the Communist party throughout the 1930s. But that is not to say that the Union itself was a Communist front. It was not. It even had its relationship strained at times, owing to the illiberal practices of the party. For example, during the presidential campaign of 1932, Communists demonstrated, heckled, physically assaulted persons, and broke up rival working-class political street meetings in New York; they sought to "expose the misleaders." The Union responded by setting up a special committee chaired by Professor William L. Nunn, to investigate the situation. It heard many witnesses and eventually turned its report over to the Communist party. The report endeavored to delineate the limits of heckling as a form of free speech. The Communists disavowed intentions of disrupting meetings or assaulting members of other political groups but insisted on the right to heckle.[79]

A major internal dispute occurred within the Union concerning the events of a textile strike in North Carolina. In 1929 Fred Beal, a labor activist, had been designated by the Communists to fight a potential wage cut at the Loray Mill in Gastonia; his ultimate goal was to organize a union at the plant. When the company fired those who followed Beal's lead, a strike ensued. After the National Guard was ordered to intervene, several people were killed, beaten, and kidnapped. The workers retaliated by killing the local chief of police. Beal and many of the strikers were arrested, and sixteen were indicted for murder. The International Labor Defense, the legal arm of the Communist party, quickly came to the defense of the men.[80] The ACLU helped to finance the Communist defense organization with monies procured from the American Fund of Public Service. The American Fund had established the Bail Fund, which was administered by the ACLU; it wrote bail in all cases involving First Amendment violations.[81] Beal and four other Communist leaders then jumped bail and fled to Russia (where they were made instant martyrs). The Union issued a strong condemnation of the five,[82] and William Z. Foster, a Communist and board member of the ACLU, resigned from the Union in protest.[83] It was after the Bail Fund had lost approximately $33,500 that the ACLU broke its relationship with the International Labor Defense.[84]

On 6 October 1930, the Board of Directors of the ACLU met to discuss the Gastonia case. The thirteen members in attendance resolved "to discontinue writing and recommending the writing of bail for members of the Communist Party." The ACLU explained its rationale as follows:

The primary reason for this action is the almost insuperable difficulties which the flight of these defendants has placed in the way of securing funds and legal defense for free speech cases involving radical propaganda. Therefore, this policy is to remain in effect until the Communist authorities make it clear under adequate guaranties that they will not support or tolerate bailjumping.[85]

Although the ACLU policy was eminently reasonable, it did not sit well with its most radical members. It did, however, continue to fight for the rights of Communists throughout the decade.

In January 1931 the ACLU came under fire from the editors of *Law and Labor*, who criticized the Union's position on free speech. The Union was on record for stating that *"it is perfectly clear that orderly progress can be achieved only by unlimited free speech*. No man should ever be locked up for what he says—even if he advocates overthrowing the government by violence, or advises the destruction of property. . . . *The only way to judge the effect of words is by acts."* To this the editors replied: "There is no respectable opinion that any government should take a revolution lying down. Advocacy of force is an invitation to the use of force as much against the advocate as for him. The constitutional guaranties of individual right cannot be warped and twisted in their meaning."[86] The article continued its attack on the Union, denouncing Baldwin's decision not to appear voluntarily before Representative Hamilton Fish's investigative committee on Communist activities. Baldwin had said that the committee was "detrimental to the interests of the country," and that he regarded an appearance before it as a "waste of my time."[87] When Baldwin finally did appear before the committee, he was asked by Fish if he upheld the right of an alien to advocate the overthrow of the government. Baldwin answered, "Sure; certainly. It is the healthiest kind of thing for a country, of course, to have free speech—unlimited."[88] Unless, of course, the country is the Soviet Union, for which Baldwin allowed exceptions to his "principle." Fish's committee offered the following conclusion of the Union:

> The American Civil Liberties Union is closely affiliated with the communist movement in the United States, and fully 90 per cent of its efforts are on behalf of communists who have come into conflict with the law. It claims to stand for free speech, free press, and free assembly, but it is quite apparent that the main function of the A.C.L.U. is to attempt to protect the communists in their advocacy of force and violence to overthrow the Government, replacing the American flag by a Red flag and erecting a Soviet government in place of the republican form of government guaranteed to each State by the Federal Constitution.[89]

ACLU supporters like to think of the organization as a nonpartisan entity that never takes a political stand. This myth has been repeated by the authors of every book about the ACLU, bar none. Take Donald Johnson, for example. In the 1960s he argued that Baldwin was a moderate: "He was just as opposed to violence, revolution, Communism, and syndicalism, as he was to the suppression of anyone who advocated these things."[90] Violence, maybe. But not to communism or revolution. In fact, he explicitly supported both. In 1934 Baldwin revealed his true sympathies in an article in *Soviet Russia Today:*

> Our critics are in error in denying us a class position. . . . All my associates in the struggle for civil liberties take a class position, though many don't know it. . . . I, too, take a class position. It is anti-capitalist and pro-revolutionary. . . . I champion civil liberties as the best non-violent means of building the power on which worker's rule must be based. . . . *When that power of the working class is once achieved, as it has been only in the Soviet Union, I am for maintaining it by any means whatever. . . . The Soviet Union has already created liberties far greater than exist elsewhere in the world. . . . It is genuine, and it is the nearest approach to freedom that the workers have ever achieved. . . .* If American workers, with no real liberties save to change masters or, rarely, to escape from the working class, could understand their class interest, Soviet "workers' democracy" would be their goal.[91]

Baldwin later came to regret this article.

The following year, 1935, Baldwin once again proclaimed his allegiance to communism. The editor of Harvard's class book sent a questionnaire to the class of 1905, asking them to offer a statement regarding their beliefs. Baldwin responded by saying, "Communism is the goal."[92] In the same year he commented, "No greater calamity could happen to the advance of mankind than the failure or defeat of the Soviet Union."[93] When Baldwin came under attack by the Hearst newspapers, he responded, "I am not and never have been a member of the Communist Party." This was true, but Baldwin could not help but add, "I am sympathetic with the economic system being worked out in Soviet Russia. I believe in the economic goal of communism—namely, sharing in common the world's wealth."[94] The credibility of the ACLU was undermined once again before the decade closed when, in March 1937, the Board of Directors issued a restatement of its principles. Replying to charges that it refused to condemn the repressive measures of communists as harshly as it condemned fascists, the board said: "If Communists engaged in such repressive tactics in the United State, we would condemn them equally. The record shows that American Communists do not."[95]

The Era of Expediency

Decades do not always begin or end on time: the 1930s began with the Great Crash of 1929; the 1960s ended with Watergate in 1973. And the

1940s began in 1938. That is when Representative Martin Dies took command of the newly created House Committee on Un-American Activities (HUAC). Dies wasted no time before criticizing the ACLU for its disloyalty. The Union responded by launching an educational campaign on the meaning of civil liberties that became its number-one priority.[96] In the Union's first annual report of the 1940s, it singled out the Dies Committee for promoting hysteria. The Committee was responsible for the passage of a federal sedition bill.[97] As we shall see, a showdown would occur between Dies and the ACLU.

The 1940 Resolution and the Flynn Affair

The most dramatic internal dispute in the history of the ACLU occurred in 1940 when the Board of Directors expelled Elizabeth Gurley Flynn, one of its original members, because she was a member of the Communist party. Flynn had long been active in radical crusades (she was an early member of the IWW), but it was not until 1937 that she joined the Communist party. Reelected to the Board in 1939, it was not until the following year that she was dismissed from it. The events surrounding this episode were—and still are—highly controversial. No other issue has haunted the Union as much. And no other issue symbolizes the polemical nature of so many of the Union's policies in the 1940s. While doing her research on Baldwin, Peggy Lamson aptly concluded that "all roads lead to Elizabeth Gurley Flynn."[98]

The Flynn affair is, to this day, a serious source of embarrassment for the ACLU. The Union would prefer to discuss it parenthetically, as an unfortunate incident. Sympathetic students of the Union have respected its sensitivity by writing very little about the case. A few examples will suffice. In 1975 the associate director of the ACLU, Alan Reitman, edited a volume on his organization; different authors were each assigned a decade to write about, beginning with the 1920s. The 1930s went to Jerold Auerbach. He covered the Flynn case, for its genesis lay in the 1930s. His treatment was fair and accurate, but he made one mistake: he wrote too much about the Flynn case to suit the ACLU. In an unusual move, Reitman included a rebuttal to Auerbach's discussion by Baldwin—it appeared in the midst of Auerbach's chapter! Baldwin was upset partly because Auerbach devoted "disproportionate attention" to this issue.[99] To be sure that the reader embraced Baldwin's criticism, Reitman included another response to Auerbach that appeared in the midst of the last chapter, written by Reitman. The second response came from ACLU official Osmond K. Fraenkel, who charged that "the large amount of space given by Jerold S. Auerbach to this episode [the Flynn case] is disproportionate."[100] Charles Lam Markmann also obliged the ACLU's sensitivity; his 434-page book on the ACLU cited Flynn's ouster only twice, and both citations were parenthetical in nature and lacked assessment. Never once did Markmann find it necessary to explain why Flynn was thrown off the staff; he was content simply to mention her allegiance to the Communist party.[101]

To understand what precipitated Flynn's expulsion, it is necessary to know something of the social currents that were evolving in the mid-1930s. The "news" of Stalin's terror and the ritualistic endorsement of his strategy by the Communist party in the United States shook the conscience of at least some civil libertarians. For a few in the ACLU it was too much to bear; they could not defend civil rights for Communists. Resignations on the West Coast were particularly heavy.[102] Board member John Haynes Holmes was convinced that Communists did not belong with him on the chief governing body of the Union. In 1934 he wrote that Communists were "a group of savages, who, like their Nazi competitors made war upon all members of the human race excepting themselves."[103] Even though Holmes was an influential member of the Union, there is no evidence that his pronouncement was well received by his colleagues. What he created, however, was the start of unprecedented factionalism within the organization. One of Holmes's most outspoken adversaries was the wealthy and radical (no contradiction, really) Corliss Lamont. Heir to a fortune built on capitalistic adventures, Lamont has remained the most embittered critic of the ACLU's policies in the forties and fifties. Needless to say, his writings on the Union have not endeared him to the organization.

According to Lamont, the first controversy to evoke hard feelings on the board involved a violent confrontation between Communists and Socialists at a mass meeting in Madison Square Garden. In 1934 the Socialist party and a number of trade unions organized a rally to protest an attack on workers in Vienna by the Austrian government. The Communists were determined to be recognized at the meeting. When one of their leaders, Clarence Hathaway, mounted the platform in an attempt to speak, he was attacked by Socialists and driven from the hall. The Board of Directors of the ACLU promptly appointed a commission to investigate the conflicting charges. When the report surfaced, it declared the Communists to be the major culprits; they had denied freedom of speech to their rivals. However, the Socialists were reprimanded too; they were cited for confiscating copies of the *Daily Worker* from Communists as they entered the meeting and chastised for assaulting Hathaway. Board member Norman Thomas was livid; he claimed that the report was designed to placate Communist sympathizers on the board.[104]

The second controversy centered on the Ford Motor Company-UAW dispute, a taxing issue for the ACLU,[105] as we have seen. The third controversy was the initial stage of the Flynn affair and concerned the role of the Dies Committee. It is hardly a moot point to suggest that the Union was apprehensive over the activities of Dies and his colleagues, but it is debatable whether Lamont's analysis is factually correct.

Early in 1939 the Dies Committee issued a report calling for an investigation of the ACLU. Since its origin in 1920, the Union had been accused of being a Communist front. Now the matter was to be resolved. The Union was nervous. Norman Thomas, Morris Ernst, and Roger William Riis tried to persuade their fellow board members that it was time for the Union to abandon its traditional policy of confining itself to the Bill of Rights. They urged that the organization take a strong stand against totalitarian governments.[106] Holmes's sympathies were with this group: "So many of us are partisans of other causes, that again and again the cause of civil rights is so bent to the advantage of these other causes as to be warped and strained beyond recognition."[107]

In the fall of 1939 the ACLU held a two-day national conference on "Civil Liberties in the Recent Emergency." Dies charged that many of the participating organizations were Communist fronts.[108] However, at the same time Dies himself was under fire from the president and the press. His committee had published the membership and mailing lists of the Washington branch of the American League for Peace and Democracy, with the implication that all of the members were under the influence of the Communist party. But criticism of the committee neither weakened it nor relieved its pressure on the ACLU. All along the Union had been trying to obtain a hearing before the committee to explain its side but it never got the chance. On 23 October 1939, Dies unexpectedly absolved the Union of the charges of communism:

> This Committee found last year, in its reports there was not any evidence that the American Civil Liberties Union was a Communist organization. That being true, I do not see why we would be justified in going into it. I mean, after all, they have been dismissed, by unanimous report of the committee, as a Communist organization.[109]

The Dies surprise came while the ACLU board chairman, Dr. Harry Ward, was testifying before the committee about the activities of another organization that he chaired, the American League for Peace and Democracy.

It was not only the unanticipated context of Dies's remark that stunned Lamont, but the content itself. Lamont denies that the report to which Dies referred ever existed: "The strange and suspicious thing about [Dies's] statement was that the Committee had made no such report." Lamont then poses the obvious question: "Why, then, did Martin Dies suddenly revise so drastically the opinion of his committee, and give the Union a clean bill of health?" His answer represents an indictment of the integrity of the ACLU. Lamont believes that Morris Ernst and Arthur Garfield Hays made a deal with Dies at the Hay-Adams House in Washington between 14 October and 23 October 1939. The substance of the deal, according to Lamont, was that Dies would cease harassing the Union if the ACLU would help to crush the Communist apparatus.[110] That such a meeting took place is not disputed.[111] What is disputed is whether a sinister quid pro quo arrangement took place. In the mid-1950s Dies wrote to Lamont, saying that he had met in Washington with Ernst, Hays, and Adolph A. Berle, Jr. (assistant secretary of state in 1939) to discuss "the possibility of united action on the part of liberals and conservatives to investigate and expose Communists in the United States." The meeting had been arranged at his insistence, but "unfortunately. . . was not productive of any fruits."[112]

Lamont, of course, asserts that the talk *was* productive: "After the high-level meeting in Washington and Representative Dies' subsequent white-washing of the ACLU, the projected hearing for the ACLU before the Un-American Activities Committee faded away entirely." As for the reciprocal response on the part of the Union, Lamont's charges are circumstantial: "Certainly, very soon after the Hays-Ernst-Dies discussion the Thomas-Ernst group on the Union's Board of Directors started a high-powered anti-Communist cleansing operation that raised havoc in the ACLU for the next fifteen years." Lamont adds that the ACLU's decision to contract its activities was also influenced by the Nazi-Soviet nonaggression pact in August 1939.[113] For Lamont, then, the scenario was no accident: Dies attacks the ACLU; Dies meets with Hays and Ernst; Dies clears the Union; the Union purges Flynn; ergo, a deal was made. Lamont's account is logically consistent but suffers from oversimplification. The questionable character of Lamont's argument will become apparent after the position of Baldwin on this affair has been addressed.

Baldwin, quite naturally, rejected Lamont's analysis entirely. When Lamson asked him whether there had been a deal with Dies, Baldwin retorted, "No truth at all! Absolutely none whatsoever! Corliss Lamont is very gullible. He'll believe anything he wants to believe."[114] Baldwin told me the same thing:

> There was nothing to it. Pure fabrication—pure fabrication. Mr. Hays and Mr. Ernst went down to Washington to talk to Mr. Dies on several occasions, and one of them was in order to get us to testify. They never allowed us to testify. We never did testify before that Committee. And they finally issued a statement saying that there was no reason for us to testify—that we were not un-American—and we never did get a chance. That's all we went down for the yet Lamont persisted even when he was on the Board, in the suspicion

that the counsel had gone there to make a deal that they would not investigate the ACLU in return for our cooperation with them—ousting a Communist from the Board.[115]

There is no way to prove or disprove definitively either of the two accounts. Yet it appears that Baldwin, like his adversary Lamont, is being less than candid. Baldwin's version does not square with Dies's letter to Lamont. Baldwin claims that Ernst and Hays met with Dies on several occasions, but only to request a hearing. Yet Dies himself says he invited the two ACLU representatives (at least once) to discuss a united attack on the Communists. Obviously, Dies, who had been relentless in his criticism of the Union, expected that if the ACLU agreed to cooperate, the organization would demand something in return. Although it is clear that Dies ceased pursuing the Union, it is not certain why he chose to do so. Dies denies there was a deal. So does Baldwin. Lamont's conviction that there was a deal rests on Dies's statement to Harry Ward and the quickly started drive in the ACLU to adopt a purge resolution. In examining these events, it is doubtful that Lamont has given us the complete record.

In his remarks to Ward, Dies said his committee had found "in its reports there was not any evidence" that the ACLU was a Communist organization. He then said the Union had been dismissed "by unanimous report" of the committee. From this statement it is not clear whether HUAC found no evidence in its numerous reports on several organizations that the ACLU was a Communist front or whether HUAC had issued one report that absolved the Union. It is clear that Lamont chose to believe the latter interpretation. The difference is important because Lamont charged it was "strange and suspicious" that there was no report. Had he chosen the other interpretation, namely, that the Union had been found innocent of Communist affiliation as a result of a diffuse survey, his accusation of a deal between Dies and the ACLU would be seriously negated. Moreover, Lamont does not give sufficient consideration to other related events that draw a somewhat different picture of the conditions as they existed.

If Lamont's version is totally correct, it seems likely that the ACLU would not have continued to attack the Dies Committee. But the record shows that, if anything, the condemnation of HUAC was just beginning. While Dies was giving the Union a "clean bill of health," the ACLU was opposing an extension of HUAC for the second time and assisting the Communist party in Philadelphia to resist the activities of the committee.[116] The following year, 1940, brought renewed action against Dies. The ACLU issued a widely circulated pamphlet analyzing the record of the committee but its denunciations were not well accepted.[117] And again in 1941 the Union worked to curb Dies's work.[118] When, in the mid-1940s, the

House of Representatives re-created the old Dies committee in the form of a standing committee on un-Americanism, the ACLU called for its abolition.[119] Finally, in the late 1940s, the Union issued a policy that put it on record as opposing HUAC as "an unconstitutional abridgment of free speech."[120]

Lamont cites the Nazi-Soviet pact as affecting the direction of the ACLU, but he underestimates the degree to which the Union was jolted by the pact. For years many civil libertarians had placed their faith in the Soviet experiment. Now they had had enough. Baldwin was particularly upset: "I think it was the biggest shock of my life. I never was so shaken up by anything as I was by that pact—by the fact that those two powers had got together at the expense of the democracies. The Nazi-Soviet pact made you feel that suddenly the Communists were different people. They had abandoned us and got into bed with Hitler. It changed everything, of course."[121] In the first annual report of the 1940s the same sentiment was expressed: the pact was cited as the event that triggered the purge resolution.[122] The oddity of it all was that it took a formal pact between the Nazis and the Soviets before American civil libertarians realized the striking similarities between the two totalitarian regimes. I asked Baldwin why his organization could state in 1937 that Communists did not engage in repressive tactics and then, three years later, pass a resolution barring Communists from the governing boards of the Union. His answer: "Well, that was a very natural reaction to the Nazi-Soviet pact . . . the distinction between Communism and Fascism [was] no longer tenable. . . . Communists in the United States were Russian servants and they were behaving like good Russians, they were behaving as apologists for the Nazis. That's why we had the 1940 Resolution."[123]

Baldwin was not the only person who was wrenched out of his intellectual cradle as a result of the Nazi-Soviet nonagression pact; scores of other liberals experienced the same awakening. Granville Hicks quit the Communist party three weeks after the pact.[124] John Haynes Holmes gave a sermon shortly after the pact was announced, in which he stated:

> If we liberals were right on certain single aspects of the Russian Revolution, we were wrong, disgracefully wrong, on the question as a whole. We were wrong because, in our . . . vision of a new world springing from the womb of this Russian experiment, we permitted ourselves to condone wrongs that we knew must be wrongs. . . . We defended, or at least apologized for, evils in the case of Russia which horrified us wherever else they appeared, and by whomsoever else they were done.[125]

Speaking of liberals, John Kenneth Galbraith later rendered a similar judgment: "During the war years they had accepted the current picture of Stalin as an amiable and avuncular figure."[126]

There can be no doubt that the Nazi-Soviet pact did more than any other event to change the course of liberalism and the policies of the ACLU. Once the distinction between communism and fascism was lost, mainstream liberals, as well as others normally associated with the Left, took a more moderate stance toward capitalism and began to voice concern over national security interests. Some persons of the Left took to criticizing their colleagues who were still unprepared to reconsider their beliefs. Norman Thomas was one of them. Six-time presidential candidate of the Socialist party and ACLU Board member from the beginning, Thomas was open about his denunciations of ACLU staff members who clung to the "old" position on communism. Lamont has never forgiven Thomas for his "betrayal" and prefers to label him as a "double-faced" Tammany Hall-like politician who was "the most egotistical man" he ever encountered.[127] Lamont, of course, was then and still is, one of the arch-apologists for Soviet repressions. He was one of four hundred intellectuals who signed an open letter vigorously supporting the Soviet Union just prior to the Nazi-Soviet agreement.[128] In that letter the progressive-minded establishment accused the fascists and "their friends" of preventing "a united anti-agression front by sowing suspicion between the Soviet Union and other nations interested in maintaining peace." What proved to be the most ludicrous accusation of people like Thomas, Holmes, Dewey, and Hook was an exculpatory statement designed to disassociate the Communists from the Nazis: "With the aim of turning anti-fascist feeling against the Soviet Union they have encouraged the fantastic falsehood that the U.S.S.R. and the totalitarian states are basically alike." Others who signed the letter included Professor Max Lerner, ACLU fellow-traveler Mary Van Kleeck, and Maxwell S. Stewart, associate editor of the *Nation*.[129] Perhaps most embarrassing of all, was the letter's appearance in the same issue of the *Nation* that announced the Nazi-Soviet pact![130]

In 1939 John Dos Passos resigned from the National Committee of the ACLU because of Communist participation in the Union's affairs.[131] Baldwin tried to dissuade him without success: "We can hardly apply in our Board or membership the test of political or other values. . . . I don't see how we could adopt any such policy without doing violence to our fundamental principle."[132] Interestingly, Baldwin wrote this to Dos Passos on 4 December 1939, after the Nazi-Soviet pact had "shaken" him and after the alleged conspiracy meeting between Dies and Hays and Ernst! It adds another dimension to the whole affair, for if Baldwin was truly convinced after the Nazi-Soviet pact that Communists were "different people," why then did he resist Dos Passos's position? I mentioned to Baldwin what he had said to Dos Passos, and then asked him why the Union proceeded to heed his advice. Baldwin replied, "Well, I suppose looking back at it—I don't remember exactly the circumstances—that I would have said: While we don't ever elect anybody that we think is unsympathetic with our principles, if we have elected them we don't examine their views. Once we have made the mistake, why we've made the mistake that's all."[133] This statement will have to suffice for Baldwin's reasoning. But Lamont's position looks even less plausible in light of Baldwin's antipurge attitude after the so-called deal was made in Washington. If Baldwin had been coopted by Dies (he had to have been if the Union had been), then why did he not agree with Dos Passos that Communists were a menace to the future of the ACLU? To be sure, Baldwin did change his mind and supported the 1940 Resolution barring Communists from key positions in the Union. Nonetheless, Lamont fails to explain why Baldwin responded the way he did to Dos Passos.

My own reading of the events that led to the passage of the 1940 Resolution lies somewhere between Lamont's and Baldwin's. There is reason to believe that the Thomas-Holmes faction (for the purge resolution) was gaining momentum prior to the Nazi-Soviet pact. The August agreement appears to have been the final straw; those who were leaning toward a purge resolution now fell in line with the Thomas-Holmes group. The October meeting with Dies no doubt entailed a discussion about the activities of the Communists and their negative impact on the ACLU and other organizations. Whether a deal was made is pure guesswork. However, it is not unrealistic to think that Dies was probably satisfied with what he had heard from Hays and Ernst—so much so that he was convinced that the Union was not a Communist organization and could, therefore, be given an *earned* "clean bill of health." If this analysis is correct, then there was no single report on the Union that was issued by the committee. As for Baldwin's reaction to Dos Passos, it is conceivable that although Baldwin failed in his attempt to keep the author on the National Committee, he may have been persuaded by the force of Dos Passos's argument. This, at least, would account for Baldwin's change of mind and ultimate support for the 1940 Resolution.

Baldwin not only backed the 1940 Resolution but wrote it.[134] Morris Ernst had drafted a similar resolution the month before, in January.[135] The actual resolution reads as follows:

> While the American Civil Liberties Union does not make any test of opinion on political or economic questions a condition of membership, and makes no distinction in defending the right to hold and utter any opinions, the personnel of its governing committees and staff is properly subject to the test of consistency in the defense of civil liberties in all aspects and all places.
>
> That consistency is inevitably compromised by persons who champion civil liberties in the United States and yet who justify or tolerate the denial of civil

liberties by dictatorships abroad. Such a dual position in these days, when issues are far sharper and more profound, makes it desirable that the Civil Liberties Union makes its position unmistakably clear.

The Board of Directors and the National Committee of the American Civil Liberties Union, therefore, hold it inappropriate for any person to serve on the governing committees of the Union or on its staff, who is a member of any political organization which supports totalitarian dictatorship in any country, or who by his public declarations indicates his support of such a principle.

Within this category we include organizations in the United States supporting the totalitarian governments of the Soviet Union and of the Fascist and Nazi countries (such as the Communist Party, the German-American Bund and others); as well as native organizations with obvious anti-democratic objectives and practices.[136]

The resolution, passed as a policy position, promoted the ACLU's new image. Those who had worked for its passage now felt relieved. It was only a matter of time before the resolution would be invoked against Flynn. But the effort would not be without a struggle. Corliss Lamont and others provided a tenacious opposition. Lamont, who published the entire transcript of the "Trial of Elizabeth Gurley Flynn," declared the 1940 Resolution to be " a thinly disguised Loyalty Oath." He contends that this decision helped launch an era of witch-hunting culminating in McCarthyism.[137]

The Flynn "trial" began at 8:00 P.M. on 7 May 1940, at the City Club of New York on West 44th Street. When the hearing before the Board of Directors ended at 2:20 A.M. the next day, Flynn had been expelled from the body that tried her. She had been given an opportunity to resign but refused. The charges had originally been brought against her on 4 March 1940 by Dorothy Dunbar Bromley, a columnist for the Scripps-Howard newspapers. It was Baldwin who chose Bromley to submit the charges against Flynn; he thought it would be a good tactic to have a woman formally broach the issue.[138] Lamont believes that Baldwin did more than initiate the proceedings; he holds that Baldwin was "pulling strings behind the scenes in all the maneuverings that led to the hearing." Furthermore, Lamont maintains that "had [Baldwin] chosen to uphold without compromise the basic principles of the Civil Liberties Union, the Flynn trial would never have taken place. His responsibility for this unhappy event was greater than that of anyone else."[139] When I asked Baldwin if he had masterminded the ouster of Flynn, he said, "Of course not. It was done collectively, [tape inaudible] all you have to do is read the record. I didn't say a word."[140] Both Baldwin and his biographer Lamson are incorrect about this point. Baldwin did say a few things, but nothing of any substance.[141] I told him about this, and, after first denying that he said anything, he finally conceded that he had spoken.[142]

At the meeting, Lucille B. Milner, secretary, read the three charges against Flynn. The first and most important one was brought by Bromley; she argued that Flynn's membership in the Communist party disqualified her from retaining directorship on the board. The second charge was filed by author and playwright Elmer Rice; he contended that Flynn should be disqualified because of attacks she made on board members in the March 19 issue of *New Masses*. Roger William Riis, writer and publicist, followed with a similar charge. Flynn, he maintained, had made hostile comments against her colleagues in the *Daily Worker* two days before her other article appeared.[143]

Before she began her defense, Flynn drew the board's attention to a few pertinent facts. She stated categorically that she was a member of the Communist party.[144] She then mentioned the resignation of Dr. Harry F. Ward and a letter of protest from three National Committee members as signs of support for her. Ward had resigned as chairman of the Board of Directors on March 2 in response to the resolution of February 5, which, he argued, advanced the principle of guilt by association.[145] The letter of protest was written by Alexander Meiklejohn, Edward Parsons, and George West on March 21. They chastised the Union for departing from its original principles.[146]

Flynn's next move was to request the disqualification of four board members from serving on her jury. She wanted the three members who brought the charges, as well as Dr. Holmes, who had first asked for her resignation, removed from the body that was to decide her status. She did not succeed.[147]

In her objections to the first charge against her, Flynn raised the most polemical question of the entire affair: Was the 1940 Resolution a radical change from the principles upon which the ACLU was founded? Flynn and her supporters were certain that it was. Others maintained that nothing essential had been altered. In a statement released to the press on the resolution, the Union claimed that no fundamental policy change had occurred: "The present resolution merely states what has been always the unwritten policy of the Union in elections or appointments."[148] By taking this position, those who favored the resolution were confronting two additional problems. If the resolution was not a change of policy, then why had William Z. Foster and Anna Rochester been elected to the governing bodies of the Union in the 1920s when it was well known that they were members of the Communist party?[149] And why had Flynn been reelected to the board in 1939, two years after she had joined the Communist party?[150] I asked Mr. Baldwin to comment on these issues.

W.D.: In the first annual report back in 1920 it states that "there is no membership in the Union in the sense of committing those who join to any dogmatic statement of principles."[151] Doesn't the '40 Resolution represent a departure from this tradition?

R.B.:   Well, it was a matter of practice not a matter of statement of principles or an examination of views. We just didn't elect people like that. We didn't regard them as sympathetic. There was a time when some of our affiliates, which were not after all under control of the National Board, did do that. We had some people who were quiet fellow travelers. They wouldn't join the party but they were fellow travelers and they gave us a lot of trouble, because they took the Communist line as opposed to our line whenever there was a conflict.[152]

Baldwin does not like to be reminded that he, too, was a fellow traveler at one time. When Lamson declared that he had been a fellow traveler, he replied, "Yes, I suppose I was. I accepted the fact that civil liberties were not suitable for Russia, but I certainly didn't approve of the dictatorship."[153]

With regard to the other issues, the commentary by Baldwin speaks for itself.

W.D.:   Do you still hold that the 1940 Resolution was not a change in the Union policy?

R.B.:   It was not a change in the sense that we had ever elected to our Board or staff any Communists, any reactionary or Klansman or anybody who didn't believe in civil liberties. We always used that test. It had to be by your connections and associations—a supporter of civil liberties national causes—that's what the organization was for. And we did not conceive Communists to be supportive of civil liberties as we understood them. They supported them insofar as they served their purposes in the United States, but they would not go to the front for their enemies. They wouldn't even go to the front for Trotskyists! They even approved Trotskyists going to jail for their opinions. But we worked with them on other common fronts until that time—until the Nazi-Soviet pact. That made all the difference in the world, because of the fact that the two became indistinguishable.

W.D.:   But William Z. Foster and Anna Rochester were both members of the Communist Party—

R.B.:   Who?

W.D.:   William Z. Foster and Anna Rochester were members of the Communist Party and they were on the governing boards of the ACLU.

R.B.:   They became—they became members after they were elected just like Miss Flynn. And we rather diplomatically dropped Miss Rochester, and Mr. Foster fortunately resigned. He was elected, originally, long before the Communist Party was exposed—openly. When it was underground, we didn't know it. He was an organizer for the A.F. of L. when he was elected. And Miss Rochester, I think we didn't know she was a Communist—appeared to be so afterwards—and she was quietly dropped. Miss Flynn was expelled openly.

W.D.: But Miss Flynn was reelected to the Board of the ACLU—

R.B.: That's right! Well, that was a great blunder. That was a great mistake. We should have known better than that. And the reason we did was because she was one of the original organizers in 1920. And we had all known her so well and were so fond of her, that we just didn't have the heart to apply any such principle to her.[154]

Baldwin tries hard to persuade but ultimately fails. The resolution was written so that the ACLU could get rid of Flynn and thereby strengthen its public image. The Union's contention that the substance of the resolution had always been an unwritten policy is pure nonsense. On the contrary, as I pointed out to Baldwin, the ACLU had pledged to stand by a written declaration of principles that were the very antithesis of those contained in the resolution. Furthermore, the election of Foster and Rochester to the National Committee and the board, respectively, must be seen as violative of the "unwritten" policy. (According to Lamont, Foster was reelected three times *after* he became an open member of the Communist party in 1921. Rochester, says Lamont, was known as a Communist when she was elected to the board in 1928. See Lamont, *Freedom Is As Freedom Does*). As for Flynn herself, her reelection to the board after she joined the Communist party is demonstrative of the vacuity of the "unwritten" policy. That Baldwin and his friends did not "have the heart" to dump her earlier may be true. Nevertheless, it does little to add credibility to the argument that the decision of 5 February was not a change in policy.

Ironically, Baldwin's activities at the time of the 1940 Resolution may not have been consistent with the tenets of the policy that he wrote. Lamson reminded him that he chaired the Spanish Relief Campaign (a united front group) after the signing of the Nazi-Soviet pact.[155] When I asked Baldwin why he participated in united front actions as late as the 1940s, he replied, "I wasn't in any—well, this is the 1940 Resolution. After that, I wasn't in any United Front after that, no."[156] Yet when Lamson questioned him as to exactly when he was involved with the Spanish Relief Campaign, he confessed, "In the forties." Then he said, without further questioning, "I can't believe I was involved in a United Front that late, but I suppose I must have been."[157] Moreover, in the mid-1940s Baldwin gave a Town Hall of the Air speech in which he concluded that communism was not a menace to the American way of life. However, in fairness to Baldwin, he was referring to the threat (surely a remote one) that domestic communism posed.

Throughout the proceedings, Flynn's supporters came to her defense. Lamont, in particular, tried to swing votes in her favor. To demonstrate the political nature of the second and third charges, Lamont offered into evidence an article by Norman Thomas in the 16 December 1939 edition of the socialist *Call*. In that piece, Thomas criticized some members of the Civil Liberties Union. Lamont argued that Flynn's hostile remarks about her colleagues were no more extreme than those of Thomas.[158] Although the article was branded "highly improper" by a special subcommittee, nothing else came of the matter.

It was Flynn's strong devotion to the Soviet Union that angered her fellow board members most of all. Her detractors argued that it was impossible for one to divide one's loyalty between support for civil liberties in the United States and endorsement of public policy in the Soviet Union. Flynn's critics never found it necessary to prove that her activities were inconsistent with civil liberties; her allegiance to a totalitarian nation was enough. That was why Ward, Lamont, and A. F. Whitney protested that Flynn was a victim of "guilt by association." Whitney, who was both president of the Brotherhood of Railroad Trainmen and a member of the National Committee, wrote Baldwin that it was unjust to expel Flynn on such a trumped-up charge: "Simple justice and fair play would again suggest that Flynn was punished not because of what she said or did, but because she belonged to a certain group."[159] I asked Baldwin what proof there was at the trial that she herself departed from the principle of supporting civil liberties. His response and the subsequent exchange went as follows:

> R.B.: Well, she testified at the trial that she supported the Soviet Constitution. The Soviet Constitution was a one-party constitution. It denied all other parties any right to campaign, to exist. She was very proud of her support of the Soviet Constitution. It's in the trial record.

> W.D.: Again though, she was also enthusiastic about the Soviet Constitution prior to the 1940 Resolution when she was reelected.

> R.B.: I don't know. We didn't have any occasion to examine her views about it. She may have been.[160]

She may have been enthusiastic about the Soviet Constitution at the time of her reelection? There clearly is no doubt about it.

Each of the three charges was voted on separately prior to a final vote on expulsion. The first vote was the most important because it would help determine the outcome of the voting to follow and because of its central significance to the trial itself. When a deadlock occurred, Chairman Holmes broke the tie by voting against Flynn. She lost 10-9. Holmes did not have to vote again. Flynn lost on the second and third charges by a margin of 12-8. On the motion to expel her, the final tally was 11-8 in favor.

For Lamont, the trial and the role played by Holmes in breaking the tie were reminiscent of the ordeal of Joan of Arc: "The Reverend Holmes' action could not help but remind me of the leading role played by Bishop Pierre Cochin some 500 years previously in the heresy trial of Joan of Arc and her final burning at the stake."[161] The trial taught Lamont a lesson he would never forget: "It proved the greatest disillusionment to me and at the same time taught me that I had to be continually on my guard in the debased world of politics against the hypocrisy of some so-called liberals. I had been far too naive in my participation in public affairs. That is what the year 1940 taught me."[162]

Virtually everyone who was either a member of the ACLU at the time of the Flynn episode or who has written about it agrees that the action was taken to insure the survival of the organization. The Union had been tainted, seriously tainted, by charges of communism and disloyalty. If the organization was to survive—especially after the Nazi-Soviet accord—it had to do something to restore its credibility with liberals. The 1940 Resolution did just that. Lamont concedes that the Union did win "respectability" as a result of its decision.[163] Baldwin concurred:

> W.D.: Well, do you think that the 1940 Resolution was a compromise in the sense that it was necessary for the survival of the organization?
>
> R.B.: Yes, Yes.[164]

I asked Reitman to comment on the Flynn affair. His assessment is sensitive to the historical context in which it emerged, and is worth quoting at length:

> A.R.: No one knows exactly what would have happened if the Resolution never had passed, or if as a consequence, Elizabeth Gurley Flynn had not been expelled from the Board of Directors of the ACLU. The Union's position before the country as an impartial defender of the Bill of Rights might have remained unchanged and its work continued undisrupted. But, given the mood of the national revulsion against the German-Russian pact as abdication of principle, and the havoc created by Soviet supporters' takeover of organizations through antidemocratic methods, it is at least a fair assumption that the ACLU might not have withstood the battering attacks which an absolute stand would have provoked, or that it might have had its civil liberties directions altered. And what was essentially a small private organization might have sunk into oblivion.[165]

In the aftermath of the 1940 Resolution, the board tried to assuage the feelings of its affiliates, many of which reacted sharply to the entire affair.[166] Ward resigned and took over the chairmanship of the Communist-front organization known as the Civil Rights Congress.[167] Most of the other fellow travelers, including Van Kleeck, resigned from the ACLU within a year after the resolution.[168]

Apparently the tenets of the 1940 Resolution were to apply only to the ACLU. The Union scolded other organizations for barring or firing Communists from their ranks. Shortly after the Union disposed of Flynn, it began to criticize the firing of some 1,000 Works Progress Administration workers in New York City alleged to be "subversives." On 25 June 1940, the Union attacked the purge as indefensible "so long as they belonged to legal organizations functioning openly." The alleged radicals were members of the Communist party and the German-American Bund.[169] At approximately the same time, the Union was condemning the U.S. Civil Service Commission for barring from employment in the civil service members of the same two "subversive" organizations.[170] One year later, the ACLU held that teachers should be allowed to join any organization they chose, and opposed the dismissal of teachers in New York City on the ground of opinion or mere membership in the Communist party. Activities alone, argued the Union, should constitute "conduct unbecoming a teacher."[171] The Union admitted that it had a hard time trying to convince the public that while it was all right for it to exclude Communists, it was not all right for other organizations to do the same.[172] I asked Baldwin about this apparent anomaly.

W.D.: Well, let's see, why was it okay for the ACLU not to have Communists on its governing committees, but it was okay for labor unions to have them?

R.B.: Well, the labor unions threw them all out.

W.D.: But the ACLU did not object, in fact supported the right of Communists to be on the governing boards of labor unions.

R.B.: I would think so. We could support the right of—

W.D.: But not on the ACLU's governing unions.

R.B.: We're not a labor union. Labor unions are masters of their own elections. They can elect anybody they want to.

W.D.: But I don't quite understand it.

R.B.: A labor union is not a civil liberties organization which is committed to the Bill of Rights. It is committed to the welfare of workers. We are committed to a single proposition which is contrary to every Communist belief.[173]

But if mere membership in the Communist party was enough to prove that a person could not be dedicated to the cause of civil liberties, why was it not sufficient to show that a teacher who belonged to such a group could not objectively approach lessons in a civics class? And if Communists were servants of the USSR, how could a labor union function well, given the unnecessary discord? Evidently Communists adversely affect only civil liberties organizations.

World War II and Civil Liberties

Throughout the 1940s and the first half of the 1950s, the ACLU maneuvered to the right. So did liberalism. When the war began, Baldwin had already realized that liberals had been duped by the Communists: "Communists have been the most conspicuous promoters of the united front; but Socialists, peace organizations, civil liberties and pro-democratic middle-class movements have promoted them, too. . . . The liberals in the Communist-inspired united fronts should have learned from previous experience that their houses were built on the shifting sands of Soviet policy and were likely to collapse at any moment."[174] For the first time, Baldwin admitted the difficulty of reconciling liberty with collectivism.[175]

It was a difficult time for the Union. It was busy fending off criticism that it was a subversive organization, while at the same time it was trying to keep its affiliates in line with its new image. For example, on 27 October 1942, Baldwin wrote to J. Edgar Hoover expressing his concern about FBI perceptions of the ACLU: "I neglected to speak to you the other day of what is a relatively unimportant matter, but one which is occasionally annoying—and that is reports that some of your agents seem to have some notion that the Civil Liberties Union is a subversive organization and that connection with it justifies investigation."[176] Two days later Hoover replied: "I can assure you that there are no outstanding instructions from this bureau which would either directly or indirectly lead any Special Agent of this Bureau to assume that connection with the American Civil Liberties Union is presumptive indication of subversive activity and therefore necessitating an investigation upon the part of this Bureau." Hoover assured Baldwin that it was not annoying for him to consider such concerns, and that he regarded such inquiry as "not unimportant, but very vital."[177]

The problem with the affiliates was most troublesome in Chicago. Late in 1944 a factional dispute arose within the affiliate over the alleged partisan line (i.e. leftist) that some members were following. The national organization became involved when the Board of Directors, in January 1945, authorized the appointment of a committee of inquiry to examine the charges. A report was to be made within thirty days; until that time, no publicity was allowed.[178] Two months later, after the delegated Chicago members had still not prepared the report, the board unanimously adopted a resolution calling upon the Chicago Civil Liberties Committee to show cause before 31 March, explaining why it should not be disaffiliated. The committee was charged with circulating an article that was both untruthful and harmful to the Union.[179] On 10 April the Chicago Civil Liberties Committee decided to disaffiliate itself from the ACLU, claiming it could better conduct its work without the "restraints" of national affiliation.[180] When asked about this episode, Baldwin told me that he blamed the Chicago secretary, Ira Latimer, for recruiting partisan members. Latimer, he said, was "a very unstable character" who followed the Communist line.[181]

As the Nazis moved throughout Europe, most liberals, including those at the *New Republic*, came to see the necessity of American intervention; Stuart Chase and Charles Beard were notable exceptions.[182] The ACLU also approved of U.S. entrance into the war, but was divided on the question of pressing for civil liberties at home while the war was in progress. Although the Union pledged at that time not to waver on civil liberties,[183] the record of its activities is uneven. There were some in the Union who deplored defending fascists in wartime. Freda Kirchwey, editor of the *Nation*, resigned from the National Committee because of her disagreement with the policy of defending free speech for fascists while the United States was at war.[184] However, it was the sympathetic positions that the Union exhibited toward the United States war effort that best demonstrated its attitude.

The ACLU did not object to the suspension of habeas corpus in Hawaii following the attack on Pearl Harbor; it simply recommended that its constitutionality be decided in court.[185] The ACLU also balked on the issue of industrial strikes in wartime. In an important policy decision, the Union concluded that although the government should not use troops to break a strike for the benefit of an employer, it was permissible to take over defense plants for bona-fide reasons.[186] A letter to President Roosevelt conveyed the same message: government takeover of a defense plant in an emergency could be justified where it was necessary to assure protection.[187] On another occasion the Union declined to intervene when the government took over the entire railroad industry in the spring of 1948.[188] However, the Union challenged a New Jersey law that authorized the governor to seize public utilities whose operations were blocked by a strike. It was believed that the law affected both private and publicly owned utilities and, therefore, was without legal merit.[189]

The issues of anonymous literature and public disclosure received the ACLU's attention. Congress had been entertaining the possibility of requiring the publishers of literature to print their names and addresses. The Union opposed such a law because of its encroachment on the rights of minorities; however, it explicitly stated that it did not mean to include foreign agents or foreign propaganda. In fact, it advocated the banning of foreign propaganda from the United States if it did not bear "the name and address of *responsible* publishers" (emphasis added).[190] Later in the decade a similar problem arose over public disclosure. Truman's Committee on Civil Rights recommended that all agencies engaged in influencing public opinion should be required to disclose to public authorities the names of those who backed them. An ACLU referendum on this question showed that a decisive majority opposed general disclosure and favored continuing the policy of "acting on particular forms of disclosure in relation to specific privileges or dangers."[191]

Although the Union's stance on World War II was far more yielding than its stance in the previous war, it did not hesitate to challenge the government on many important civil liberties issues. Most notably, it opposed the first sedition prosecution since World War I, done under the authority of the Smith Act. In 1941, the Roosevelt administration, at the prodding of the Teamsters Union leadership, brought charges against twenty-nine members of the Trotskyite Socialist Workers party in Minneapolis. They were indicted and convicted for conspiring to advocate the overthrow of the government.[192] The ACLU raised funds and assisted the Civil Rights Defense Committee in its efforts to protect the rights of the Trotskyists and Teamsters.[193] There were many other issues, particularly free speech issues, on which the Union refused to sway from its principles.[194]

When Baldwin headed the Bureau for Conscientious Objectors in the NCLB, he was an avowed pacifist, and even spent a year in jail for refusing the draft. At that time, he notified his local draft board that he was "opposed to the use of force to accomplish any ends, however good."[195] Twenty years later, Baldwin switched his position. World War II was different—it required a different response.[196] Even before World War II Baldwin had given a speech approving of the participation of Americans in the Lincoln Brigade for the Loyalists, during the conflict in Spain: "Even as a pacifist I justified it on the ground that it was a police action in aid of a legal government."[197] From then on, each war would be appraised on its own merits. The necessity of American involvement in World War II, and the threat that Hitler, Mussolini, and Tojo posed, were unlike the conditions surrounding World War I. A blanket defense of conscientious objectors could not, therefore, be entertained. After Pearl Harbor, the board passed a policy stating that "no civil liberties issues are involved in the exercise of the government's right to exact civilian service if it is democratically organized and adequate protection is made for conscientious objectors."[198] This position was similar to the Union's policy on military conscription in wartime: If the rights of conscientious objectors were not abused, the principle of conscription in time of war was not a violation of civil liberties.[199] In essence, the Union remained sensitive to procedural safeguards but did not object to conscription. Baldwin told me that because alternative service was not provided for in World War I, the Union's position on conscription was more unyielding.[200] The circumstances of World War II, however, were equally decisive.

Pacifists who refused to register for the draft did not receive the support of the ACLU in World War II. In a statement published before registration day, the Union strongly advised all conscientious objectors to complete the forms and stipulate their position. In the more than two hundred cases that immediately surfaced, the Union declined to defend any of the nonregistrants.[201] Even in cases tried after the war, the ACLU refused counsel to nonregistrants, many of whom were Quakers, on the grounds that "no practical legal service can be rendered admitted violators of the law."[202] As for the rights of GIs, the Union held that enlisted men ought to have the same rights as officers in appearing before congressional committees and in addressing private communications to their congressmen and to the president.[203] In cases where troops were charged with disobeying military orders, however, the Union took a laissez-faire stand.[204] On the issue of peacetime compulsory military service, the board voted to sustain it but was quickly overridden in a referendum.[205] The final policy declared that "universal military service inevitably is an infringement upon the liberties of the individual."[206] This policy, which was issued in January 1945, was reaffirmed two years later.

When the war began, a number of sedition cases were brought to the attention of the ACLU. The Union's first response was to judge each case as it arose,[207] but as the number of cases grew, it became obvious that a policy decision had to be made. One case, in particular, motivated the Union to act. In July 1942 a seditious conspiracy case brought in the District of Columbia against twenty-eight people (later increased to thirty-three) from all over the country caught the attention of the Union and lawyers everywhere. The Union, via its Southern California branch, resisted the removal to Washington of two defendants who the ACLU was convinced had not taken part in the alleged crime.[208] This was the extent of the Union's participation. In a referendum vote that was unanimously adopted by the board, the ACLU declared that it would not participate in cases where there were grounds for believing that the defendant was cooperating with or acting on behalf of the enemy. In making such determinations, the Union pledged, it would consider such matters as "past activities, and associations, sources of financial support, relations with enemy agents, the particular words and conduct involved, and all other relevant factors for informed judgment."[209] The Union, of course, has the right to determine its own clients.

The ACLU of the 1940s did not object to government loyalty tests, but it did object to the government's method of declaring people disloyal on the basis of mere membership in a subversive organization.[210] The board appointed a special committee to study the question of loyalty tests. In the fall of 1947 the committee's draft report read: "No violation of civil liberties is involved in the government's dismissing or in refusing to employ persons who, because of divided national loyalties or otherwise, are found to be unfit."[211] Although the Union did not approve of the loyalty test that the government had adopted,[212] it did conclude in its policy that the government did have the right "to exact loyalty from employees and to dismiss those who are found to be unfit."[213] The Union specifically said that the government, in considering the applications of Communists for sensitive positions, could fairly deny them a job.[214] When I asked Baldwin why the ACLU did not oppose the idea of a loyalty oath, he said: "Well, you have to compromise in many cases, and principles are not pure—we would like to think so."[215] What is perhaps most troublesome about the Union's position on loyalty oaths at that time is that authors who have written about this issue have been less than candid. For example, William Preston, Jr., has maintained that "the loyalty-security issue was certainly enemy number one on the ACLU's most wanted list for the decade."[216] Such a statement hardly squares with Baldwin's account or, for that matter, the Union's record on the loyalty issue.

The internment of 120,000 Japanese Americans during World War II was the most flagrant denial of civil liberties to occur in the 1940s and one of the ugliest chapters in American history. One would think that such an unprecedented event would have ushered forth every bit of energy that the most respected civil liberties organization in the world could muster. Yet the evidence shows that the ACLU haltingly compromised on the issue. It was against the evacuations, as they were administered, but did not oppose the principle of establishing military zones and removing persons who threatened the national security. The Union opposed the president's proclamation of 19 February 1942, as well as the mass evacuations, the race discrimination involved, and the employment of the military in the campaign.[217] But even on the last score, the Union did not condemn the president's action: "Considering the speed with which so many people were moved from their homes and occupations, the military authorities did an extraordinary job with a minimum of complaint."[218] The official policy of the Union read as follows: "The government in our judgment has the constitutional right in the present war to establish military zones and to remove persons, either citizens or aliens, from such zones when their presence may endanger national security, even in the absence of a declaration of martial law."[219]

Naturally, this was one issue about which I had to ask Baldwin:

W.D.:   Why did the ACLU support the right of the government to establish military zones during World War II?

R.B.:   That is probably the most debatable question you could raise. It was a very tough one. And, of course, the government was all wrong about it. But the fears that were expressed of Japanese submarines off the Pacific Coast—and there had been one and after Pearl Harbor—was so profound on the Pacific Coast that you just could not tolerate it—they would not tolerate it—the presence of people they suspected of being sympathetic with the Japanese.[220]

Dwight MacDonald criticized the Union for not acting quickly enough. He also called the Union's response "feeble and confused."[221] When I asked Baldwin about the validity of this charge, he told me that the ACLU was receptive to the needs of the Japanese and employed many of them in its offices. He also offered the following explanation:

We had one hell of a time with the, one hell of a time with that issue all during war. I was going to Washington every week on seeing Mr. Dillon Myer who was head of the Japanese Relocation Agency and laboring with him over letting people out—not closing up the camp. They were trying to close up the camps too soon. People had been taken from them. They had no home. But they wanted to close it up anyway. They were too quick to start and too slow to end.[222]

As with so many other issues, the ACLU's stand on the internment of Japanese on the West Coast was similar to that of liberals in general. It should be remembered that the evacuations were carried out as a result of the orders delivered from President Roosevelt's desk; his claim to liberalism is undisputed. Earl Warren, who later became the most liberal chief justice of the United States in the twentieth century, oversaw the evacuations as attorney general in California. Walter Lippmann, another outstanding liberal, gave his support to the internment. So did such leftists as Carey McWilliams and Vito Marcantonio. The Communist party of the United States also defended Roosevelt's order.[223] The ACLU's Northern California branch—the most leftist of all the affiliates—backed Roosevelt's decision.[224] Even the leadership of the Nisei, the second-generation Japanese, supported the order.[225] One person who did not was J. Edgar Hoover.[226] Looking back on the internment, Baldwin agreed that it was a "terrible thing" but added: "But, well—perhaps in wartime it's very difficult to say that national security shouldn't be the first consideration. After all, you have to win a war. You can't lose it."[227]

As the war was winding down, the Union turned its attention to a new arena: international civil liberties. The ACLU created a Committee on International Civil Liberties to study the possible role that the Union could play in fostering respect for democratic principles abroad.[228] Before the war ended, it had already been involved in agitating for the resettlement of hundreds of thousands of political, racial, and religious refugees who had been uprooted by the war. Other concerns were the rights of native peoples in island colonies and military bases, as well as the political status of Puerto Rico.[229] When the war ended, the issue of international censorship was given top priority by the ACLU. Worldwide freedom of press, radio, motion pictures, and travel for journalists and students was urged by the Union. It sent a petition to the secretary of state demanding that these rights be embraced by the government.[230] It also intervened on behalf of American journalists who had been subject to exclusion or censorship in Yugoslavia, Eastern Europe, China, and parts of the British Empire. The confiscation and destruction of Nazi books and publications by American authorities in Germany was roundly scored by the Union.[231] On the issue of conscription, it supported a congressional resolution calling on the government to press for the universal abolition of conscription among nations.[232]

In the mid-forties, liberals everywhere supported Wendell Willkie's vision of "One World."[233] They settled for the United Nations. So did the ACLU. In fact, President Eisenhower's support for the United Nations prompted Baldwin to vote for him—the only Republican for whom he ever voted.[234] The Union was instrumental in drafting the International Bill of Rights for the United Nations, and participated in the Joint Committee of U.S. Agencies on Human Rights, a group recognized as an unofficial advisory body to the State Department.[235]

Perhaps nothing symbolized the Union's new image in the 1940s better than Baldwin's affinity with General Douglas MacArthur. On 9 January 1947, Baldwin received a letter from the War Department requesting his services in Japan and Korea. The Union was delighted. Baldwin, surprised and encouraged, wanted to make sure that he could function as a free agent and decided not to go unless MacArthur said it was all right for him to go at his own expense and on his own terms.[236] Baldwin's trip was financed by the Union (he later paid back all of the $731.16).[237] For three months he assisted the Japanese and Koreans in forming associations to promote and protect civil liberties, the Japanese Civil Liberties Union among them.[238] Baldwin was active in persuading MacArthur and, through him, the Congress to establish the "Bride's Act," which made it possible for the Japanese wives of American GIs to enter the United States despite the strictures of the Oriental Exclusion Act. The United Nations Association in Japan and the Japanese American Citizens League in Salt Lake City were both the creation of Baldwin.[239] It was not Baldwin's work that was unusual; it was for whom he was working and his sentiments toward MacArthur that stood in stark contrast to his behavior and attitude in the previous two decades.

When Baldwin returned to the United States, he wrote that MacArthur was one of the few men in public life who had "an almost missionary spirit" of promoting democracy: "On every point we discussed I found his at once sensitive to the highest concepts of our democratic ideals."[240] He later said that MacArthur "was one of the few generals who was ever a thoroughgoing pacifist."[241] Experiences such as this allowed Baldwin to boast that he had "boxed the compass" from Emma Goldman to Douglas MacArthur.[242] That he did—and always in style.

After the war liberals had fractionated into two distinct groups—those who supported Henry Wallace and those who followed the ADA. Historian Alonzo Hamby regards Vice-President Wallace as "the most visible and courageous advocate of the liberal cause" in the postwar period.[243] Hamby indentifies Wallace as a liberal who sang songs of praise to the Soviet Union, bragging about its achievements in "ethnic" and "educational" democracy. Wallace regarded Soviet entrance into the war as a defensive move, quite out of step with its professed concern for world peace. As long as the United States did not "double-cross" the USSR, lasting peace was possible.[244] Some liberals, including Wallace and Secretary of War Henry L. Stimson, recommended that we share some atomic knowledge with the Soviets. Freda Kirchwey of the *Nation* went further: "That Russia should be given full information about the atomic bomb is so evident that the question no longer seems arguable."[245] The *New Republic* offered its advice: "It is time that the United States awoke to the truth that nothing is gained for us vis-à-vis Russia by 'getting tough.'"[246]

Some liberals, like Dwight MacDonald, took an anti-Soviet stand without abandoning their hostility to capitalism, but they would have nothing to do with the anticommunist movement.[247] Others did. Trotskyite James Burnham relinquished all ties with the Left and went on to be one of the great conservatives of the United States. He came to recognize, as others did, that the repressions in the Soviet Union were the logical outgrowth of Marxism.[248] At *Partisan Review*, Marxist Philip Rahv and liberal William Phillips joined the conservative tide by reminding liberals that had it not been for the success of the United States in World War II they might not be around to criticize their country.[249] In England, Arthur Koestler and George Orwell voiced similar sentiments.[250] Orwell, in particular, had long had enough with leftists: "One sometimes gets the impression that the mere words 'Socialism' and 'Communism' draw towards them with magnetic force every fruit-juice drinker, nudist, sandal-wearer, sex-maniac, Quaker, 'Nature Cure' quack, pacifist and feminist in England."[251] It was the Americans for Democratic Action, however, that did more than any single organization to rid liberalism of association with Communists. The "vital center" had emerged when people like ADA Chairman Wilson Wyatt broke clean with the "Communist dupes" who followed Henry Wallace.[252]

The Cold War

An optimistic appraisal of the state of civil liberties characterized the four annual reports of the war years. During the first two years a remarkable lack of hysteria was evident.[253] This extraordinary record was repeated in the third year.[254] Aside from the zealous activities of the American Legion and the harassment of the Jehovah's Witnesses,[255] the Union noticed little in the way of repression. In the last year of U.S. involvement in the war, the Union exclaimed that there was an "almost complete absence of repression."[256] The overall record of civil liberties during World War II was far superior to that during World War I.[257] The relative constraint exercised by the federal government led the ACLU to praise the president's leadership (this despite what happened to the Japanese). When FDR died, the board noted his death "with deep grief" and hailed him for having brought "unmatched leadership both at home and abroad" to the cause of civil liberties.[258]

The gains in civil liberties continued in the year following the war,[259] but it was the last good year for some time to come. In the last few years of the decade, the national mood swung in a reactionary direction. As the fear of communism increased, the state of freedom in the land deteriorated. Hysteria,[260] confusion,[261] and insecurity[262] impaled the progress of the previous years. The Union charged that private pressure groups such as the American Legion and Catholic agencies, along with the behavior of local police forces, created an inauspicious climate for civil liberties.[263] As the decade came to a close, intolerance had soared to its highest level in the history of the ACLU.[264] The Cold War had begun.

The year 1950 was an historic one for the ACLU: Roger Baldwin stepped down from his position as executive director. The man who "was the ACLU" was replaced by Patrick Murphy Malin. Malin and his successors—Pemberton, Neier, and Glasser—exercised strong leadership but none of them would command the power and allegiance that Baldwin had. Baldwin was one of a kind—one of the most courageous and ambitious men in American history.

Alan Reitman, who knows more about the ACLU than anyone, has said that in 1950 the Union became a "grass-roots" organization.[265] It is true that the ACLU became decentralized after Baldwin's departure, but affiliate autonomy did not occur until sometime after 1950. In 1951, for example, the Union revised its constitution and by-laws. Previously, when a new policy was adopted or an old policy revised, the Board of Directors had to act in accordance with the results of a national referendum consisting of the combined vote of the National Committee, the affiliates, and the board itself.[266] This policy was now amended to read "except where it [the board] believes there are vitally important reasons for not doing so—which it shall explain to the Corporation members."[267] The interesting aspect about the new policy is the Union's characterization of its action. It declared the policy to be an adventure in "democratization and systematization." The "democratization" was supported, curiously enough, by an overwhelming majority of the National Committee and the boards of the local organizations.[268]

Corliss Lamont understands the board's decision as an abridgment of the power of the affiliates; it was a reaction to their recalcitrant behavior. Lamont argues, correctly, that ever since the 1940 Resolution, the affiliates had supported stronger policies on civil liberties than the national body. Given this condition, Lamont reasons, it was not surprising that "the Cold War group on the Board decided it was time to curb the power of the affiliates." He concludes, in his typically exaggerated way, that the new provisions in the by-laws meant that the Board of Directors constituted an "inner-dictatorship within the ACLU."[269] He blames the new executive director for exercising weak leadership: "Malin weakly went along with the right-wing Directors and cooperated with them in taking the Civil Liberties Union further along the road of compromise and political partisanship."[270]

The ACLU's swing to the right in the early 1950s was representative of many, though not most, liberals at that time. Most liberals had lost their infatuation with the USSR but could not bring themselves to side with the anticommunists. To be anticommunist has always been associated, in the liberal mind, with reactionary forces. Certainly Joseph McCarthy helped to sustain the liberals' belief but, with or without McCarthy, the idea was so impervious to reason that nothing could shake it. If the revelations of Whittaker Chambers could not rattle liberals, nothing could. Indeed, as William Barrett has argued, "the innocence of Alger Hiss virtually became a Liberal crusade in some quarters."[271] According to Barrett, Philip Rahv was struck by the fact that in the Hiss case, "a large segment of the American public—particularly on the Liberal side . . . were simply unwilling to believe that Communism existed as a continuing and organized conspiracy that meant the United States no good, and that this conspiracy had been able to penetrate the American Government."[272]

The attack on liberals in the 1950s came most prominently from *Partisan Review*, the leading anticommunist publication on the left,[273] and from *National Review* on the right. In 1955, William F. Buckley, Jr., founded *National Review* with the realization that ideas have consequences.[274] But perhaps the biggest stir in the liberal community was the 1952 piece that Irving Kristol wrote in *Commentary*. Kristol, another one-time leftist, moved to the right, challenging the liberals' assessment of communism. In the *Commentary* article he argued that, notwithstanding

McCarthy's demagoguery, the American people knew that McCarthy, like them, was anticommunist. The same could not be said of most liberals.[275] Kristol railed against Henry Steele Commager for perceiving communism as being on a continuous line with liberalism and democratic socialism.[276] He gave liberals no quarter:

> Did not the major segment of American liberalism, as a result of joining hands with the Communists in a Popular Front, go on record as denying the existence of Soviet concentration camps? Did it not give its blessing to the "liquidation" of millions of Soviet "kulaks"? Did it not apologize for the mass purges of 1936-38, and did it not solemnly approve the grotesque trials of the Old Bolsheviks? Did it not applaud the massacre of the non-Communist left by the GPU during the Spanish Civil War?[277]

Kristol's article was hailed by John Haynes Holmes, Ernest Angell, Norman Thomas, and others,[278] but it was critically received by most liberals. Alan F. Westin of the ACLU made the most direct response. He claimed that "we defend the civil liberties of Communists to preserve our own rights and to advance the national welfare."[279] To Westin, we jeopardized the rights of all Americans when we failed to defend the rights of Communists.[280] His position was in stark contrast to Kristol's: "So long as liberals agree with Senator McCarthy that the fate of Communism involves the fate of liberalism, and that we must choose between complete civil liberties for everyone and a disregard for civil liberties entirely, we shall make no progress except to chaos."[281] To this day, the liberal-conservative split on this issue has remained unshaken.

McCarthy's work and the atmosphere of fear that he cultivated prompted the Union to declare McCarthyism "the chief threat to our civil liberties on the inside." "Tyrannical Soviet Communism," the Union said, "[was] the chief threat to our civil liberties from the outside."[282] The internal threat of McCarthyism was evident throughout the country. In Washington, D.C., a former junior high school teacher, who was indentified as a Communist, was denied a license to practice piano tuning on the ground that he was "under Communist discipline." And while the Wisconsin legislature was considering a loyalty oath for liquor dealers, in Indiana professional wrestlers and boxers were swearing their allegiance to the United States.[283]

The Union heartily endorsed the censure of Senator McCarthy.[284] One of the main reasons that it wanted him censured was his unauthorized use of confidential information. The ACLU "welcomed" the following conclusion of the Watkins Committee: "The conduct of Senator McCarthy in inviting Federal employees to supply him with information, without expressly excluding therefrom classified documents, tends to create a disruption of the orderly and constitutional functioning of the executive and legislative branches of the Government, which tends to bring both into disrepute."[285] Although the ACLU opposed McCarthy and the House Un-American Activities Committee, it did not question the necessity and validity of the Senate Subcommittee on Internal Security. Nor did it oppose the Kefauver Committee on Interstate Crime.[286] That the Union could resist denouncing the existence of a governmental committee on subversives suggests how far it had come from the days of Sacco and Vanzetti.

McCarthyism carried over into the media arena in the 1950s. Politically controversial persons were blacklisted by the radio and television industry. Board member and writer Merle Miller conducted an inquiry into such practices and concluded that both anticommunists and Communists were guilty of blacklisting attempts. The Union issued a statement on the matter, declaring that the government was the only proper authority for designating positions where security risks might be present. Competency, the statement said, was the only legitimate test for employment in the radio and television industry.[287]

Despite the Union's criticism of McCarthy, Corliss Lamont maintains that the orgainization "sold out" on a number of important matters. His most serious charge against the Union in the 1950s concerns the three new policy statements that the board adopted after an alleged series of manipulatory schemes were completed. According to Lamont, after the new amendment to the by-laws regarding new or revised policies was passed, the board debated three new controversial policy positions back and forth until May 1953. The first statement was an attack on the Communist party. This policy, argues Lamont, enlisted the ACLU in the Cold War "by deflecting the organization from its proper business—concentration on civil liberties—and engaging it in the general battle against world communism." Lamont claims that the second statement violated the First Amendment and the United Nations Charter by leaving unchallenged congressional interrogation of American employees of the U.N. on matters of personal belief and association. "The third statement," writes Lamont, "put the ACLU on record as discarding, in effect, the Fifth Amendment's safeguard against self-incrimination when invoked by teachers, U.N. employees and others before Congressional investigating committees."[288]

What troubles Lamont most about the policies is that they were adopted in a manner not consistent with the principles of good civil libertarians. After the board passed the three statements, several directors, including Lamont, initiated a national referendum on the matter. The result: rejection of the three policies. At this time, Lamont maintains, Malin started maneuvering to overturn the vote. Malin began sending letters to the affiliates asking for further information about their votes. In the process, the Chicago affiliate changed its decision from negative to affirmative. Even though the deadline for the referendum had passed, Malin reported to the board that the poll had resulted in a victory for the affirmative. Lamont says that he objected, claiming that it was illegal to alter the ballot totals after the referendum had been concluded. In addition, he states that the Chicago switch was improper because it was based on "a hasty and incomplete telephone poll." Lamont registered his complaints, but to no avail: "The Board, however, in a jeering mood, voted me down.[289]

Lamont did not give up easily. He quickly phoned the chairman of the Chicago affiliate to protest the action. When Lamont's complaint was delivered at the next meeting of the Chicago group, the members decided that the second vote was unacceptable; they reverted to their original negative vote. Lamont relates what happened when Malin informed the Board that the negative vote had won the national referendum:

> But the Cold War group, tight-lipped in its fury, was determined to have its way; and shortly afterwards put through a Board resolution (the first one of its kind in the history of the ACLU) to override the referendum under cover of the new veto provision in the By-laws. The three controversial policy statements stood, adopted officially by the Union.[290]

Lamont's description of the internal machinations of the Union is not to be found, nor is it even implied, in the annual reports. The policies of which he speaks are noted[291] but there is no indication that their adoption was the result of a painful, if not internecine, struggle.

For Lamont, the battle was costly. In early November of 1953, he was nominated for a new three-year term as a member of the Board of Directors, but the chairman of the ACLU, Ernest Angell, along with Morris Ernst, Norman Thomas, and James Lawrence Fly, threatened to resign if his name appeared on the ballot.[292] On 16 November the board rescinded his renomination. Lamont was then confronted with an offer to accept a petition endorsing his renomination by twenty-five rank-and-file members. On November 30 he declined the offer and quit. Lamont's farewell statement was strong but not caustic. He pledged to continue working with the Union on such issues as censorship and race relations—wherever the Union had not faltered in its commitments to civil liberties. His relationship with the affiliates would remain close in spite of any discord with the national body. Predictably, Lamont did not pass up the opportunity to attack his opponents. He claimed that if he were to accept the latest offer to renominate him, it might well be "hopeless and a waste of time." He acknowledged that the disagreements were so far-reaching that little could be gained by his efforts. The board, Lamont said, had gotten itself involved in a "disastrous tangle over policy, finances, office administration, democratic procedures and illegal By-laws." Lamont pressed further by concluding that if he were renominated now, "the same high-handed group that forced the withdrawal of my Board nomination would in all probability renew the controversy and create a terrible furor which would again plunge this organization into bitter dissension."[293] Whatever one thinks of Lamont, one cannot say that he does not speak his mind.

The three polemical policy statements that engendered the debate must now be considered. The first was an attack on the Communist party. Actually, there had been several assaults on the party. For example, on St. Patrick's Day, 1953, Merlyn Pitzele made the following motion before the board:

> The Communist Party in the United States is an organization operating conspiratorially in the service of a foreign government and is a real danger to civil liberties. An organization of this character can obviously not be simply an organization of "advocates" and "teachers."[294]

Mrs. Bromley offered an amendment to Pitzele's motion—"the act of membership in such an organization does not automatically involve the support of a conspiracy"—but it was defeated. It is ironic to note that Bromley—the very person who brought the guilt-by-association charge against Flynn thirteen years earlier—would try, albeit unsuccessfully, to expunge such a provision from a related board policy. Pitzele's motion was put to a vote: it resulted in a tie, and was then delivered to a special committee for modification and future consideration.[295]

On 15 March 1954, the Union once again assumed the offense and condemned the Communist party. The board held that "it is actually an international conspiracy to seize power—political, social, economic—wherever it can." The Union added that the party rejects, in theory, "all the concepts of civil liberties which the ACLU exists to defend and in practice it crushes every assertion of individual dignity and freedom which may conflict with the Party's commands." And in a move to demonstrate the social (as well as political) distance between the Union and the Communist party, the ACLU asserted: "Like all patriotic citizens the Board of Directors of the ACLU expects the government diligently to seek out and punish lawbreakers, especially those guilty of treasonable acts against our country; and to provide for the integrity of federal employment."[296]

Had these very statements been submitted for approval to the board during its first era, they would have been voted down resoundingly; the authors would no doubt have been lambasted for Red-baiting. But this was a different era—the era of expediency.

The attack on the Communist party, which the annual report lists, was the product of a tripartite committee of representatives from the affiliates, the National Committee, and the National Board of Directors. The committee had this to say about the Communist party: "It is both a political agitational movement and a part of the Soviet conspiracy. Insofar as it is the first, its members have all the rights of members of other parties; to the extent that it is the second, its members may in some particulars be restricted by law."[297] With this policy statement, the Union reaffirmed its opposition to allowing Communists on the governing boards of its organizations. Lest someone doubt the ACLU's sincerity in this regard, the Union repeated the same policy on three other occasions—all falling within a few years of each other.[298]

The second policy statement that irked Lamont concerned American employees of the U.N. Lamont claims that the Union's position was to leave unchallenged congressional interrogation into the personal beliefs and associations of these workers. Lamont has extended himself once again. The Union was careful to qualify its position: "[The ACLU] opposes inquiry, by the United States or any other member state, into the beliefs or associations of its nationals employed by the United Nations, except in connection with possible subversive activities."[299]

The third policy statement that infuriated Lamont involved the Union's position on Fifth Amendment protections. He claimed that the Union failed to recognize the safeguard against self-incrimination when invoked by U.N. employees and others before congressional committees. What the ACLU actually said was that although it would oppose any employment penalty based solely on the claim of the privilege, it would not oppose such penalty "if the matter under investigation involves possible unfitness for a particular employment."[300] Given the historical context in which this policy emerged, it is fair to say that the Union's reservations were based on a fear of communism.

One does not have to repair to the writings of Lamont to realize that the ACLU practiced organizational apostasy in the 1950s. In 1951 it went so far as to credit national security as the foundation upon which civil liberties were grounded. In the same year it exhorted the government to "do its utmost to prevent or punish treasonable and revolutionary acts."[301] On many issues, the Union's position had traveled to the right. For example, the ACLU's tolerance for sacrificing civil liberties policies when threats to national security appeared imminent marked many of its policies in the 1950s. In the previous decade, it had found loyalty tests to be constitutional, providing certain standards were met. Now it was prepared to accept the need for government security programs. The Union wanted everyone to know what it meant when it decided to support the government's contention that something stronger than a loyalty test was needed. Therefore, it formulated its own definition of what constitutes a security program: "*A security program* is aimed at locating and removing those whose presence (through disloyalty *or otherwise*), may involve an actual risk to the country's security."[302] That the Union thought it proper to accent "or otherwise" is indicative of how far it had departed from its radical antigovernment position of the 1920s and 1930s. Amazingly, the ACLU chose to adopt an ambiguous policy on such a delicate issue. The inclusiveness of its position removes any doubt as to what its objective entailed: the ACLU was enlisting in the war on communism.

The Union's policy on security programs applied to "sensitive" positions, i.e. jobs that closely affect military or international affairs. It contended that persons in such positions ought to be subject to "governmental checkups."[303] Although periodic reviews of "sensitive" positions were encouraged as a means of limiting them to the smallest number that was acceptable, the ACLU made clear its wish that however many positions were under consideration, the number should be compatible with national security interests. Also, it recommended that administrative measures be designed to "minimize access to security materials by those for whose work they are not essential."[304] The ACLU specifically applied its policy to Communists who worked on sensitive programs. It said that "no Communist *or Communist sympathizer* should be connected with the atomic bomb or other atomic weapons" (emphasis added).[305] Such a policy would have had the effect of barring many a liberal (certainly Lamont) from working on the bomb.

In the 1950s the ACLU reversed its position on teachers' rights. Back in the forties, the board had backed the Committee on Academic Freedom's assertion that teachers should not be dismissed for "mere opinions or mere membership alone."[306] It had also argued that Communists and fascists had as much right to teach as those who did not share their political ideology, providing indoctrination was not being conducted in lieu of teaching.[307] But in the early 1950s, the Union held that while it was permissible for teachers to present their own opinions, it was not permissible if the opinions were derived from a source that compromised teachers' commitment to a search for unbiased truth: "Commitments of any kind which interfere with such pursuit are incompatible with the objectives of academic freedom."[308] Although only a minority of liberals felt that membership in the Communist party alone was sufficient grounds to bar a teacher from teaching,[309] the ACLU thought otherwise:

> When a teacher surrenders his independence of judgment by affiliation with any totalitarian group or party, Ku Klux Klan, Fascist or Communist, which imposes dictatorial orders, he flouts that liberty of the individual conscience which the ACLU is organized to protect and betrays the principle on which sound education and the very preservation of democracy depend. School

authorities clearly have a right and duty to guard against the employment of such teachers especially at the grade school level.[310]

Back in the 1940s the Union had taken a referendum of the board and National Committee on whether compulsory public disclosure of lobbying groups should be permitted. A decisive majority had opposed general disclosure (allowing for certain grave considerations).[311] However, the contributing members of the Union had voted 609-194 in favor of compulsory disclosure.[312] The lack of unanimity on this issue helps explain its tentative approach to the subject in the 1950s.

In 1950 the House Select Committee on Lobbying Activities subpoenaed Edward A. Rumley, an official of the Committee for Constitutional Government. The congressional committee demanded that he produce the name and address of each person who had given his committee $500 or more in the past three and a half years, along with the date, amount, and purpose of each payment. Rumley refused to provide the information, holding that compulsory disclosure of the names of purchasers of books was a violation of the First Amendment.[313] The Union balked at participating in his defense, and decided not to enter the case; no civil liberties violation had occurred.[314] The Supreme Court, however, ruled unanimously (7-0) that Rumley's claim for protection was valid. In the spring of 1953 Justice Frankfurter wrote that a sensitive constitutional issue would arise if the investigating committee was allowed to inquire as to private persons to whom Rumley sold books.[315] The ACLU's noninterventionist position in this case illustrates how weakly it opposed compulsory public disclosure of agencies that attempted to influence government decisions.

In 1950 the new executive director, Patrick Murphy Malin, noted that events in Korea had raised the specter of World War III. He cautioned against too hasty a reaction: "One of the most serious threatened costs is the curbing of individual freedom in the name of national security."[316] In its policies regarding the Korean war, the Union continued to oppose universal military training while accepting the need for a draft: "The grim facts of our troubled times have compelled the Union to recognize the imperative claim imposed upon us all by the necessity to maintain our national security." The Union maintained that "the most efficient way to provide military forces is by means of conscription and the assignment of men through Selective Service."[317] This was not a new policy but it was worded more positively. However, the Union's policy on those who instruct inductees not to register with their draft boards was a new policy. In World War II the ACLU declined to defend those who refused to register with their local draft boards. In the Korean conflict, the Union refused to defend those who merely advocated noncompliance. The Civil Liberties Union insisted that "it has never intervened in any of the prosecutions for advising violation of the draft law."[318] That may be so, but the annual reports never mention this before the mid-1950s. At any rate, the Union refused to defend Mrs. Manuel Miller of Bethel, Vermont, for advocating abstention from registering for the draft. The ACLU not only declined to intervene in Miller's behalf but went one step further by declaring that its decision was based "on the ground that counseling non-registration was a direct incitement to an illegal act."[319]

The Cold War clearly had an impact on the immigration and naturalization policies of the ACLU. But on deportation, the Union held its ground. Its policy was anathema to the provision of the McCarran Internal Security Act of 1950 that called for the deportation of all persons who are or ever were members of the Communist party.[320] The Union held that past or present membership in any totalitarian party, whether communist, fascist, or Falangist, was not grounds for deportation in most instances. At the very least, such organizations should be classified by a judicial body to be a criminal conspiracy. The ACLU declared that "to deport for mere membership in an organization is to adopt the principle of guilt by association, which is an unnecessary and undesirable policy in this situation."[321] (Apparently, the Union did not feel it was guilty of violating this principle within its own organization.) This policy was not a new one; a similar one can be found in its first annual report.[322]

On immigration, the ACLU issued a policy that departs from its original one: "The ACLU will not oppose the refusal of permanent immigrant status to present members of the Communist, Fascist, Falangist, or other totalitarian parties."[323] The Union defended its policy by reminding us that permanent immigration must be selective due to the number of persons who may enter the United States each year. Therefore, it reasoned that "it is not unjustifiable to exclude members of these organizations, since they are dedicated to the overthrow of democratic government."[324] This policy was in sharp contradistinction to its original one: "No person should be refused admission to the United States on the ground of holding objectionable opinions."[325]

The Union's policy on naturalization also reversed its policy of 1920. At that time, the ACLU took an absolutist position: "Citizenship papers should not be refused to any alien because of the expression of radical views, or activities in the cause of labor."[326] Now the union felt that its earlier language was too strong: "The Union will not oppose the denial of citizenship to persons who are members of the Communist, Fascist, Falangist, or any other totalitarian party at the time they apply for naturalization." The ACLU added that such persons could not be trusted to abide by the Constitution, as required by the oath of allegiance.[327]

The Union's policy on passports engendered considerable debate. The original 1920 policy held that no one should be denied a passport for mere membership in a radical group or for opinions that were thought subversive.[328] But in 1952 the ACLU altered its position: those who might endanger the safety of the nation could be restricted in their travel.[329] Then, in another new policy, the restrictive sanctions on subversives was dropped; Secretary of State John Foster Dulles was exercising too much discretionary authority.[330] At the same time, however, the Union declared that a passport could be denied if the United States was at war with the country in question. Also, if the citizen was under any legal obligation to remain here by reason of criminal or civil process, then a passport could be denied.

Midway through the decade, the Union noted that the American people were reacting against the accumulation of protective laws and regulations.[331] A new interest in the meaning of the Bill of Rights was emerging. The Union, of course, applauded this development. It followed the turn of events by commissioning journalist Allen Raymond to make a study. His report, "The People's Right to Know," approved by the Union, concluded that there was a trend toward ever-increasing secrecy within the federal executive branch. The Truman and Eisenhower administrations were singled out as the culprits.[332] But just when a more relaxing climate was being nurtured, the Soviet Union launched its sputniks. The ACLU was once again concerned about the possibility of war: "The security of the United States, and the peace and freedom of mankind, are in much greater danger internationally than they were a year ago." Malin, speaking for the Union, criticized a report issued by the Commission on Government Security in June 1957 for recommending "a multiplication of negative rules and mechanisms—in basic neglect of the old Notre Dame football axiom that the best defense is a good offense!" Referring to 1957 as the "portentous year of the sputnik," Malin added that only "the blindest" would not recognize the need for the nation to employ "a host of the most competent citizens the country possesses" in "all parts and at all levels of our government."[333]

As the decade progressed the Union slowly relaxed its position on loyalty tests and security programs. In testimony before a subcommittee of the Senate Committee on Government Operations in the spring of 1955, Ernest Angell, chairman of the Union's Board of Directors, criticized many of the procedures of the security program. He called for more exacting criteria and a more impartial review board but did not challenge the need for a security program.[334] In June 1957 the Union moved to strike the "confidential" category in the classification of documents. It supported, in a nonpolicy statement, many of the findings of the Loyd Wright Commission on the government's security program, and approved the commission's recommendation that the internal security system should not reach all persons who have access to defense plans.[335] The Union's sentiments were significantly different from its earlier decision not to oppose such provisions.[336] In June 1958, one year after the Wright Commission report, a special ACLU committee recommended the abolishment of an overall loyalty program. The Board of Directors adopted the statement as policy.[337]

If the Union was moving toward a strong defense of civil liberties as the decade closed, it was against the background of an inconsistent and often poor record of supporting the Bill of Rights. Aryeh Neier once admitted that "it was tough in the 50s to defend Communists and we ran away."[338] Nonetheless, the ACLU continued its opposition to the Smith Act of 1940. Although the courts had upheld the legality of the act, which made it illegal to advocate the violent overthrow of the government, the Union felt that the law was both "unconstitutional and unwise." However, it was not until the board meeting of 3 April 1950 that the ACLU formally opposed the Smith Act. On 23 June 1951, the Union issued its strongest statement condemning the sedition bill. At that board meeting, the Union maintained that the distinction between "discussion" and "advocacy" was not sufficiently clear to warrant punishment for "advocating" revolution. Furthermore, the Union argued that the clear-and-present-danger rule should not be misconstrued as to mean clear and probable danger.[339] Although the act was aimed at internal threats, its real target was the Communist party; as the Union indicated, party members were under the authority of the Soviet Union. Therefore, the act was passed as a concern for the national defense. The inconsistencies of the Union's performance were exemplified by its refusal to come to the aid of the International Workers Order (IWO). This organization, which had 160,000 members and assets of more than $6,000,000, was ordered by a New York court to disband because it was "a political front for a revolutionary group." The Union did not support the IWO when it appealed the decision because "it found no civil liberties issue."[340]

The ACLU's record in the 1940s and 1950s shows why it can accurately be dubbed the "era of expediency." The Union backed a government takeover of defense plants in time of war; the unbridled expression of the workers to strike was not recognized in this instance. It supported the existence of a loyalty oath. It set limits on free speech by ascribing to a "clear-and-present-danger" position. It supported the Hatch Act. Internally, the board ruled that it had the exclusive power to rule on vitally important issues without consultation with the affiliates. It ruled against defending the right of teachers to teach, especially at the grade school level, if they were affiliated with a totalitarian association. It would not okay the advising of nonregistration for GI candidates.

In the 1940s the ACLU passed the 1940 Resolution. It supported the government takeover of defense plants in time of war. It adopted a sedition policy that put it on record for refusing aid to those who cooperated with or worked for the enemy. It did not argue against a loyalty test. Originally, it supported peacetime military service. It found civilian service in wartime to be constitutionally sound. Military conscription was not opposed during war. The ACLU did not help those who refused to register with their local draft board. Military zones were unopposed. It formally opposed totalitarian political and economic systems.

In the 1950s it was much the same. The affiliates had their power curbed because of their insistence upon a nonexpedient line. An anticommunist policy was passed. The Union did not oppose a security program. It found no difficulty with the government's investigating the lives of those who worked in private defense industries. It opposed Communists who ran for office in labor unions. Teachers who belonged to totalitarian groups could have their rights abridged. Pacifists, the Union claimed, did not have the right to refuse to partake in civil defense drills. Advising nonregistration for the draft was taboo. Its last three restrictive policies were aimed at screening out subversives; its policies on immigration, naturalization and passports were designed to weaken the Communist base.

The pattern of expediency that emerges from the evidence (especially when contrasted with the Union's record in its era of emergence) reflects the operative goal of the ACLU in its second era: organizational survival. The only other alternative—to stand fast on its principles—did not recommend itself, primarily because of the near-certain adverse consequences that would have arisen from such an unrealistic decision. The elasticity of the Union's concern for protecting national security during this era highlights its unstated goal of organizational survival. The two major causes of the ACLU's change in value patterns emanated from its external environment: the effects of the Nazi-Soviet pact and McCarthyism.

For Lamont, at least three-fourths of the Union's second era was characterized by expediency:

> From 1940 to 1955 the Civil Liberties Union compromised on many basic issues and often took an apologetic attitude in defending the Bill of Rights. It watered down its criticisms of the House Committee on Un-American Activities, adopted a weak position on the Government's loyalty-security program, boasted of its close and friendly relations with the FBI, approved the Internal Security Acts exclusion of Communists and Fascists as immigrants to the United States, and worst of all, refused at any time to denounce the compilation and use of the U.S. Attorney General's list of subversive organizations.[341]

Lamont's last charge, that the Union flatly refused to denounce the attorney general's list, is an exaggeration. While it did not challenge the compilation of the list, it did raise procedural objections by demanding a fair hearing for all the "subversive" organizations listed. It even filed a brief in one case before a Circuit Court of Appeals requesting a hearing for an organization that challenged the attorney general's characterization.[342]

The ACLU-FBI Connection

What caused the ACLU to follow an expedient course? Its disillusionment with the Soviet Union? The Cold War? McCarthyism? Yes, all three episodes acted as causal agents in determining the Union's performance in the 1950s. But there was one more episode that heretofore has not been mentioned: The relationship between the ACLU and the Federal Bureau of Investigation. For about seven years in the 1950s the ACLU courted the FBI by supplying the bureau with information about itself, its activities, and some of its members.[343] When I read about this in the *New York Times* in the summer of 1977, I was able to understand more clearly the etiology of the Union's behavior in the 1950s. An analysis of this episode will uncover the Union's motives. It will also raise some questions surrounding the ACLU's behavior once it learned of the information.

On 3 August 1977 (the day before the *Times* story broke), Norman Dorsen, chairman, and Aryeh Neier, executive director, issued an official statement on the ACLU-FBI connection. The ACLU had obtained approximately 10,000 documents on the ACLU for the period 1943-76 from the FBI's central office files. The material, which was made available upon a request under the Freedom of Information Act (FOIA), was the second set of documents on this matter; the ACLU had previously obtained and released to the press the FBI files for the period 1920-43. In the later block of documents, the files show that during the McCarthy era, certain ACLU officials maintained an ongoing relationship with the FBI by providing and obtaining "information about the political beliefs or affiliations of other ACLU members and officials, particularly those who were thought to be Communists."[344] Most of the contacts were made between 1953 and 1959.[345]

The materials that certain ACLU officials gave the FBI included the kind of information that any researcher could have found, as well as inside information about the organization. Minutes of the meetings of various state affiliates, drafts of position papers, memoranda, lists of officers, and gossip about internal feuds were all supplied to the FBI.[346] Specific information about the FBI files was offered by Neier in a piece that he wrote for the ACLU-sponsored publication, *Civil Liberties Review.* On the basis of the information, Neier charged five key officers of the ACLU with maintaining questionable contacts with the FBI.

The most famous officer of the ACLU who established an ongoing relationship with the FBI was the late Morris Ernst. Ernst had at one time successfully defended James Joyce's *Ulysses,* which the Customs Service was trying to ban as obscene.[347] Ernst cultivated a close relationship with J. Edgar Hoover by passing bits of information about the ACLU to him. Neier claims that the few ACLU documents that Ernst gave the FBI showed him speaking out in the interests of the bureau when an internal dispute arose over the FBI.[348]

Neier was far more upset with Irving Ferman than with Ernst. Ferman was the Union's Washington officer between 1952 and 1959, and regularly provided the FBI with information on people within the Union. For example, he passed on to his friend Louis B. Nichols, assistant director and number-three man in the bureau, minutes of the Massachusetts Civil Liberties Union that contained information about the Union's plan to attack the Smith Act. In one of the ACLU documents that Ferman passed on to the bureau, he went so far as to say that "there is no question in my mind but this is a product of Communist coercion."[349]

Herbert Monte Levy, staff counsel for the ACLU from 1949 to 1955, also maintained regular contact with the FBI. He was concerned, as was Executive Director Patrick Malin, about the activities of the local affiliates. Both men requested the assistance of the FBI in determining whether or not there were Communists on the boards of some state affiliates.[350]

The fifth officer who dealt with the FBI was John de J. Pemberton, Jr., the executive director who succeeded Malin. He did not establish an incestuous relationship with the FBI, but he did ask William C. Sullivan, assistant director of the Bureau, in 1964 (after the McCarthy era) for "public source" information on a suspected Communist in the Georgia CLU. According to his successor, Neier, this was Pemberton's only questionable contact with the FBI.[351]

The most revealing aspect of Neier's brief article was not the information on the ACLU-FBI connection (he added little to the original *Times* story) but, rather, his attempt to personalize the blame: We are expected to believe that only five men participated in, and knew about, the civil liberties transgressions of the fifties. "The Board of Directors seem to have known nothing about the exchange of information with the FBI."[352] This statement of Neier's appeared in the 1977 year-end issue of *Civil Liberties Review.* There is good reason to believe that when Neier wrote this, he knew it was not true. Two weeks after the *Times* story broke, one of the members of the Board of Directors in the early 1950s publicly announced that the entire board knew of the ACLU-FBI transactions. Corliss Lamont posted his remarks in a letter to the *New York Times*. Lamont relates the comments of the then-executive director of the ACLU, Patrick Malin, which he purportedly made to a full meeting of the board: "I was down in Washington a couple of days ago and dropped in on J. Edgar Hoover at the FBI. I asked him whether Corliss Lamont was a member of the Communist Party, and he said, 'No.'" Lamont adds that he complained about Malin's conduct but "no other member of the Board present raised the slightest objection."[353]

Lamont was not the only board member to argue that all of the top brass at the time knew about the role of the FBI. Herbert Monte Levy, one of the accused, answered Neier's article in a letter to the ACLU-sponsored magazine: "Pat Malin and I were officers of the ACLU, but at all times subject to and carrying out board policy. The board of directors knew that selected FBI contacts were made by its executive personnel to help achieve ACLU objectives, as former Board member Corliss Lamont confirmed in a letter written to the New York *Times* last August."[354]

One could argue that the charges of Lamont and Levy were bogus and opportunistic. But the evidence would not support such a claim. Lamont's incident of the ACLU-FBI connection was no revelation; he had made the same charge ten years earlier. Commenting on the effects of the 1940 Resolution, Lamont wrote: "One result in the Civil Liberties Union itself was that its National Office checked with J. Edgar Hoover as to whether one individual or another was a member of the Communist Party."[355]

Given this evidence, it would be difficult to believe that the officers of the ACLU in 1977 could have been surprised when they "learned" about the questionable behavior of the Union in the 1950s from the FBI documents. Even a cursory examination of the annual reports and board minutes of the 1950s would have shown the acquiescent role of the Union toward government authorities. In the early 1950s the board reaffirmed "the long-understood policy of complete disclosure of any information about the Union requested by a governmental body."[356] And when it was brought before the board that the FBI was gathering information about defense attorneys in unpopular cases, Ernst told his colleagues that it was part of the proper FBI practice of reporting everything and evaluating nothing.[357] One more curious note: During the years 1953 to 1959—the very years when the now embarrassing contacts were made—the ACLU advertised on the last page of its annual reports for those years its qualifications for membership. It read "The ACLU needs and welcomes the support of all those—and only those—whose devotion to civil liberties is not qualified by adherence to Communist, Fascist, KKK, or other totalitarian doctrine."[358]

There is some question as to what happened between the time the ACLU received the FBI documents and the appearance of the *Times* story. The *Times* said that 10,000 pages of material had been released to the ACLU "in recent months"[359]—meaning the few months preceding August 1977. On the day of the *Times* piece, Neier issued a memo to the Board of Directors, the affiliates, and the National Advisory Council stating that the ACLU is "in the process of obtaining" the FBI files. He did not say when the ACLU received the documents.[360] But in the article he wrote for *Civil Liberties Review*, he said that the Union obtained the documents in July 1977.[361] Oddly enough, in an introductory statement to Neier's article, an editor states that the Union received the documents in June 1977.[362] What difference does it make whether the ACLU received the FBI documents in June or July or "in recent months?" It makes a big difference: 10,000 pages of documents are a lot of pages to analyze. If, as Neier says, the ACLU received them in July (the *Times* story appeared on 4 August), then either the ACLU had some pretty fast readers or only a cursory search of the material had been conducted. And what of Anthony Marro of the *New York Times*? Did he read all 10,000 pages, or did he simply report what someone in the ACLU said was in the documents? If an ACLU source acted as the sole gatekeeper, one can only conclude that the documents may contain additional information on the esoteric performance of the Union in the 1950s. It is instructive to note also that once the fourteen members of the Executive Committee learned of the FBI files, they did not share this information with the Board of Directors, the affiliates, or the National Advisory Council. Neier's rationale for this decision included the need to preserve privacy and insure fairness for those who were mentioned.[363] Therefore, most of the contributing members to ACLU policy learned of the FBI files the same day as everyone else.

Predictably, when the news hit the front page of the *Times*, ACLU activists were aghast. Neier and Dorson labeled the contacts "inexcusable and destructive of civil liberties principles."[364] Edward J. Ennis, who was a general counsel to the ACLU at the time, said that the information "came as a surprise to me," and claimed that such action had never been endorsed by the Board of Directors.[365] Ennis's comment, which was contradicted by Lamont and Levy, was not the most defensive reaction to the news. Board member George Slaff declared: "This wasn't the organization, it was a couple of bad apples, a couple of individuals."[366] Once again, an attempt was made to personalize the blame and exculpate the organization. As organizational responses go, there is nothing unusual about such a position. What is noteworthy is that this is not a senior member of the Pentagon or General Motors offering the "bad apples" thesis, but a high-ranking official in the nation's leading civil liberties organization.

Nearly a year after the ACLU received the documents, I asked the national office if I could see them. I was told that no decision had been made on the availability of the files but that one was to be made soon.[367] Alan Reitman told me that a special board committee had been set up to study the whole question of the FBI files. The concern for protecting the privacy of the individuals who were involved was receiving serious attention.[368] But there were other concerns as well.

Neier introduced the subject of the FBI files on the ACLU to the board in September 1977. He claimed that the FBI had "frustrated" ACLU efforts to protect the privacy of individuals named in the documents. As it turned out, the frustrating efforts of the FBI amounted to the placement of the files in a reading room for interesting documents released under the FOIA. Neier complained that this action had been taken after the Union had established very strict guidelines for access to the files, including access by the press. In addition, the *National Catholic Register* had obtained a copy of the documents; three front-page stories had been printed on the matter.[369]

There were mixed feelings on the board regarding the proper role of the ACLU on this issue. Eventually, a voice vote favored the establishment of a special committee to study ACLU-FBI abuses so that such practices would be avoided in the future. This vote carried over the objection that such a use of resources would distract the ACLU from its everyday activities. It was also argued that the activities under question were those of a different historical era, and that the Union should concentrate on the future.[370]

When a motion was made to grant access of the files to all board members, several people objected. One called it "elitist" in giving board members special privileges; another maintained that no board member had a right to know private facts about any other board member that may appear in the files. Someone pointed out that full access was then possible both under FOIA and in the FBI's reading room. At this time, the vote for a special committee to propose guidelines for the disposition of the files passed. Five board members and two non-board members were selected for this assignment.[371]

What caused the ACLU to establish such a close relationship with the FBI in the 1950s? Neier and Dorsen have offered a sensible explanation: "The FBI files demonstrate that in the 1950s some people in the ACLU feared that they or the organization would be labeled Communist because the ACLU was defending the civil liberties of Communists. That fear produced or contributed to the incidents now revealed."[372]

Levy's account is similar:

Under the circumstances as we then knew them . . . it was thoroughly advantageous to the ACLU and to the cause of civil liberties to enlist the aid of the

> FBI whenever we could do so in support of civil liberties—then under severe attack by McCarthyism—and to intend to the good offices of the FBI to set the record straight when anyone mistakenly claimed ACLU was a Communist organization.[373]

Ferman's position strengthens the Neier-Dorsen-Levy explanations. Ferman, who headed the Washington office at that time, maintains that "it was largely the responsibility of my office to maintain the contact with the FBI in the '50s." He argues that such contact "did much good to the cause of civil liberties and to the ACLU." Specifically, Ferman mentions that it was through Louis B. Nichols of the FBI that a huge, irresponsible HUAC report on the ACLU had been killed. "Had this document been issued, it would have been a prelude to long, fruitless, and perhaps perilous public hearings."[374] There is no reason to dispute Ferman's account. The ACLU was in trouble and could ill afford a damaging government report on its operations in the fifties.

In the last week of 1982 Alan Reitman of the ACLU allowed me access to the FBI files on the ACLU. What I uncovered supports and strengthens the charges that have already been made. Even though the FBI will make available to researchers the identical files held by the Union, I have elected to limit my comments to those men already exposed: Ernst, Levy, Ferman, Malin, and Pemberton. In the interest of privacy, I will not mention by name other ACLU personnel who also placed themselves in a compromising position. It should be noted, however, that the five men who have been identified were the prime participants in this affair.

Public officials have long been skeptical about the ACLU, but Harry Truman, was not among their number. On 24 November 1945, he wrote to John Haynes Holmes expressing his admiration for the Union:

> I send you warm greetings upon the completion of twenty five years of fighting for the civil rights of all Americans. . . . I believe with your members that whatever a man's political thinking, or whatever his background, environment or education, he must, if he be a real American, respect the aims of organizations such as yours. The integrity of the American Civil Liberties Union and its workers in the field has never been, and I feel, never will be questioned. Officers, directors and members of the Union have performed outstanding service to the cause of freedom.[375]

Truman could not have been more wrong in his statement that the Union's integrity had never been questioned. It was questioned from the very beginning by many public officials, including the New York legislature. Hamilton Fish made several charges against the Union's integrity. Martin Dies conducted an investigation on the ACLU in the late 1930s and early 1940s. And J. Edgar Hoover was suspicious of the ACLU all along. On 1

December 1925, he had sent a memo to the attorney general indicating his apprehension about the Civil Liberties Union over the past "several years."[376]

During the McCarthy era, questions were often raised regarding the ACLU's integrity. Not coincidentally, this was precisely the time when the Union was the least radical or leftist in its inclinations. Nonetheless, both governmental and nongovernmental sources suspected the Union as a radical organization. On 21 August 1952, the FBI released a statement that said, "No investigation of the American Civil Liberties Union has been conducted by this Bureau." However, it did note the fact that the California Senate's Fact-Finding Committee on Un-American Activities had labeled the ACLU as a "Communist-front or 'transmission belt' organization." That was in 1943. But the most recent report on the ACLU, the HUAC statement of 14 May 1951, did not list the Union as a subversive organization.[377]

Even though the HUAC report did not list the ACLU as subversive, FBI personnel were still leery of the Union. On 23 August 1952, a memo was sent from D. M. Ladd of the FBI to A. H. Belmont offering information on ACLU staff members. No investigation of Levy, Malin, or Angell had been made by the FBI, but Ladd said, that both Angell and Levy had been active in the National Lawyers Guild, a Communist-inspired organization. Louis Nichols of the FBI did not think too much of Levy: "I fear Levy is like most of these fuzzy thinking pseudo liberals. They chant and bellow about need for tolerance and fairness but are in fact the most intolerant and the most unfair." The bureau did make "an applicant type investigation" of Edward Ennis during the fall of 1950. It found him to be "of good character and reputation and loyal to the United States," notwithstanding his involvement with the National Lawyers Guild in the 1930s (which he quit when he learned of the Communist influence in it).

Private individuals and radio stations often wrote to Hoover asking him to state whether the ACLU was a Communist front. Hoover typically gave the same form-letter response; a reply to a radio station inquiry date 2 May 1962 is an example:

> With respect to your inquiry, the FBI is strictly an investigative agency of the Federal Goverment and neither makes evaluations nor draws conclusions as to the character or integrity of any organization, publication or individual. In this connection information contained in our files must be maintained as confidential in accordance with regulations of the Department of Justice. In view of the foregoing, I am unable to comment in the manner you have suggested, nor can I advise you of a source where this information can be obtained.[378]

"Superpatriots" frequently inquired as to the status of the ACLU. This letter, representative of the lot, was written to Hoover on 23 September 1966:

> I met you at the Mayflower when having lunch with our mutual friend, Eddie Fox; you autographed your "Study of Communism" for my son. I am taking the liberty of writing you personally to wish you the best and ask you to advise me on the "American Civil Liberties Union." The LEAF (Let's Elect Americans First) Society is one which is actively against the Communist movement; comprised of Masons. I was retired for physical disability—belong to the SAR and am violently anti-communist and pro-American. But not to the extreme of many and in the military I was unable to "sound off" much. The talk to-day was a result of us trying to find out what this Union is about; I predicted it was a Commie front type, with a name like that; the talk convinced me further. I told some members that I had met you and they asked if I would find out if it is so listed or considered by the FBI. (If is is not, it certainly ought to be if to-day's talk is any indication of their thinking—such as against the loyalty oath.) Please believe me, most of us were convinced; if you or one of your aides (of course, I'd like to hear from you personally), will give me an opinion I shall read it to our members upon receipt—we meet every Friday for lunch.

Three days later Hoover responded:

> Your letter of September 23rd, with enclosure, has been received, and I certainly appreciate your best wishes.

> While I would like very much to answer your inquiry, I cannot do so since regulations of the Department of Justice specifically state the files of the FBI must be maintained as confidential. I am sure you will understand the reason for this policy. You might like to know, however, that this Bureau has not investigated the American Civil Liberties Union.[379]

On 25 August 1952, the American Legion passed a resolution at its convention in New York City calling for the U.S. attorney general, the House Un-American Activities Committee, and the Subversive Activities Control Board to investigate the ACLU to determine if it was a Communist or Communist-front organization. On the same day, in a news release, the Union said that "the suggestion that the ACLU is a Communist or Communist-front organization is preposterous." The next day it said that it was willing "to cooperate fully with governmental agencies in any investigation of its activities." On 27 August Governor Adlai Stevenson addressed the American Legion and defended the Union. Editorial comments between 27 and 30 August took Stevenson's position. The *New York Times* said the Legion's resolution was "as unwarranted a slur upon a useful and thoroughly patriotic organization as could be devised." The *New York Post* argued that "the last place to look for subversive activities is in the ACLU." The *Daily Compass* and the *Washington Star* said the Union was the victim of a "smear." The *Trenton Evening News*, the *St. Louis Post-Dispatch*, and the *San Francisco Chronicle* branded the charge "preposterous." The *Pittsburgh Post-Gazette* wrote: "The absurdity of the charge that the Union is a Communist front is indicated by facts that the Legion could have acquired from readily available sources." The Syracuse *Post-Standard* was concerned about "the increasing tendency of many organizations such as the American Legion, to condemn anyone who does not subscribe 100 percent, sight-unseen, to any blind, unreasoning hatred of a group, even Communists. . . ." The *Minneapolis Morning Tribune* said of the Legion, "Many persons associate any vigorous championship of civil rights with subversion." The Providence *Evening Bulletin* and the *Oregonian* also came to the defense of the Union. Perhaps the *Atlanta Constitution* said it best: "In their zeal, American Legion leaders have sometimes lost sight of the basic principles of Americanism they so revere." Only the New York *World-Telegram and Sun* was not supportive: "The American Civil Liberties Union has only itself to blame for the American Legion resolution urging government investigation.[380]

Criticism of the ACLU did not come exclusively from right-wing organizations. Even the Columbia Broadcasting System (CBS) was irritated by Union activities. On 3 June 1952, Assistant Director Louis Nichols of the FBI sent this memo to one of his colleagues:

> As a matter of interest, _____ CBS, advised me this morning that in April the American Civil Liberties Union filed a complaint with the Federal Communications Commission against CBS, DuMont, New York Daily News station, and several other stations urging that their licenses be held up because they have embarked upon program blacklisting applicants for jobs either with the networks or as artists, and submitted as evidence Merle Miller's book, "The Judges and the Judged." CBS advised the FCC that even if everything the American Civil Liberties Union said was true, it was none of their business or that of the FCC.[381]

Like other liberals today, the ACLU of the 1980s regards the McCarthy era as a time when civil liberties abuses were rampant. It is ironic to read, then, the praise that the ACLU had for J. Edgar Hoover during the heyday of Senator McCarthy. On 20 March 1952, D. M. Ladd sent a memo to Hoover relaying the sentiments about Hoover that a leading ACLU official had expressed to him on a recent visit: "He stated he always enjoyed coming in and talking to you about civil liberties in a general way, that he had found you knew more about that subject than he did; that he had been trying to catch you off base on civil liberties for many years, but had not been able to do so." Another top ACLU official wrote to Hoover on 25 July 1952, congratulating him on an article in the Winter 1952 issue of the *Iowa Law Review*. In that article, "Civil Liberties and Law Enforcement: The Role of the FBI," Hoover argued that civil liberties and law enforcement were both vital to the interests of a democratic society. "The FBI, in fulfilling its responsibilities, is respecting civil liberties."[382] He admitted that there were "enemies of civil liberties in the field of law enforcement" but said that he was doing what he could to rid law enforcement agencies of such persons.[383] Hoover was clear about his philosophy on democracy: "The state is strong because the individual is strong, free and virile; the individual is strong because the state is strong, secure and solid. They are essential ingredients for maintaining America as the home of the free, the brave and the just."[384] The major threat to democracy, he maintained, was communism.

> Communism represents a different kind of enemy, an enemy new in the ideological patterns of human thought. The nation never before has been faced with an external enemy of such danger. Communism is not hostile to one sector of our society, but to non-Communist civilization itself. It would obliterate, completely and ruthlessly, everything we cherish. Moreover, it is not only an external enemy; through ideological infection, thousands of its agents have been planted in our midst. It has a shocking—almost unbelievable—way of converting individuals born, reared and educated in America to its fold. Not only that, but its converts are often difficult to identify—lying like serpents in ambush in an industrial firm, labor union, school, or church, waiting for the opportunity to strike.[385]

In his letter to Hoover, the ACLU official said of the article: "I have read it with great interest. It describes what we at the Union have long known, the sincere interest that the Bureau has, and the determined efforts it is making, in safeguarding both national security and individual rights."[386]

Herbert Monte Levy was unrestrained in his applause for Hoover's article. On 15 July 1952, he wrote to Hoover:

> I have just finished reading your article on civil liberties in the Iowa Law Review. I hope you will not think it presumptuous of me to state that I think it is a perfectly magnificent job. While of course there are some points in it on which I would disagree with you, I only wish that all government officials and private persons showed the same regard for civil liberties that you do. . . . I have always been impressed by the fact that there are hardly ever any complaints that third degree methods are used by FBI agents; indeed, in the three years that I have been associated with the American Civil Liberties Union, I have heard only one such complaint, which I frankly felt to be so patently lacking in veracity that I did not pursue the matter any further.[387]

In a memo from Nichols to one of his colleagues dated 12 September 1952, the assistant director disclosed that Levy had admitted to him "in an off the record manner" that he was personally against the ACLU stand on the Smith Act.[388] But to his credit, Levy did not always mouth the FBI line. On 19 March 1952, he wrote to Hoover indicating his concern about questionable FBI tactics:

> Within recent weeks, we have received reports to the effect that the F.B.I. in loyalty and security cases involving persons who are attorneys, has inquired as to whether such attorneys have ever represented Communist or left-wing clients. We should greatly appreciate being advised by you as to whether or not this information is correct. It would seem to us that representation of unpopular or Communist defendants should not be a consideration with respect to the issue of the attorney's loyalty. In these days, when it is so difficult to secure attorneys to represent unpopular clients, it would seem that such action if true, might be an additional deterrent and a substantial one, to such representation.

Hoover replied on 24 March: "Since inquiries of the type you discuss are entirely contrary to our policy, I would appreciate your letting me have at an early opportunity full details concerning the reports to this effect which have come to your attention."[389]

Morris Ernst was interested in the same matter as Levy, but his role was compromising. On 15 February 1952, Nichols said in a memo:

> Morris Ernst confidentially advised me that at a meeting of the American Civil Liberties Union on January 21, 1952, James Lawrence Fly reported that the FBI includes information in loyalty investigations involving attorneys on cases wherein they have served as defense counsel in unpopular cases.
>
> Mr. Ernst stated that he replied to this by stating that the FBI would be subject to criticism if they did not report everything and evaluate nothing.[390]

Corliss Lamont regards Ernst as a "paranoid" anticommunist who served as Hoover's personal lawyer.[391] Whatever, it is certain that Ernst did have a very friendly relationship with Hoover and other top FBI officials. On 13 February 1952, he wrote what he called a "fan letter" to Nichols, Hoover's assistant. Offering his help on a matter of interest to the FBI, Ernst said: "The girl I thought you should send for promptly is _____. She was of mighty aid in the Newspaper Guild fight conducted to fire out the communist leadership."[392]

It is easy to see why Neier was most upset with Irving Ferman: his duplicity was the most extensive of any ACLU staff member. Called J. Edgar Hoover's "fast friend" by Ernst, Ferman was often in touch with

Hoover. A letter from Ferman to Hoover dated 6 January 1955 offers a view of Ferman's politics:

> I read with interest your report issued on January 5, 1955.
>
> I would like to personally endorse your mentioning the need for vigilance against Communist subversion in the face of the widespread support of the theory of "peaceful co-existence" in a way suggesting appeasement, rather than mutual respect of power status. This kind of theory of peaceful co-existence is leading to a dangerous form of subversion in surprising areas.[393]

Ferman also kept close contact with Nichols. On 4 January 1957, Ferman said:

> I am attaching herewith a copy of the December 28th minutes of the Illinois Division of the ACLU, and call your attention to item 4.
>
> This is another indication of how much this gang really believes in free speech. I will enjoy knocking heads together one of these days. It looks as if Don Meiklejohn is a chip off the old block.

Item 4 of the minutes of the Illinois affiliate's Executive Committee for 28 December 1956 reads:

> As a result of a review of Dr. Whitehead's book on the FBI appearing in the *New Republic*, written by ACLU Washington staff member, Irving Ferman, Don Meiklejohn moved that the National office be asked to urge strongly upon ACLU officers and staff—both national and affiliates—the importance of distinguishing between statements made in an individual capacity and those made when representing ACLU to some section thereof.

On 9 January, Nichols replied to Ferman:

> I appreciated your note of January 4, and I quite agree with you on the unfairness of the comment made in Chicago about your position in reviewing "The FBI Story" in the "New Republic." Free speech to some people is determined by which foot the shoe pinches.[394]

Perhaps Ferman's most ignoble statement was the letter to J. Edgar Hoover of 10 December 1956:

> My dear Mr. Hoover:
>
> I have your letter dated December 7, 1956, concerning my review of "The FBI Story."

My only wish is to have a forum someday to express my feeling that the FBI has been the positive force, perhaps the strongest, for the preservation of our liberty during the cold war period.

With best wishes for a happy holiday season,

Very truly yours,
Irving [Ferman][395]

Patrick Murphy Malin also was involved in the ACLU cabal. Nichols's memo dated 11 January 1957 shows how:

For record purposes, Pat Malin, the Executive Director of the American Civil Liberties Union (ACLU), came in to see me. He was in town and had nothing particular to see me about. He did state he had been on the alert for any complaints directed at the Bureau in connection with the interview program and so far none have come to him. . . . He then told me he had been on the alert for the advancement of names to the ACLU who might be the tools of communism. So far he had not spotted any and if we got any word of this he would appreciate being tipped off.[396]

And, finally, Malin's successor, John de Pemberton, Jr., continued the ACLU-FBI connection into the 1960s. In a memo to A. H. Belmont on 13 February 1964, William Sullivan wrote:

This time Mr. Pemberton contacted me to say that the American Civil Liberties Union (ACLU) is very anxious not to admit any person who is communist or procommunist to its organizations. He said there is a man in Georgia who is trying to move in on the ACLU chapter there and he is suspicious of this man, believing him to be connected with communism. Mr. Pemberton gave the man's name as _____ and asked if there was any public source information to which we could refer him on this man. I explained to Mr. Pemberton that our files are completely confidential and that, of course, no material could be provided.[397]

Corliss Lamont regards this chapter of the Union's history as unforgivable:

In my opinion the collaboration between the ACLU leadership and the FBI was a scandalous betrayal of American civil liberties. It stemmed directly from the fanatical anti-Communism of the times, typified by the rantings of Senator Joseph McCarthy. Many ACLU personnel swallowed McCarthy's moonshine about a terrible Communist threat and became more concerned with exposing and crushing Communists than with preserving civil liberties.[398]

Lamont's analysis is the kind of interpretation that one would expect from someone who is infinitely more alarmed by anticommunists than Communists. But it should be remembered that the ACLU's swing to the right long preceded its swallowing "McCarthy's moonshine," and was in fact a natural response to an organizational imperative—survival. It was also a reaction, rationally based, to the motives and aspirations of Communists, as the Union belatedly learned after the Nazi-Soviet accord. At any rate, the kind of symmetry that the ACLU acknowledged in the 1940s and 1950s between the interests of national security and civil liberties would vanish in the next decade. As with the liberal community in general, national security would be regarded as the province of governmental attention, not the domain of civil libertarians.

The 1940 Resolution Reconsidered

Throughout the 1960s many members of the ACLU took umbrage at the principles of the 1940 Resolution. What constitutes a respectable position on communism for an organization devoted to the Bill of Rights? In its 1966 policy guide, the Union restated its earlier position to defend the civil liberties of any person—regardless of how unpopular her or his beliefs may be. However, membership in the Communist party warranted special consideration:

> In considering the rights of members of the Communist Party, the American Civil Liberties Union recognizes that problems have arisen because of the dual nature of the Communist movement. It is both a political agitational movement and a part of the Soviet conspiracy. Insofar as it is the first, its members have all the rights of members of other parties; to the extent that it is the second, its members may in some particulars be restricted by law.[399]

Although this policy restated the Union's position on defending Communists, it did not approach the more sensitive question of the right of Communists to serve on its governing boards.

When the 1940 Resolution came under attack in the mid-1960s, a joint committee was established to work out an acceptable policy on the qualifications for membership on the Union's governing boards. The joint committee comprised the five members of the Constitution Committee and the six members of the Special Committee on the 1940 Resolution.[400] Their task was to propose an amendment to the ACLU constitution, and they succeeded by proposing a revision that was unanimously adopted by the board in 1967, and that gathered at least a two-thirds majority of the Union's electorate.[401] Section 7(D) of the constitution now stated that those who served on the governing bodies of the ACLU "shall be unequivocally committed to the object of this Union . . . and to the concept of democratic government and civil liberties for all people."[402] The Union added that its goals should be sought "wholly without political partisanship."[403]

Corliss Lamont, no longer an ACLU member, continued to criticize the organization. Finding the language of Section 7(D) offensive, he reacted against the inclusion of the last two words "all people." He noted that the language of the Objects Clause "all people throughout the United States and its possessions" was "carefully omitted."[404] For Lamont, this meant that the Union had only made progress in disguise: "Hence Section 7(d) automatically brings the Civil Liberties Union back to the 1940 Resolution and enables it, for instance, to bar as officers those who gave moral support to some foreign state perhaps one recently freed from colonialism, that considers certain non-democratic controls justified."[405]

Lamont's claim that the ACLU had not really moved beyond the 1940 Resolution is not without merit. The Union was not content to simply settle for the position embodied in Section 7(D). David Carliner, who chaired the Constitution Committee, told board members that some of the rank and file wanted the inclusion of some kind of statement in the constitution that would preserve the integrity of the organization. The following statement was passed as part of a board resolution to clarify Section 7(D):

> Therefore, be it resolved that the interpretation of the requirement stated in Section 7(D) should be understood to preclude support of those principles which reject or qualify individual liberties and minority rights for all people equally, regardless of race, sex, religion or opinion; or which reject or qualify the freedoms associated with the forms and processes of political democracy.[406]

It was this statement that incensed Lamont most of all. He maintained that it was "reminiscent of the 1940 Resolution because it involves the Civil Liberties Union in determining which foreign governments 'reject or qualify minority rights' and what individuals are to be excluded after such determination." He added that the statement was "so broad and vague that it could apply to most political scientists and commentators on public affairs."[407]

Did the 1967 Resolution constitute a break with the 1940 Resolution? Or was it mere subterfuge? The evidence shows that it was both. When Baldwin told me that the 1967 Resolution was broader than its forerunner, I responded by saying it was less specific. He replied, "It's less specific but it's very clear that you cannot believe in any totalitarian system, you cannot support any totalitarian system or any racist system." He added that the Resolution "makes it very clear that we don't want people like that. The 1940 Resolution is stronger today than it was in 1940."[408]

A somewhat different, less conclusive, interpretation is held by Reitman. I asked him if the ACLU was now opposed to the 1940 Resolution. Reitman's response was helpful:

> At one point the 1940 Resolution was part of the Constitution of the ACLU. It was eliminated from the Constitution, I believe in the late 1960s, and is no longer a part of the Constitution and by official action of the Board, the Board today does not subscribe to that Resolution. However, at the time that the 1940 Resolution text was removed from the Constitution, there was inserted in the Constitution a section indicating that members of the governing council's staff, leadership at least, must adhere to the principle of democratic rights to all persons. The important distinction is that the Resolution does not specify by name the Communist Party, Fascists, KKK, or other political groups by name that was the most odious part of the 1940 Resolution.[409]

Reitman's interpretation of the 1967 Resolution appears to be more accurate than that of either Lamont or Baldwin. Just before the board passed the 1967 Resolution, Herbert Prashker asked his fellow members if the new resolution rendered the earlier one obsolete. Carliner responded that it "superseded" rather than "repeals" the 1940 Resolution. Its aim was to eliminate the offensive terminology (references to communists, fascist, racist doctrines) while leaving unchanged the substantive position of the 1940 Resolution.[410] Immediately after Carliner's remarks, the new resolution passed.

Approximately six months after the 1967 Resolution, Lamont's book *The Trial of Elizabeth Gurley Flynn* appeared. It was hailed by the Marxist publication *Monthly Review* but ignored by the *New York Times* and other influential organs. But its effect on the ACLU was not lost. Lamont began to lobby the Union to rescind its expulsion of Flynn. George Slaff, president of the Southern California affiliate, took up Lamont's cause by imploring the Board of Directors to reconsider the case. "The Catholic Church," Slaff told the board, "reversed the trial of Joan of Arc and canonized her."[411] Ergo, the ACLU should exonerate Flynn. Although nothing came of the matter, Slaff persisted, and in April 1976 emerged victorious. He argued that Flynn had been unfairly tried and convicted of guilt by association. Furthermore, there was no evidence that she had done anything that violated the ACLU constitution. During the discussion of Slaff's resolution, it was mentioned that the Union should separate itself from its "Red-baiting" policies of the 1940s and 1950s. By a vote of 32-18 the board rescinded the 1940 decision that ousted Flynn. Flynn was praised for being a great defender of the rights of labor who led many struggles for economic and constitutional rights.[412]

More important than the vote to recognize Flynn was the board's conclusion that "the expulsion of Ms. Flynn was not consonant with the basic principles on which the ACLU was founded and has acted for fifty-four years." The board also agreed that language should be drafted to indicate its happiness with the removal of the 1940 Resolution from the ACLU constitution in 1967.[413] This settles the argument. Recall that Baldwin claimed that "the 1940 Resolution is stronger today than it was in 1940."[414] There is no question but that the strictures of the 1940 Resolution have vanished from the Union. Indeed, two years before the board's vote on Flynn, it declared that "no member of any political party or any other association in the United States is ineligible for membership on the Board of Directors of the Union or any affiliate or on the staff thereof by reason of being a member of such party or association."[415] This resolution makes it impossible for the Union to expel a Communist from its governing boards simply because of political affiliation. Further proof that the ACLU will accept any person on its staff, regardless of how compromising he or she is on civil liberties, is the fact that William Kunstler was selected to be on the Union's National Advisory Council in the 1980s.[416] In 1979 Kunstler admitted his selective concern on civil liberties to Nat Hentoff: "I do not believe in public attacks on socialist countries where violations of human rights may occur."[417] Evidently, Kunstler's ire is aroused only when violations of human rights occur in the United States.

National Security in the 1960s and 1970s

In the 1960s and 1970s the ACLU relaxed its policies regarding national security: it has steadily moved away from its positions of the 1950s. The only group of citizens that the Union believes may rightfully be expected to abide by the imposition of a loyalty oath is public officeholders. (And even here, the Union makes clear that oaths should not go beyond the constitutional provision in Article VI that requires allegiance to the Constitution.) All others, including teachers, should not be required to take a loyalty oath. To impose oaths on teachers, the Union reasons, would be "discriminatory and demeaning."[418] This became policy in 1968. A few other changes are worth noting. In the two policy guides of the 1960s, the Union included its 1954 position "ACLU and Communism."[419] Renamed in 1971 "ACLU and Totalitarianism," the latest policy includes only a short statement on the Union's opposition "to any governmental or economic system which denies fundamental civil liberties and human rights."[420] Dropped from this policy is any reference to communism as both "a political agitational movement and a part of the Soviet conspiracy."[421] Two other restrictive policies were dropped completely: "Attorney General's List" and "State and Local Employee Investigation."[422]

At the beginning of the 1960s the ACLU strengthened its original anti-HUAC position by making the committee's elimination "a prime order of business."[423] It called for the repeal of the Subversive Activities Control Act as well.[424] In November 1964 it came to the defense of Communist-front organizations. The Union argued that there was a fundamental difference between a Communist-action organization and a Communist-front group. The latter, it said, "is by definition only indirectly related to a foreign power bent on the forcible overthrow of the United States government, and does not operate to advance the objectives of world Communism but only to aid and support them."[425] In the 1970s it allocated more of its resources to the issues of secrecy in government, political surveillance, and privacy than it had in any previous decade.[426] The Union came down hard on the use of undercover agents, informers,[427] and the practices of the Central Intelligence Agency (CIA), FBI, and Internal Revenue Service (IRS).[428] With regard to the intelligence agencies, the ACLU drew up several recommendations. One of its goals was to check the power of the executive by giving the Congress more oversight in the affairs of the CIA and FBI. While many of its suggestions were voiced by other liberals in the mid-1970s, some of the Union's prescriptions were controversial from the perspective of mainstream liberals, never mind conservatives. Some of these ideas were (a) to abolish all CIA clandestine activities, (b) to prohibit entirely wiretaps and tapping of telecommunications, and (c) to prohibit all domestic intelligence and political information-gathering.[429] In short, the ACLU sought to reduce substantially the scope and influence of the CIA and FBI. This goal has remained on the Union's agenda in the 1980s.

In the 1966 and 1967 policy guides, the ACLU's position stated in "Access to Government Information" was that "there can be no quarrel with the principle of 'executive privilege' to withhold information. . . ."[430] When the next policy guide appeared in 1971, the "executive privilege" caveat was stricken.[431] The 1976 policy is the Union's clearest, and current, statement on this issue. It contends that the public's right to know "outweighs any governmental interest in concealing military action the government is taking or sponsoring. . . ."[432] The "Pentagon Papers" case involving the *New York Times*, wherein the Union filed an *amicus* brief, is referenced in its latest policy guide. The Union has maintained, however, that government agencies can withhold "truly secret information directly relevant to national security"; it lists "technical details of military operations or weaponry" as an example of what it means.[433] As for declassification, the ACLU's position is: "The Union supports the establishment of an independent agency within the federal government to represent the public interest in the declassification of records hitherto kept secret and to work for increased disclosure."[434] The ACLU's position on classified information has been uneven. For example, in the 1950s the Union sharply criticized Senator McCarthy for inviting federal employees to supply him with classified documents.[435] But in the 1970s the Union felt that former CIA agent Vincent Marchetti had a perfect right to break a contractural agreement by disclosing information that was more sensitive than the documents that McCarthy had sought.[436]

In the session of Congress that ended in June 1938, a bill was passed that required foreign agents to register with the State Department. The ACLU did not at that time oppose the bill,[437] nor did it do so for the next forty years. Indeed, it recognized the right of the authorities to require the registration of agents of foreign governments and certain other principals; it was proper to identify the material distributed by them and fell securely within the responsibility of those who pursued the interests of national defense and foreign relations.[438] But in 1978 the ACLU ruled against the Foreign Agents Registration Act because "its system of regulation and disclosure has a chilling effect on the right to speak out on any issue."[439]

The Vietnam War and the Rights of Dissidents

Many junior faculty members today look back upon their college years in the 1960s as a period of activism. Their nostalgia is matched only by their determination to resurrect the drama of that period. And drama there was. Midway through the decade, the ACLU announced that the gravest threats to civil liberties were "undoubtedly the pressures arising from the war in Vietnam."[440] In the late 1960s the Union singled out rapid social change as the prime catalyst of antidemocratic behavior.[441] For the ACLU, those who threatened civil liberties came from the Right. In 1964 it passed a policy on the "Ultra-Right" wherein it registered its position on the civil liberties of the John Birch Society.[442] It has never issued a policy on the "Ultra-Left," and has chosen not to address the activities of the Students for a Democratic Society (SDS), the Weathermen, or the Black Panthers in a policy statement.

Opposition to the Vietnam war and sympathy for dissidents were orginally more pronounced amongst the affiliates than amongst the members of the national Board of Directors. The New York chapter was particularly outspoken. In 1966, the NYCLU challenged a law that was designed to (a) make it unlawful for any American to assist by material means any group engaged in armed hostilities against U.S. troops, and (b) make it unlawful to attempt to impede physically the movement of troops or supplies to a front where U.S. soldiers were fighting. The NYCLU did more than oppose the legislation; it sought to disrupt a congressional committee hearing on it. One of the NYCLU lawyers refused to listen to the instructions of the chairman of the committee and proceeded to institute his own rules of conduct, which included the right to talk when asked to yield to another party. As was common in those days, federal marshals were called upon to escort the irate lawyer from the chamber. His colleagues protested that his rights had been abused and noted that he was only five feet two inches tall.[443]

Protesters in the 1960s—both nonviolent and violent—frequently justified some of their illegal activities by referencing "civil disobedience." It is fair to say that at no time in American history was civil disobedience invoked more often than in the 1960s. Everyone from exemplary practitioners such as Martin Luther King to those who had never read Thoreau cited civil disobedience as a justification for illegal actions. This issue created somewhat of a dilemma for the ACLU. Its sympathies and ideological bent were clearly on the side of the lawbreakers, but it risked losing its credibility if it ruled that people are entitled to break any law that their conscience so directs. As is wont to happen in such situations, a compromise was struck—but not until the ACLU issued its second policy position on civil disobedience; originally it had taken a more hard-line approach.

The ACLU first broached the issue of civil disobedience in February 1967. The following definition was devised: "Generally speaking, civil disobedience is the willful, nonviolent and public violation of valid laws because the violator deems them to be unjust or because their violation will focus public attention on other injustices in society to which such laws may or may not be related." The Union's involvement would be limited to acts that "can reasonably be defended as an exercise of a constitutional right." It declared that "the way to correct injustice in a free society is to change valid laws by persuasion, not by their violation."[444] A year later, on 12 January 1968, the National Board cited its policy on civil disobedience as its reason not to involve itself in the case of Dr. Benjamin Spock, who was under federal indictment on charges of conspiracy to counsel and abet young men to avoid the draft. Four of the state affiliates—New York, Southern California, Massachusetts, and New Jersey—split with the National office and offered to defend those who challenged the draft laws.[445] It set the stage for the ACLU to reconsider its policy.

Less than a month after the board said it would not involve itself in the defense of Spock (and his codefendent, the Reverend William Sloan Coffin), it voted, on 1 February, to file an *amicus* brief on his behalf. Aryeh Neier, then head of the NYCLU, was not satisfied. Neither was Emil Oxfeld of the New Jersey affiliate, nor Melvin Wulf of the national organization. The board caved in, and on 2 March it voted (26-20) to furnish money and counsel to the accused. The significance of this move was captured by Yale lawyer Joseph W. Bishop, Jr.: "The distinction is no mere legal technicality.

Counsel for the defense do not represent the Union, as do the counsel who prepare a brief for in the role of friend of the court. They represent the accused, and it is their obligation to raise any available defense, whether or not that defense has anything to do with the Bill of Rights."[446]

In October 1968 a revised policy on civil disobedience was adopted. Much of the language in the 1967 policy was used again, but there were some important changes. The latest policy omitted the suggestion that to correct injustice, one should use persuasion to change valid laws. Its most striking new provision was the following: "The ACLU will continue to defend individuals who violate laws, which, either in themselves or as applied in circumstances, the ACLU believes to be unconstitutional or to interfere with the existence of constitutional right, whether or not the courts previously ruled otherwise, or whether or not such violations are called civil disobedience." The Union's participation would now be extended to satisfy the hard-line activists on the Board.[447]

By the late 1960s the saturnine ACLU of the 1950s was a thing of the past. Gone were the days of cooptative ventures with government officials. The Union had made an about-face and embarked on a frontal assault on government, as well as other public figures. The radicalization of liberalism that took place in the sixties can be attributed to six causes: demographics, economic prosperity, Vietnam, the civil rights movement, the media, and college faculty. By the late 1960s the ranks of young people had swelled to unprecedented numbers as a result of the baby boom following World War II; young people, who tend to be the most idealistic segment of the population, are essential to any activist movement. Activism typically flourishes in times of economic prosperity, and the 1960s was certainly such a time. The Vietnam war and the civil rights movement provided the affluent youth of the sixties with causes they could seize upon, venting their alienation and anger in a forceful manner. The media's role was to magnify the activism, and thereby stimulate more of it by focusing on the most egregious displays of unlawful behavior, e.g. students who shut down colleges by taking over the presidents' offices. Many faculty members, another idealistic lot, fanned the flames of discontent by exhorting students to enroll in courses such as "Confrontation Politics." The abdication of responsibility and authority by many persons in leadership positions provided suitable "role models" for SDS types. The ACLU's contribution should also be added.

The ACLU was quite busy in the spring of 1971 defending the rights of the Berrigan brothers and launching a crusade to protest the treatment of the Mayday protesters. The Board of Directors voted 49 to 5 "to provide direct representation to any or all of the six defendants in the Berrigan case who might want ACLU representation."[448] Joseph Bishop's comment on the Berrigan case is accurate and perceptive: "The statutes which they are accused of violating seem clearly constitutional: neither blowing up government, nor even kidnapping Henry Kissinger, has yet been held to be a protected form of symbolic expression."[449] Neier of the ACLU said the organization acted on behalf of the Berrigans because it saw a "frameup."[450] In the Mayday caper, thousands of young people rioted and brought traffic to a halt in Washington in an attempt to shut down the government. The police moved in, sweeping 14,000 youths into a "concentration camp" called R.F.K. Stadium, home of the Redskins. The ACLU rushed to their defense and instituted a $12 million lawsuit in their behalf, which they eventually won. No doubt civil liberties were put aside by the police, but, as William Safire has argued, the events surrounding the Mayday "demonstrators" were serious:

> These rioters were not gentle souls carrying candles, but largely the toughs and crazies who marred the peace movement. As they proceeded to slash tires, terrorize motorists and pedestrians, and roll cans of garbage into the streets, the District of Columbia police moved to prevent anarchy. . . . The real threat of mob rule had been averted with a minimal application of force. The civil liberty of the law-abiding citizen to walk on a public street or drive to work had been protected.[451]

Much of the domestic violence that took place in the late 1960s and early 1970s was supposedly a form of dissent directed at U.S. policy in Vietnam. Roger Baldwin once said of President Kennedy that he was "really one of us in spirit."[452] He was also one of those who gave us Vietnam. Nisbet has identified the architects of the war:

> Intellectuals more than any other group in American life pushed the United States into full political and military intervention in South Vietnam under President Kennedy. Kennedy, it appears, was indecisive and apprehensive for a long time. But not McNamara, Rusk, Rostow, Bundy, Galbraith, and Schlesinger, nor a Pentagon intellectual named Daniel Ellsberg. All of them favored the fullest possible political intervention, even to the extent of deposing of President Diem, and most of them were equally in favor of military intervention.[453]

The "best and brightest," namely, the Harvard brain trust, washed their hands of the whole affair once events proved dismaying.

The ACLU's position on the Vietnam war sheds further light on the consciousness of liberals during the 1960s and 1970s. During Johnson's tenure as president, the Union said that "it would avoid making value-judgments about the worth and wisdom of a particular Government foreign policy. 'We neither favor nor oppose our nation's involvement in the war in Vietnam.'" It also maintained that "there was probably no constitutional legal challenge that could be brought against conscription, as such, or the monthly draft calls."[454] By the late 1960s the Union had reversed itself and moved, in several court cases, to test the constitutionality of the draft law. It also defended draft-card burners as exercising their freedom of expression. The high court did not see it that way: the Union lost 7-1 in *O'Brien v. United States*.[455]

By 1970 the ACLU could no longer resist making "a value judgment about the worth and wisdom of Government foreign policy": it declared its formal opposition to the Vietnam war on 2 June 1970. This was an unprecedented decision—never had the Union officially opposed any war in its fifty-year history. There were two major issues that the Union addressed: the war's unconstitutionality, and its adverse effect on civil liberties at home. The war was held responsible for several domestic social problems ranging from violations of academic freedom to "the festering sores of urban neglect."[456] Only eleven board members out of the fifty-four who voted rejected the policy; there was one abstention.[457] The ACLU's decision to oppose the war in Southeast Asia (which Baldwin labeled "a little farfetched")[458] departed radically from its position in World War II when it declared it took "no official position on national defense or foreign policy."[459] It also departed from its neutral position in the Korean war. I asked Reitman why the Union opposed the Vietnam war but not the Korean war. He replied:

> There was no opportunity for the public's will to be expressed at the time of the Vietnam war in terms of any declaration except what was referred to as Congressional intent . . . whereas the Korean war I believe there was some clear discussion of that, and I'm not sure if Truman acted under emergency powers left over from World War II or whether he acted in terms of a Congressional declaration.[460]

The historical record shows that Truman acted "on his own" in ordering U.S. forces to Korea.[461] Furthermore, according to New York University political scientist Louis Koenig, Truman failed "to involve Congress substantially in his early Korean decisions."[462] The Congress, of course, appropriated the monies that were necessary to conduct both wars. The Supreme Court, it should be remembered, refused to hear a case challenging the constitutionality of the Vietnam war.

In another new policy that reflected the ACLU's antipathy toward the war, the board struck from "International Civil Liberties" its earlier pledge not to "intervene in the actions or operations by the U.S. armed forces of a purely military nature."[463] This policy of noninterference in military matters guided the Union's decision-makers from the end of World War II to 1973.[464]

The ACLU did not abide by its own passport policy in the 1960s. Its policy in the sixties restated its traditional support for freedom to travel, noting that when "the country is engaged in war or when a criminal or civil action is pending against the individual desiring to leave the country" a passport may be denied.[465] However, at about the same time that it was busy drawing up its passport policy, the Union was engaged in the courts defending the right of a Yale professor to secure a passport so he could travel to Hanoi. Staughton Lynd had made a private visit to Hanoi and Peking and consequently had his passport revoked when he returned to the United States. Lynd refused to promise that he would not travel to restricted countries again if he received a new passport; North Vietnam was a restricted country. The United States was at war with North Vietnam, yet the ACLU claimed that the refusal to grant Lynd a passport was not justified by "any showing of overriding public interest."[466]

The Union's position on the draft dovetailed with its changing policies on the war. In World War II, when conscription was inaugurated in August 1940, the ACLU did not oppose the draft law.[467] In 1966, at the height of conscription during the Vietnam war, the Board of Directors delivered a revised policy that touched on several important issues. "Compulsory military service," it declared, "whether in time of war or peace, is always a severe deprivation of civil liberties."[468] However, the Union did not go so far as to say that conscription was an absolute deprivation of civil liberties. In the interests of national security, it was permissible to conduct a draft "in time of war or the imminent danger of war."[469] The Union went on to say that it would "examine separately each occasion for required military service, to the best of its ability, in order to decide and express an opinion whether conscription's limitations on individual freedom is justified by world and national conditions."[470] This part of the Union's policy on conscription, while worded somewhat more cautiously than its previous decision, did not depart from the principles of its policies in the 1940s. However, at that time, the issue was dichotomized to reflect the difference between peacetime and wartime conscription.

That the ACLU gave the edge to supporting the privacy of one's conviction can be seen by examining the other parts of this policy. Nonreligious, ethical convictions were accorded the same legitimacy as religiously based objections to the war.[471] Special treatment for students should not be given by the draft boards; deferments were discriminatory.[472] It was legitimate to refuse participation in a particular war, as opposed to all wars, if the individual found that conscience dictated against involvement. Compulsory nonmilitary activity, it was argued, should not be required of those objectors who cannot accept civilian service.[473]

The ACLU's growing objections to the war led it to devise a policy on conscription that fit with its political ideology. In February 1969 it passed a new policy governing the draft:

> The present Selective Service law as presently administered and in present circumstances is a violation of civil liberties and constitutional guarantees, and ACLU should act to oppose the present draft law in the judicial legislative and public forums.[474]

Notice that the Union found no problem with the draft until it turned cold toward the war. This was clearly a political decision. And some ACLU members said so themselves. When this policy was being discussed, some board members said that it was really a smoke screen for having the Union take a political stand against the war. Others felt that the wording was so vague that it could be construed to mean anything the reader wished it to mean.[475] In an attempt to steer the ACLU away from a political statement, board member Fraenkel proposed a substitute motion to delete the phrase "under present circumstances." His motion lost by only one vote, 24-23.[476]

During World War II, the ACLU maintained that GIs had the right to address the president or members of Congress, but made clear that soldiers could be treated differently than civilians in other areas of free speech. Then in 1962, it strengthened its previous stand: "Government restrictions on the speech of military personnel is not an unconstitutional restraint of freedom of expression."[477] But as the Vietnam war progressed, so did the Union's reactions to it. In 1971 it announced its new policy:

> The First Amendment guarantees and protects the freedoms of speech and association of members of the armed forces. Expressions may be restricted or punished only if it presents a clear and present danger of directly causing violation of a valid military law of a high degree of gravity.[478]

The policy never mentions who will decide which military laws are "valid" and are of "high degree of gravity." There also seems to be some confusion over whether First Amendment guarantees are applicable to soldiers in time of war: before Vietnam the consensus was no; after the war started, the consensus was yes. Then in 1975, the ACLU issued a new policy that retained nearly all of the stipulations of its 1971 policy, except this time the qualifying statement regarding a "clear and present danger" was stricken. Now armed forces personnel were to enjoy First Amendment guarantees "to the same extent" as civilians.[479] Does this mean that a combat troop has the right to distribute literature to the front line urging insubordination, desertion, and sabotage? Evidently so! Such ratiocination appears to be the exclusive property of civil libertarians. Once again it is worth recalling that during World War II (a war to which the Union did not object), it refused to defend GIs who were charged with disobeying military orders.[480]

That the ACLU does not believe the military is capable of rendering a fair trial is incontestable. During the Vietnam war, Charles Morgan, Jr., of the Southern Regional Office spoke for many of his colleagues when he said that "there's just no point in having any sort of trials conducted within the military. The military is incapable of understanding the Constitution."[481] But the ACLU does. As the war was winding down, it recommended that the military discharge system be reformed so as to do away with less-than-honorable discharges. The Union claimed that a disproportionate number of these discharges went to Blacks (never mentioning whether they deserved them) and that the overwhelming majority of them had not committed a crime (again, no documentation was offered).[482] In addition, those who received such discharges labored under "a heavy and unnecessary stigma."[483] In short, the ACLU would like to extend all the benefits that an honorable discharge entails to those who have won the Purple Heart, as well as to those who proved to be disloyal.

Watergate

No issue of government lawlessness ever engaged the ACLU more deeply than Watergate. The Watergate episode demonstrated once again that when respect for civil liberties decreases, the ACLU's coffers increase. For the Union, Watergate was a bonanza. In the annual report of 1972-73, Neier wrote: "We are enjoying an unaccustomed popularity because we were the first major group to call for impeachment and to launch a systematic campaign."[484] Of President Nixon, Neier said: "He has relentlessly trenched the Constitution."[485]

The Union's war on Nixon was led by Charles Morgan, Jr., chief of the Washington office, who was in the forefront of the call for impeachment. To other influential Union members, Morgan was acting too quickly. He was criticized by Edward Ennis and others for his zeal, and when Neier did not come to his defense as strongly as he would have liked, Morgan resigned.[486] Interestingly, when Morgan quit the ACLU, he established his own law firm—one that is committed to the protection of large corporations, such as Sears, Roebuck, from government regulation.[487]

The ACLU is proud that it was the first major organization in the country to call for a campaign to impeach the president.[488] It did so by taking full-page advertisements in newspapers across the nation. This action did not please Baldwin. He said, "I don't like it. It's too hysterical. It's an unnecessarily emotional commitment for an organization that's as legalistic as the ACLU. It's not in keeping with the Union's way of behaving, which is to go into the courts."[489] Notwithstanding the view of its founding father, the Union persisted in its efforts right up to its *amicus curiae* brief in *United States v. Nixon*.[490] The Supreme Court ordered the president to hand over the tapes he possessed regarding conversations in the Oval Office. Shortly thereafter, he resigned.

Two major policies were passed concerning the Watergate incident: the first covered the impeachment of Nixon: the second addressed the question of procedures governing the Senate trial. The internal debate that these policies fostered left many a Union member with hard feelings toward colleagues. The board minutes regarding these two policies tell more about the ACLU's politics than they do about Nixon's.

At the end of September 1973, Marvin Schachter of the Southern California CLU presented to the national Board of Directors his affiliate's resolution calling for the Congress to initiate impeachment proceedings against Nixon. Schachter was worried that the Union had not had enough sense of outrage theretofore.[491] William Van Alstyne spoke in opposition to the proposed resolution and offered a substitute proposal. (Much of what follows is taken verbatim from the Board Minutes of 29-30 September 1973.) He stated that the abuses listed, although colorably unconstitutional, were not issues adjudicated by the Supreme Court at the time of abuse. For example, the Supreme Court had never said that the president needs a declaration of war by Congress, and the issue of impoundment had not reached the Supreme Court. These abuses of presidential power, argued Van Alstyne, do not fall within the language of the Constitution regarding impeachment, and there was no precedent for saying that they do.

With regard to the alleged violations of existing criminal statutes, Van Alstyne asserted that they were an appropriate subject for impeachment proceedings but he believed that the effort was premature because the hard evidence implicating the president personally was very thin (at the time.) He proposed adoption of a resolution calling upon the House to authorize a committee to determine whether grounds exist for impeachment.

An alternative formulation calling upon the House to impeach Nixon was presented by Sheldon Ackley for the New York CLU. It was suggested that this general statement should be followed by a bill of particulars.

At the outset of the debate, a number of board members urged no action on the impeachment resolution or opposed it. Mel Straus argued that the Union should take no action (at that time). The ACLU should exercise discipline and self-restraint, to maximize the opportunity to exploit the Watergate affair for civil liberties purposes. He asserted that the Union could not attach itself to the separation of powers principle and at the same time hold the president culpable in the absence of a judicial decision.

David Isbell also advocated no action, stating that the ACLU should avoid the self-delusion that what it says will come about. There is no civil liberties value in calling for impeachment. The Union should address itself to the acts involved, the specific violations of civil liberties, but not to the man himself. Pragmatically, Isbell noted, there would be a good chance of acquittal and thereby vindication of the president.

Larry Speiser questioned whether the Union wanted to be in the position of lending credibility to the arguments of Nixon and Agnew that they could not be reached by the courts but only through the impeachment process. He also suggested that at that time Congress was the worst possible forum. Monroe Freedman argued that although there was more than probable cause for impeachment, even without the events of Watergate, board members should not express their individual feelings through the institution of the ACLU. Calling for impeachment would be regarded by many as a political blow at a vulnerable enemy. Many of the illegal acts and abuses of presidential power had been initiated before the Nixon administration, and the ACLU had not called for impeachment then. The individual can take such an arguably inconsistent position, but the institution of the ACLU could not afford to do so. It was also argued that the impeachment provision of the Constitution was itself anti-civil libertarian: instead, the procedure should be one of voter recall.

Several arguments were advanced in favor of calling for impeachment immediately: the Union should do so for educational purposes, emphasizing the civil liberties issues involved; impeachment was the only means of placing the charges against the president; the actions of the president did not conform to the civil liberties standards of the country; the high crime of President Nixon lay in administering a government of lawlessness; 70 percent of the American people believed that the president violated the law. After a few other arguments in favor of impeachment were heard, a motion that no action be taken was defeated overwhelmingly. Then, after consideration of three alternatives, the board voted 51-5 to urge the House of Representatives to initiate impeachment proceedings.

A bill of particulars was accepted by a vote of 49-0. The entire resolution was then accepted by the same vote. The bill of particulars, which was presented by David Carliner, declared that there was substantial public evidence of President Nixon's participation in high crimes and misdemeanors. Reference was made to Nixon's approval of the "Huston plan" for domestic political surveillance and espionage. Nixon was accused of usurping the war-making powers of Congress by ordering the bombing of Cambodia and then concealing this information from the Congress and the people. Nixon's involvement with the "plumbers" unit and the Ellsberg case were among the other charges.[492]

The board minutes that were just cited show how convinced most of the members were of Nixon's guilt. I asked Reitman whether this statement of policy came close to charging Nixon guilty prior to the Senate trial (which never did occur). He responded, "No, I think that was an organizational policy statement—not a statement of law."[493] Unquestionably. But that does not relieve the objection. Many board members wrestled with the same problem.

At the board meeting of 12 June 1974, the question of the ACLU position on influencing the Senate during its trial of the president was considered.[494] Norman Dorsen argued that the ACLU should refrain from taking a position before or during the trial so as to avoid prejudgment. Comments supportive of Dorsen's position stated: (a) the integrity of the ACLU is questioned if it lobbies during the course of the trial; (b) it is improper for the ACLU to lobby on evidentiary matters; (c) it is a violation of civil liberties to lobby for conviction—the Union's purpose is to defend individual rights, not press for prosecution; and (d) previous public statements calling for impeachment clearly made the distinction that the Union was not calling for conviction.

Those who differed with this account said: (a) the ACLU is an advocate in the proceedings and not a neutral arbiter of civil liberties; (b) the ACLU will have to come out for conviction because it has already taken the lead in calling for impeachment; (c) the board should not take a neutral position on the trial, for the Senate proceeding is not a criminal trial but a political remedy provided in the Constitution; and (d) everybody is going to be involved in lobbying the Senate, including the president, therefore, the Union should also lobby for conviction.

Ira Glasser, then executive director of the NYCLU, moved that the ACLU take action on the civil liberties questions that were factually not in dispute because no valid defense would be possible. Neier pointed out that this proposal was the worst possible position to take for it cast doubt on the September position on impeachment in which items were enumerated that were factually in dispute but that were still believed to be valid grounds for impeachment. It was then decided 30-26, that the board should adjourn until after the House issued the articles of impeachment, if any.[495] As it turned out, the only final policy statement that the June meeting produced concerned the televising of the trial and due process safeguards.

Two unusual developments occurred when the Union took up the question of procedures for the trial. A majority of board members declared: (a) the Senate trial should be televised, and (b) Nixon should not be given the right to claim Fifth Amendment privilege against self-incrimination.[496]

Although some members maintained the Union's traditional position of opposing the televising of courtroom proceedings so as not to induce altered behavior in trial participants, most believed that in this case, the participants would be well enough acquainted with the television medium and used to a large measure of public visibility and public scrutiny that behavior alterations due to exposure would be much less likely than in an ordinary trial. Furthermore, the Union concluded, "the public has a right to be 'present' at this grave, profound and unique event which brings the whole of the constitutional scheme under scrutiny."[497]

When eight safeguards of due process for the president during the Senate trial were first considered by the board, his right to claim the Fifth Amendment privilege against self-incrimination was included. But then the rejoinders emerged. One member suggested that if the president did use the protection of the Fifth Amendment, he should forfeit his office. Another member contended that if the president invoked the Fifth Amendment, the Senate may draw a negative inference! It was finally decided to delete any reference to this safeguard of civil liberties. The board added that the standard of evidence required for conviction should be that of "clear and convincing evidence."[498]

The ACLU's decision to recommend that Nixon's Fifth Amendment right be forfeited was the first and only time in its history that the Union went on record advocating the suspension of civil liberties guarantees for any individual. Not surprisingly, the Union called President Ford's pardon of Nixon "deeply objectionable in its moral and political assumptions."[499] What is surprising is that the ACLU's denunciation of amnesty for Nixon appeared in the same annual report, and in the same section, as its call for universal and unconditional amnesty for the war resisters of the Vietnam era![500] Instances like this demonstrate the lack of nonpartisanship that colors ACLU thinking.

Civil Liberties, Communism, and the State Under Reagan

Illegal aliens have long been a problem for Washington. The Reagan administration, like those that have preceded it, has been unable to find a solution. At issue is the right of the United States to secure its borders from illegal immigration, while at the same time preserving civil liberties for those who are either directly or indirectly involved. No one doubts that there has been much corruption and abuse of established procedures by the authorities in this area. The ACLU has not been silent and has raised serious questions regarding the practices of immigration lawyers in the United States.[501] In 1982 it assailed federal roundups of illegal aliens as "playing with people's rights to score a public relations victory."[502] The

Union has been particularly critical of the Reagan administration's handling of illegal immigration from Mexico and Haiti. It called the detention of Haitians a discriminatory and unconstitutional policy.[503]

The ACLU's strongest criticism of government immigration policies has centered on employment sanctions. In 1977 it introduced the policy "Employment of Undocumented Aliens," wherein it voiced opposition to legislation that penalized employers for hiring illegal aliens. The Union held that such legislation would exacerbate existing patterns of racial and ethnic discrimination in employment. Furthermore, it opposed the use of social security cards and other governmentally issued documents as a condition of employment. It claimed that such a practice would create an "employment passport," resulting in a "universal identifier of all persons in the United States."[504] The controversy surrounding immigration came to a head in 1981 when the final report of the Senate Subcommittee on Immigration and Refugee Policy was released.

On 30 June 1981, William French Smith, the attorney general, presented the Reagan administration's position on immigration to the subcommittee. The substance of his testimony was as follows:

> We have lost control of our borders. We have pursued unrealistic policies. We have failed to enforce our laws effectively. . . . The Administration proposes five related initiatives to curtail illegal immigration: 1) increased enforcement of existing immigration and fair labor standard laws; 2) a law imposing penalties against employers who knowingly hire illegal aliens; 3) a new experimental temporary worker program for up to 50,000 Mexican nationals annually; 4) legal status for qualifying illegal aliens currently residing in the United States; and 5) international cooperation within the western hemisphere to enforce immigration laws and discourage illegal immigration.[505]

Smith also said that the Reagan administration was opposed to the creation of a national identity card.[506]

Shattuck offered the ACLU's position on 6 May 1981. He said the Union was not opposed to the policies on asylum of the Select Commission on Immigration and Refugee Policy, the legalization of certain categories of undocumented aliens in the United States, or the provisions regarding due process; the enforcement of employer sanctions was another matter. Shattuck expressed the ACLU's concern over a worker-identification system, noting that immigration officials would view such a system "as an invitation to conduct dragnet searches of places frequented by foreigners or those who look foreign. The resulting invasion of privacy and discriminatory focus on those who are 'foreign-looking' would be severe."[507] He said the Union would like to endorse, as an "alternative" to employer sanctions, the commission's recommendation that existing wage and working-standards legislation be enforced.[508] The Union has been consistent on this issue and has opposed the repeated attempts by Senator Alan Simpson and Representative Romano Mazzoli to reform immigration policy by making it a crime knowingly to recruit or hire illegal immigrants.[509]

The Reagan administration's move to curtail the release of government documents drew fire from the ACLU and other organizations in the 1980s. Increased authority was given to public officials to classify government data. Although White House spokesman Larry Speakes said there was "no central directive to cut back on the availability of information,"[510] the ACLU did not see it that way. The Union was concerned about any changes that the Reagan administration would make regarding the Freedom of Information Act. Shattuck argued that "this is certainly not an open-government. This makes the act itself more important than ever. We will look skeptically at proposals to change the actual language of the statute."[511] Although the FOIA reforms worried the Union, it reserved its sharpest criticisms for Reagan's proposals regarding national security and dissent.

In 1982 Ira Glasser warned that the symptoms of McCarthyism were beginning to reappear. Amongst his concerns was the petition to revive the House Un-American Activities Committee. Glasser also put the Union on record as opposing a bill that would make illegal the disclosure of names of covert U.S. intelligence agents.[512] This bill, which passed the House by a vote of 315 to 32, and won in the Senate 81 to 4,[513] was prompted by the activities of former CIA agent Philip Agee. Agee's disclosure of the names of CIA agents had resulted in the death of one of the men. Glasser was also exercised over the appointment of a Senate committee charged with the responsibility of holding hearings on terrorism.[514] Shattuck opposed such a committee, contending that no investigations of terroristic organizations ought to be made by the government.[515] No suggestions were put forward by the ACLU on this subject: a laissez-faire approach was advocated. Charles Mohr of the *New York Times* succinctly captured the feelings of the Union in his appropriately titled article, "A.C.L.U. Says Fight to Stop Terrorism Imperils Rights."[516] The irony in the ACLU's attitude was clearly not lost on Mohr.

The issue of nuclear weapons and reactors has become a central concern for both liberals and conservatives in the 1980s. Since 1959 the ACLU has maintained that there are no civil liberties questions involved in nuclear weapons testing.[517] But this policy has not always been followed by the Union. For example, in the early 1970s the Union filed suit to enjoin the shipment of nerve gas from Okinawa to Oregon.[518] What civil liberties issue is involved here is unclear. In the 1980s the Union took to defending nuclear freeze activists from detractors of the movement, accusing them of

McCarthyism. Not only was Reagan criticized for impugning the integrity of the activists but the *Washington Post* was also singled out for such "Red-baiting" smears. The *Post* simply went on record as charging the Women's International League for Peace and Freedom as a Soviet front.[519] Evidence to the contrary was not forthcoming from the ACLU.

To the ACLU in the 1980s, and to the well-educated segments of the liberal community in general, to be an outspoken anticommunist is to be a McCarthyite. Time and again we hear that the Reagan administration is returning us to the days of McCarthyism. That such labeling might itself be a McCarthyite tactic seems never to be recognized. So it is that liberals who aspire to remain in good standing with their ideological kin often resort to defending the rights of Communists—in every endeavor—lest they be accused of engaging in Red-baiting. It was for this reason that the ACLU in 1977 dropped from its policies its decision not to oppose the refusal of permanent immigration status to "present members of Communist, Fascist, Falangist, or other totalitarian parties."[520] Since 1950 the Union had accepted this policy,[521] but as the 1980s grew near, its attitude toward communism changed.

Another indicator of the Union's change of heart was its defense of Dorothy Blitz. Blitz, a member of the Communist Workers party, took a part in a CETA training program in brick masonry in 1981. Her congressman, Dan Daniel, took issue with Blitz's enrollment in the government program: "I do not believe it was the intention of Congress that individuals whose stated policy is the overthrow of our system be the beneficiary of that system." In December 1981 Congress passed the "Blitz Amendment," a law that prohibits persons who advocate the violent overthrow of the government from partaking in the CETA program. After Blitz gave birth to her child, she applied to return to work but was rejected. Enter the ACLU. "This is a throwback to lawsuits that we thought were over and done with," protested ACLU President Norman Dorsen. He added, of course, "This is a throwback to McCarthyism."[522] In May 1982 a federal judge upheld the Union's position. But in January 1983 the ACLU lost in the Supreme Court: it vacated the lower court's ruling as moot.[523]

No one angered the liberal-Left intelligentsia in the 1980s more than Susan Sontag. Her standing in leftist circles came to an abrupt end on 6 February 1982. She had committed the biggest sin of all at New York's Town Hall: she told the truth about communism. In the audience that night were many liberal-Left notables, all of whom had come to show support for Solidarity in Poland and to condemn the martial law in Warsaw. Sontag told members of the audience that they were responsible for telling lies about communism for decades. Why had the Left not been honest? "The answers are well-known," Sontag said. "We had identified the enemy as Fascism. We heard the demonic langugage of Fascism. We believed in, or at least applied, a double standard to the angelic language of Communism." Communism, she argued, was nothing more than "Fascism with a human face." She even indicated that reading only the *Reader's Digest* between 1950 and 1970 would have yielded a more accurate picture of communism than reading only the *Nation* or the *New Statesman*. The reaction of many of her listeners—men and women who pride themselves in defending civil liberties and free speech—was to boo and shout insults.[524] Sontag later said: "I have gotten so many grotesque attacks as a result of this Poland speech; they're violent, sneering, vituperative in a way which is very different from expressing strong disagreement. I'd never been the object of it before."[525] Nor had she ever "betrayed" the Left before. Aryeh Neier, who was at Town Hall the night of Sontag's speech, said shortly afterward that he had expressed her views before, but that he "would not care to in the *Reader's Digest*."[526] Like other liberal-leftists, Neier feels more at home writing for the *Nation*. As long as he continues to do so, his credentials as a bona-fide intellectual will remain untarnished.

On 26 January 1982, the Americas Watch Committee, led by Neier, and the ACLU, under the direction of Morton Halperin, issued *Report on Human Rights in El Salvador.*[527] It became evident that the Union's role as a voice for civil liberties would no longer be confined to the United States. Since the 1920s the Union had made occasional references to U.S. island possessions in Puerto Rico and the Virgin Islands but, at least until Vietnam, it did not seek to affect U.S. foreign policy. The El Salvador report is unprecedented to the extent that the Union went on record as an early and leading spokesman for civil liberties in another country. True, the ACLU has supported the U.N. Charter, but that has not inspired it to denounce the holocaust in Cambodia. El Salvador is different: a right-wing authoritarian regime, in the midst of a civil war, is receiving aid from the United States. Although there has never been a civil war where human rights violations did not occur, the ACLU prefers to treat El Salvador differently: it has chosen to (a) call our attention to the violations and (b) call for the Congress to deny aid to the regime. Defensively, the ACLU argues that the way a sovereign government treats its citizens is a legitimate concern for the international community.[528] No doubt it is. But when no report is issued on the monstrosities of Pol Pot, reasonable people will wonder what kind of passion is at work when only El Salvador is criticized.

On one page in *Report on Human Rights in El Salvador*, the Union asks the Congress to deny military aid to El Salvador. On the following page, it says that it does not "take sides" in the war.[529] The "objectivity" of the report is underscored once again when the two organizations pronounce the scheduled elections in El Salvador as offering "little hope" to the war--

torn country.[530] When the election came, 1.5 million voters cast their ballots—some while being shot at by the guerrillas. The support that the regime received did not impress the ACLU or other liberals. Renewed attempts were made to deny the elected citizens the right to military aid. When on 29 July 1982, the Congress began hearings on the president's "certification" of "progress" in economic reforms and human rights, the chorus from the Left grew louder. The Congress was busy asking many questions about El Salvador but, as Elliott Abrams, the assistant secretary of state for human rights and humanitarian affairs, pointed out, there was a series of pertinent questions that the politicians chose not to ask:

> With the certification requirement, Congress nowhere asks who the people of El Salvador support, the Government they elected or the guerrillas who attack it? It does not ask about human rights violations by the guerrilla forces. It does not ask whether a cutoff of military aid would curb human rights violations or whether it would hurt our influence with the military and retard the training programs that we hope will produce more professional, disciplined Salvadoran soldiers. It does not ask whether there is any evidence of growth in support for the guerrillas. In the end, is it not odd that Congress, acting in the name of human rights, specifically asks what the President of the United States thinks of progress in El Salvador but not what the Salvadoran people think?[531]

The same questions have eluded the ACLU. In January 1982 the Board of Directors, by a vote of 38-18, passed a resolution on El Salvador urging the president not to certify that nation's compliance with internationally recognized human rights standards. Just as impressive was the board's decision not to adopt a resolution that would have had the effect of rescinding its opposition in the event that the president offered evidence to the contrary.[532] The board knew that the elections in El Salvador were slated for March, but it opted to commit itself in January instead of waiting for the next meeting in April.

There is little doubt that in the years to come the ACLU will move to extend its influence on U.S. foreign policy. A clear indication of its intentions was revealed at the board meeting of June 1983. A new policy entitled "ACLU Role in International Civil Liberties Matters" was adopted. The Union announced that it was its belief that "the United States Constitution requires the same standard of conduct for government personnel (whether civilian or military) overseas as it requires at home." Specifically, the board claimed that "a policy of secrecy" encouraged civil liberties violations.[533] A few months later, when President Reagan authorized the landing of troops in Grenada, the ACLU applied its new policy and, of course, found that civil liberties violations had indeed occurred. Ira Glasser fired off a letter to the president informing him of the ACLU's outrage.[534]

It is striking to note that the ACLU, dedicated as it is to freedom, could not summon the moral courage to call attention to the absence of civil liberties in Grenada before the U.S. involvement. In Glasser's letter to the president, and in his letter to the ACLU membership, there is no mention of either the events that precipitated the U.S. action or the effects of Reagan's decision. Glasser prefers not to comment on the fact that since 1979 Grenada had become a depository for Soviet weapons. He prefers not to talk about the fact that Soviet, East German, Bulgarian, and North Korean advisers were active on the island. He prefers not to address the issue of the Soviet, Libyan, and North Korean embassies on Grenada. He prefers to be silent on the fact that the Cuban-built airport was not being constructed for the benefit of People's Express. He prefers not to mention that the Grenada National Democratic Movement—the only organization capable of rendering freedom to the islanders—was sent into exile in 1981. He prefers not to call attention to the execution of the Grenadian government leadership by a group of Marxist gangsters. He prefers not to take into consideration the fact that the Organization of East Caribbean States, as well as Jamaica and Barbados, requested our assistance. He prefers not to utter a word on the loud welcome that the "invading" forces received from the "invaded" medical students and the Grenadian people. Most distressing of all, he prefers not to ask whether the U.S. initiative succeeded in bringing civil liberties to a tyrannized people. The only thing that concerns Glasser and his organization (as well as many liberals) is why Mike Wallace did not have the opportunity to interview the troops while they were landing.

If it is fair to say that Roger Baldwin "boxed the compass" from Left to Right, it is accurate to conclude that the ACLU has traversed the ideological spectrum from Left to Right and back again. Whether it ever moves right again is doubtful. Being associated with anticommunism is enough to forfeit one's stature in the liberal community. Look what happened to Daniel Patrick Moynihan: He screamed about the Soviet Union and was instantly branded a "neoconservative." One can be sure that the ACLU will not let that happen to itself. It learned its lesson in the fifties—it will not "sell out" again.

Notes

1. Robert Nisbet, *The Twilight of Authority* (New York: Oxford University Press, 1975), p. 178.
2. Arthur Schlesinger, Jr., "Is Liberalism Dead?" *New York Times Magazine*, 30 March 1980, p. 79.
3. Barton Bean, "Pressure for Freedom: The American Civil Liberties Union," Ph.D. diss., Cornell University, 1955, pp. 1-14.

4. Charles Forcey, *The Crossroads of Liberalism* (New York: Oxford University Press, 1961), pp. 226-27.
5. Ibid., p. 233.
6. Paul L. Murphy, *World War I and the Origin of Civil Liberties in the United States* (New York: W. W. Norton, 1979), pp. 147-50.
7. Forcey, *Crossroads of Liberalism*, p. 237.
8. Ibid., p. 242.
9. Ibid., p. 254.
10. Ibid., p. 252.
11. Ibid., p. 247.
12. Ibid., p. 248.
13. Ibid., pp. 248-49.
14. Ibid., pp. 227, 233, 275.
15. Murphy, *World War I and the Origin of Civil Liberties*, p. 149.
16. Forcey, *Crossroads of Liberalism*, p. 256.
17. Ibid., p. 273.
18. Murphy, *World War I and the Origin of Civil Liberties*, pp. 107-12.
19. Nisbet, *Twilight of Authority*, p. 179.
20. Murphy, *World War I and the Origin of Civil Liberties*, pp. 153-57.
21. Ibid., p. 80.
22. Quoted, Donald Johnson, *The Challenge to American Freedoms* (Lexington: University of Kentucky Press, for the Mississippi Valley Historical Association, 1963), pp. 56-57.
23. Murphy *World War I and the Origin of Civil Liberties*, pp. 99-100.
24. Johnson, *Challenge to American Freedoms*, pp. 63-71.
25. Quoted, Bean, "Pressure for Freedom," p. 45.
26. Johnson, *Challenge to American Freedoms*, pp. 73-77.
27. Ibid., pp. 136-45.
28. Paul L. Murphy, "Communities in Conflict," in *The Pulse of Freedom*, ed. Alan Reitman (New York: W.W. Norton, 1975), pp. 4-5.
29. Ibid., p. 8.
30. AR 1, pp. 12-13.
31. AR 3, pp. 7-8.
32. AR 5, pp. 3, 14.
33. AR 6, p. 10.
34. AR 8, p. 6.
35. Charles Lam Markmann, *The Noblest Cry: A History of the American Civil Liberties Union* (New York: St. Martin's Press, 1965), p.56.
36. AR 18, pp. 28-29.
37. Eric Foner, "Sacco and Vanzetti," *Nation*, 20 August 1977, p. 141.
38. Quoted, Peggy Lamson, *Roger Baldwin: Founder of the American Civil Liberties Union* (Boston: Houghton Mifflin, 1976), p. 169.
39. AR 4, p. 17.
40. Quoted, Louis Joughin and Edmund M. Morgan, *The Legacy of Sacco and Vanzetti* (Chicago: Quadrangle Books, 1964), p. 243.
41. Foner, "Sacco and Vanzetti," p. 141.
42. Quoted, Joughin and Morgan, *Legacy of Sacco and Vanzetti*, p. 255.
43. Ibid. Joughin wrote this comment himself.
44. AR 7, p. 20.
45. Quoted, Lamson, *Baldwin*, p. 171.

46. Quoted, Corliss Lamont, *Yes to Life* (New York: Horizon Press, 1981), p. 138.
47. Joughin and Morgan, *Legacy of Sacco and Vanzetti*, p. vii.
48. Ibid., p. 505.
49. Francis Russell, "Son of Sacco," *National Review*, 17 August 1973, p. 889.
50. Ibid., pp. 887-90.
51. Francis Russell, "Sacco and Vanzetti Fifty Years Later: The End of the Myth," *National Review*, 19 August 1977, p. 939.
52. Katherine Anne Porter, "The Never-Ending Wrong," *Atlantic Monthly*, June 1977, p. 40.
53. Foner, "Sacco and Vanzetti," p. 141.
54. AR 3, title page.
55. "American Civil Liberties Union and Communist Activity," *Law and Labor*, February 1931, p. 24.
56. "Robert W. Dunn, 81, a Co-Founder of American Civil Liberties Union," *New York Times*, 23 January 1977, p. 28.
57. Quoted, Lamson, *Baldwin*, p. 141.
58. Murphy, *World War I and the Origin of Civil Liberties*, p. 154; Bean, "Pressure for Freedom," p. 54.
59. ACLU Papers, Reel 16, Vol. 115.
60. Quoted, Paul Hollander, *Political Pilgrims* (New York: Oxford Univesity Press, 1981), p. 349.
61. Quoted, Lamson, *Baldwin*, p. 142.
62. Ibid., p. 143.
63. Ibid., pp. 180-81.
64. See chapter 8 of Hollander, *Political Pilgrims*, for a splendid discussion of the "techniques of hospitality."
65. Lamson, *Baldwin*, p. 183.
66. Ibid., p. 185.
67. Ibid., p. 187.
68. Ibid., p. 188.
69. See Hollander, *Political Pilgrims*.
70. William O'Neill, *A Better World* (New York: Simon and Schuster, 1982).
71. Edmund Wilson, "An Appeal to Progressives," *New Republic*, 14 January 1931, p. 238.
72. Arthur Schlesinger, letter to the editor, *Commentary*, July 1952, p. 84.
73. William Barrett, *The Truants* (Garden City, N.Y.: Doubleday, 1982), p. 90.
74. This statement was made in 1952. See "Plight of the U.S. 'Liberals'—Signs That an Era Is Ending," *U.S. News and World Report*, 14 July 1969, p. 41.
75. George H. Nash, *The Conservative Intellectual Movement in America* (New York: Basic Books, 1976), pp. 86-88.
76. Barrett, *Truants*, p. 84.
77. Ibid., p. 8.
78. Sidney Hook in symposium "What Is a Liberal—Who Is a Conservative," *Commentary*, September 1976, p. 69.
79. AR 12, pp. 19-20.
80. Murphy, "Communities in Conflict," p. 36.
81. AR 10, p. 38.
82. Ibid., p. 11; Murphy, "Communities in Conflict," p. 37.
83. AR 10, p. 33.
84. Ibid., p. 39.

85. Bd. Mid., 10/6/30, p. 1.
86. "The American Civil Liberties Union Sticks Out Its Tongue," editorial, *Law and Labor*, January 1931, p. 7.
87. Ibid., pp. 7-8.
88. "American Civil Liberties Union and Communist Activity," editorial, *Law and Labor*, February 1931, pp. 23-24.
89. Ibid.
90. Johnson, *Challenge to American Freedoms*, p. 199.
91. Roger Baldwin, "Freedom in the U.S.A. and the U.S.S.R.," *Soviet Russia Today*, September 1934, p. 11.
92. Quoted, Lamson, *Baldwin*, p. 192.
93. Quoted, Cletus Daniel, *The ACLU and the Wagner Act* (Ithaca, N.Y.: Cornell University, New York State School of Industrial and Labor Relations, 1980), p. 81.
94. Ibid., pp. 129-30.
95. AR 16, p. 15.
96. AR 17, p. 52.
97. AR 18, p. 4.
98. Lamson, *Baldwin*, p. 226.
99. Quoted, Jerome Auerbach, "The Depression Decade," in *The Pulse of Freedom*, ed. Alan Reitman (New York: W.W. Norton, 1975), p. 70.
100. See Alan Reitman, ed., *The Pulse of Freedom* (New York: W. W. Norton, 1975), p. 251.
101. Markmann's two references to Flynn can be found on pages 94 and 220 of his *Noblest Cry*.
102. AR 14, p. 17.
103. Quoted, Auerbach, "Depression Decade," p. 68n.
104. Corliss Lamont, *Freedom Is As Freedom Does* (New York: Horizon Press, 1956), pp. 265-66.
105. Ibid., pp. 266-67.
106. Ibid., p. 267. See also Thomas to Executive Committee, 3/6/39, ACLU Papers, Vol. 2063.
107. Quoted, Auerbach, "Depression Decade," p. 64.
108. Lamont, *Freedom Is As Freedom Does*, p. 268.
109. Ibid. See also AR 18, p. 18.
110. Lamont, *Freedom Is As Freedom Does*, pp. 268-69.
111. Baldwin admits that the conference was held. See Lamson, *Baldwin* , p. 233. In my interview with Baldwin he acknowledged the same.
112. Lamont, *Freedom Is As Freedom Does*, p. 269.
113. Ibid., p. 270.
114. Ibid., P. 233.
115. Interview with Baldwin.
116. AR 18, pp. 18-19.
117. AR 19, pp. 22-23.
118. AR 20, p. 48.
119. AR 24, p. 47.
120. AR 26, p. 80.
121. Quoted in Lamson, *Baldwin*, p. 201.
122. AR 18, p. 6.
123. Interview with Baldwin.

124. Walter H. Waggoner, "Granville Hicks, Critic and Leader in Proletarian Movement, Is Dead," *New York Times*, 19 June 1982, p. 18.
125. Quoted, Irving Kristol, letter to the editor, *Commentary*, July 1952, p. 84.
126. John Kenneth Galbraith, "An Agenda for American Liberals," *Commentary*, June 1966, p. 31.
127. Lamont, *Yes to Life*, p. 131.
128. "U.S. Urged to Seek New Tie with Russia," *New York Times*, 14 August 1939, p. 15.
129. Ibid.
130. Irving Kristol, letter to the editor, *Commentary*, May 1952, p. 500.
131. AR 18, p. 46.
132. Quoted, Auerbach, "Depression Decade," p. 65.
133. Interview with Baldwin.
134. Lamson, *Baldwin*, p. 228.
135. Auerbach, "Depression Decade," p. 65.
136. AR 18, pp. 48-49.
137. Corliss Lamont, ed., *The Trial of Elizabeth Gurley Flynn by the American Civil Liberties Union* (New York: Horizon Press, 1968), pp. 22-23.
138. Lamson, *Baldwin*, p. 234.
139. Lamont, *Trial of Elizabeth Gurley Flynn*, p. 13.
140. Interview with Baldwin.
141. Baldwin's few comments at the trial can be found in Lamont, *Trial of Elizabeth Gurley Flynn*, pp. 35, 78, 121, 135, 166. Lamson wrote that Baldwin had not said a word at the trial on p. 223 of *Baldwin*.
142. Interview with Baldwin.
143. Lamont, *Trial of Elizabeth Gurley Flynn*, pp. 35-36.
144. Ibid., p. 45.
145. Ibid., pp. 209-11.
146. Ibid., pp. 212-15.
147. Ibid., pp. 47 and 57.
148. Ibid., pp. 185-86.
149. Lamont, *Freedom Is As Freedom Does*, p. 273.
150. Lamont, *Trial of Elizabeth Gurley Flynn*, p. 48.
151. AR 1, p. 19.
152. Interview with Baldwin.
153. Lamson, *Baldwin*, p. 230.
154. Interview with Baldwin.
155. Lamson, *Baldwin*, p. 202.
156. Interview with Baldwin.
157. Quoted Lamson, *Baldwin*, p. 204.
158. Lamont, *Trial of Elizabeth Gurley Flynn*, p. 142.
159. Ibid., p. 220.
160. Interview with Baldwin.
161. Lamont, *Yes to Life*, p. 135.
162. Ibid., p. 136.
163. Ibid., p. 133.
164. Interview with Baldwin.
165. Interview with Reitman.
166. Bean, "Pressure for Freedom," p. 223.
167. Ibid., p. 278.

168. Daniel, *ACLU and the Wagner Act,* p. 134.
169. Lamont, *Trial of Elizabeth Gurley Flynn,* p. 23.
170. AR 18, p. 11.
171. AR 19, p. 33.
172. AR 27, p. 6.
173. Interview with Baldwin.
174. Roger Baldwin, "Liberalism and the United Front," in *Whose Revolution,* ed. Irving DeWitt Talmadge (Westport, Conn.: Hyperion Press, 1975), pp. 169,175.
175. Ibid., p. 183.
176. *FBI Files on the ACLU,* located at the ACLU's national headquarters, New York City.
177. Ibid.
178. Bd. Min., 1/8/45, p. 3.
179. Bd. Min., 3/19/45, p. 1.
180. Bd. Min., 4/16/45, p. 1.
181. Interview with Baldwin.
182. Alonzo Hamby, *Beyond the New Deal: Harry S. Truman and American Liberalism* (New York: Columbia University Press, 1973), p. 13.
183. AR 20, p. 10.
184. Ibid., p. 60.
185. AR 21, p. 32.
186. AR 20, p. 38; Bd. Min., 6/25/41, pp. 1-2.
187. Letter to President Roosevelt, in Bd. Min., 6/27/41.
188. AR 26, p. 34.
189. AR 27, p. 40.
190. AR 19, pp. 45-46.
191. AR 26, p. 80.
192. William Preston, Jr., "Shadows of War and Fear," in *The Pulse of Freedom,* ed. Alan Reitman (New York: W.W. Norton, 1975), p. 87.
193. AR 20, pp. 27-28.
194. Preston, "Shadows of War and Fear," pp. 95-99. See also the "freedom of the press" and "censorship" sections of the annual reports of the 1940s.
195. Quoted, Lamson, *Baldwin,* p. 86.
196. Ibid., p. 237.
197. Quoted, ibid., p. 203.
198. AR 20, p. 61.
199. Ibid.
200. Interview with Baldwin.
201. AR 19, p. 31.
202. AR 27, p. 44.
203. AR 20, pp. 24 and 61.
204. AR 21, p. 26.
205. AR 26, pp. 79-80.
206. Ibid; AR 23, p. 60.
207. AR 20, p. 5.
208. AR 21, p. 35.
209. Bd. Min., 10/19/42, pp. 1-2.
210. AR 25, p. 31.
211. Bd. Min., 10/21/47, p. 1.

212. AR 26, p. 23.
213. Ibid., p. 80.
214. AR 27, p. 6.
215. Interview with Baldwin.
216. Preston, "Shadows of War and Fear," p. 81.
217. AR 21, p. 29.
218. Ibid., p. 24.
219. Ibid., p. 28.
220. Interview with Baldwin.
221. Lamson, *Baldwin*, pp. 238-39.
222. Interview with Baldwin.
223. Thomas Sowell, *Ethnic America* (New York: Basic Books, 1981), p. 172.
224. William Petersen, *Japanese Americans* (New York: Random House, 1971). pp. 77-79.
225. Sowell, *Ethnic America*, p. 171.
226. Baldwin acknowledged Hoover's role to Lamson; see Lamson, *Baldwin*, p. 239.
227. Ibid.
228. AR 22, p. 55.
229. AR 23, pp. 9-10.
230. Ibid., pp. 45-46.
231. AR 24, pp. 31-33.
232. Ibid., p. 45.
233. Hamby, *Beyond the New Deal*, p. 15.
234. Lamson, *Baldwin*, p. 193.
235. AR 26, p. 58.
236. Lamson, *Baldwin*, pp. 241-43.
237. AR 26, p. 75.
238. AR 25, p. 8.
239. Lamson, *Baldwin*, p. 248.
240. Quoted, ibid., p. 251.
241. Quoted, Dave Goldberg, "ACLU Founder Roger Baldwin: Recalling the Past, But Thinking Ahead," *Pittsburgh Post-Gazette*, 1 August 1978, p. 23.
242. Lamson, *Baldwin*, p. 241.
243. Hamby, *Beyond the New Deal*, p. 22.
244. Ibid., p. 26.
245. Quoted, ibid., p. 99.
246. Quoted, Barrett, *Truants*, p. 243.
247. Ibid., p. 90.
248. Ibid., p. 88.
249. Ibid., pp. 55, 56, 78, 79.
250. Ibid., pp. 80-83.
251. Quoted, Hollander, *Political Pilgrims*, p. 417.
252. Wilson Wyatt, "Creed for Liberals: A Ten-Point Program," *New York Times Magazine*, 22 July 1947, p. 37.
253. AR 20, p. 3; AR 21, p. 3.
254. AR 22, p. 5.
255. AR 18, pp. 33-34.
256. AR 23, p. 5.
257. AR 21, p. 3.

258. Bd. Min., 4/16/45, p. 1.
259. AR 24, p. 5.
260. AR 25, p. 4.
261. AR 26, p. 4.
262. AR 27, p. 3.
263. Ibid., p. 7.
264. Ibid., p. 9.
265. Alan Reitman, "Introduction," 1976 *Policy Guide*, p. 2.
266. Lamont, *Freedom Is As Freedom Does*, pp. 279-80.
267. AR 29, p. 13.
268. Ibid.
269. Lamont, *Freedom Is As Freedom Does*, pp. 279-80.
270. Ibid.
271. Barrett, *Truants*, p. 93.
272. Ibid., p. 194.
273. Ibid., p. 189.
274. Nash, *Conservative Movement in America*, p. 148.
275. Irving Kristol, "'Civil Liberties,' 1952—A Study in Confusion," *Commentary*, March 1952, p. 229.
276. Ibid., p. 230.
277. Ibid., p. 233.
278. Alan F. Westin, "Our Freedom—And The Rights of Communists," *Commentary*, July 1952, p. 33.
279. Ibid., p. 40.
280. Ibid., p. 37.
281. Kristol, "'Civil Liberties,' 1952," p. 236.
282. AR 29, p. 8.
283. AR 31, pp. 38-39.
284. AR 30, pp. 3-4.
285. AR 31, p. 82.
286. AR 29, p. 78.
287. Ibid., pp. 28-30.
288. Lamont, *Freedom Is As Freedom Does*, pp. 280-81.
289. Ibid., p. 281.
290. Ibid., pp. 281-82.
291. AR 30, pp. 25-27.
292. Lamont, *Freedom Is As Freedom Does*, p. 282.
293. Bd. Min., 11/30/53, p. 3.
294. Bd. Min., 3/17/53, p. 1.
295. Ibid., p. 2.
296. Bd. Min., 3/15/54, p. 2.
297. AR 30, p. 26.
298. Bd. Min., 3/15/54; AR 31, p. 28; AR 32, p. 19.
299. AR 30, p. 27.
300. Ibid.
301. AR 28, p. 6.
302. Ibid., p. 17.
303. AR 30, p. 87.
304. AR 28, p. 18.
305. Ibid., p. 20.

306. AR 19, p. 34.
307. AR 27, p. 71.
308. AR 29, p. 68.
309. Hamby, *Beyond the New Deal*, p. 400.
310. Bd. Min., 10/15/51, p. 1.
311. AR 26, p. 80.
312. AR 27, p. 70.
313. Bd. Min., 9/25/50, pp. 1-2.
314. Bd. Min., 1/8/51, p. 3; Bd. Min., 9/8/52, p. 1.
315. AR 29, pp. 35-36.
316. AR 28, p. 5.
317. AR 29, pp. 75-76.
318. AR 31, p. 68.
319. Ibid.
320. AR 29, p. 49.
321. AR 30, p. 33.
322. AR 1, p. 17.
323. AR 30, p. 33.
324. Ibid.
325. AR 1, p. 17.
326. Ibid.
327. AR 30, p. 33.
328. AR 1, p. 17.
329. AR 29, p. 46; AR 34, p. 36.
330. AR 34, p. 36.
331. AR 31, pp. 21-22.
332. AR 32, pp. 7-8.
333. AR 33, pp. 5-6.
334. AR 31, pp. 70-71.
335. AR 33, p. 12.
336. AR 29, pp. 42-43.
337. AR 34, p. 74.
338. Quoted, J. Anthony Lukas, "The ACLU Against Itself," *New York Times Magazine*, 9 July 1978, p. 11.
339. '76 PG, #92.
340. AR 29, pp. 103-04.
341. Lamont, *Freedom Is As Freedom Does*, p. 278.
342. AR 26, pp. 24-25; AR 27, pp. 11-12; AR 29, pp. 41-42.
343. Anthony Marro, "FBI Files Disclose '50s Tie to ACLU," *New York Times*, 4 August 1977, p. A1.
344. Statement from Norman Dorsen and Aryeh Neier, 3 August 1977.
345. Marro, "FBI Files Disclose '50s Tie to ACLU," p. B5.
346. Ibid.
347. Ibid.
348. Aryeh Neier, "Adhering to Principle: Lessons from the 1950s," *Civil Liberties Review*, November/December 1977, pp. 26-27.
349. Ibid., pp. 27-28.
350. Ibid., pp. 29-30.
351. Ibid., pp. 30-31.
352. Ibid., p. 31.

353. Corliss Lamont, letter to the editor, *New York Times*, 17 August 1977, p. 20. Lamont is a curious character. He admits that other board members knew of the ACLU-FBI connection, yet he said in his memoirs that he was "profoundly shocked" by the "revelations" that appeared in the *Times*. See *Yes to Life*, p. 140. Evidently his capacity for shock is limitless. One can only conclude that he was "shocked" to read about the extent and the duration of this relationship.
354. Herbert Monte Levy, letter, *Civil Liberties Review*, March/April 1978, p. 5.
355. Lamont, *Trial of Elizabeth Gurley Flynn*, p. 22.
356. AR 28, p. 80.
357. Bd. Min., 1/21/52.
358. See the last page of ARs #30-35. In March 1967 this statement was dropped from the organization's membership card. Lamont, *Trial of Elizabeth Gurley Flynn*, p. 24.
359. Marro, "FBI Files Disclose '50s Tie to ACLU," p. B5.
360. Memo from Aryeh Neier to the Board of Directors, Affiliates, National Advisory Council. Re: FBI Files on the ACLU, 4 August 1977.
361. Neier, "Adhering to Principle," p. 26.
362. "The ACLU and the FBI: Over 50 Years of Constant Surveillance," *Civil Liberties Review*, November/December 1977, p. 17.
363. Memo from Neier, 4 August 1977.
364. ACLU statement by Dorsen and Neier, 3 August 1977.
365. Marro, "FBI Files Disclose '50s Tie to ACLU," p. B5.
366. Anthony Marro, "ACLU Aides Fear Effects of Former FBI Ties," *New York Times*, 5 August 1977, p. A20. I was in the ACLU headquarters doing research when Marro's second article appeared. One staff member complained to a colleague that one article about the ACLU-FBI connection was enough. Apparently the *Times* thought differently.
367. Letter from Mimi Schneider, secretary to Jack Novik, 24 May 1978.
368. Interview with Reitman.
369. Bd. Min., 9/24-25/77, p. 7.
370. Ibid.
371. Ibid., pp. 7-8.
372. ACLU statement by Dorsen and Neier, 3 August 1977.
373. Quoted, Marro, "ACLU Aides Fear Effects of Former FBI Ties."
374. Irving Ferman, letter, *Civil Liberties Review*, March/April 1978, pp. 5-6.
375. *FBI Files on the ACLU*, located at the ACLU's national headquarters, New York.
376. Ibid.
377. Ibid.
378. Ibid.
379. Ibid.
380. Ibid.
381. Ibid.
382. J. Edgar Hoover, "Civil Liberties and Law Enforcement: The Role Of the FBI," *Iowa Law Review*, Winter 1952, p. 194.
383. Ibid., p. 178.
384. Ibid., p. 176.
385. Ibid., p. 186.
386. *FBI Files on the ACLU*.

387. Ibid.
388. Ibid.
389. Ibid.
390. Ibid.
391. Lamont, *Yes to Life*, p. 130.
392. *FBI Files on the ACLU.*
393. Ibid.
394. Ibid.
395. Ibid.
396. Ibid.
397. Ibid.
398. Lamont, *Yes to Life*, p. 141.
399. '66 PG, #85.
400. Bd. Min., 12/2-3/67, p. 25.
401. Ibid., p. 31.
402. Ibid., p. 26.
403. Ibid.
404. Lamont, *Trial of Elizabeth Gurley Flynn*, p. 25.
405. Ibid.
406. Bd. Min., 12/2-3/67, p. 26.
407. Lamont, *Trial of Elizabeth Gurley Flynn*, p. 26.
408. Interview with Baldwin.
409. Interview with Reitman.
410. Bd. Min., 12/2-3/67, p. 31.
411. Quoted, Lamont, *Yes to Life*, p. 138.
412. Bd. Min., 4/10-11/76, pp. 12-14.
413. Ibid.
414. Interview with Baldwin.
415. Quoted, John Caughey, "McCarthyism Rampant," in *The Pulse of Freedom*, ed. Alan Reitman (New York: W. W. Norton, 1975), p. 160.
416. Bd. Min., 6/20-21/81.
417. Quoted by Hollander, *Political Pilgrims*, p. 400.
418. '81 PG, #110.
419. '66, '67 PGs, #85.
420. '71 PG, #91; '81 PG, #99.
421. '66, '67 PGs, #85.
422. '66, '67 PGs, #s 92-93.
423. AR 36, p. 40.
424. '81, PG, #100.
425. Ibid.
426. AR '71-'72, p. 3; AR '74, pp. 3-4; interview with Baldwin.
427. '81 PG, #111.
428. Ibid., #112.
429. Ibid.
430. '66, '67 PGs, #10.
431. '71 PG, #10.
432. '76, '81 PGs, #7.
433. Ibid.
434. Ibid.
435. AR 31, p. 82.

436. AR '71-'72, p. 22.
437. AR 17, p. 18.
438. AR 19, pp. 45-46; '66, '67, '71, '76 PGs, #10.
439. '78, '81 PGs, #10.
440. AR 42, p. 74
441. AR 43, p. 2.
442. '81 PG, #44.
443. William F. Buckley, Jr., "Needed: Another Investigation," *National Review*, 6 September 1966, p. 875.
444. '67 PG, #38.
445. "A 'Liberal' Group Speaks Out Against Draft Violation, Rioting," *U.S. News and World Report*, 12 February 1968, pp. 68-69.
446. Joseph W. Bishop, Jr., "The Reverend Mr. Coffin, Dr. Spock, and the ACLU," *Harper's Magazine*, May 1968, p. 58.
447. Bd. Min., 10/5-6/68, p. 7. See also '76 PG, #38.
448. Joseph W. Bishop, Jr., "Politics and ACLU," *Commentary*, December 1971, p. 54.
449. Ibid.
450. Aryeh Neier, letter to the editor, *Commentary*, March 1972, p. 12.
451. William Safire, *Safire's Washington* (New York: Times Books, 1980), p. 146.
452. Quoted, Lamson, *Baldwin*, p. 255.
453. Robert Nisbet, *Prejudices* (Cambridge: Harvard University Press, 1982), p. 313.
454. AR 42, p. 54.
455. AR 43, p. 12.
456. '76 PG, #108.
457. Bd. Min., 6/2/70, p. 9.
458. Interview with Baldwin.
459. AR 19, p. 8.
460. Interview with Reitman.
461. James MacGregor Burns and Jack Peltason, *Government by the People*, 6th ed. (Englewood Cliffs, N.J: Prentice Hall, 1966), p. 421.
462. Louis Koenig, *The Chief Executive,* rev. ed. (New York: Harcourt, Brace and World, 1968), p. 360.
463. '66 PG, #401.
464. Ibid. and '76 PG, #401.
465. '66 PG, #100; AR 37, p. 31; AR 39, pp. 36-37; AR 40, pp. 42-43.
466. AR 42, p. 57.
467. AR 26, p. 79.
468. '66 PG, #99; AR 42, pp. 53-54.
469. Ibid.
470. Ibid.
471. Ibid. See also AR 39, p. 35; AR 42, p. 55.
472. Ibid.; AR 42, pp. 52-55.
473. Ibid.
474. Bd. Min., 2/15-16/69, p. 9.
475. Ibid.
476. Ibid., p. 10.
477. '66 PG, #37. See also AR 37, p. 12; AR 38, pp. 35-36.
478. '71 PG, #37.

222   The Politics of the ACLU

479. '76 PG, #37.
480. AR 21, p. 26.
481. Quoted in Bishop, "Politics and ACLU," pp. 53-54.
482. AR '72-'73, p. 19.
483. Ibid. See also '76 PG, #245.
484. AR '72-'73, p. 2.
485. Ibid., p. 1.
486. Lukas, "ACLU Against Itself," p. 18.
487. George Kannar, "Sears Shall Overcome," *New Republic*, 10 March 1979, pp. 18-19.
488. AR '74, p. 3.
489. Quoted, Lamson, *Baldwin*, p. viii.
490. AR '74, p. 4.
491. Bd. Min., 9/29-30/73, pp. 24-29.
492. Ibid.
493. Interview with Reitman.
494. Bd. Min., 6/12/74, pp. 14-18.
495. Ibid.
496. Ibid., pp. 10-13; '76 PG, #112.
497. '76 PG, #112.
498. Ibid., and Bd. Min., 6/12/74, pp. 10-13.
499. AR '74, pp. 4-5.
500. Ibid.
501. Howard Blum, "Unscrupulous Professionals Prey on Captives of Immigration Maze," *New York Times*, 15 January 1980, p. A1.
502. Peter Kihss, "Civil Liberties Union Assails Raids for Making 'Scapegoats' of Aliens," *New York Times*, 3 May 1982, p. A17.
503. ACLU, *Civil Liberties in Reagan's America*, October 1982, pp. 57-60.
504. '77 PG, #327.
505. William French Smith, *Congressional Digest*, October 1981, pp. 232-38.
506. Ibid.
507. John Shattuck, *Congressional Digest*, October 1981, pp. 233-39. See also the ACLU publication, "Testimony of John Shattuck on the Final Report and Recommendations of the Select Commission on Immigration and Refugee Policy before the Subcommittee on Immigration of the Senate and House Judiciary Committees," 6 May 1981.
508. Ibid.
509. "Immigration on Fast Track in Both House and Senate," *Civil Liberties Alert*, March 1983, p. 1.
510. David Burnham, "Government Restricting Flow of Information to the Public," *New York Times*, 15 November 1982, p. 1.
511. Philip Taubman, "Government to Defend Lawsuits Aimed at Release of Documents," *New York Times*, 5 May 1981, p. A18.
512. Ira Glasser, "The Coming Assault on Civil Liberties," in *What Reagan Is Doing to Us*, ed. Alan Gartner, Colin Greer, and Frank Riessman (New York: Harper and Row, 1982), pp. 234-35.
513. "Bill to Penalize Uncovering of Agents Passed by Senate," *New York Times*, 11 June 1982, p. A20.
514. Glasser, "Coming Assault on Civil Liberties," p. 235.
515. Charles Mohr, "A.C.L.U. Says Fight to Stop Terrorism Imperils Rights," *New York Times*, 19 May 1981, p. B11.

516. Ibid.
517. '81 PG, #125.
518. Bishop, "Politics and ACLU," p. 56.
519. Barry Steinhardt, "Reagan, Red Baiting and the Nuclear Freeze," *Civil Liberties Record*, January 1983, p. 2.
520. '77 PG, #323.
521. '76 PG, #322.
522. ACLU, *Civil Liberties in Reagan's America*, pp. 18-19.
523. "Communists' Rights," *New York Times*, 11 January 1983, p. 9.
524. "Susan Sontag Provokes Debate on Communism," *New York Times*, 27 February 1982, p. 27.
525. Quoted, Charles Ruas, "Susan Sontag: Past, Present and Future," *New York Times Book Review*, 24 October 1982, p. 11.
526. Aryeh Neier, "Communism and the Left," *Nation*, 27 February 1982, p. 232.
527. Americas Watch Committee and ACLU, comps., *Report on Human Rights in El Salvador* (New York: Vintage Books, 1982).
528. Ibid., pp. x-xi.
529. Ibid., pp. viii-ix.
530. Ibid., p. xlviii.
531. Elliott Abrams, "El Salvador: Are We Asking the Right Questions," *New York Times*, 29 July 1982, p. A23.
532. Bd. Min., 1/23-24/82, p. 4.
533. ACLU Policy #401, 2d revision to '81 PG.
534. The letter that Glasser sent President Reagan was dated 15 November 1983. The following month he sent a similar letter to the members of the ACLU.

4

Civil Liberties, Civility, and the Social Order

Free Speech

"Congress shall make no law . . . abridging the freedom of speech, or of the press; or of people peaceably to assemble and to petition the Government for a redress of grievance." Those words are the heart of civil liberties. Following Justice Holmes, they have typically been interpreted as meaning that the free trade of ideas is guaranteed by the First Amendment. Since *Winters v. New York* in 1948, the Supreme Court has steadily, though unevenly, widened its interpretation of the First Amendment to go beyond the exposition-of-ideas position. But it has never taken an absolutist position, nor has any serious student of the Constitution. Not even Justice Hugo Black, who once said: "It is my belief that there *are* 'absolutes' in our Bill of Rights, and that they were put there on purpose by men who knew what the words meant, and meant their prohibitions to be 'absolutes'. . . ."[1] That Black did not adhere to his own interpretation of the First Amendment can be seen in his dissents in *Cohen v. California, Tinker v. Community School District,* and other cases.[2] Similarly, Dr. Alexander Meiklejohn, a former member of the ACLU National Committee, is often cited as an absolutist. He once said, "The phrase 'Congress shall make no law . . . abridging the freedom of speech,' is unqualified. It admits of no exceptions . . . under any circumstances . . . they established an absolute, unqualified prohibition of the abridgment of the freedom of speech."[3] However, even Meiklejohn admitted that "in any well-governed society, the legislature has the right and duty to prohibit certain forms of speech."[4]

The Supreme Court has recognized certain excepted categories of speech that may be proscribed, among them are cases involving obscenity, libel, incitement to riot, and when a clear and present danger can be established. In addition to tests addressing the latter two categories, the court has applied the bad-tendency test and the balancing test. Hard cases make for unsatisfactory laws, and also make it difficult for legislators and judges to develop an airtight prescription for dealing with such cases. But decisions must be made as to where to draw the line, and it is the faith of every democrat that those decisions be respected by everyone. A rule of law requires no less. Additional problems are posed when we begin to define what exactly constitutes speech. Surely there is a difference between speech and action, but even here the difference is not always empirically obvious. Utterances are recognized as speech, but what about nonverbal expression? Should all symbolic expression be accorded the same protection that is given to speech? Sound arguments have been advanced by both advocates and opponents of symbolic speech. Does the burning of one's draft card as a protest against war merit protection as an exercise of symbolic speech? The Supreme Court thinks not. The ACLU disagrees.[5]

One's interpretation of free speech ultimately reflects one's perception of the meaning of democracy. Irving Kristol has argued that the traditional (and now conservative) idea of democracy saw democratic institutions as a means toward the realization of the good society; it was not indifferent to the ordering of the quality of public life. He describes the contemporary, i.e. liberal, perception of democracy as "a set of rules and procedures, and *nothing but* a set of rules and procedures, whereby majority rule and minority rights are reconciled into a state of equilibrium."[6] In essence, freedom is seen as an end in itself, not as a means toward the good life. Because it is the liberal position that concerns us, it is appropriate to consider its stand. Thomas Emerson and Franklyn Haiman have made the two most cogent and recent contributions to the liberal's idea of freedom. Both men focused on the meaning of free speech.

Following a long line of distinguished legal scholars, including Meiklejohn, Chafee, and Leonard Levy, Thomas Emerson has written a book, *The System of Freedom of Expression*,[7] that has been heralded as a classic in the literature on the First Amendment. Emerson insists that we distinguish between "expression" and "action." Expression is entitled to absolute protection under the First Amendment, "even where the results of expression may appear to be in conflict with other social interests that the government is charged with safeguarding." This is what he means by his "full-protection" theory. Action, however, "can be controlled, subject to other constitutional requirements, but not by controlling expression."[8] He rejects the various tests that have been applied by the Supreme Court in addressing limitations on free speech, namely, the bad-tendency test, the clear-and-present-danger test, and incitement test, and the ad hoc balancing test. Although he is critical of the absolute test, his own interpretation of the First Amendment gravitates toward that position.

A careful scholar, Emerson acknowledges that the line between expression and action is sometimes blurred. For Emerson, there is such a thing as "verbal acts," or what the Supreme Court calls "fighting words."[9] Not insensitive to the context in which speech occurs, Emerson notes that "for reasons peculiar to each case, certain sectors of social conduct, though involving 'expression' . . . must be deemed to fall outside the system [of full protection]. The areas that must be excluded embrace aspects of the operations of the military, of commercial activities, of the activities of children, and of communication with foreign countries."[10] Notice that Emerson distinguishes between expression and "expression." This has left him vulnerable to Sidney Hook's charge that he engages in "semantic legislation" whenever he believes that certain forms of speech should be legally punishable.[11] Hook's criticism stems from his defense of the court's excepted-category approach and the tests, such as the clear-and-present-danger test and the ad hoc balancing test, which Emerson finds wanting.

A different sort of criticism is afforded by Franklyn Haiman. In his role as national secretary of the ACLU, Haiman has been an influential contributor to free speech issues. His book *Speech and Law in a Free Society* has been praised by Norman Dorsen of the ACLU and many others. Haiman's quarrel with Emerson is over the parameters of freedom of expression. Emerson simply does not go far enough in the absolutist direction to please Haiman. Like Hook, Haiman objects to Emerson's distinction between expression and "expression." Words, he maintains, cannot be transformed into acts "by the magic of redefinition."[12] The idea of a "verbal act" is unacceptable to Haiman. For Haiman, there should be no category of speech that, by definition, is outside the protection of the First Amendment. Context may be considered, albeit not broadly. The First Amendment ought to cover "a broad range of symbolic conduct, whether oral or written, rational or emotive, verbal or nonverbal. Even behaviors which are not normally engaged in for communicative purposes [can be viewed] as potential candidates for First Amendment protection when functioning symbolically."[13] Practically every form of "communication" short of physical assault, including most every instance of defamation, ought to be legal.[14]

The position taken by Emerson, and most especially Haiman, ascribes to what Kristol labeled the liberal idea of democracy. Haiman explicity acknowledges that he sees freedom as an end in itself.[15] It is for this reason that he can defend George Carlin's broadcast of four-letter words over the air waves at times when children are likely to listen.[16] It is for the very same reason that he can defend the right of a draft resister to parade through a public building with the inscription "Fuck the Draft" on his jacket.[17] If we do not like what we hear or see, we can simply turn the channel or avert our eyes. That is the democratic remedy according to Haiman.

The American Civil Liberties Union does not follow the liberal line on free speech—it leads it. No other organization has done more to affect our perception of free speech in a democratic society. Often successful in the courts, the Union's interpretation of the First Amendment closely parallels that of Haiman's on most free speech cases. Unquestionably, the ACLU sees freedom as an end in itself (this departs from its earlier commitment to defend civil liberties in service to labor and against capitalists). Like Haiman, the ACLU views *all* methods of communication as conveying information and opinion.[18] Two recent cases demonstrate the Union's position. When the South African rugby team asked local authorities in this country for the right to play on a publicly owned playing field, it was initially denied. The ACLU went to work arguing that playing rugby was a form of free speech covered by the First Amendment.[19] In 1983 one of the first cases that the newly formed Scranton chapter of the ACLU involved itself in was the defense of rock singer Ozzy Osbourne. Osbourne had been banned from playing in a concert at the Catholic Youth Center in Scranton. He was unwanted because of his past activities, which included biting off the head of a bat while peforming (for which he received twenty-seven rabies shots) and urinating on the Alamo shrine. The Union affiliate rushed to Osbourne's defense, citing the usual First Amendment argument. It took three attorneys to plan the defense of the entertainer. The case was given front-page coverage by the ACLU's Pennsylvania news record, which noted that the Scranton lawyers had established "a vigilant ACLU" in the city.[20]

In the ACLU's first annual report in 1920, it flatly stated that it "puts no limit on the principle of free speech."[21] The Union was busy during the 1920s, defending the free speech rights of persons who needed an organization such as the ACLU to secure their rights. Free speech in the twenties had nothing to do with rugby matches or rock performers; elementary, straight First Amendment cases were the typical ACLU fare. A few examples will suffice. On 27 January 1924, a Lenin memorial meeting held in Wilkes-Barre, Pennsylvania, was broken up by a city policeman and members of the American Legion. The Legionnaires forced an audience of four hundred, chiefly aliens, to salute the American flag at gunpoint. The mayor sent a collect telegram to the ACLU stating that in the future he would submit the names of "all meetings of this character" to the Legion for its approval.[22] In Washington, Georgia, Charles E. Falloon was arrested for challenging the local clergy by contending that there is "no proof that Jesus ever lived as a man, much less as a God."[23] In 1927 a man in New York City spent two days in jail for failing to remove his hat when the national anthem was played at ceremonies for Lindbergh. The court decided he should be punished even though he said he kept his hat on only because he was sensitive about his baldness.[24] Albert Phifer of Reading, Pennsylvania, was luckier; he was acquitted by a jury after he was charged with a crime for having said, "To hell with that," when asked as a witness in court to swear on the Bible.[25]

Free Speech for Whom?

"My demand for freedom to speak," argues Sidney Hook, "is at the same time a demand that the freedom of those who desire to prevent me from speaking should be curbed."[26] This fundamental truism has yet to be accepted by many members of the liberal community. Ambassador Jeane Kirkpatrick's free speech was routinely violated on college campuses in 1983 by students and faculty who shouted her down. As Diane Ravitch has said, "Such campuses are still hostage to the concessions they made to radical students in the late 1960s."[27] A decade earlier, Harvard professor James Q. Wilson wrote that he had been affiliated with five institutions in his adult life—the Catholic Church, the University of Redlands, the United States Navy, the University of Chicago, and Harvard University—and, "If I were required to rank them by the extent to which free and uninhibited discussion was possible within them, I am very much afraid that the Harvard of 1972 would not rank near the top."[28] One would think that the ACLU would quickly come to the aid of any person who was denied free speech on a college campus, but its record on this score is uneven. Although it has always disapproved of attempts to silence a speaker, it has often failed to exert the kind of muscle that it possesses when such attempts occur. Joseph Bishop commented on the ACLU's reaction to the deliberate disruption of prowar speakers at Harvard in March 1971: "There have been no interventions, no briefs *amici curiae,* no press releases supporting authorities to prevent or punish such violence." On the contrary, Bishop noted, the Union sought to have an injunction overturned in the Supreme Court when the University of Connecticut sought to enjoin its students from disrupting the activities of recruiters representing corporations with defense contracts.[29] Such decisions by the ACLU raise serious questions about its commitment to free speech for everyone. But at least the Union has made improvement from the days when *it* took people to court for saying things that it did not like.

The ACLU vs. the *American Mercury*

In December 1936 Harold Lord Varney wrote critically about the ACLU in the *American Mercury.* The ACLU did not like what he said, so it threatened a libel suit against the publication. The article, "The Civil Liberties Union—Liberalism à la Moscow," was a searing indictment of the Union's alleged nonpartisan position. Although much of what Varney said was true, he no doubt exaggerated the record of the Union. But there was nothing libelous about the article, even given the relatively loose libel laws that existed at that time. Varney was exercising his First Amendment right, but the Union did not see it that way. The series of events that followed the publication of the Varney piece has all the drama of a Watergate-type scandal. Those who have done in-depth research on the ACLU have conveniently omitted any detailed discussion of this incident.[30] It is being told here for the first time.

Varney was piqued at Roger Baldwin's admission that the ACLU would uphold the right of any American citizen or alien to advocate the overthrow of the government. Furthermore, he was irked at Baldwin's duplicity when violations of civil liberties occurred in the Soviet Union. Baldwin, it will be recalled, wrote in *Liberty Under the Soviets:* "Repression in Western democracies are violations of professed constitutional liberties and I condemn them as such. Repressions in Soviet Russia are weapons of struggle in a transition period to Socialism." From this and similar passages in the Union's record, Varney concluded:

> If any informed observer of temporary American Radicalism were asked to single out the organization which is doing the most fruitful work to advance the so-called Class War in America today, his answer would be immediate! He would name the American Civil Liberties Union. Indeed, it is doubtful if, without the ACLU, there would exist a Red problem in the Republic in anything approaching its present seriousness.[31]

Just as disturbing to Varney was Baldwin's belief that only the rich enjoy civil liberties. Varney cited the observation by Baldwin:

> For although I am an advocate of unrestricted civil liberty as a means of effecting even revolutionary changes in society with a minimum of violence, I know that such liberty is always dependent on the possession of economic power. Economic liberty underlies all others. In any society, civil liberties are freely exercised only by classes with economic power—or if by other classes, only at times when the controlling class is too secure to fear opposition.[32]

This prompted Varney to reply:

> What a sweeping admission that the whole program of the American Civil Liberties Union is but a deceptive prelude to the Proletarian Revolution! Under Mr. Baldwin's artful leadership, it is a mobilization of unsuspecting Liberal idealism to the materialistic services of the Kremlin.[33]

The ACLU quickly issued a strong reply to Varney's charges, maintaining that it "takes no position whatever on the class war and defends all comers without distinction." The Union wrote this *before* it defended its first capitalist client, the Ford Motor Company, and *after* its admitted alignment with the "propertyless" class. It then said of the man "who was the ACLU" that "Mr. Baldwin's personal views on economics and politics have nothing to do with the Union's program; nor have the views of any of the other officers on the philosophy of liberty or their economic and political predilections."[34] In a memo that the Union issued responding to Varney's criticism, it enumerated twenty-six charges that it regarded as false. It disputed the idea that "almost invariably the Union's crusades connect somewhere with the devious strategy of the Party [Communist] Line." It also found bogus the suggestion that "where radical interests conflict with civil liberties, the Union frankly becomes a partisan organization."[35]

So far, no big deal: Varney criticizes the ACLU; the Union criticizes Varney. Then the ACLU draws up its libel suit against the *American Mercury* and Varney, citing legal precedent.:

> It is not penalizing or curtailing freedom of opinion or criticism to hold that the article appearing in the defendant's magazine is libelous per se. Read as a whole and not treated in shreds it exposes the plaintiff to "public contempt, ridicule, aversion or disgrace"; it induces an evil opinion of the plaintiff "in the minds of right thinking persons. . . ." It would seem that this offending article does more than express an opinion; in any event it is for the jury "to decide whether the defendant went beyond the limits of fair criticism." Quite logically, the article might directly affect the plaintiff's credit or the management of its business.[36]

Neither Paul Palmer, the editor of the *American Mercury*, nor Baldwin relished the idea of bringing their dispute before the courts. A compromise was to be worked out by both parties. Palmer agreed to a proposal made by Arthur Garfield Hays of the ACLU that the famed journalist H.L. Mencken be invited to write an article about the Union in the *American Mercury*. The expectation was that Mencken would defend the ACLU against Varney's charges. Baldwin then discussed this matter with the Board of Directors, which concluded that it would be better to have someone else write the article, someone "who [is] presumed to be less committed to our viewpoint." Baldwin told Palmer that Mencken was associated "with what passes for radical views in the minds of those whom we most want to reach." Relaying the board's decision to Palmer, Baldwin recommended that one of four men be solicited to write the article: three were former commanders in the American Legion, the fourth was attorney Elihu Root.

But there was a hitch: Baldwin told Palmer, "It is understood that both you and we reserve the right to reject the article if it does not suit our common purpose on which we appear to be in agreement." Once the article received the ACLU's editorial blessings, Baldwin added, it could be printed and the suit would be dropped. The letter was dated 12 January 1938.[37]

A few days later Palmer replied to Baldwin. Furious, he reminded Baldwin that it was the ACLU's idea to have Mencken do the piece in the first place. Palmer had already traveled to Baltimore to request Mencken to do the article, and Mencken had agreed. Palmer was now left in the embarrassing position of having to disinvite the great Mencken. Just as disconcerting was Baldwin's insistence that he be allowed to preview and reject the article if he did not like it. That had not been part of the original agreement. According to Palmer, Hays had previously said that "he would withdraw the suit and accept, sight unseen, whatever Mencken wrote." Palmer added, "I confess that I simply do not understand such a volte-face."[38]

Upon receipt of Palmer's letter, Baldwin sent a memo to the board indicating that he and Hays felt that the board had erred in not accepting that Mencken would write the article. He said that Hays recommended that "we should not reserve the right to reject the article, but to correct it factually and to insist upon the proper editorial comment in introducing it."[39] The board agreed to have Mencken write the article but demanded that it have the right to reject if it the members did not like it: "Otherwise there would hardly be any point in accepting the publication of Mencken's article as satisfaction of our claims." Baldwin wrote Hays of the board's position, and stated, "Although I know how ingracious it will appear to ask Mr. Mencken to do this work, the right of rejection [must be] in our hands. I can hardly imagine that we would exercise it." A carbon copy of this letter was sent to Palmer.[40]

Baldwin received replies from both Hays and Palmer. Hays responded first: "Of course, one thing the Board seems to me not to appreciate is the danger of our trying the law suit against the *American Mercury*. My thought was that since Mencken is honest in his views and certainly not a reactionary so far as civil liberties are concerned, it [is] rather presumptuous on our part to insist upon censoring the article."[41]

Palmer was, understandably, angered and perplexed by the Union's behavior. He reminded Baldwin that the original agreement was to have an impartial investigator write the article, to have it published without the ACLU's permission, and to have the suit dropped upon publication. There was also no agreement that the *American Mercury* publish a retraction of the Varney piece. Troubled by the Union's unreasonableness, Palmer wondered, "Is this the American Civil Liberties Union definition of an 'impartial' investigation? It would seem that the investigation will be impartial if it meets with your approval; but prejudiced if it does not." He then said that he planned to print the Mencken article without changing a word of it. But he held out an olive branch to Baldwin by promising that he would give him the option of rejecting Mencken's article when it was finished, but before it was submitted to the ACLU, in return for dropping the suit. He closed with: "You made the offer, you selected the man, and I have accepted your offer and your selection in every particular."[42]

Baldwin would not budge. With his usual candor, he responded: "I think that the best thing to do is to have Mencken go ahead with the article, let us see it, and have the suit withdrawn if it meets with our approval." He added that there was not "a chance in the world" that the board would withdraw the suit without reserving the right to censor the article.[43] Once again Palmer reiterated the terms of the original agreement and refused to yield any further. "It seems to me," he wrote, "that the position of the A.C.L.U. has been changed several times since we came to that [original] agreement."[44]

More hard feelings developed between Baldwin and Varney when, in March 1938, the *Forum* printed an exchange between Varney and Ernest Sutherland Bates, debating the merits of the ACLU's nonpartisanship. Varney contended that Baldwin was the key figure in the Union and that the nonradicals in the organization did not carry much weight. He nailed Baldwin for his comment in the Harvard alumni news record that "communism is the goal." Bates criticized Varney for quoting out of context, arguing (no doubt correctly) that Baldwin's phrase was meant to have generic significance, i.e. it did not refer to the Communist party but to the idea of a classless society.[45] Baldwin clarified his stand in a letter to the *Forum* date 28 March 1938. He noted that his view of democracy was based on the belief that a "classless society without property castes or controls by violence" would eventually materialize.[46]

Mencken's article on the ACLU was submitted to Palmer on 31 March. The ACLU received a copy of it simultaneously. Unexpectedly, the Union was not pleased. Mencken argued that although Varney could not "scientifically" demonstrate each and every one of his charges, his inferences had "sufficient support in the record (allowing a reasonable something for the heat of controversy) to justify him in reaching and uttering them." He chastised Varney for confusing the ACLU's defense of Communists with support for their cause, maintaining that Varney's logic would mean that the Union could be held "equally responsible for the doctrines preached by other groups that it has defended, for example, the sect called Jehovah's Witnesses." Mencken then bared the truth about the ACLU: it was not a nonpartisan organization. It was a fact, he said, that some of the Union's "most important and active officers [were] actually strong partisans of the Left" and that they had sufficient influence to affect the operations of the organization; their influence was enough to cast "a resonable doubt" over the ACLU's disinterestedness." He even went so far as to say that Varney had not completely exposed all the partisan officers who served the Union, and then considered the evidence against Baldwin, the executive director, and Dr. Harry F. Ward, chariman of the ACLU.

Mencken began by appraising the ACLU's defense of Baldwin's ability to separate his politics from his decision-making in the organization. The Union's statement admitted to no bias whatsoever: "Mr. Baldwin's personal views on economics and politics have nothing to do with the Union's program." Furthermore, the ACLU maintained that Baldwin was merely "the agent of the board in carrying out its decisions, and has only the influence in the board or the Union of a paid executive who carries out group decisions." Mencken was not so naive as to accept this defense: "All this seems to me to be nonsense. No one familiar with the conduct of such organizations will believe for a minute that Mr. Baldwin is the mere lackey of the board. . . . He may influence it without opening his mouth in argument. The very statement of the case before it must be colored inevitably by his private notions of the true, the good and the beautiful." Mencken then took Baldwin to task for his defense of civil liberties violations in the Soviet Union:

> I can imagine nothing feebler than this. No thorough-going friend of civil liberties can subscribe to it. If the bosses of Russia are free to abolish civil liberties in order to attain some chosen political end then the bosses of the United States are free to suspend them in order to attain some other end. It is perfectly possible to think of his condonation of the Russian war upon civil liberties as a mere transient aberration born of a brief visit to Moscow Zion and his exposure to the seductions there on tap. Other if not better men have succumbed to the same marihuana. Let him now make plain that he is actually in favor of civil liberties *in themselves*, as essential to the primary dignities of man, in Russia as well as the United States, and all will be forgiven.

Harry Ward received the same treatment. Mencken lambasted Ward for acting as chairman of the Communist-front group, the League for Peace and Democracy (previously known as the League Against War and Fascism), while at the same time serving as chairman of the ACLU. "It seems to me," Mencken wrote, "that his retention of both offices was, and is a considerable impropriety, and that he cannot complain if it has cast doubts upon the *bona fides* of the Union." Mencken also noted that Ward had never publicly disassociated himself from the Communists with whom he worked so closely at the league. "He cannot, any more than Mr. Baldwin," contended the Baltimore journalist, "be a defender of civil liberties on one side and a consorter with its avowed enemies on the other. So long as the two chief officers of the Union permit themselves that dichotomy, or anything resembling it in the eye of a reasonable man, they must bear responsibility for any damage that ensues to the organization."

Mencken offered pieces of advice to the ACLU. First, Baldwin should either publicly repudiate his defense of civil liberties abuses in Russia or quit the ACLU. He can always "join one of the many organizations which are in favor of [civil liberties] everywhere save in Russia." Second, Ward should do likewise by distancing himself from the agents of Moscow. Third, in the Union's defense of Nazis, it should not seek out Jews to do the work: "The job is manifestly one for *Goyim*. No Nazi not insane will ever believe that a Jew not twice insane is actually hot to succor him. All the evidence in the book runs the other way." Fourth, there were too many radicals in the Union to convince people that it was a nonpartisan organization. The board was "overloaded with avowed radicals, some of them either Communists or members of the I Am Not a Communist, But — — — Association." Mencken suggested "that interlocking directorates arouse just as much suspicion, and with just as much reason, in the field of reform as they do in Wall Street."[47]

At this point, Baldwin wrote to Mencken[48] and to Palmer[49] telling them that he had referred the matter to Hays, who was representing the Union. He also wrote to Ward: "Mencken has written a very bad article for the American Mercury which possibly can be revised to do the job Mr. Hays thought could be done."[50] Baldwin's letter to Hays was more explicit:

> Here is Mencken's article for the Mercury. As you will see, it is factually incorrect in ascribing to me and to Dr. Ward views which do not hold by putting the emphasis in the wrong places. It is a very superficial treatment of what ought to be couched in terms of economics, not civil liberty.
>
> It looks to me as though we will have to labor with Brother Mencken a little further, for I feel confident he will state the case clearly, if we give him the dope. What is your view?[51]

Ward, perhaps the most radical of the board members, was the most upset. The mere fact that Mencken had mentioned that the League for Peace and Democracy, with which he was associated, had changed names was enough for Ward to charge that Mencken had revealed "gross prejudice"; it was as "slanderous as anything that Varney wrote." For Ward, Mencken, like Varney, was a fascist: "Mr. Mencken's statement shows that in one important point he is as much a Fascist as Varney. He is in this statement a definite red-baiter thus using the tactic by which Fascists deceive the people into supporting them."[52]

Hays wrote to Mencken on 25 April defending Baldwin and Ward. He said he was "shocked" by the article, stating that "you have done very much the same as Varney." Hays, like his colleagues, was frank: "Your criticisms of both Roger and Dr. Ward are definitely unfair, if not libelous. We who have worked with them for years are proud of our association with them and were I not a believer in free speech, I'd like to 'knock the block off' anyone who doubted their integrity and sincerity." After engaging in more invective, Hays pleaded with Mencken to rewrite the article: "Damn it all, Henry, are you so cynical that you have forgotten that there are some honest men in the world?"[53]

The ACLU got its way: Mencken rewrote the article toning down his criticism, saying that he had no objection if the Union and Palmer agreed not to publish it.[54] Hays told Baldwin that the second article was an improvement over the first and sent him a copy of it.[55] But for Baldwin, the new article was "not good enough. It will leave readers with a very bad and false impression." He then added, "If the Mercury would publish a paragraph from Ward and me, I think it might do."[56] Baldwin told Ward that he and Hays would not agree to publication of the article unless they had the opportunity to include their own statements.[57]

Baldwin and Hays were ready to accept publication of Mencken's second article provided that they had input, but Ward would not go along with idea, maintaining that the article "will do more harm than the original." It was decided that the board should vote, by postcard, on what to do.[58] The response, at first, was largely critical of Mencken and supportive of Ward's position. Dorothy Kenyon replied that Mencken "wallops us." Roger William Riis complained, "The article is punk and impertinent and misses the point—all points." Another board member wrote, "Mencken is a more effective Red-baiter than Varney and certainly as vicious." Elizabeth Gurly Flynn said, "Agree with Dr. Ward." But John Haynes Holmes contended that "The article should be accepted and published just as it stands."[59]

Meanwhile, Baldwin was busy writing to Mencken, defending his views on civil liberties. He said that he did not condone the abridgment of freedom in Russia but conceded: "If I do not see suppression in Fascist and Communist countries with the same eye, it is because Fascist countries offer no chance of economic progress while Soviet Russia does."[60] That such logic could have been used to defend Hitler, for the economy progressed under him from the days of the Weimer Republic, seems not to have caught Baldwin's attention.

In June 1938 Mencken agreed to make more changes in his article that were recommended by the ACLU.[61] Still not satisfied, Baldwin sent a letter to the members of the Board of Directors asking them to cast a formal and decisive vote on the matter at the upcoming meeting. He said that he thought an approval of the article was the "least undesirable" alternative. Ward, he mentioned, was as resolute as ever, holding that the article "would be quite as injurious as the Varney article, even with a critical reply from our Board of Directors attached in the same type."[62]

In July 1938 the board voted 14-6 to permit the publication of Mencken's article along with a rejoinder from the Union. The suit was to be dropped as well. Voting "no" were Flynn, Riis, Ward, R.S. Childs, A.J. Isserman, and Mary Van Kleeck.[63] Flynn was outraged: "I do not care to sign the letter to H.L. Mencken, which I feel is entirely too apologetic and conciliatory, towards his attitude which would reduce Civil Liberties to an absurdity. Nor do I relish being featured as exhibit A—'Our only Communist' etc."[64]

The matter was not yet settled. Mencken informed Baldwin that Palmer wanted Varney to have the opportunity to reply to the board's criticism.[65] Baldwin objected and told Palmer that Varney should not be given the right to reply: "Otherwise controversy will not be concluded."[66] Palmer could not hold back any longer:

> I confess that it strikes me as a little short of extraordinary that an organization such as the ACLU, supposedly dedicated to the freedom of expression and the observance of fair play, should deny an opponent a privilege which it demands for itself. . . . Up to this point, I was tolerant of all your changes, hedges, and additions. Why, I don't know. Perhaps I have ingrained in me the tolerance and respect for the freedom of expression of other people which is the boast of the ACLU. . . . I have an old-fashioned idea of the prerogatives of an editor, who in America, at least, has the right of free expression and the duty to defend it because it is a right held in trust for the American people. An attempt to dictate to me that I should not offer Mr. Varney an opportunity to reply, coming from men who profess the defense of civil liberties— and professionally, too—is to me astounding.[67]

Baldwin gave up. The article by Mencken, "The American Civil Liberties Union," was published in the October 1938 issue of the *American Mercury*. The libel suit was dropped.[68]

How does one account for the ACLU's move to censor an article of which it did not approve while acknowledging that its claim to fame is the defense of the First Amendment's right of free speech? Writing at the time of the ACLU-Varney-Mencken controversy was Albert Jay Nock, the astute conservative social critic:

> I do not recall a single Liberal of my acquaintance who impressed me as having the least interest in freedom, or a shadow of faith in its potentialities.

On the contrary, I have always found the Liberal to have the greatest nervous horror of freedom, and the keenest disposition to barge in on the liberties of the individual and whittle them away at every accessible point.[69]

Nock's criticism is overdrawn, but it is nonetheless true that many of those who have called the loudest for free speech are amongst the most intolerant of speech that criticizes them or their beliefs. Even the most celebrated advocate of free speech, John Stuart Mill, was given to intolerance when he himself was the object of criticism. When Elizabeth Gaskell, the biographer of Charlotte Brontë, included a letter by her subject saying of Mill, "I feel disposed to scorn his heart," Mill chided Gaskell on her responsibilities as an author and argued that the letter should never have been printed! He told her that she had disregarded the "obligation which custom founded on reason has imposed, of omitting what would be offensive to the feelings and perhaps injurious to the moral reputation of individuals." He wrote this shortly *after* his classic essay *On Liberty*.[70]

The real reason that the ACLU attempted to muzzle the free speech of the *American Mercury* has already been discussed in Chapters 2 and 3: The ACLU was more interested at that time in advancing the cause of radical labor than it was in promoting free speech. Civil liberties, as Baldwin acknowledged, was a tool used to foster liberal-left programs. Therefore, there was nothing incongruous about the Union's reaction to Palmer, Varney, or Mencken; its commitment to free speech was quite selective.

Freedom of the Press

The First Amendment to the Constitution was not made binding on the states until the passage of the Fourteenth Amendment in 1868. But it was not until 1925, in a case in which the ACLU participated[71]—*Gitlow v. New York*—that the Supreme Court established with certainty that "we may and do assume that freedom of speech and of the press which are protected by the First Amendment by the Congress—are among the fundamental personal rights and 'liberties' protected by the due process clause of the Fourteenth Amendment from impairment by the States."[72] Moreover, when the First Amendment was adopted in 1791, it was accepted as a prohibition on the use of prior restraint. But it was not until 1931 in *Near v. Minnesota*, that the Supreme Court expounded with clarity the veracity of the principle; prior restraint was confined to a limited, workable tenet of constitutional law. The ACLU was also active in this landmark decision.

Jay Near was an anti-Semite, anti-Catholic, anti-Black, anti-labor, and anticommunist newspaper correspondent writing for the *Saturday Press* in Minneapolis in the late 1920s. His bigoted writing got him into trouble with the local authorities when he accused them of permitting a Jewish gangster to have free rein in gambling, bootlegging, and racketeering. He also maligned the local newspapers, the grand jury that had been activated, and all Jews. On 21 November 1927, County Attorney Floyd Olson filed a complaint with Hennepin County District Judge Mathias Baldwin, accusing the *Saturday Press* of defaming Charles Davis, head of the Law Enforcement League; Frank Brunskill, chief of police; George Leach, mayor; the Minneapolis *Tribune*; the Minneapolis *Journal*; the Hennepin County Grand Jury; and the entire Jewish community—he also included himself. Olson charged that the *Saturday Press* was "a malicious, scandalous, and defamatory publication." He wanted the court to restrain publication of the newspaper. Judge Baldwin complied with Olson's wish. The so-called Minnesota Gag-Law of 1925 did not permit such material to be printed.[73]

On 25 May 1928, in a unanimous decision, the Minnesota Supreme Court sustained the Gag-Law. Chief Justice Samuel Bailey Wilson said that the Constitution "was never intended to protect malice, scandal and defamation when untrue or published with bad motives or without justifiable ends." Then, in a statement that was reiminiscent of the eighteenth-century English common law position, Wilson said: "There is no constitutional right to publish a fact merely because it is true."[74] Fortunately for Near and, more importantly, freedom of the press, someone told Near about Roger Baldwin and the ACLU.

In June 1928 Baldwin responded to Near's request for assistance by committing $150 toward Near's defense. Baldwin realized that the Gag-Law was unconstitutional and did not want to pass up the opportunity to participate in what was shaping up to be a decisive court battle. He was also keen enough to know that the key to the case rested on a challenge to the concept of prior restraint. The ACLU stated its stand with precision: "Heretofore the only control of the press has been by prosecution for criminal or libelous matter after the offense. We see in this new device for previous restraint of publication a menace to the whole principle of the freedom of the press." The Union knew that precedent would be determined in this case: "If the Minnesota law is constitutional, then the 14th Amendment and inferentially, the 1st Amendment, no longer protects the press against previous restraints."[75]

From the time that the Minnesota Supreme Court had issued a "temporary" restraining order, the ACLU had been preparing its briefs for an eventual U.S. Supreme Court test. However, through the efforts of Chicago attorney Weymouth Kirkland, in cooperation with Robert McCormick of the Chicago *Tribune,* the Union was squeezed out of the case. The powerful Kirkland was persuaded that he and his associates could do a better job of representing Near than the relatively young Civil Liberties Union.[76] In the end, Near won and prior restraint was rendered ineffective in all but the most serious, egregious cases concerning public welfare. Chief Justice Charles Evan Hughes championed the rights of the press: "The fact that the liberty of the press may be abused by miscreant purveyors of scandal does not make any the less necessary the immunity of the press from previous restraint in dealing with official misconduct."[77] Had it not been for the catalyst role that the ACLU played, the court's famous 1931 decision might not have been delivered.

The ACLU did not participate in the Supreme Court landmark case of 1964, *New York Times v. Sullivan,* but it did support the decision. In that ruling, the court limited state power to punish criticism of public officials to cases where a statement was made "with actual malice—that is, with knowledge that it was false or with reckless disregard of whether it was false or not." After an eighteen-month review of libel and free speech, the Union declared that it would not back a libel suit by persons in political life unless they could prove "with convincing clarity" that the statement conformed to the high court's ruling in *Sullivan.*[78] The ACLU's new libel policy was amended a few years later to include "persons in public life"—meaning public figures about whom false statements were made. This position emerged as a result of the Pauling case. Dr. Linus Pauling, Nobel laureate, had sued columnist William F. Buckley, Jr., for calling him a Communist collaborator. A New York State Supreme Court judge dismissed the $1 million libel suit because Pauling had "made himself a public figure engaged voluntarily in public discussion of matters of grave public concern and controversy."[79]

Two major freedom of the press decisions in which the Union did participate were the "Pentagon Papers" case and the *Progressive* magazine suit. The Nixon administration had sought to prevent the release of what it regarded as sensitive information concerning the U.S. involvement in the Vietnam war. The Pentagon Papers detailed the historical background of U.S. decisions affecting its role in Vietnam from 1945 to 1968. The Union filed an *amicus* brief arguing that the dissemination of public information regarding the U.S. role was essential to the working of the democratic process. It was successful.[80] The *Progressive* case, in which the Union was also successful in prohibiting prior restraint, was equally controversial.

On 8 March 1979, the Justice Department, acting on behalf of the Department of Energy, ordered the *Progressive,* a liberal journal of opinion, to refrain from publishing an article by Howard Morland entitled "The H-Bomb Secret—How We Got It, Why We're Telling It." It was the first time in the history of the United States that a publication had prior restraint invoked against it in a national security case.[81] On 5 April the ACLU was asked to represent the editor of the *Progressive,* Erwin Knoll. It agreed. The government was afraid that nations that did not possess the bomb would now acquire ability to do so; there was also concern over the role that terrorists might play. In a statement issued on 9 April, the ACLU said: *"The connection between publication of the Progressive article and any 'sure,' 'direct,' 'immediate,' or 'irreparable' harm to the United States is a connection that has not been made by the government."*[82] The Carter administration successfully suppressed the article for six months before finally withdrawing its objection. On 17 September the Justice Department announced that it was abandoning its efforts because of the publication of a letter by Charles R. Hansen in the *Press Connection*, a Madison, Wisconsin, newspaper, disclosing information about the bomb. As a result, the Justice Department concluded that it was pointless to pursue its efforts against the *Progressive*.[83] The *New York Times* congratulated the ACLU for its work.[84]

In the 1980s a plethora of libel cases have been launched against the media. General William Westmoreland filed suit against CBS for inaccurately portraying his role in the Vietnam war. Dan Rather of CBS was summoned to court in May 1983 to defend himself against allegations that he misrepresented the activities of a physician in "60 Minutes." Mobil Oil Corporation brought suit against the *Washington Post*. Media "watchdog" groups have provided resources to those who feel that they have been libeled by television or the press. A study done by the Libel Defense Resource Center in New York showed that juries award damages against news media defendants in nearly 90 percent of all cases; however, 70 percent of the verdicts are eventually dismissed by trial or appellate judges.[85] Meanwhile, the ACLU's Board of Directors was reconsidering its policy on libel.

The ACLU has long supported the Supreme Court's position on libel, but it has become increasingly clear in the 1980s, that the Union is preparing to break with the conventional reasoning on this issue. For example, in 1981, its official policy on libel declared that "false statements involving character assassination do not forward the process of a marketplace of ideas." At that time, the Union was also on record for opposing the awarding of punitive damages in all libel cases except in suits brought by persons that did not involve "public discussion with respect to political, governmental, economic, religious or social matters."[86] In 1983, the board dropped these positions entirely. The deletion of these positions, held by nearly everyone to be reasonable, tells volumes about the ACLU's latest interpretation of the First Amendment. The only right of action for defamation that the Union said was not violative of the First Amendment was the following:

> In cases brought by private individuals, not involved in a public matter, against all defendants there should be no liability unless the plaintiff can

prove with clear and convincing evidence that the false and defamatory speech was made with the knowledge of its faisity or with reckless disregard as to its truth or falsity and with intent to damage an identifiable party's reputation.[87]

It may not be long before the ACLU considers all libel laws to be violative of the First Amendment. That is the position taken by at least one of its influential members, jounalist Nat Hentoff.[88] Hentoff's commitment to free speech is total—for everyone—without regard for all but the most catastrophic conditions. He is not naive regarding the occasional reckless- ness of the press. Indeed, he has publicly stated that "the press—aside from its own fiercely valued First Amendment rights—doesn't give much more of a damn about the rest of the Bill of Rights than any other segment of the citizenry. I have no more faith in voluntary self-restraint by the press than I have in any similar exercises by the FBI."[89] What recourse the defamed should have is not suggested by Hentoff.

Free Speech in Broadcasting

The ACLU's policies regarding free speech in broadcasting address the issues of equity and diversity in television and radio. On the subject of equity in the media, the Union's position has been to see to it that political dissidents have the same free speech rights that others enjoy. One of its first major concerns in this area arose in 1939 when the Federal Communica- tions Commission (FCC) mandated that international broadcasting "re- flect the culture of this country and promote international good-will, un- derstanding and cooperation." That was enough to provoke the ACLU to make a formal protest against the FCC, charging that the order con- travened the provisions of the Federal Communications Act prohibiting interference with free speech. At that time, the Union also contended that "equal time" on the radio be given to every candidate for political office. Communists, it said, did not receive equal time.[90]

Up until 1960, the ACLU supported Section 315 of the Federal Com- munications Act requiring broadcasters to allot equal time for political candidates. Then it changed its position by endorsing the concept of "equi- table time"; this was supposed to enhance the chances of minority views to be heard.[91] In 1967 it switched its position again, arguing that the con- ditional aspect of Section 315 (equal time) be changed to "a definite obliga- tion for a station to present candidates' broadcasts."[92] In 1972 the board went even further by declaring that "some television time should be made available at no charge during political campaigns to candidates for the offices of President, Vice-President, Senator, Congressman, and Governor."

For other political candidates it urged that time and space be given in the media "at the lowest commercial rate."[93]

In the mid-1960s the ACLU voiced its support of the FCC's "fairness doctrine." It backed the FCC in its attempt to secure air time for persons or groups attacked on radio or television; the doctrine encompassed other elements related to the fairness of reply to the media.[94] The application of the fairness doctrine did raise, however, some difficult questions. For example, in April 1964 the United Church of Christ petitioned the FCC to allow the licenses of two Jackson, Mississippi, television stations to expire on the grounds that the stations systematically ignored Black interests. The ACLU asked that a hearing be held in order to determine if the Black population was being consistently and intentionally misrepresented.[95] When I asked Alan Reitman what difference it would have made even if Blacks were intentionally being misrepresented, he responded by saying that such issues were difficult ones for the Union. He did not rule out (nor did the organization) the Union's support of the FCC in such cases.[96] When the FCC ordered one of the stations to "immediately cease discriminating programming patterns," the Union did not come to the assistance of the station.[97]

The ACLU leadership comprises mostly White, well-educated, upper-middle-class persons. Their values and tastes are not representative of Americans who are not so affluent. This can be seen quite clearly in the Union's position on diversity in the media. To many well-educated folk, much of what is shown on television is boring and sterile. There is no civil liberties problem here. Nonetheless, the Board of Directors of the ACLU thinks that this condition ought to be changed. In the early 1960s the ACLU decided that the FCC should intervene to protect programming in the "public interest, convenience and necessity."[98] In the eyes of the Union, there was "too much conformity" on television.[99] In addition, network shows suffered from "over-commercialization."[100] It was such reasoning that motivated the Union to defend the FCC's attempt to influence television stations to provide more "public service" programming during prime-time viewing. The ACLU struck back at broadcasters who complained about unwarranted interference by the FCC; the Union accused them of "raising the cry of censorship."[101] What is most perplexing about all this is the Union's fickle attitude toward "public-interest" considerations affecting the media. For example, in 1978, when the board addressed the question of communications monopolies, it recommended: "An ad-hoc public interest test should determine whether divestiture of cross-owned media should be required."[102] But nowhere does it say what constitutes the "public interest." Yet in the same year it found, with regard to an FCC regulation, that "no significant sanction such as denial of license renewal may be imposed for failure to comply with vague or ambiguous standards of performance such as failure to operate in the public interest. . . ."[103] Apparently the criterion of the "public interest" can be seen as acceptable or unacceptable depending on the issue—or depending on how it strikes the ACLU's fancy.

The Union's inconsistencies and imposition of its values on the media were also evident in its 1960s rulings in "Curbs on Network Control of Programming." It did not look favorably on a proposed FCC rule aimed at restricting network control of television and programming to no more than 50 percent of the programming shown during prime time (excluding news and public affairs programs). The Union feared that such a move would reduce rather than promote diversity. Its apprehension stemmed from the notion that the remaining 50 percent of prime time would fall under the aegis of advertisers. It claimed that advertiser-supplied programming was, for the most part, "uniformly uncontroversial and non-diversified." The Union was worried that increasing diversity of program sources would not increase diversity of content. The proposed rule would merely insure "an even greater preponderance of what is today considered 'popular' fare with the resulting lack of diversity."[104] The Union was so incensed over the mediocrity of "popular fare" that it broke with its previous policies[105] by arguing that the commission should "concern itself actively with the problem of diversity of program content."[106] In 1974 it added that because of the "rating game," there existed a tendency to appeal to "the lowest common denominator."[107] This is still its position today.[108]

Censorship

In the ACLU's first annual report it went on record opposing censorship by any group or agency in the country; the Post Office was singled out as the major threat to freedom of expression in 1920.[109] In the following year, the Union again registered its concern regarding the Post Office's power of censorship; it noted, however, that such powers had not been exercised.[110] It was not until 1929, with the advent of talking movies, that censorship emerged as "an important new issue" for the Union. The Union dispatched Arthur Garfield Hays to challenge the Post Office's frequently used authority to censor from the mails material it held to be "libelous, obscene and lascivious."[111] In a critical court case, the Union provided assistance to Mary Ware Dennett of Brooklyn, whose pamphlet, *The Sex Side of Life*, had been used for about seven years by educators and social workers. The Post Office Department held that it was obscene, and in 1929 Dennett was convicted and sentenced to pay $300 or serve three hundred days in jail. A defense committee organized by the Union raised $3,320. The Circuit Court of Appeals sustained the Union's position and set aside Dennett's conviction by unanimous decision in 1930.[112]

State courts, legislatures, and private groups continued their efforts toward censorship in the 1930s. The Supreme Court of Massachusetts sustained the conviction of Theodore Dreiser's *An American Tragedy*.[113] The play *Lysistrata* was banned in a number of cities, while at the same time the NAACP was successful in persuading the police to ban the film *Birth of a Nation*.[114] Through the work of the ACLU, James Joyce's classic *Ulysses* was finally admitted into the United States after Judge John M. Woolsey of the District Court in New York passed on its admissibility.[115] The Union exclaimed that the decision was "a milestone in progress toward sanity."[116] To combat censorship in the media more effectively, the Union organized the National Council of Freedom from Censorship in 1931 as a branch of its activities. Among its successes was the Customs Bureau decision allowing *Contraception* by Dr. Marie Stopes to be admitted into the country; it was the first book of specific birth control information to be admitted since 1890.[117]

Preoccupied with war issues in the 1940s, the ACLU's involvement in censorship matters was limited mostly to promoting diversity in the media.[118] In the 1950s and 1960s the increase in violence and sex in the media became the target of censors and regulators alike. In every instance they were met by opposition from the ACLU. In the mid-1950s, for example, crime comic books were criticized by a number of segments in the population. It was claimed that such publications had a negative effect on youngsters; some advocated prohibition, while others favored self-regulation by publishers. The Union countered by maintaining that "it should be proved beyond doubt that crime comics produce juvenile delinquency so regularly and in such degree that the offensive publications really constitute a clear and present danger to society." And even if such a cause-and-effect relationship could be demonstrated, the Union said, "it should be shown that no means other than censorship can offer protection."[119]

In 1968 the Motion Picture Association of America devised a voluntary classification system whereby movies would be classified according to their audience appeal. A "G" would be given to movies that were suitable for general audiences; an "X" signified suitability for persons over the age of sixteen; and intermediate categories were also established. This voluntary rating system has been widely accepted as an appropriate source of useful information, but not everyone was satisfied. The ACLU was not. The Union not only objected to the classification system but saw it as acting as "a prior restraint on the creative process." It was particularly upset about the "X" rating because "the administration of classification based on content will tend to act as a prior restraint upon film producers." Because children were barred from "X"-rated movies, it deprived parents of "the right to determine for themselves what pictures their children may see."[120]

The courts have never sustained such an elastic definition of prior restraint, nor has there been a grass-roots movement by parents organized to secure their right to permit their youngsters to see pornographic movies. Civil libertarians' efforts to do so would no doubt garner few supporters outside their ranks.

In the early 1980s a number of local school boards across the country sought to ban certain books from public school libraries. The 1981 Christmas edition of the *New York Times Book Review* featured a front-page discussion of the controversy in an article by Colin Campbell, "Book Banning in America." Campbell noted that such classics as *1984, The Merchant of Venice, The Catcher in the Rye, The Grapes of Wrath,* and *The adventures of Huckleberry Finn* were among the books that were targeted; many contemporary works were also held objectionable, including *Jaws*.[121] In 1977 the ACLU passed a new policy called "Selection of School and Library Materials and Pressure Group Attacks," wherein the board asserted its support for "the principle of free inquiry and diversity at all educational levels." The Union did say, however, that it recognized "the right of parents and students to some measure of protection from compulsory use of instructional materials which they believe assault religious and moral beliefs."[122] Unfortunately, the board gave no indication of what it meant by according "some measure of protection" to parents and students.[123]

The ACLU's most publicized case involving school board censorship in the early 1980s involved the 1975 decision of the Island Trees school board of New York to remove nine books from its libraries. The New York affiliate challenged the decision and won in the Supreme Court in June 1982. The high court drew a distinction between a school board's right to remove books for reasons of "pervasive vulgarity" or "educational suitability" and its lack of authority to deny students "access to ideas" with which the board disapproves. The Island Trees school board had banned books that it held were "anti-American, anti-Christian, anti-Semitic, and just plain filthy."[124] In August 1982 after the Supreme Court ruling, the school board voted 6-1 to return the nine books to its libraries.[125]

Testing the Limits of Free Speech

In 1983 Nellie and Charles Babbs of Dodge City, Kansas, captured the attention of ABC's "Nightline" and made the pages of the *New York Times.* The cause of their notoriety stemmed from the bigoted broadcasts of their local radio station KTTL-FM. They denounced Blacks, Roman Catholics, Asians, and Jews—especially Jews. Jews were referred to as "the children of Satan."[126] The editors of the *New York Times* were moved to argue that it was "enough to test one's faith in a marketplace of uninhibited debate," but added: "Still, that's what free speech is all about."[127] The ACLU no doubt agreed.

The ACLU has always subscribed to what Roger Baldwin referred to as the "Voltairian doctrine": "If the person you hate has no rights, then the person you like may have no rights either. And in order to defend the people you like, you have to defend the people you hate."[128] It is for this reason that the Union has defended the rights of the Klan and Nazis as well as anarchists and Communists. Those who preach race, ethnic, or religious hatred have typically won the legal (though not moral) support of the ACLU. In the mid-1940s it opposed laws that would have barred racial and religious hate literature.[129] In the 1980s it denounced a New York State law forbidding the utterances of racial or ethnic slurs.[130] The law was enacted after a sharp rise in anti-Semitic incidents was reported.[131]

The ACLU's record on First Amendment cases has not been as uniform as one might suppose: It has made a number of exceptions to its Voltairian position. Recall that it took eighteen years before it would defend the free speech rights of capitalist employers.[132] Baldwin later retold the Union's stand on what Henry Ford could and could not do:

> Mr. Ford could go to the chamber of commerce and tell the businessmen that he was opposed to unions and he could be recorded in all the newspapers as having said so. But what he could *not* do was to put a notice on the bulletin board of his factories telling the workers not to join the UAW because that would be threatening them that if they did join he'd fire them. It was a very fine distinction between free speech and coercion.[133]

The ACLU of the 1980s still holds to that position. It emphasizes the right of free speech for employers but adds that "a statement which is demonstrated to be part of a campaign of intimidation may be proscribed."[134] Why can free speech be proscribed for employers who conduct a campaign of intimidation but not for Nazis who do the same? Baldwin's answer was "Nazis haven't any power over anybody."[135] Yet. And what should be done if, by exploiting the resources of the ACLU, they get power? That American Nazis may possess what Dennis Wrong describes as "possible power,"[136] i.e. power that has not been mobilized in the past but that may be in the future, is not a relevant consideration for civil libertarians.

Even before the Ford case, the ACLU recognized the limits of free speech. In 1933 the Union organized a national protest against the governor of California, James Rolph, Jr., for publicly approving of the hanging of two kidnappers by a mob in San Jose. The Union claimed that the governor's irresponsibility was a "threat of incitement elsewhere."[137] About a year later the Union claimed that the police in Bridgeport, Connecticut, had the right to stop a demonstration conducted by the American League

Against War and Fascism because it interfered with a nearby concert.[138] In the early 1940s the ACLU refused to come to the aid of Joseph Mc-Williams, leader of a semifascist organization, because "disorder usually accompanied the meetings." It admitted that it was the police, not Mc-Williams's followers, who initiated the violence but nonetheless claimed that it would not support the leader's plea of "peaceful assembly."[139]

In 1949 the board accepted[140] (and still does today)[141] the Holmesian provision regarding "clear and present danger." Expressions of opinion are protected by the First and Fourteenth Amendments except when: "1) They become an integral part of conduct violating a valid law; or 2) They are a direct incitement to specific and immediate violation of law; or 3) They threaten a danger of unlawful acts so great and so immediate that time is lacking for answer, or if need be, for other protective measures against the threatened acts."[142] The Union applied this policy in the mid-1950s when it refused to defend a woman who was charged with urging prospective inductees to evade the draft. The Union held that counseling nonregistration was as direct incitement to an illegal act.[143] However, it did not invoke this logic during the Vietnam war.

David Hamlin, one-time executive director of the Illinois CLU, has written that "in Chicago, the tradition of defense of First Amendment freedoms is just as rich as the city's penchant for offense—the ACLU is a part of the tradition."[144] Hamlin exaggerates. In the early 1960s, when the Philadelphia affiliate was defending the American Nazi party, the Chicago affiliate refused to defend the racist White Youth Corps. The corps was convicted of charges of starting a riot while parading before a movie theater showing a Sammy Davis, Jr., picture by carrying inflammatory signs. The majority of the Chicago board felt that while the group had a right to hire a hall and expound its offensive views peacefully, "people walking in a public street or standing in line to buy theater tickets, are entitled to protection from verbal assault."[145] This logic was abandoned by the affiliate in 1977.

The ACLU affiliates have not been consistent in their approach to what constitutes a "clear and present danger." The New York affiliate, however, has shown greater consistency than most. It was the NYCLU, together with the national office, that defended George Lincoln Rockwell's free speech in the 1960s. Rockwell, a White supremacist and leader of the American Nazi party, led his troops throughout the country trying to fan the flames of racism. When he was denied a permit to march in New York City by Mayor Robert Wagner, the local affiliate rose to the Nazi's defense. Arguing against the mayor's attempt to stop Rockwell, the NYCLU claimed that the "clear-and-present-danger" test was not applicable: "In the Union's view, speech can be limited only when a speaker urges immediate violent action and there is a real danger that his followers will act then and there on his incitement. This 'clear and present danger' limitation applies only to violence urged by the speaker. It does not apply to threats of violence by his opponents."[146]

Explaining the Union's "clear-and-present-danger" position in 1970, Roger Baldwin wrote: "We accept [it] for a long time. . . . The Supreme Court found it handy if vague enough to arouse dissent among the Justices. We found it vague, too, and fell back on the law of incitement to an act committed or attempted."[147]

What about the right of a private pressure group to lobby against the distribution of material that if finds offensive? The ACLU has not had an easy time answering this question. In the 1950s and 1960s it waged war on the right of the Citizens for Decent Literature (CDL) to organize boycotts of theaters that showed what the group labeled offensive movies. The Illinois CLU disapproved of the distribution of placards to stores that agreed to abide by the CDL's "code of decency."[148] Affiliates in Washington and Wisconsin protested attempts at film classification by the Roman Catholic Legion of Decency.[149] And today, as we have seen, the Union opposes as a "prior restraint" the Motion Picture Association's voluntary classification system. Disturbed by the boycott attempts to limit certain material, the board, in 1977, stated that "in situations where the result or the likely future consequence of such activity will be to remove material or close down a media outlet, the ACLU may call attention to these consequences, and urge media officials to respect the principle of public access to all materials."[150] Perhaps realizing the vagueness of this wording, the board redefined its position on "Private Pressure Groups" in 1981. It said it would call public attention to situations where "the likely consequences of private pressure group activities would be inimical to civil liberties, and particularly if the consequences would be to restrict a free and diverse marketplace of ideas."[151] It is still not clear what the Union would do or recommend in such cases. And how does one achieve whatever end the Union seeks without infringing on the right of people to protest against expression they do not like?

That the ACLU does not believe in unrestrained free speech on all occasions can be verified by examining its policies on captive audiences, libel, filibustering, and blockbusting. In 1950 the Union came to the defense of passengers in buses and streetcars who were being bombarded with music, advertisements, and "public announcements." It said that such broadcasts "violated free speech by denying riders the freedom not to listen, and due process by depriving persons of the liberty to use their conscious minds as they should like."[152] The Union today continues to score those who violate this right and does not oppose "reasonable regulation," i.e. those regulations that apply to time, place, and manner without regard for content—

content-neutral regulations.[153] As for libel, we have seen that the Union has not completely dropped its animadversions of those who defame others. On the subject of filibustering, the board recently exclaimed that it was "unalterably opposed to the practice of filibusting" because such a tactic frustrates "the information of a wise decision by the majority." It said that it supported "reasonable legislative rules permitting closure."[154] Also supported by the ACLU are blockbusting statutes that prohibit "false or deceptive statements concerning changes in the racial, religious, or national origin character of a neighborhood."[155] Such statutes are endorsed because of the social utility that they serve.

The Union's political interest in defending laws that afford a desired social outcome is not limited to blockbusting statutes. We can assess the Union's priorities in other cases where free speech collides with social equality. Such an occasion was provided in 1981 in Pittsburgh when Judge Gerald Weber mandated that five school districts be merged so as to promote racial integration. One of the teachers affected by the ruling, Jay Bush, protested the mandate. Weber then filed an order enjoining all employees of the new school district from expressing any public protest against his decision. The Pennsylvania chapter of the CLU agreed with Weber, stating that public criticism of his mandate was "often racist in content." So now judgment was being passed on the content of speech by the civil libertarians. How did the PCLU justify its position? By arguing that the school children had the right "to be provided with equal educational opportunities." Certainly they did. But what about Bush's right to dissent? He was told that he "should resign and then be entirely free to speak against [the order]." Joseph Sobran saw the anomaly: "This is not an indefensible position. But it is also not the position one expects of the ACLU, which boasts of its efforts to defend and expand the right of protest, as in the armed forces, among other places."[156]

Free Speech for Klansmen and Nazis

Not all liberals are prepared to defend the free speech rights of those who would silence dissent if they came to power. There are many sound arguments that can be made in defense of this position, but it is not the position that is associated with contemporary liberal thought. The Voltairian doctrine of defending everyone's right to free speech is the accepted wisdom of liberalism. Why is this position maintained? Ever since John Stuart Mill asserted that we can never be certain of the truth, and therefore all discourse must be entertained, liberals have never tired of repeating this maxim. The rationalism and optimism of liberals moves them to accept what Mill said: "Truth, if it has fair play, always in the end triumphs over error, and becomes the opinion of the world."[157] It is not necessary for liberals to add "it is hoped"; their faith in humans is too strong to require such reservations.

We now know why it is necessary for liberals—and certainly civil libertarians—to defend Klansmen and Nazis in the United States: the truth, being relative, can be established only by allowing it to emerge through open discourse. In his study of liberals, James Burnham put his finger on this "truth": "Since we cannot be sure what the objective truth is, if there is any such thing, we must grant every man the right to hold and express his own opinion, whatever it may be; and, for practical purposes as we go along, be content to abide by the democratic decision of the majority."[158] This position has become a staple of liberal thought. When John Shattuck of the ACLU was asked why it was necessary for his organization to defend the diatribes of Nazis in Skokie, Illinois, he replied that "there is no way you can pick and choose among particular words as to which are impermissibly offensive and which are not. What is offensive to one person may not be to another."[159] Another high-ranking official in the Union, Franklyn Haiman, understands the same logic: "Whether or not one believes, theoretically, in the existence of absolute truth, a democracy presumes that we can never be certain it has been attained by any fallible human being. Thus, reliance is placed on a free marketplace of ideas."[160]

David Hamlin, a defender of the Nazi Frank Collin's right to march in Skokie, took umbrage at the arguments of his critics: "They implied—and an astonishing number seemed to actually believe—that Collin could gain support for his doctrine if and when he aired it." Hamlin's solution to the proliferation of Nazi ideas is characteristically liberal: "The only sure way to reject such ideas is to examine them fully, to attack them for their flaws, to reject them for their inhumanity, and the only way to examine, attack, or reject is to listen to them first."[161] Haiman underscores this position. Speaking about democracy, he said: "It operates on the premise that although demagogues may succeed now and then, here and there . . . in the long run they and their deceptions will be rejected."[162] Aryeh Neier, who was the executive director of the ACLU during the Skokie incident, rose to the defense of the Nazis by referencing his support for John Milton's view that "truth will prevail in a free and open encounter with falsehood."[163] The present head of the ACLU, Ira Glasser, is equally optimistic: "A basic belief of democracy is that if all speech is permitted, the people will be wise enough to sort out the truth."[164] Such boundless optimism cannot be shaken by recalling Hitler's rise to power in Germany. Nothing, absolutely nothing, can shake the liberal's faith in the eternal wisdom of the people and in their ability to forgo the appeals of those who advocate genocide. It is perhaps the liberal's most tenaciously held, sacrosanct belief.

Not everyone in the ACLU has been supportive of the rights of right-wing extremists. In the 1930s Andrew Furuseth was dropped from the National Committee of the Union because of his membership in the Klan and because of his view (regarded as an action by his colleagues) that the criminal syndicalism laws should receive wider application.[165] This was done at a time when no Communist was being expelled from the governing bodies of the organization. In the 1980s Paul D. Boas, an ACLU lawyer, placed himself in nomination for a seat on the Pittsburgh CLU's Board of Directors, advertising his refusal to defend the Klan or Nazis (but not Communists) if elected.[166] But these instances are the exception to the rule. Since the 1920s the ACLU has been offering its services to the Klan. In its early days, it mounted a vigorous protest against the New York City Police Department for breaking up Klan meetings.[167] When its legal aid was offered to the notorious group, the Klan refused cooperation.[168] In the 1930s the Union again came to the Klan's defense, but toward the end of the decade it announced that the Klan did not have the right to parade with masks in Toledo, Ohio; anonymity was not condoned.[169] It no longer holds to this restriction.[170]

The ACLU's defense of Klansmen is in accordance with the law. In 1969 the Supreme Court, in *Brandenburg v. Ohio,* overturned the conviction of a Klansman for a racist speech; Clarence Brandenburg had been arrested for violating the state's criminal syndicalism law. The court ruled that "the constitutional guarantees of free speech and free press do not permit a state to forbid or proscribe advocacy of the use of force or of law violation except where such advocacy is directed to inciting or producing imminent lawless action and is likely to incite or produce such action."[171] The Union often cites this decision as supportive of its position.

It was not just the Union's defense of the Nazis in Skokie that provoked dissension amongst civil libertarians in the 1970s. The ACLU's defense of the Klan in California and Mississippi engendered similar discord. According to Pulitzer Prize-winning journalist J. Anthony Lukas, the Klan cases "stirred much more debate than Skokie within the organization's [ACLU's] ruling bodies."[172] In both cases the Union was roundly scored by the National Lawyers Guild.[173] The California case emerged in November 1976 when thirteen Black Marines armed with clubs, knives, and screwdrivers attacked seven Whites they thought were Klansmen. As it turned out, none of the five White Marines who were hospitalized belonged to the Klan.[174] The Marine Corps brought criminal charges against the Blacks and ordered fifteen Klan members to different bases around the country. The case divided the Southern California affiliate into two factions. The Los Angeles regional headquarters represented the Blacks. The San Diego chapter defended the Klansmen. At first, the Los Angeles group tried to restrain the

San Diego chapter from giving legal assistance to the Klan, but when twenty members of the San Diego Board of Directors unanimously re-affirmed their support of the lawsuit, the Los Angeles affiliate was left powerless. Both factions represented their clients on largely the same grounds—Marine Corps bias, intimidation, harassment, and denial of due process. The San Diego chapter sought $775,000 in damages for ten Marine Klansmen who were summarily transferred to other bases.[175]

The Mississippi case aroused even greater hostility within the ACLU. It grew out of an attempt by the Klan to hold a rally in a public school playground on a Saturday. The Harrison County Board of Education, which had been implementing a school desegregation plan, denied the request.[176] At that time, the Board of Directors of the Mississippi affiliate voted 8-7 to defend the Klan in a First Amendment case. Following this decision, ten of the twenty-one affiliate board members resigned from the Union—including all seven Black members. When this case was brought to the attention of the national office in September 1977, Aryeh Neier maintained that it was a straight First Amendment case. By a 29-19 vote, the board approved a resolution affirming its support of the Mississippi affiliate's decision.[177]

In the December meeting of the National Board, the case surfaced again. Norman Dorsen read a letter from Edwin King, the Mississippi affiliate's representative to the board, who was bothered by the board's September vote. His letter was pointed: "I am sorry the Board did vote to commend the chapter. I personally do not think it appropriate to commend a Board that has just lost almost half its membership and would prefer that no action had been taken especially something which only further alienated our Black members."[178]

The Mississippi affiliate did not support the Klan throughout the legal process. When the Klan sought to switch its suit from the state to federal court, the Mississippi board reversed itself and refused to take the case, citing Klan violence against Blacks. The Klan was successful, however, in receiving the support of the ACLU (the board voted 47-15 to back the Klan). According to Lukas's account, King charged that Neier told him that the ACLU had to represent the Klan because Jews would never understand if it defended the Nazis in Skokie but not the Klan in Mississippi.[179]

Skokie

In the 1960s Frank Collin was a member of George Lincoln Rockwell's Nazi Party of America. He was expelled from the organization rather quickly. Why? According to David Hamlin, executive director of the Illinois CLU at the time of the Skokie incident, the FBI exposed Collin as being Jewish and Rockwell responded by ousting him. COINTELPRO documents released by the FBI offer evidence of Collin's ethnicity. Mike Royko, the Chicago street reporter, also presented evidence that Collin was Jewish. Collin, of course, denied this. At any rate, after he was expelled he formed the National Socialist Party of America. It was a small organization, headquartered in Chicago, and supported by fascists like Collin.[180] Its goal of racial purification is to be achieved through the extermination of Jews, non-Whites, and whomever else its members do not like.

In the summer of 1976 Collin made plans to have his group demonstrate in Chicago's Marquette Park. The Chicago authorities held that the parks were "booked up" and then sought an injunction against Collin's demonstrations. Although that did not work, the police arrested Collin in the park area. The police were under instructions to arrest him if he said "anything derogatory." When he told his marchers that the police were ordering him to move, he was arrested. Later, he was acquitted. But that did not stop the Chicago authorities: the Park District administrators resurrected an old, infrequently used law that required the posting of insurance in the amount of $250,000 before a permit to demonstrate could be granted.[181] It was this event that started the most publicized and costly episode in the Union's history.

Collin called the ACLU to inquire about the insurance proviso. The Union quickly filed suit on his behalf in federal district court, but Collin was not about to wait for the litigation proceedings. He decided to take his crusade outside the city, and requested permission to march in many of the suburbs. All but one of the requests were either flatly rejected or simply left unanswered. The exception was Skokie. The Park District Board of Trustees of Skokie told Collin that he would have to post $350,000 in insurance prior to his demonstration. That was all Collin needed to gain the kind of exposure his group had always sought.[182]

The majority of the people who live in Skokie are Jewish:[183] approximately 10 percent are survivors of the Nazi persecution in Germany.[184] It was not surprising that most of the residents objected to Collin's plans, but Collin persisted. He wrote to the Village of Skokie announcing his intent to picket the Village Hall on 1 May 1977; this was his way of protesting the Skokie Park District insurance requirement. Shortly before Collin's planned rally, Harvey Schwartz, the Village attorney, filed a petition on behalf of the Village against Collin in the Circuit Court of Cook County. The Village sought an injunction barring Collin and his gang from parading in Skokie, in uniform, on 1 May. Collin immediately telephoned the Illinois Division of the ACLU.[185]

The Union represented Collin in court but lost: the injunction was issued. The ACLU quickly appealed the ruling. Again, it lost: the Illinois Appellate

Court denied without opinion. Collin then announced his plans to march in Skokie on 30 April, claiming that the injunction barred a march on 1 May but said nothing about 30 April. The Skokie lawyers then succeeded in banning Collin and his followers on 30 April and thereafter. The new injunction was intended to bar Collin permanently from exercising his First Amendment "right" in Skokie.[186]

Still not satisfied, the Village of Skokie drafted and passed three more ordinances aimed at preventing Collin from continuing his challenges. The first ordinance required a permit, issued by the Village for any demonstration. In addition, insurance in the amount of $350,000 had to be posted; Village authorities had the right to waive this requirement. The second ordinance banned the display of symbols offensive to the community, and parades by political groups in "military style" uniforms were banned. The third ordinance prohibited the distribution of literature that engaged in "group libel."

Meanwhile, the ACLU succeeded in approaching U.S. Supreme Court Justice John Paul Stevens for a stay of the injunction. Stevens treated the stay petition as one requesting a review of all procedural issues in the case (a petition of *certiorari*). The high court granted the petition on 14 June 1977, and thus the Illinois courts had to respond. In the meantime, Collin announced his plan to march in Skokie on 4 July. The Illinois Court of Appeals, which was under orders to expeditiously rule on the merits of the case, replied that Collin would be given a hearing on 6 July 1977! When the court met, it sent the entire matter back to the lower court for further hearings.[187]

In 1978, after a series of more legal tests, Collin won the court's approval to march in Skokie. Ironically, the Skokie march never took place. Instead, Collin wisely chose to march in other suburbs and in Marquette Park that summer.[188] He said that his plan to march in Skokie was "pure agitation on our part to restore free speech."[189]

The Skokie case did not engender a new policy decision by the ACLU: the Union had been defending the Nazis and other groups devoted to the elimination of civil liberties since its inception. But the reaction of civil libertarians to this case was dramatically different from that to previous cases involving the same issue. I asked Reitman why the ACLU lost so many members as a result of defending the Nazis in this particular case as opposed to previous ones. His response was lengthy and illuminating. What he said, in part, is as follows:

> There are a number of reasons why I think we have the reaction that we have today in terms of Skokie. One is the matter of proportion, we're just that much larger an organization and so, therefore, resignations proportionately

would be greater. Second, a large number of people, I think, joined the ACLU in the early '70s because of two basic causes—one, the anti-Vietnam war cause, and two, the Nixon impeachment cause. And while we saw those things in clear civil liberties terms, many members, I think, came in as an expression of their political opposition to the war and to Nixon himself. We don't ask a member to declare what his belief is. We have our literature which prints our program. A person reads the program and joins. But given the psychological and sociological dimensions of those two major historical events, a large number of people came in who perhaps came in not as fully educated civil libertarians but under the political momentum of the moment. And, therefore, when a controversial case comes up which people don't like because the group in question is disliked, and because the two issues which they joined on are no longer the pressing issues of the day, people may feel so unsettled that they would leave the war. Third, I think there is a special situation with repect to the American Jewish community. We have no way of knowing how many members of the ACLU are Jewish. But it's fair to say that given the general liberal tradition of the Jewish community that a large number of Jewish people belong to the ACLU. And, therefore, one has to examine the following: This is a period of great upset in the Jewish community. There is a deep concern about the plight of Soviet Jews; there is a deep concern about the security of Israel. Those factors, as well as other factors, have led to the search of what is called the Jewish identification, the Jewish identity. And when you get involved in a Skokie case where you see the enemy so clearly out there, even though it's not a realistic enemy in terms of numbers, but philosophically, it's so clear and it's so clearly opposed to Jews and what Jews represent, these psychological internal factors come up and people simply say—I must assert myself and my assertion is to disagree with the ACLU.[190]

Many members of the ACLU asserted themselves by quitting the organization. Neier's introduction to the 1977 annual report was aptly entitled "A Year of Testing." In that year, there was much negative fallout as a result of the Union's decisions to defend the Nazis and the Klan—as well as of the embarrassing revelations concerning the ACLU-FBI connection in the 1950s. By June 1977 membership had slipped by 12,000.[191] Overall, the Union lost at least 75,000 members. In 1977 it was forced to cut its budget by 15 percent, laying off staff members and dropping several important programs.[192]

The fallout from the Skokie case could have been tempered had the ACLU not chosen a Jewish lawyer to defend the Nazis. David Goldberger said he could not find another attorney in the Chicago CLU to defend Collin,[193] but the national ACLU could have found one had it tried. Goldberger's presence antagonized many in the Jewish community, and it is no secret that Jews have supported the ACLU more than has any other ethnic group. Goldberger paid a heavy price for his role in Skokie; he was personally and professionally vilified, physically threatened, and forced to move his wife and two children several times from their house.[194]

The ACLU made a modest comeback in 1978 and 1979. In December 1977 Neier launched an "Emergency Development Campaign."[195] In February 1978 a decision was made to have Goldberger write a letter to all ACLU members explaining his position and asking for continued assistance. The appeal was a success: 25,000 members donated $550,000 above their regular contributions. Nonetheless, overall membership was still down from the Watergate period. And in June 1978 the "Convocation on Civil Liberties" was held to drum up more support.[196]

Crime and Civil Liberties

Harvel Wilder was arrested at the age of thirteen for stealing a car for a joy ride. He was sent to New York City's Spofford Juvenile Center in the South Bronx for a short stay. When he was released, he continued to do what he did before: steal, fight, and generally behave in an antisocial manner. In and out of juvenile detention centers for the next two years, Wilder stopped going to school altogether when he was fifteen. He was turning professional and would now "earn" a few hundred dollars a night "working" the streets. Old people, young people, Black, White, male, female—it mattered not to Harvel whom he hit; he never discriminated against anyone. This went on for years before he was sent to Coxsackie State Prison. Arrested twelve times, and convicted for half as many, Wilder was known to the police as a "career criminal." He explained his contact with the law with the aplomb that is nurtured by frequent association with our nation's criminal justice system: "I'd go to court and they'd say, 'Well, the lawyer's not here and such and such not here.' So they'd let me go, give me a date to come back to court and I never come back—till I got busted again." He was eligible for parole within two years after his last conviction in 1980.[197]

On 11 March 1979, Steven Gladstein, nineteen, escorted seven young children to a hockey game at Madison Square Garden. After the game, Dennis Mannix, twenty-three, began hurling anti-Semitic remarks at Gladstein and the children, who were wearing yarmulkes. Gladstein unavailingly told Mannix to stop. Gladstein then pulled out chukka sticks—two sticks chained together—from his pocket. Mannix seized the sticks, walked to his car to get a hammer, and then beat Gladstein over the head with the hammer. Five days later the victim died in Bellevue Hospital of a cerebral contusion. Mannix was convicted of homicide in 1980. His sentence: five years' probation. That was it. State Supreme Court Judge Peter J. McQuillen announced that "vengeance had no place in the penal law."[198] Case closed.

The experiences of Wilder and Mannix have been shared by thousands in the United States. The public knows it. The police know it. Judges know it. And so must the ACLU. The criminal justice system, as liberals and conservatives would agree, has not been working well. In 1981 Chief Justice of the United States Warren Burger spoke for many Americans when he questioned: "Is a society redeemed if it provides massive safeguards for accused persons" but fails to afford "elementary protection for its decent, law-abiding citizens?" He called for "swift arrest, prompt trial, certain penalty and—at some point—finality of judgment."[199] His last plea was an end to the system of multiple appeals; he said that such a practice ought to be limited to "genuine claims of miscarriage of justice."[200] Burger's speech was quickly endorsed by liberals and conservatives alike. The *New York Times* praised him for defining the issue for public debate.[201] Carl Rowan, the liberal columnist, said that Burger spoke "a pathetic truth when he said that we Americans have become hostages to crime." Rowan added: "I agree with the chief justice that it is lunacy to put known robbers, rapists and other hoodlums back on the streets pending trials that won't take place for months."[202] The American Bar Association, not always on a cordial basis with the chief justice, enthusiastically endorsed his speech.[203] Just about everyone liked it. But not the ACLU. Barely an hour after Burger spoke to the American Bar Association, Bruce J. Ennis, the national legal director of the Union, presented himself before the press to deliver a strong denunciation of the speech. He opposed Burger's criticism of the multiple appeals practice and took issue with the recommendation that bail standards be tightened before a suspect is released.[204]

The Bill of Rights says nothing about a citizen's having the right to demand that government's first duty is to protect him from being molested. It also says nothing about the rights of crime victims. The ACLU, which is dedicated to the defense of the Bill of Rights, concludes that it is not its responsibility to attend to the right of citizens to go about their business without the fear of being victimized. A free society, of course, needs to protect the rights of those (all of us) who may be victimized as well as the rights of the accused. Striking a balance between liberty and order has always been one of the most difficult jobs facing a democracy. As the ACLU sees it, its job is to ensure liberty; police officers are expected to maintain order. This idea has been set from the top for quite a long time. When Baldwin headed the Union he once said that he would not serve on a jury, maintaining that he would never take part in convicting anyone. When asked how society could exist without any punishment, he replied, "That's your problem."[205] Neier gave a similar response when I questioned him about the Union's reticence about the victims of crime. Specifically, I wanted to know why the ACLU did not see fit to issue a statement regarding the plight of thousands of teachers who have been assaulted, brutalized, and raped by their students. At first Neier countered by saying that he was unaware of this condition[206] (though it has often been reported),[207] then he said: "We have a few police agencies in this country that employ about 500,000 police officers, and the ACLU is no substitute for them in prosecuting crime."[208] The issue, of course, has nothing to do with the ACLU's playing surrogate for the cops. Neier made it clear to me that he was unhappy with this line of questioning.[209]

There is one recommendation that the Union makes on how to stem crime: strong gun control legislation. It adopted its first gun-control policy in the late sixties, calling for strict federal legislation that would require the registration of firearms and the licensing of owners and dealers. One of the ACLU's major concerns was that any gun-control legislation should not discriminate against persons on the basis of moral or mental reliability. It specifically said that "to deny a license to any person convicted of any felony or ever committed to an institution by a court for reasons of alcoholism, narcotics addiction, or mental incompetence, or to any non-citizen, would be to deny both the wide variety among types of offenses classified as felonies and the possibility of rehabilitation."[210] It is doubtful that this policy is representative of liberal thought; it appears to be the sole position of the ACLU Board of Directors.

In 1971 the Union took the position that the ownership of guns, any guns, aside from guns owned by the militia, was not constitutionally protected. Recognizing that it is not unlawful to own a gun, the board addressed the question of state regulation of firearms. Although it dropped its specific reference to the rights of convicted felons, alcoholics, drug addicts, and the mentally incompetent to own a gun, it nonetheless adhered to its previous reasoning when it declared that an applicant's "personal history" should not be a consideration for a gun permit.[211]

The ACLU's objections to gun ownership led it to become a participating member in the National Coalition to Ban Handguns. In 1982, however, the board voted to change its status to that of an affiliate member of the organization. Its reasoning was political: It did not want to be publicly identified with the coalition on its letterhead, publicity, or research reports.[212] At the same board meeting, the Union ruled on police use of deadly weapons. The men and women in blue were summoned to establish new procedures in apprehending criminals. Nondeadly techniques, including alternatives to firearms, should be adopted by police officers; only as a last resort, the Union counseled, should deadly physical force be used.[213]

It goes without saying that the National Rifle Association (NRA) and the ACLU do not share the same position on gun control. The NRA, a powerful Washington lobby, has been largely responsible for the lack of strict gun control legislation in the United States. It has been particularly disturbed by Union attempts to influence the status of gun control in local communities. For example, when the authorities in Morton Grove, Illinois, passed a law banning all handguns, the ACLU did not come to the defense of those who asserted privacy rights and freedom of choice. When the authorities in Kennesaw, Georgia, passed a law requiring a firearm in every home (allowing for religious-belief exemptions, physical disability, and convicted felon exceptions), the Union filed a suit in Federal District Court in Atlanta seeking to have the ordinance declared unconstitutional.[214] Its behavior in both instances dovetailed with its policy position on gun control.

The Rights of the Accused

When the rights of the accused are mentioned, one thinks immediately of the four famous Supreme Court cases of the 1960s: *Mapp, Miranda, Escobedo,* and *Gideon.* The Union was active in some of these cases and offered public approval of all of them. In the high Court's *Mapp* decision, it ruled that illegally seized evidence was not admissible in state criminal trials. The Union hailed the decision as a "milestone in the history of civil liberties."[215] In a new policy statement, the ACLU affirmed the court's *Escobedo* and *Miranda* rulings. In *Escobedo* the Union supported the notion that the accused is entitled to counsel during police interrogation.[216] *Escobedo* was extended in *Miranda* to include the stipulation that the police must read the accused the accused's rights; the accused has the right to remain silent and obtain the services of a lawyer.[217] The Union's victory in *Gideon* led it to adopt a policy approving of legal defense for the poor.[218] The rights of the accused received another shot in the arm when in June 1969 the board opposed "all forms of preventive detention and the application of all conditions of bail unrelated to assuring the appearance of the defendant at a trial."[219]

In the late sixties and early seventies, the Union turned its attention to the disposition of arrest records. Its basic proposition was that those who have been arrested and acquitted should not be subject to any reprisals by employers and others. To accomplish this end, the Union advocated automatic expungement of arrest records after acquittal. For those who have been convicted, it favored the "expungement of records of conviction after a certain number of years of good behavior following completion of sentence."[220] The Union cited the case of ghetto residents who rioted in the 1960s as an illustration of its concern; they should not be subject to undue restrictions and penalties upon release by the authorities.

The rights of the accused have frequently been raised in cases where government agents have sought to uncover criminal behavior. The ACLU has been quite vigilant in these cases. For example, in the 1950s it took a strong stand against wiretapping[221] and the use of lie detectors.[222] The

Abscam undertakings by the Federal Bureau of Investigation in the late seventies and early eighties provided another opportunity to scrutinize government practices in the war on crime. Begun in the spring of 1978, the initial Abscam activities were representative of typical, and noncontroversial, actions by the FBI to thwart the efforts of organized crime through its usual "sting" operations. But as the investigations progressed, so did the FBI's enthusiasm for extending its reach. Its new target was corruption in government, first in New Jersey and then in Congress. How it conducted itself proved to be as important as its findings. Perhaps more so.

In October 1982 the ACLU released a report, "The Lessons of Abscam," prepared by Jerry J. Berman, legislative counsel of the Union's Washington office. It is a spendid example of the ACLU at its best; reasonable, informative, and constructive, it typifies what a civil liberties organization ought to be. The essential problem in the Abscam affair lay in the provisions of the FBI's own charter: it allowed the FBI to target undercover operations against persons on less than a finding of reasonable suspicion of criminal activity.[223] The ACLU report suggested that "persons should be targeted only when there is sufficient and reliable evidence that they are engaged or likely to engage in criminal activity of the type under investigation."[224] The report was balanced in its appraisal of FBI responsibilities and the need to protect civil liberties: "We need a law that would give the FBI the authority it needs to conduct investigations—including undercover operations—as well as substantive investigative standards and authorization procedures to protect civil liberties."[225] The entire report reflects the same kind of reasonable analysis, including the six recommendations that the ACLU made to rectify any future problems in this area.[226]

The right to a fair trial is central to the rights of the accused, but establishing the right is not easy. One of the most vexatious matters for civil libertarians has always been the reconciliation of two important and conflicting rights: freedom of the press versus freedom to a fair trial. There is no easy and satisfactory solution to this dilemma; tipping the scales one way is done at the expense of other values. If the ACLU has shown a preference for one value over the other, it has been on the side of the right to a fair trial. During the McCarthy hearings in the 1950s, the Union maintained that "newspapermen deserve no special exemption from questioning about illegal acts" but went on to criticize the senator's tactics as unacceptable.[227] In 1953 the Union went on record opposing newspaper, radio, and television coverage of court proceedings.[228] It reaffirmed its position five years later.[229] At the same time, it adopted a policy statement "opposing all attempts at legislating a compromise between conflicting civil liberties principles involved in freedom of the press and an individual's right to know his accuser."[230] As the Union moved into the 1960s, it voiced its support for Justice William O. Douglas's opinion that a public trial was "for the benefit of the accused, not the press."[231]

The issue of a fair trial versus freedom of the press reached new heights in the 1960s: Billie Sol Estes, the notorious swindler; Dr. Sam Sheppard, the alleged murderer of his wife; and Lee Harvey Oswald, the believed assassin of President Kennedy were the protagonists. In a 5-4 decision, the Supreme Court threw out the case against Estes because his right to a fair trial was jettisoned by allowing television coverage of his trial; the ACLU's friend-of-the-court brief was upheld by the court.[232] The Union came to the defense of Sam Sheppard for a similar reason: his right to a fair trial had been sacrificed by the sensational pretrial publicity that was accorded to him by the press.[233] The ACLU brief noted that a free press "without justice is an empty view." It urged a reversal of Sheppard's conviction, hoping that "cynical use of freedom of the press as a weapon to obtain a conviction will not be tolerated." The ACLU won.[234] The Union's strongest language was reserved for the media's behavior in the events surrounding Oswald's abduction by the authorities. "Oswald's transfer from the city to the county jail was arranged by the police," the Union charged, "to suit the convenience of the news media and took on the quality of a theatrical production for the benefit of reporters, photographers, and television cameramen." Although the Union's 3,500-word statement on the Oswald affair excoriated law-enforcement officials, much of the blame was visited on the media: "The news media must themselves accept their share of the responsibility to assure fair trial by curbing their pressure on police and prosecuting officials to publicize the case.[235]

Since the 1950s, the Union has taken the position that television coverage of courtroom trials should not be permitted.[236] The only exception to its policy was the proposed Senate trial of President Nixon. It argued that because the participants were "well acquainted with the television medium . . . behavior alterations because of the exposure would be much less likely than in an ordinary trial."[237] In another shift in policy, the board in 1973 took a strong, albeit not absolute, stand in favor of a reporter's privilege not to disclose sources to the authorities in a case pending trial. In the 1950s it acknowledged a reporter's privilege but also recognized that the implications for due process were serious. The 1970s policy seemed to give the edge to the reporter.[238] Indeed, in the *Branzburg* case of the early seventies, the ACLU participated *amicus* in a losing effort to sustain a reporter's privilege. What was most interesting about the case, however, was the Union's support in Congress for federal legislation designed to overturn the *Branzburg* decision.[239] This is just another example of the ACLU's readiness to support court-stripping attempts by the legislature when it disapproves of the high court's thinking.

Anyone who has boarded a plane in the past ten years or so has experienced the practice of an airport search of his or her possessions. Usually, it involves nothing more than passing through a detector designed to reveal weapons being brought on board. It is done so as to protect the safety of all passengers. Most people regard this practice as a sensible precaution against hijackers and assorted terrorists. But not the ACLU. The Union sees this requirement not as a minimal intrusion into a person's privacy but as a blatant violation of the Fourth Amendment's guarantee against unreasonable search and seizure. Particularly disturbing to the Board of Directors is the fact that most people, including civil libertarians, have "accepted and indeed welcomed such procedures."[240] The Union applies the same logic with regard to checkpoints set up by the police in an attempt to uncover intoxicated motorists; it does not regard such practices as a minimal intrusion. Complaining about the Maryland checkpoint operation, an ACLU lawyer said: "If you refuse to stop or roll down your window or be properly sheeplike, you'll discover how 'minimal' the police consider the matter . . . of course, drunken driving is awful, and, of course, roadblocks may 'work.' But there are dozens of offenses as vile as drunken driving."[241] As George Will sees it, "The ACLU would sacrifice lives on the theory that tyranny lies down the road from the checkpoints." He also reminds the ACLU that "the Founding Fathers, in proscribing 'unreasonable' searches and seizures, allowed for reasonable ones."[242]

The rights of juveniles have not been overlooked by the ACLU. It even has a Juvenile Rights Project designed to monitor and promote the rights of youngsters. Ever since the Union's victory in *Gault*, establishing due process rights for juveniles, "kid power" has attracted a large audience. Just what the status of a juvenile is, or should be, is nonetheless an open question. Rutgers criminologist Jackson Toby has said: "Under our 'no fault' juvenile justice system, children can get away with most crimes, even fairly serious ones such as burglary and mugging, because they are not considered to be responsible for their actions."[243] While Toby's statement is undeniably true, it is not the kind of utterance that one would ever hear from an ACLU lawyer. The Union's sole concern is with the rights of the juveniles who commit the burglaries and the muggings.

Should juveniles be treated as juveniles or as adults? Apparently the ACLU is somewhat confused over this question. On the one hand it seeks to abolish all laws that penalize acts committed by a juvenile but that are held to be legal if done by an adult. On the other hand it calls for protective measures to be instituted so as to advance the rights of children.[244] For example, when it comes to the rights of children, the Union views children as adults. But when it comes to the disposition of a sentence or the treatment accorded by the authorities, the children are often seen as children, deserving of unequal treatment. On the issue of rights, the ACLU won in 1981 in a class-action suit in New York against pretrial detention for juveniles; the Family Courts previously had the right to detain them for five days.[245] And on the subject of nocturnal curfews, the Union has moved to strike down such laws wherever they occur.[246] Such a law was imposed by Mayor Maynard Jackson of Atlanta in 1981 when scores of Black children were found missing or dead.[247] According to the ACLU, the mayor violated the rights of the children of Atlanta by ordering them off the streets after 9 P.M.

Prisoners' Rights

The ACLU has no policy on the victims of crime but has eight policies addressing the rights of prisoners. Prisoners' rights were not a major concern of the Union until the late 1960s. For example, in the early sixties when prison officials confiscated the autobiography of an inmate who wrote it in jail, the Union held that it was not technically a violation of civil liberties.[248] If the inmate had written his autobiography at the end of the decade, instead of at the beginning, the ACLU would have filed suit in his behalf.[249] In December 1969 the board passed a policy advocating basic rights for prisoners: "Prisoners remain subject to the Constitution and while incarcerated should suffer only restrictions of those constitutional rights which are necessary concomitants to the valid purpose of incarceration."[250] The Union argued then,[251] as it does now,[252] that greater concern should be shown for rehabilitation. "Such an effort is essential," the argument goes, "to reduce crime and violence."[253] If only it would. Robert Martinson, who is the nation's leading authority on rehabilitation, came to the following conclusion after reviewing all the rehabilitation studies available in the English language: "I am bound to say that these data, involving over two hundred studies and hundreds of thousands of individuals as they do, are the best available and give us very little reason to hope that we have in fact found a sure way of reducing recidivism through rehabilitation."[254] James Q. Wilson knows why: "Today we smile in amusement at the naïveté of those early prison reformers who imagined that religious instruction while in solitary confinement would lead to moral regeneration. How they would smile at us at our presumption that conversations with a psychiatrist or a return to the community would achieve the same end."[255]

In 1978 the ACLU established a policy, "Criminal Sentences," that went further than any previous policy advancing the rights of convicted criminals. Once again, the Union moved a few steps ahead of the liberal community in the formation of public policy. Imprisonment, the board said, was "harsh, frequently counter-productive, and costly." It plainly opposed "general deterrence as the basis for incarceration" as well as "mandatory sentencing schemes that do not allow for non-incarcerative options."[256] The concept of deterrence serves the function of utility, i.e. it is designed to mitigate the future prospects of crime. The ACLU rejects this reasoning. But, as Ernest van den Haag has noted,[257] the only other traditionally accepted rationale for incarceration speaks to the question of justice, i.e. that it is right and proper that persons who violate the rights of others be punished by the state for their infractions. The ACLU has nothing to say on this justification for incarceration, holding that incarceration should be "the penalty of last resort." What does the ACLU recommend we do with convicted criminals? Put them on probation and send them back to where they came from in the first place? What if they are recidivists, i.e. repeat offenders, the so-called career criminals? The Union is silent on this matter. "Probation should be authorized by the legislature in every case, exceptions to the principle are not favored, and any exceptions if made, should be limited to the most serious offenses, such as murder or treason." If punishment, instead of probation is to be levied, the Union recommends that "a fine should always be the preferred form of penalty."[258] It is not certain what the appropriate fine might be for rape, but, then again, that is not part of the ACLU's business, is it? One thing is certain: When convicted criminals do get sentenced to prison (harsh as it is), the ACLU will be there, as the Massachusetts affiliate was in the early 1970s, to see to it that inmates are accorded protective labor legislation—including minimum wage.[259]

Much of the Union's activities for prison reform grew out of its involvement in the Attica prison uprising at the start of the 1970s. Some inmates had taken prison guards as hostages, demanding that inmates be granted certain rights. The bloody outcome is well known. Neier and I discussed the Union's role.

> W.D.: Why did the ACLU oppose administrative reprisals against the Attica inmates?
>
> A.N.: Why did we oppose administrative reprisals? I'm not certain that we did.
>
> W.D.: In one of the annual reports, I believe it was one of the ones in the early 1970s, the ACLU took the position against the administration.
>
> A.N.: Against the administration. It doesn't say that we took the position against any administrative reprisals.[260]

Neier is wrong. The Union's first annual report of the 1970s (which he wrote) says that the ACLU "obtained a federal court consent order barring administrative reprisals against the prisoners."[261]

Capital Punishment

A person who commits a "heinous" crime in Louisiana can be sentenced to death. On 4 November 1979, Walter Culberth, Jr., killed Annie Simms in Louisiana by stabbing her five times. He was convicted by a jury and sentenced to death. One year later, the Louisiana Supreme Court overturned the death sentence by ruling 6-1 that the crime was not heinous; there was no evidence that Culberth had tortured his victim even though she did not die instantly.[262] The Culberth case highlights the uncertainties and multiple issues surrounding the death penalty. The overwhelming majority of Americans favor the death penalty, but their sentiment is rarely put into practice by the authorities. On this issue conservative intellectuals represent the attitude of the public more accurately than liberals. The issue has not always been so clear-cut: John Stuart Mill once appeared before Parliament to oppose a motion to abolish capital punishment. But even then, Mill admitted that his position was at variance with what he called "advanced liberal opinion."[263]

The ACLU is widely known as one of the most persistent critics of the death penalty. It has been active in appealing the death sentence even when its assistance has not been wanted by the candidate for execution. What is not widely known is that the Union did not always oppose capital punishment. In the early 1950s Ethel and Julius Rosenberg were tried and convicted for conspiracy to commit espionage. Specifically, they were sentenced to death for transmitting the secret of the atomic bomb to the Soviet Union in wartime. The ACLU watched the case closely and found that no civil liberties violation had taken place during the proceedings. The only question left was whether any violation of civil liberties was involved by imposing the death sentence. The Board of Directors said there was none.[264] I asked the present associate director of the ACLU, Alan Reitman, who at that time was the assistant director, why the Union had failed to oppose capital punishment in the 1950s. He replied: "There is nothing in my knowledge concerning an organizational decision not to oppose capital punishment."[265]

When the board reviewed the briefs filed by counsel for the Rosenbergs, it drew up six reasons for its rejection of the arguments made by those who favored the commutation of the death sentence. To the contention that the sentence of death for espionage was unprecedented, the board countered, "The sentence is not so disproportionate to the severity of the crime as to amount to a denial of due process." Many maintained that the sentence was motivated by political and/or religious considerations, but the Union said, "There is no evidence to substantiate these contentions." Some argued that others who were involved in the conspiracy did not receive the death penalty, but the civil libertarians answered that "all of them turned State's evidence, thus providing a reasonable basis for different sentences." Another argument was that the Rosenbergs were victims of their time: if they had been sentenced for their act when the United States and the USSR were allies, instead of adversaries, they might have received a lighter sanction. The ACLU said: "But the conspiracy was found to have continued during at least the beginning of the cold war, and the trial judge also had a reasonable basis for consideration of present world circumstances, in evaluating the seriousness of the results of the crime committed several years earlier." As to the contention that the defendants should be given special consideration because their children would be left orphans, the Union reasoned that this was not a civil liberties issue. Finally, responding to the reasoning that world opinion would consider the sentence "barbaric," the board said: "This is a question of international policy, not of civil liberties."[266]

Not until the end of the 1950s did the ACLU indicate that capital punishment might be considered a civil liberties problem.[267] On 4 April 1965, the Union reversed its position and declared the death penalty to be unconstitutional. The new policy was preceded by a campaign against capital punishment conducted by the Southern California affiliate in the wake of the execution of Caryl Chessman in May 1960.[268] The campaign inspired the national ACLU to launch a two-year study of the issue. The new policy argued that the death penalty denied equal protection of the laws, was cruel and unusual punishment, and removed the guarantees of due process. The death penalty denied equal protection of the laws by discriminating "against the poor, the uneducated and the Negro." Similarly, it violated due process because of its "fundamental unfairness. . . . The punishment does not fit the crime. It is directed almost exclusively to the most disadvantaged members of society."[269]

In 1972 in *Furman v. Georgia* the Supreme Court declared all existing state and federal death penalty laws unconstitutional due to the arbitrary and discriminatory manner in which they were implemented. It did not say that capital punishment violated the Eighth Amendment's provision against cruel and unusual punishment. Within four years, some states had revised their death penalty laws to meet the stipulation in *Furman*. By 1981, thirty-five states had a death penalty law on the books and the Senate Judiciary Committee had voted for a federal death law. The laws were based on the revised death penalty laws of Georgia, Texas, and Florida, of which the Supreme Court had approved.[270] In 1976 Gary Mark Gilmore was the first person to be executed under the new code.

The ACLU mobilized the efforts of its Capital Punishment Project to stop the execution of Gilmore but failed. The project had founded the

National Coalition Against the Death Penalty (NCADP), which also failed to save Gilmore. The State of Utah told Gilmore that he could appeal the death sentence conviction, but he elected to die, saying that he had a "right to die."[271] Gilmore's statement was a reaction to ACLU attempts to save him. He wanted nothing to do with the ACLU: "I do not wish to have other people's purposes to be forced on me."[272] Aryeh Neier defended his organization's right to "butt in," arguing that the Union's quarrel was with the state, not Gilmore. "Capital punishment is barbarous," Neier exclaimed, holding that the state was engaging in "savagery."[273] The courts did not think so. Three years later, in 1979, the Union tried to stop the execution of John Spenkelink. Again it failed.[274] In 1981 the Union proved unsuccessful in stopping the execution of Steven Judy. Judy had raped and murdered a woman and killed her three small children. At his sentencing, he told the jurors, "You better vote for the death penalty, because if you don't I'll get out and it may be one of you next or your family."[275] The jury voted the way Judy instructed it to. The ACLU intervened and lost again. Like Gilmore (and Jesse Walter Bishop in 1979), Judy was not interested in an appeal. Neither was Frank Coppola, who also was executed for murder. The ACLU experienced defeat yet another time.[276]

On 27 April 1981, Hugo Adam Bedau, John J. Donohue, and Henry Schwarzschild testified before the Senate Committee on the Judiciary as to the ACLU's views on capital punishment.[277] Bedau is a philosopher at Tufts University and an authority on capital punishment; Donohue is a lawyer sympathetic to the Union's perspective; and Schwarzschild is the director of the ACLU's Capital Punishment Project, as well as the NCADP. All of the men argued, of course, against capital punishment. They tried to persuade the committee not to adopt S.114, a bill to establish rational criteria for the imposition of the sentence of death. Bedau asserted that capital punishment was not a deterrent to crime. Omitting the work done by others in the study of deterrence (Jack Gibbs, James Q. Wilson, Ernest van den Haag, Walter Berns, and many others), Bedau told the senators that "there is no such evidence" that capital punishment deters crime.[278] Bedau's rejection of capital punishment is so strong that he questioned the usefulness of distinguishing between first and second degree murder, arguing that people who die as a result of an accident "are just as dead as the victims of the most ghastly murder."[279] Schwarzschild maintained that the death penalty was racist and sexist because half those on death row were Black and only 9 of the 750 candidates were women.[280] He did not propose any solution to this alleged problem. In any event, the committee was not impressed by such logic; it voted for the bill.[281]

On 7 December 1982, the State of Texas executed Charles Brooks, Jr., for the murder of David Gregory in 1976. What was unusual was that Brooks was the first person to be executed by lethal injection. Schwarzschild denounced the method as a "yearning for hi-tech efficiency" and claimed that compared to other methods of execution it was "more obscene because it provides the illusion of humaneness in the killing."[282] But had Brooks died before a firing squad, it would not have changed things for Schwarzschild or the ACLU: killing is always wrong (save possibly for war, self-defense, and abortion). The Union had rushed to Brooks's defense but got nowhere: the U.S. Supreme Court dismissed the ACLU's application for a stay of execution as "unsubstantial."[283] By the spring of 1983, eight states had already prescribed execution by injection; other states were considering its merits.[284]

The War on Crime

In the late 1970s many communities, associations, and students of crime began to focus on the rights of victims. Victimology became a new discipline as victimologists turned out one research report after another detailing the need for a bill of rights for victims. From feminists who focused on the rape victim to fundamentalists who stressed the plight of other victims of crime, there emerged a grass-roots effort to lobby in behalf of those who have been victimized. In June 1982 the voters of California passed the Crime Victim's Bill of Rights in a voter-initiated referendum. The people of the nation's largest state had spoken clearly: they wanted (a) an end to lenient bail practices; (b) tighter plea-bargaining provisions; (c) an end to the rule that illegally obtained evidence cannot be used in prosecution; (d) longer prison terms for career criminals; and (e) the right of victims to be heard at the parole hearings of their assailants. Not everyone agreed with the voters. The ACLU did not,[285] nor did the editors of the *New York Times*.[286].

While Californians were asking their representatives to get tough on crime, legislators in Pennsylvania were doing just that; a mandatory minimum-sentence law of five years in prison was passed for those convicted of violent crimes with a firearm, those who are repeat offenders, and those who commit a violent crime on public transportation. Pennsylvania was not the first state to adopt mandatory sentences for violent crimes, but its drive to advertise the new code was unique: television advertisements warned, "Commit a crime with a gun in Pennsylvania and this is what you're in for." The crackdown was well supported in both the White and Black communities. It was not supported by the Philadelphia chapter of the ACLU. Hilda Silverman, who chaired the state CLU said: "We objected to the bill because it precluded non-incarcerating options, will have a negligible effect on reducing crime and could lead to overcrowding and unconstitutional conditions in prisons."[287] Consistent with ACLU policy, Silverman's objection to incarceration stems from the belief that criminals ought to be placed on probation and reintegrated into the community.

The war on crime in the 1980s has been led by President Reagan. It did not take him long to appoint a task force on crime and to draw up a list of reforms addressing the issue. The rights of victims were central to the Reagan plan. He railed against "excessive litigation" that was stymieing the courts, and added, "Our legal system has failed to carry out its most important function—the protection of the innocent and the punishment of the guilty." [288] As a corrective, the administration pushed for mandatory sentencing for use of a firearm in federal felony convictions, more money for state correctional facilities, tighter drug-law enforcement, and a substantial increase in law-enforcement personnel. The two most controversial recommendations that were made centered on bail provisions and the exclusionary rule. The administration suggested that bail be denied to persons who were found by convincing evidence to endanger individuals or the community, for those whose release on bail would not guarantee appearance in court, and for those who had a prior record of committing a crime while on pretrial release. As for the exclusionary rule, it was recommended that evidence should not be excluded in court if the police officer obtained it while acting in reasonably good faith and in the belief that he or she was respecting the law.[289] The ACLU fought the Reagan initiative.

The ACLU believes that pretrial detention and modification of the exclusionary rule not only are unconstitutional but would not work. No one can be sure how effective the changes would be in reducing crime, but virtually no one aside from the ACLU believes that they would have absolutely no effect. Loren Siegel, an attorney and special assistant to Ira Glasser, flatly said: "The American Civil Liberties Union believes that not only is pretrial detention unconstitutional, it will not do anything to stop violent crime."[290] Siegel's boss said the same thing about the exclusionary rule changes: "*If the rule is relaxed, there will be no effect on violent crime.*"[291] Much of the Union's sentiment against the Reagan idea of allowing evidence to be presented in court that was obtained in reasonable "good faith" by the police officer reflects a certain uneasiness with regard to the likely application. Martin Garbus of the ACLU put it this way: "The good-faith exception would encourage prosecutors and police officers, who know better, to say that they did not understand the law or that somehow they got their facts wrong. Police officers, professionally committed to stopping crime, would often shade the truth to insure convictions."[292] No doubt some would. And that is the danger that such a proposal holds. But as others have pointed out, there are risks involved in clinging to the present, unmodified *Mapp* decision. What public interest is served, one might ask, when a police officer opens the trunk of a car without a warrant (after the motorist is caught for speeding) and finds the corpses of a woman and her two children, only to have the case thrown out in court because the evidence was ruled inadmissible? The killer in this case walked away scot free.[293]

Morality and the Law

How far can laissez-faire capitalism be advanced without endangering the cohesion of the social order? This is a question that has been thoroughly examined and answered by American liberals. But they have shown very little interest in examining, never mind answering, how far a laissez-faire attitude can be advanced regarding morality without similarly endangering the cohesion of the social order. Modern-day liberalism favors extensive public control of the economic order, but recoils at the suggestion that the moral order is deserving of at least some public policing. It was not always that way. John Stuart Mill believed in laissez-faire in both the economic and moral spheres of society. His hostility to public interference with matters of morality was so strong that not even today's liberals have been able to go beyond his position. But such a position has a price. Commenting on Mill's stand, Gertrude Himmelfarb has argued that the effect of societal nonintervention in all areas of morality is to weaken "the status of morality and its hold upon the individual. Philosophers can keep in mind the distinction between social neutrality and moral relativity. But the ordinary person cannot be expected to appreciate such niceties."[294] And as Daniel Bell has observed, none of the great Western religions has ever accepted Mill's laissez-faire morality. The common thread that runs through the religions of the West is an appreciation for the nature of humankind: "When there is no restraint, when mere experience is the touchstone of what should be permitted, the impulse to explore everything, to seek all sensations . . . leads to debauchery, lust, degradation of others, and murder. The lesson they have all drawn is that a community has to have a sense of what is *shameful*, lest the community itself lose all sense of moral norms."[295]

In no other area of society do the liberal values of optimism, rationalism, secularism, and antitraditionalism reach such a crescendo and become more visible than in the realm of morality. In describing the mind-set of the unrepentant rationalist, the English political philosopher Michael Oakeshott has said: "At bottom he stands (he always *stands*) for independence of mind on all occasions, for thought free from obligation to any authority save the authority of 'reason.' His circumstances in the modern world have made him contentious: he is the *enemy* of authority, or prejudice, of the merely traditional, customary or habitual."[296] That tradition stands in the way of progress, that it is restraining and without ennobling influences has become the creed not only of literary intellectuals but, as Edward Shils has noted, of social scientists (especially sociologists) as well.[297]

Aside from Daniel Patrick Moynihan[298] and a few others, there were not too many liberals in the 1960s who warned of the societal consequences that are wrought when individuals abandon their interest in practicing self-restraint. But by the 1980s, a number of those associated with liberalism and Left politics began to think through the effects of what Hadley Arkes has called "the legalization of vice."[299] Princeton scholar Michael Walzer contemplated the possible effects and then drew an appropriate question: "I imagine a human being thoroughly divorced, freed of parents, spouse, and children, watching pornographic performances in some dark theater, joining (it may be his only membership) this or that odd cult, which he will probably leave in a month or two for another still odder. Is this a liberated human being?"[300] After Reagan won the election, Henry Fairlie treated the readers of the *New Republic* to a stinging article entitled "Who Speaks for Values?" Certainly not liberals, he argued: "For years liberals have been warned that they were trampling on the decent feelings of most ordinary people. But they casually have gone on with their effrontery, and now they have reaped their predictable reward. Will they learn even now?"[301] Even Tom Hayden chided liberals for pushing permissiveness too far.[302]

It was the insouciant attitude that liberals displayed toward issues of morality that encouraged Jerry Falwell and his Moral Majority to emerge as a loud voice for traditional values. Falwell and his followers, along with others on the New Right, began to launch a crusade against permissiveness by focusing on marriage, the family, the schools, and the media. The institutions of marriage and the family were under attack, Falwell said, and the media were the number-one culprit. The Coalition for Better Television and its affiliate, the National Federation for Decency, both associated with the Moral Majority, announced that they would organize boycotts against the sponsors of television shows that they labeled as offensive. They were not without some success.[303] The schools were targeted for reform, bringing a chorus of criticism from liberal commentators. It was not as if liberals had not done the same. Albert Shanker, president of the American Federation of Teachers, blasted the National Education Association for pushing its political propaganda into the classroom.[304] But such liberal forays did not generate much reaction. At center stage remained the Moral Majority, an organization that the Reverend Timothy Healy, president of Georgetown University, said was akin to the Ku Klux Klan.[305] The ACLU outdid all of Falwell's critics by accusing the Moral Majority of seeking to "overthrow" traditional values.[306] It has fought Falwell tooth and nail, most conspicuously over the Family Protection Act.[307]

Although the Moral Majority does not represent a majority of Americans (no organization does), the Reverend Falwell's concern over the status of the family and the nation's public schools is shared by most citizens. Neither the family nor the schools has fared well in recent times. It is because these institutions are looked upon as the primary agents of socialization that social scientists have been busily engaged in examining their condition. The one-parent family, a reflection of the high incidence of illegitimacy and divorce, is a reality for millions of children in the United States. The report card on the schools is equally dismaying.

The Family and the Schools

Conservative social critics have long deplored the changes in the schools that began in the 1960s. They have pointed to a decline in educational standards and a general disregard for the rigors of scholarly endeavors. In the 1970s many of those on the left delivered similar appraisals. Christopher Lasch scored liberals for their "faith in the wonder-working powers of education," and argued that the quality of education had decreased as a result of the campaign for mass education.[308] In the spring of 1983, the National Commission on Excellence in Education, along with the Twentieth Century Fund report on education, issued a strong warning to educators and the public: the quality of education had dipped to a worrisome new level. Functional illiteracy was widespread and growing. Competence in grammatical and mathematical skills was shockingly low. Mastery of fundamental knowledge in the natural sciences seemed to exist almost nowhere. The word was out: tighten standards and demand more work.

Although there are many serious problems at the college level, most of the concern has been given to the conditions affecting the quality of education at the elementary and secondary levels, where instruction is mandatory. The concept of compulsory education, which is supported by the ACLU,[309] has long been seen as a necessary property in a society that promises equal opportunity. It follows that whenever the quality of education is undermined, so, too, is the value of equal opportunity. It is, after all, the children of the poor who suffer most when education in general declines. And judging from recent studies on education in our cities, it is apparent that many children, particularly students from disadvantaged backgrounds, will never realize equal opportunity in life. More than one-third of New York City's public high school students are "chronically absent" from class, making it impossible to teach them;[310] almost half drop out of school.[311] The problem is not confined to New York City; for example, the dropout figure in Pittsburgh is 35 percent.[312] It is a nationwide scandal.

Given the unfortunate state of so many public schools, it is not at all surprising that thousands of parents have placed their children in private schools. Protestant-run schools have experienced a flood of applicants,[313] and Catholic schools have taken in a record number of non-Catholic students, many of them Black. Black-run private schools have witnessed a similar resurgence of interest.[314] Those who elect to send their children to private schools are, of course, forced to pay for public education as well. Conservatives have rallied to their side, advocating the voucher plan and the tuition tax credit program. Liberals, who are associated with the interest of the poor, have almost uniformly denounced these proposals. The middle-class National Association for the Advancement of Colored People,[315] the *New York Times*,[316] and the ACLU[317] have all opposed these freedom-of-choice measures. The Union does so on the grounds that religious schools would be receiving, in effect, a public subsidy.[318]

The ACLU's role in matters of the family and the schools has been at once both encouraging and discouraging. Surely it favors good families and schools; its intent is above reproach. But owing to its civil libertarian vision, which equates equal rights for individuals with individual liberty, it has often taken the position that children are entitled to equal rights vis-à-vis adults. As good as this might seem to students of freedom, the consequences that inexorably flow from such a position are less than salutary. If children are seen as deserving of equal rights, it makes untenable the exercise of legitimate authority that is ascribed to parents and teachers. All authority rests on inequality; attempts to equalize unequal relationships cannot be achieved without undermining authority.

The record of the ACLU shows that it supports the institution of marriage (monogamy but not polygamy),[319] the family, and children's rights. It is when the rights of parents conflict with the rights of children that a dilemma is presented to the ACLU. For example, should parents be notified when their teenage daughter (under eighteen) avails herself of contraceptives from a federally supported family-planning clinic? The Union, which won in court,[320] maintained that parental notification violated the rights of minors.[321] Previous cases affecting the family typically have seen the ACLU defending the institution against the encroachments of the state. The Union's first significant case in defense of family rights occurred in the mid-1920s. A juvenile court judge ordered Russell Tremain, a nine-year-old from Bellingham, Washington, taken from his parents because they refused to allow him to salute the flag in school exercises. The boy was placed for adoption in "a patriotic and Christian family."[322] He spent more than a year and a half in the state's Children's Home Society before the ACLU succeeded in returning him to his parents.[323] The Union's policy today on state intervention in parent-child relationships is well thought through, placing a heavy burden on the state to show why a child ought to be removed from his or her parents. Barring cases of documented abuse or neglect, the parents' rights ought to be respected.[324] Good foster care, the Union maintains, is preferable to placement in a state home for abandoned children.[325]

The ACLU's thinking and court action on issues affecting the authority of teachers and school administrators has been more controversial than its policies on the rights of parents. Once again, the central question is how much authority should adults in legitimate positions be expected to yield in the name of children's rights. Disciplining students, so that all can learn, is at the heart of the controversy. Programs that mandate that students be taught the responsibilities of citizenship—like programs in New York City[326]—are helpful but may not be enough. The degree and kind of anti-social behavior found in the public schools demands that other, more serious steps ought to be taken. At least that is the opinion of many school administrators and teachers. However, the ACLU, which does not sub-scribe to punitive measures in general, opposes many of the attempts to restore civility in the classroom. It does so in behalf of its commitment to student rights.

Over the past decade or so the ACLU has worked to strike from the law restrictive dress codes, paddling, and student searches. The purpose of a dress code is symbolically to separate, in the minds of students, school and nonschool activities. The expectation is that if students approach the class-room with respect, it will set a tone of seriousness that is appropriate for educational objectives. Educator Neil Postman, who once counseled against dress codes, has, along with many others, revised his thinking.[327] And Secretary of Education Terrel Bell has moved to eliminate the rule that allows high school students to file federal complaints about restrictive dress codes.[328] But the ACLU has not budged: it still champions the stu-dents' right to determine their own styles of dress. The Union's flat rejec-tion of paddling, under any circumstances, stems from its conviction that when the Supreme Court upheld the practice it actually gave "the right of school authorities to beat children."[329] Invoking student rights once again, the civil libertarians have consistently sought to bar school authorities from searching the possessions of students.[330] Although the Union's posi-tion is not completely unqualified, in practice its reluctance to side with school officials in such cases renders its qualifications nonexistent.

Truancy is a major problem, particularly in urban schools. The City of Newark was faced with this problem in 1982 and provided an answer: Do what has traditionally been done and assign a truant task force to retrieve the absentees. This tactic, which worked well, meant that student-age persons were to be questioned as to their status when walking the streets during school hours. If they did not cooperate, they were taken to an "identification center" where the process would continue. The *New York Times* applauded the program,[331] as no doubt most of the parents did, but, predictably, the local CLU saw things differently. Jeffrey E. Fogel, executive director of the New Jersey CLU, said he was amazed by the *Times's* support for the truancy program, arguing that there were "grave civil liberties implications" in such a program. What was so grave about the tactic was that it might encourage further "abuses." Fogel was straightforward: "We could by extension of such logic round up every person in downtown Newark not wearing a tie and jacket, hold them in 'identification centers' and thereby reduce daytime crime."[332] And by extension of Fogel's logic, the authorities could put the kids in concentration camps. So far neither "logical" step has been taken.

As with so many of its policies, the ACLU did not begin to take a strong, liberal stand on the civil liberties of students until the late 1960s. Even then it acknowledged that if there was "compelling evidence" that a pregnant or married high school student had a negative effect on other students, the school administrators could bar the student from class.[333] The Union no longer approves of this sanction.[334] Indeed, since its victory in *Tinker* in 1969, it can safely be said that the Union has eschewed almost any support for school-imposed restrictions on student behavior. *Tinker*, which secured freedom of expression rights for high school students,[335] launched the ACLU headlong into the field of student rights[336] as lawyers such as Richard Emery[337] sought to challenge school regulations on a wide variety of issues.

Tinker was preceded by a 1968 ACLU document, *Academic Freedom in the Secondary Schools*.[338] An outgrowth of board decisions on student rights,[339] the publication enumerated "fundamental principles" that recognized "that freedom implies the right to make mistakes, that students in their schools should have the right to live under the principle of 'rule by law' as opposed to 'rule by personality,' and that deviation from the opinions and standards deemed desirable by the faculty is not in itself a danger to the educational process."[340] Gerald Grant, a sociologist at Syracuse University, has observed that the "fundamental principles" laid down by the Union "pushed academic freedom to a new limit." The idea that deviation from faculty standards is not ipso facto dangerous "blurred the line," Grant said, "between speech and action." He noticed, too, that the long-standing paternalistic feature of "rule by personality" was now to be dismissed. In summary, Grant charged: "In every area of discipline, the

ACLU statement takes a lawyerly view of the need to reduce adult latitude and discretion in favor of specific definitions and rules."[341]

The ACLU has not overlooked the rights of college or elementary students either. Most conspicuously, it has pushed for participatory democracy in the classroom. It has urged the nation's colleges and universities to "take whatever steps are necessary to enable students to participate in an effective capacity with the faculty and administration . . . at every level" of education. Did the ACLU mean by this that students should help decide course offerings and curriculum? Yes, it said so. Did it mean that students should be allowed to help determine grading standards? Of course.[342] At the grade school level, the Union has called upon teachers to encourage their students to vote on different issues and conduct elections for student representatives. But what if the child is a problem student? Does it matter? Not at all. The Union claims that "the right to vote or to run for office should not be withdrawn as a disciplinary measure." Why? The ACLU's answer is disingenuous: Participation in elections is "a form of preparation for future citizenship."[343] One is forced to ask what lesson a child is likely to draw about the meaning of citizenship if she or he realizes that the way one conducts oneself has no bearing on suitability for holding office?

The ACLU has not uniformly defended the rights of children against the authority of adults. No one knows that better than Walter Polovchak. In January 1980 Michael and Anna Polovchak arrived in Chicago with their three children, Natalie, seventeen; Walter, twelve; and Michael, five. The family had been given permission to emigrate to the United States so that Mr. Polovchak could be reunited with his two sisters. After a few months in Chicago, the Polovchaks decided to return to the Soviet Union. More accurately, the parents decided to return; the two older children wanted to stay, and did. As a result, they made history in the annals of civil liberties.

The parents could not do much to Natalie; she was almost eighteen and no longer a minor. Walter's situation was different. His parents asserted their right to take him into custody and return him to the Soviet Union. But Walter asserted his right to live in freedom, claiming that he would be persecuted for his religious beliefs if he were to go home.[344] In stepped the ACLU—on the side of Walter's parents. Under Illinois law, the principle of "the best interests of the child" must prevail. Julian Kulas, a noted attorney in the Chicago Ukrainian community, and Henry Mark Holzer, a Brooklyn Law School professor, argued that it was in Walter's best interests to stay in the United States. The ACLU argued that the parents' Ninth and Fourteenth Amendment rights were being violated. Regarding the Ninth Amendment, the Union contended that it was well understood that one of the fundamental rights that the state could not deny was the "integrity of the family." The Fourteenth Amendment guarantees due process, and thus

The Politics of the ACLU

Mr. and Mrs. Polovchak had a right to challenge the constitutionality of the Illinois statute.[345] The ACLU lost in the juvenile court, but won on appeal in the Court of Appeals. The appeal process then went further.[346]

Marcia Robinson Lowry, chairman of the Children's Rights Project of the ACLU, said that there was dissensus within the National Board of Directors over this issue; some argued that the Union should be defending Walter.[347] To be sure, this is a difficult case, one that does not neatly split along ideological or constitutional lines. The ACLU's concern for the "integrity of the family" is heartening, but difficult to believe. Shortly after the Polovchak case emerged, the New Jersey CLU sought to defend a Chilean child in circumstances almost identical to Walter's.[348] Why is it okay to send a kid to the home of the Gulag but not permissible to send a kid to Chile? Is it because Chile is a right-wing authoritarian state and the USSR is only a left-wing totalitarian state?

Natalie and Walter have repeatedly charged that they were ignored and ill-treated by their parents. Walter even relayed his feelings to Congressman Peter A. Peyser of New York.[349] Nevertheless, Harvey Grossman, who represented the boy's parents, argued that the best thing that could have happened would have been for the government to back out of the case and allow the family to settle its own problems: "They don't have to live in America or in the Soviet Union. There are lots of other places beside the United States or the Ukraine."[350] This assumes that the freedom to emigrate at will is a realistic possibility for Soviet citizens. The record shows that it is not.

When Walter turns eighteen in October 1985, his parents will lose any claim to custody.[351]

Victimless Crimes

Liberals do not hesitate to call on the state to intervene in the economic affairs of men. Conservatives wish the state would mind its own business and allow the free market to thrive. Liberals wish the state would mind its own business and allow consenting adults to do as they please in establishing their own moral code, just so long as others are not affected. Conservatives do not hesitate to call on state intervention in the moral affairs of men. For some liberals and conservatives this is a dilemma: When should the state intervene in the regulation of economic and social life? There may be no satisfactory answers. And in the writings of an astute liberal or conservative writer, the apparent contradictions may appear less than what they seem.

As with all issues, not every liberal will take a laissez-faire attitude toward morality and the state, and not every conservative will align himself or herself with an interventionist approach. But there is no denying that those who have spoken the loudest in favor of a hands-off position have been liberals, while conservatives have pushed for legislative reforms in the area of morality. This divide can be seen most clearly in the subject of "victimless crimes."

Two sociologists who have thoroughly examined the subject of victimless crimes are Edwin Schur[352] and Gilbert Geis.[353] Both have concluded that the state should not try to regulate consensual conduct among adults where there is no obvious third-party victim. Schur's basic point is that "the persons involved in exchanging (illicit) goods and services *do not see themselves* as victims."[354] The kinds of conduct that Schur and Geis are referring to include, but are not limited to, gambling, narcotics, homosexuality, prostitution, and pornography; abortion once fell into this category, but has been rendered moot since *Roe*. The ACLU follows the thinking of Schur and Geis. Its policy on victimless crimes states: "The ACLU opposes the definition of behavior as criminal when such behavior, engaged in either alone or with other consenting adults, does not in and of itself harm another person, or directly force such person to act unwillingly in any way."[355] In addition to the victimless crimes that have already been mentioned, the Union includes suicide on its list.

The ACLU's views on suicide are tentative: it acknowledges the right to kill oneself, but endorses societal intervention as well. It maintains that "society may intervene to prevent an act of suicide and thus assure that the individual has had the opportunity rationally to consider whether to take this irreversible action."[356] The policy reflects the persuasiveness of Mary Coleman, who, at a board meeting, argued that societal intervention was necessary because there is a biomedical change that occurs in the brain when a person is suicidal.[357] From the board's policy, it is not at all clear whether the Union would recommend societal intervention (volunteers? the police?) in cases where the person contemplating suicide had been denied the opportunity to kill herself or himself on a prior occasion. If the person has had the chance to consider the action rationally and still wants to go ahead with it, should the person then be permitted to do so? Rational suicide, as the case of Jo Roman disclosed, is a realistic phenomenon. Labeled as a new rights martyr, Roman killed herself in 1979 after notifying her husband (a psychologist) and about a hundred friends in advance that what she was going to do was quite rational. Her wish was respected by everyone: the police were not called until four hours had elapsed from the time of the suicide.[358]

On the related issue of euthanasia, the ACLU has taken the position that it should be legal, provided that the element of volition is assured. Consensual euthanasia is regarded by the ACLU as "a legitimate extension of the right of control over one's own body." For this reason, the Union urges that state legislatures make "living wills" legally valid documents.[359] The Due Process Committee, which brought the issue to the board, failed in its attempt to devise a policy on nonconsensual euthanasia,[360] and so far the Union has not developed one.

Narcotics

The buying and selling of illegal drugs is commonplace in most big cities. Teenagers have found it to be relatively simple to purchase whatever drug they desire.[361] State legislators have attempted to thwart the easy access by passing laws forbidding the selling of drug paraphernalia in "head shops." They have been unsuccessful, thanks to the efforts of the ACLU to have such laws stricken as being unconstitutionally vague.[362] But the campaign against illicit drugs continues, for nearly every president in recent times has declared a war on drugs. None of the programs has worked very well. As a result, it has become more acceptable to propose either the regulation, decriminalization, or wholesale legalization of drugs. Arguments that cite the drain on the court system and government resources[363] have proven popular in some circles. By regulating marijuana, for instance, we could tax the buyers and sellers and thereby help cut the federal deficit.[364] Giving addicts free heroin, we are told, would stem the crime rate.[365] But despite these benefits, the public and the courts do not appear to be persuaded that it is in society's best interest to change the drug laws. The ACLU, however, is trying to change that view.

The ACLU did not enter the debate on the legality of drugs until it became a national issue in the 1960s.[366] In 1966 the Board of Directors moved to accept a policy on drug addiction that embraced a medical understanding. It noted that "addiction is at bottom an illness to be treated and not a crime to be punished." This position was actually a restatement of contemporary liberal thought on the subject. Although the Union's policy adequately addressed the problem of heroin use, it did not touch on the question of marijuana use. Marijuana's widespread use in the sixties and its alleged nonaddictive properties made necessary a distinct policy on less-than-"hard-core" drugs. Late in 1967 the Due Process Committee brought before the board a policy suggestion that recommended that marijuana be treated differently from "hard-core" narcotics: a reduction in criminal sanctions to the level of a misdemeanor was advised. The board did not accept this idea and maintained that there was insufficient evidence demonstrating the harmlessness of marijuana.[367]

In the course of one year, the ACLU not only dropped its concern over the possible harmful effects of marijuana but proclaimed that the use of the drug was a constitutional right. This was one of the fastest turnarounds in the Union's history. Its new policy declared: "The use of marijuana involves protected constitutional rights, including the right to privacy. Intrusion by government on such a constitutionally protected act places a burden of justification upon government. That burden has not been met."[368] The Union did not take up the question of the sale of marijuana until 1970, when it came out in favor of "reasonable regulations" in that regard. Two years later, the board voted for the decriminalization of marijuana, offering as one of its reasons for opposing criminal penalties the argument that they "interfere with honest efforts to educate young people about the dangers of drug use and to combat the problems of drug abuse."[369]

The Union was able to settle its policy on marijuana with relative ease, but struggled over the question of "hard core" drugs. Does one have the right to shoot heroin into one's veins or does heroin addiction have societal consequences that warrant against its legalization? The Due Process Committee pondered this question at the outset of 1969. Taking the extreme libertarian position was committee member Jeremiah Guttman: "The right *not* to live should be as basic as the right *to* live. Whether a person chooses to end his life with a bullet through the brain, fifteen years of alcoholic indulgence or five years of heroin should not be material." All that Guttman would counsel is the right of libertarians to alter the social conditions that "lead people" to addiction, but he would not countenance punishment. Commenting on this position, Ronald Bayer, an official at a New York methadone clinic said: "It is interesting to note here that Guttman, like many others associated with the ACLU, though positing a radical individualism as the basis for the defense of liberty, relied upon a form of social determinism to explain the prevalence of addiction." After five more years of debate in the Due Process Committee and at the Biennial Conference, the board voted in its present position: "Examples of behavior that should be exempt from criminal prohibition include, but are not limited to, gambling, attempted suicide, sexual relations, or the introduction of substances into one's own body."[370] The right to kill oneself with heroin had finally been sustained by the civil libertarians.

Homosexuality

In 1957 a British Parliament study called the Wolfenden Report recommended that "homosexual behavior between consenting adults in private should no longer be a criminal offense." The report, subject of much controversy at the time, did not condone homosexual acts; it simply said that it was not the law's business to try to legislate against homosexuality. Several years later, England adopted the report's recommendation.[371] The impact of the report was not immediately felt in the United States. Laws proscribing homosexual conduct remained on the books, and there was hardly a stirring in the heterosexual or homosexual ranks over the report's conclusion. But as with other social movements in the postwar period, the decade of the 1960s saw the awakening of protest among those who felt socially dispossessed: Homosexuals organized to claim their rights.

The gay rights movement began in New York and California in the late 1960s. It was the riot that took place between gays and the police at the Stonewall bar in Greenwich Village in 1969 that brought the homosexual movement unparalleled notoriety. It was a perfect example of a modern protest movement, i.e. it centered not on rights taken away but on rights not yet enjoyed.[372] What gave the new movement its force was its political nature. Not satisfied to settle for an end to harassment and discrimination, the gay rights contingent sought to advance positive rights; it wanted nothing short of individual liberation and societal affirmation of its status. Homosexuality was not only not bad, it was good, or at least as legitimate as heterosexuality. To accomplish the goal of legitimation, gay activists pressed for a major transformation of society. No gay could experience individual liberation until the society itself had become liberated from the prejudices of the past. The New York Gay Liberation Front succinctly voiced its objective in its founding statement: "Gay Liberation is a revolutionary homosexual group of women and men formed with the realization that complete sexual liberation for all people cannot come about unless existing social institutions are abolished."[373]

Dennis Altman was one of the first gay rights activists to write a serious work on homosexuality. He spoke for many of his associates when he charged that the nuclear family was a source of tyranny. Children would be better off living in a communal setting, Altman argued. His main objective was to see to it that children were raised communally by both heterosexuals and homosexuals. Children, he contended, do not "belong" to their parents; this is an extension of the cult of property. The problem, according to Altman, was that homosexuality would never be seen as an equal variant of sexual preference unless gays had a hand in raising children: "As long as homosexuals are denied any role in child-rearing . . . it is unlikely that children can grow up with other than a distorted view of what is natural."[374] It would not be long before the issue of child custody for gays emerged as a heated controversy.

The ACLU issued its first policy on the rights of homosexuals on 7 January 1957. It was not a very progressive policy, but then again liberals in general would not take up the cause of gays until ten years later. The Union admitted that it was only occasionally called upon to defend the rights of homosexuals, and made clear that it did not consider the issue to be of serious concern to civil liberties. In fact, the Union said the issue was beyond its province. It was not the business of the ACLU, the board said, "to evaluate the social validity of laws aimed at the suppression or elimination of homosexuals." Homosexuality constituted a common-law felony, argued the ACLU, and "there is no constitutional prohibition against such state and local laws on this subject as are deemed by such states or communities to be socially necessary or beneficial." Homosexuals were regarded by the Union as belonging to a "socially heretical" and "deviant group." As such, homosexuality may be regarded as "a valid consideration in evaluating the security risk factor in sensitive positions." The right to due process and the right not to register as a homosexual in a local community were the only rights that the Union was willing to defend.[375]

On 13 December 1965, the Board of Directors met to reconsider its policy on homosexuals. Once again it said that it was only occasionally called on to act on behalf of gays. Nonetheless, the board asserted that privacy rights require that homosexuals receive coverage and added that "the Union supports the idea that this kind of sexual behavior between consenting adults in private, as distinct from acts in public and improper public solicitation, should not be made the subject of criminal sanctions." This was the same position that the Wolfenden committee had taken in 1957, and that was the extent of the Union's changes. It still regarded homosexuals as members of a "socially heretical" and "deviant group" and continued to argue that gays could be screened as a security risk in "sensitive" employment.[376]

Eleven months later the board assembled to draw up another new policy on homosexuality. The minutes of the board meeting indicate that for the first time the ACLU was ready to consider the whole range of consensual sexual conduct; incest was also discussed as a civil liberties matter.[377] The heart of the revised policy read: "The right of individual privacy, free from government regulation, extends to private sexual conduct, heterosexual or homosexual, of consenting adults." The Union made clear that its policy applied only to private behavior and recognized the right of the public to be protected from "solicitation, molestation, and annoyance in public facilities and places"; minors, in particular, deserved protection against "adult corruption." It is evident from these statements that although the ACLU stopped labeling gays as deviant and the like, it nonetheless felt it prudent to guard against the advances of homosexuals. As for government employment, the Union maintained that no person should be disqualified because of private sexual conduct. But there were a few caveats: "If a homosexual employee becomes an irritating force by making sexual advances on the job which interfere with his or a fellow worker's performance, then the normal Civil Service procedures governing work performance can be invoked." It issued no caution regarding the irritating sexual advances that straights might engage in on the job. The ACLU went further by arguing that "in certain jobs there may be relevancy between the job and a person's private sexual conduct, including homosexuality." The government, however, bears a "very heavy burden of proof" in showing that homosexuality ought to be weighed as a matter for job denial. The Union concluded by saying that "the government should be permitted to rely upon present homosexual conduct or conduct so recently past that it clearly appears that the applicant is presently a practicing homosexual."[378]

In 1973 the National Sexual Privacy Project was founded by the ACLU to protect the rights of prostitutes, homosexuals, bisexuals, transvestites, and transsexuals; heterosexuals were also included.[379] But the ACLU's 1967 policy on homosexuals remained unchanged. It was not until April 1975 that the Union delivered a new policy. By that time the American Psychiatric Association had stricken homosexuality from its list of mental illnesses; homosexuality was now regarded as a "sexual orientation disturbance." The Union's 1975 policy, which is also its current one, went far beyond any of its previous policies: "Homosexuals are entitled to the same rights, liberties, lack of harassment and protections as are other citizens." This libertarian position allowed of no exceptions. In every respect, discrimination was condemned whether in employment, public or private ("sensitive" jobs or not), housing, immigration, or naturalization. Now the Union even opposed criminal restraints on "public solicitation for private sexual behavior between or among adults of the same sex."[380] With regard to children, the original proposal stated that the state had a legitimate interest in controlling sexual behavior between adults and minors by criminal sanctions. But this idea was scratched when Ruth Bader Ginsburg argued that such wording implied approval of statutory rape statutes. These statutes, she held, were of questionable constitutionality. David Isbell's motion was then carried; it simply contended that the state has an interest in protecting children from sexual abuse.[381]

Perhaps the most controversial aspect of the Union's policy on homosexuality is its endorsement of child custody rights for gays.[382] It is the Union's belief that if the court is going to deny custody to a parent, it should not be done arbitrarily or because of "personal preference for one style or mode of life over another. A court may give no consideration whatever to the parent's political beliefs or activities, religious opinions, or sexual preference."[383] In one of its most important victories, the ACLU succeeded in December 1981 in securing child custody for a lesbian. The woman's twelve-year-old son had spent summers and school holidays with his mother until 1978 when his father went to court to have the boy adopted by the father's new wife. The Union defeated the father's objections in the Virginia Supreme Court after losing the initial round in a lower court.[384] It has been quite active in this area in recent years. The campaigns of Anita Bryant and the New Right have not proven to be as successful in the courts as they have in the legislatures of local communities.

Prostitution

A prostitute whom feminist Kate Millet knows once told her: "All prostitutes are in it for the money."[385] It is because prostitution is such a lucrative business that the supply always seems to keep up with the demand. How a prostitute earns her or his money varies widely. Some are discreet and seem to bother no one; call girls who work out of a hotel are an example. Others work bars, night clubs, or casinos waiting for an offer. Those who work the streets sometimes wait for johns to approach them. But increasingly, prostitutes have become more aggressive, accosting young people in public. These are the cases that attract the most attention. The problem is not limited to controlling the advances of street prostitutes. The areas where prostitution flourishes in the United States are also the areas that invariably have a high crime rate. The 42d Streets are well known for the high incidence of muggings, beatings, narcotics, and the like. It is as though prostitution acts as a magnet for attracting deviants and degenerates of all kinds. There is not a city in the country that has not faced some degree of difficulty in confronting this situation: Sexploitation, and its attendant violence, is a ubiquitous phenomenon in urban areas.

Prostitutes have not been untouched by the sexual revolution of the 1960s. As with other segments of society, the profession of prostitution witnessed a change in standards, roughly equivalent to the changes in the normative order of society. Elementary rules of public decency were discarded as sexual mores became relaxed. The residents of Long Island City, Queens, have complained about prostitutes who use their parks as bathrooms and their streets as bedrooms. Nancy Schuln, president of the Boerum Hill Community Association in Brooklyn, has protested: "You just can't believe it unless you see it. Lookouts roaming around, prostitutes having sex on stoops and in parked cars, women out in the middle of the street in their underwear."[386] Under public pressure to do something about prostitution, New York Mayor Edward Koch instituted the "John Hour," a public broadcast of the names of men who had been convicted for patronizing prostitutes. His effort did not last long, for critics of his policy, namely, the New York Civil Liberties Union, mounted a protest against it.[387]

The ACLU's policy on prostitution was formulated in 1975. It supports decriminalization and opposes state regulation of prostitution. Citing the element of individual choice and concern for laws that discriminate against women, the Union does not address the right of a community to protect itself against unwanted sexploitation.[388] I asked Baldwin why the Union had nothing to say regarding the right of a community to oppose, through the law, prostitution. His reply: "Well, I don't think we defend solicitation. We defend the right of a person to be a prostitute."[389] Baldwin was mistaken. The organization that he founded was already on record defending solicitation.[390] I then inquired as to why the ACLU held as objectionable zoning ordinances designed to control the proliferation of "massage parlors" and prostitution in general. "Does the ACLU say there is nothing wrong with allowing this activity to spread throughout New York into communities that don't want it?" "It looks thay way," he told me. "I suppose as long as you concede the right of a woman to be a prostitute that you can't tell her where she can live."[391] Or work.

The ACLU attorney who has been most active in defending the rights of prostitutes is New York attorney Richard Emery. Emery, who has brought a federal court challenge against New York's law prohibiting "loitering for the purpose of prostitution," explains that he is against prostitutes who harass or trespass on the rights of citizens but defends their right to loiter.[392] To be sure, police officers might find the distinction untenable. Emery, like the ACLU, regards prostitution as a minor offense, not worthy of legal sanction. Yet when the New York Court of Appeals declared that accused prostitutes were not entitled to a trial by jury because of the pettiness of their offenses, Emery objected. He said, representing the local affiliate, that prostitutes should be permitted a trial by jury even though the offense was minor in the eyes of the law (and in the eyes of the ACLU). Emery worked his way out of his position by invoking the following logic: "It's not a serious offense in society's eyes. But imagine if you or your daughter were accused of prostitution. It would certainly seem quite serious then, something you'd be entitled to have a jury decide."[393] Emery gave no indication of how many people are erroneously charged with prostitution each year. No doubt the figure is infinitestimal. It is hard to know exactly what motive Emery had in this case, but it is not at all unreasonable to think that his real intent was to have prostitution declared a major offense so that prostitutes would be given trials, the effect of which would be to make a public scandal over crowded court cases and ultimately lead to a public outcry in favor of decriminalization.

Pornography

It is paradoxical, but nonetheless true, that the rise of the women's movement has coincided with a rise in pornography. Whether there is a cause-

and-effect relationship at work here is purely speculative. Certainly feminists have not intended to benefit the purveyors of pornography. Many of them, Susan Brownmiller and Gloria Steinem in particular, have lobbied hard, but without much success, against pornographic material. A number of organizations have been established by feminists to combat what they see as the objectification of women and men. Women Against Pornography, Women Against Violence in Pornography and Media, Women Against Violence Against Women—not to mention hundreds of local associations—have been founded in the past decade or so to demand a ban on pornographic movies and literature. There have been occasional success stories: Larry Flynt, owner of *Hustler* magazine, was prosecuted in Atlanta and convicted under the state's obscenity law; he lost on appeal to the Supreme Court. But he is still in business.

Edward Shils has noted that until relatively recently freedom of expression meant "the liberty of expression, in an intellectual form, of a substantive belief." In other words, free speech was regarded as the free marketplace of ideas. But no longer, observes Shils: "The liberal defenders of pornography have extended liberalism to justify actions and works that were not intended to enjoy the benefits of a liberal regime."[394] The ACLU is one of those liberal defenders. Indeed, the ACLU is *the* liberal defender of pornography in the United States; it simply has monopolized the defense of pornographers everywhere. Its reason: Pornography is free speech covered by the First Amendment—a constitutional right. Aryeh Neier, for example, sees absolutely no difference between the censorship of pornography and the censorship of political discourse, it all adds up to "expurgating the First Amendment." "Pornography may be a crime against women," says Neier, "but it is not necessarily a crime against the state."[395]

The absolutist interpretation of the First Amendment as applied to pornography has never been sustained by the Supreme Court. The court has held that obscenity must be limited to sexual matters[396] and has gone further by acknowledging that sex and obscenity are not synonomous.[397] However, such stipulations have not stood in the way of court's decisions not to accord pornography the same legitimacy as political discourse. In 1957 in *Roth v. United States*, the court upheld a federal statute making it a crime to mail material that was "obscene, lewd, lascivious, or filthy" or "other publication of an indecent character." The majority said that "obscene material deals with sex in a manner appealing to prurient interests"; contemporary community standards were the proper guidelines for application.[398] In 1973 in *Miller v. California*, the high court defined obscenity as "works which, taken as a whole, appeal to the prurient interest in sex, which portray sexual conduct in a patently offensive way, and which, taken as a whole, do not have serious literary, artistic, political, or scientific value."[399] It offered as examples "patently offensive representations or descriptions of ultimate sex acts, normal or perverted, actual or simulated," or of "masturbation, excretory functions and lewd exhibition of the genitals."[400]

Not too long ago in this country if one wanted to avail oneself of pornographic material one had to travel into the "adult bookstore-movie" sector of a city. No more. Now there are porn movies on television in the living room if there is access to a cable channel that offers such fare. And increasingly Americans are watching. In fact, porn movies on cable have proved so popular that the supply is having a hard time keeping up with the demand. In Manhattan, on New York's public access channel, viewers have the opportunity of watching Al Goldstein's "Midnight Blue," which he describes as featuring four-letter words and frontal nudity;[401] simulated sex acts are also offered. His show, which on occasion has made slanderous attacks on Catholics, is scheduled to go nationwide. Public access TV includes talk shows—in the nude. For those New Yorkers who like live, spontaneous porn, there is the "Ugly George Hour." George Urban, a former teacher and Ph.D. candidate, parades around the sidewalks of New York with a video camera on his back, asking young women to take off their clothes in a storefront, a hallway, or wherever so that his audience may take a "gander."[402] The popularity of porn movies is not limited to big cities. Allentown, Pennsylvania, has its share too; Don Berner, of Twin Counties Cable TV in Allentown, turned down the "Ugly George Hour" because he considered it too mild for his X-rated channel.[403] And in Columbus, Ohio, Warner Amex's Qube cable subscribers have paid more money to watch pornographic movies than any other type of programming.[404] Morality in Media, an organization dedicated to stopping the proliferation of porn shows, has not met with much success. The ACLU has had something to do with the organization's ineffectiveness.[405]

The controversy surrounding pornography is not simply an American issue; the English, among others, have been forced to address it. In July 1977 the British Home Secretary appointed a task force to review the laws concerning obscenity, indecency, and violence in publications and to assay the status of film censorship. In November 1979 the Committee on Obscenity and Film Censorship presented its findings, along with its commissioned recommendations, to Parliament. It gave considerable thought to the still-popular notion of John Stuart Mill that there is no rational basis for censorship of any kind, given human fallibility in discerning the truth of any idea; only a "free market" of ideas can provide the public with a basis for judgment. The committee, though impressed with Mill's contribution to the subject of free speech, found his popular notion not "entirely convincing,"[406] but did maintain that there ought to be a presumption in favor of free expression.[407]

The committee's recommendations made the U.S. "Report of the Presidential Commission on Pornography and Obscenity" appear milder than it did when it was released in 1970. The committee offered several suggestions regarding the restriction and prohibition of pornographic material. Offensive material should be restricted out of concern for the public's legitimate interest in this area. Prohibitive sanctions would be acceptable on the basis of the harm done to society. The strictures would apply only to pictorial work and not to printed matter. "The principal object of the law," the committee declared, "should be to prevent certain kinds of material causing offence to reasonable people or being made available to young people."[408] The committee readily admitted that what is offensive to reasonable people "is not a matter of simple verifiable fact," but added that the concept of a reasonable person (one who takes a balanced view) was already well known to the law. Magistrates are trained and paid to make difficult but necessary judgments.[409]

The committee recommended that restrictions should apply to matter and performances that offend reasonable persons by virtue of portraying "violence, cruelty or horror, or sexual, faecal or urinary functions or genital organs." Prohibition should be authorized when the material involved the exploitation for sexual purposes of any person where either the person is under sixteen or "the material gives reason to believe that actual physical harm was inflicted on that person." A live performance should be prohibited if

(a) it involves actual sexual activity of a kind which, in the circumstances in which it was given, would be offensive to reasonable people (sexual activity including the act of masturbation and forms of genital, anal or oral connection between humans and animals as well as between humans), or

(b) it involves the sexual exploitation of any person under the age of sixteen.[410]

The committee recommended that a statutory board be established to take over the censorship powers of local authorities; the licensing of cinemas should continue to rest with local authorities. The function of the Film Examining Board ought to be "to establish the policy and principles of film censorship within the criteria laid down by statute" as well as "to hear appeals against the decisions of the examiners."[411]

Although many Americans would no doubt endorse the proposals of the British committee, the ACLU would certainly reject them. Franklyn Haiman's perspective on obscenity is representative of his organization's views on the subject. It is not clear whether Haiman believes there is such a thing as obscenity in the first place. For example, when he discusses indecent pictures, he does so by writing about "indecent" pictures.[412] When speaking about obscene phone calls, he tells us about "so-called" obscene phone calls.[413] His discussion of indecent language, which he accurately describes as "words, either printed or spoken, and often of four letters, that refer to sexual and excretory organs or processes," is preceded by his insistence that what is being addressed is "so-called" indecent language.[414] That Haiman may not regard indecent language to be indecent is one thing, but surely he knows that there are certain words—in any language—that are held by the large majority of people to be indecent, obscene, and vulgar. It is not as though Haiman does not recognize that people have a capacity to engage in vulgarity. Indeed he understands why. To those who say that pornography strips people of their humanness and reduces them to mere bundles of animal function, Haiman replies: "I would suggest that we *are* members of the animal kingdom who have bodily needs and instincts and something is awry if we try too desperately to hide or deny that fact."[415] Attempts to restrict pornography, then, are really attempts to deny people their animal nature. Something is awry when this happens.

Although the ACLU always opposed censorship, its activities in this field did not usually deal with sexually obscene material before the 1950s. In the 1920s it rallied to the defense of O'Neill's *Strange Interlude* and Voltaire's *Candide*; it also tried to block the censorsing of Lawrence's *Lady Chatterley's Lover*.[416] The Union had an opportunity to make an issue out of obscenity in 1927 but declined. An eighteen-year-old New Yorker, David Gordon, was tried for having written a political poem held to be obscene. The ACLU's position was selective: "While we had at first declined to go into this case of 'obscenity,' we aided after its purely political character became evident."[417]

In the early 1950s novelist Henry Miller caused quite a stir with his two books, *The Tropic of Capricorn* and *The Tropic of Cancer*. Both were banned by U.S. Customs for alleged obscenity; the ban was upheld by Judge Louis E. Goodman of the Federal District Court in San Francisco. The Northern California CLU became involved in the case when a Stanford University professor, J. Murrau Luck, called on the civil libertarians to challenge the right of Customs agents to seize Miller's books; the books were denied entry into the country when Luck attempted to mail them to his home in Palo Alto from Paris. The Northern CLU argued that "at most only 13% of *The Tropic of Capricorn* was objectionable." The court rejected "any such quantitative test," maintaining that "the conclusion is justified that either the alleged literary ability of the author deserted him or that he had his eye on the box office."[418] The affiliate's willingness to concede that part of Miller's book was objectionable was in line with the ACLU's attitude toward obscenity at that time, when it said that it had "no quarrel whatsoever with appropriate laws which punish obscenity or incitement to immediate illegal acts."[419] It was not until 1957, at the time of *Roth*, that the board clearly stated its policy on obscenity:

> The constitutional guarantees of free speech and press apply to all expression, and there is no special category of obscenity or pornography to which different constitutional tests apply. To be constitutional, an obscenity statute at the very least, must meet the requirement of definiteness; and also require that, before any material can be held to be obscene, it must be established beyond a reasonable doubt that the material presents a clear and present danger of normally inducing behavior which validly has been made criminal by statute.[420]

When private organizations began to mount campaigns against the proliferation of obscene material, the ACLU braced itself for another battle. It did not oppose educational crusades whose goal was to dissuade the public from buying certain literature, but it did not endorse organized boycotts of merchants who sold the material. The Roman Catholic Church was especially active in promoting such boycotts. Cardinal Spellman of New York urged Catholics to boycott the theaters where *The Moon Is Blue* was showing.[421] When *Baby Doll* appeared in 1956, parishioners in Albany were asked not to attend participating theaters.[422] The Union's policy, issued in May 1957, condemned such activities. The National Organization for Decent Literature (NODL), a Catholic organization, was the target of the Union's attack. Although the NODC was a private advisory organization, without any legal power, the Union charged it with "censorship of what the American people . . . may read" as well as seriously violating the principle of freedom.[423]

In the 1960s the ACLU was steadfast in its insistence that obscenity is covered by the First Amendment, no matter how obnoxious the expressions.[424] Applying this position, the Union defended Ralph Ginsburg, publisher of *Eros* and other erotica.[425] The Union held that unless it could be shown that obscene material caused antisocial behavior in normal adults, censorship in any form must be prohibited.[426] The same logic applied to children. If the material in question led children to violate a criminal statute, then it could be censored. The Union demanded nothing less than definite proof that a causal relationship existed between exposure to obscenity and delinquency.[427]

The ACLU not only defended the purveyors of pornography but did its best to stop those who sought to stamp out such literature. The Union was outraged to learn that the Citizens for Decent Literature (CDL) had drawn up a list of objectionable publications that the police had used in a clean-up campaign. The ACLU held that the mere existence of such a list was tantamount to censorship.[428] Furthermore, the Union was infuriated by the CDL's attempts to organize a boycott of bookstores and theaters that featured obscene material. The ACLU contested this action as censorship because its goal was to shut down these establishments.[429] Interestingly, the Northern California CLU defended the right of a Sacramento television station employee to distribute handbills outside his struck station requesting the public not to patronize the station's advertisers.[430] Apparently, the local affiliate did not see its action as abetting censorship.

In another extension of its policy on obscenity, the ACLU complained to the U.S. Department of Health, Education, and Welfare that it was endorsing censorship by distributing a pamphlet that described how citizens of Lebanon, Tennessee, tackled youth problems. The pamphlet told of how a citizens' committee sent seals of approval to merchants who refused to sell pornographic material.[431] I asked Neier why the ACLU objected to this action. He argued that the government should not be in the business of promoting or deterring the sale of private publications. When I asked if it were acceptable for private citizens to engage in such action, he commented that "if private individuals want to do it, fine."[432] However, the ACLU did not see it that way. When this case arose in the early 1960s, the Union said that the awarding of seals of approval by private individuals was objectionable because it would "inevitably result in a general boycott, thus imposing the committee's will by means of economic sanctions."[433] I told Neier that the Union had taken the position that the citizens' action constituted a secondary boycott. He replied: "No. The word secondary boycott is not a term of ours. They [sic] don't have any special meaning."[434] Neier is mistaken. The ACLU has frequently used this term as a synonym for *general boycott*.[435]

If John Doe receives unsolicited pornographic material through the mail, should he not have the right to request the postmaster not to deliver any more such material? The ACLU says no. The case arose in the 1960s when some citizens protested that they were being inundated with unwanted obscene literature. The Supreme Court, in *Rowan v. U.S. Post Office*, asserted that "the right of every person 'to be left alone' must be placed in the scales with the right of others to communicate." It said that citizens had the right not to be captives in their own homes.[436] The Union disagreed, warning that precensorship was at work in these cases.[437] I asked Reitman to clarify the Union's position. He said that the Post Office should not be involved in this affair, maintaining that the government should not be party to censorship. The best solution, Reitman advised, was simply to throw the objectionable, unsolicited mail away.[438] Haiman comes to the same conclusion, arguing that "offensive mail can easily be thrown away immediately after an initial encounter with it."[439] This was obviously not a satisfactory remedy for the outraged citizens who were the unwilling targets of pornographers. The ACLU's answer is that if individuals were allowed the freedom to determine what they do not want sent to their homes, we would be permitting them to act as their own censors.[440] This should not be, the civil libertarians argue, because such decisions regarding obscenity represent a "subjective judgment" on the part of the citizen.[441]

In 1970 the ACLU strengthened its policy on obscenity by voicing its adamant rejection of any restraint, under any obscenity statute, of the right "to create, publish or distribute materials to adults or the right of adults to choose the material they read or view." The 1970 policy made an exception for "statutes which prohibit the thrusting of hard-core pornography on unwilling audiences in public places." But three years later, Haiman, who opposes every conceivable restraint on pornography, successfully persuaded the board to rescind this proviso.[442] In 1977 the board added to its objections all zoning plans that restricted the availability of pornographic books, movies, and other communications media.[443] In the following year the Union made explicit its objection to restrictions on pornography in the broadcast media.[444]

Child Pornography

The selling of sex is a multibillion-dollar business in the United States. William Serrin, who investigated the sex business for the *New York Times*, concluded: "It is a rapidly growing, still immature industry, a significant part of New York and the nation's economy."[445] There is virtually nothing that one cannot buy in the sex industry; whips, chains, vibrators—sex stimulants of every kind—can be bought with Visa or Mastercard as well as cash. The advertising industry has not passed up the opportunity to make a buck either. Teen-aged models, and those not yet in their teens, can be seen in seductive positions advertising the latest fashions. When Calvin Klein was asked about Brooke Shields's suggestive poses in his advertisements, the designer said of the jeans: "The tighter they are, the better they sell."[446]

Since at least the 1970s, the appetite for sex has extended to the commercialization of child pornography. Father Bruce Ritter, the founder of New York's Covenant House, a shelter for runaway boys and girls in the Time Square area, has said the word is out: "johns prefer chicken"—children, that is. Indeed, pedophiles who prefer to have sex with minors need not go to the trouble of finding young boys or girls walking the streets of Times Square. On cable television in New York, there have been commercials offering viewers the right to purchase "a young boy" for $65.[447] Child pornography is one of the most lucrative businesses for organized crime in the country. In 1982, when the authorities seized Catherine S. Wilson, one of the major "kid porn" operators in the nation, she was making $525,000 a year. She owned a Cadillac, a Rolls Royce, and a Lincoln. She also collected welfare. After being charged with a felony, Mrs. Wilson was releasd on $5,000 bail.[448]

It would be a mistake to think that all the children who are being exploited sexually are kidnapped by "kid porn" operators. Many of the children are being sold to people like Mrs. Wilson, the mother of five children,[449] by their parents. In 1977 a Colorado couple sold their twelve-year-old son for sexual purposes for $3,000. A Rockford, Illinois, social worker was convicted for allowing his three adopted sons to perform sexual acts before a camera for $150 each. In some cases, the parents have agreed to perform incest with their children. Gonorrhea of the throat in infants as young as nine and eighteen months has been reported.[450] That is not altogether unusual. Father Ritter has said that when the Covenant House doctors and nurses inspect a child who complains of a sore throat, they immediately do two throat cultures: one for strep throat, the other for gonorrhea. Most of the time it is the latter.[451]

Father Ritter knows more about child sexploitation than any other individual in the nation. He has made it his life's work to provide an alternative to children who are beaten, raped, tortured, and held prisoner. In the first five years of his program, over 25,000 children sought assistance from the Covenant House staff. They come from all over the country, running away from abusive or neglective parents. When Father Bruce (as he prefers to be called) contacts the parents, they typically say, "You keep them. If you send them home, we'll have them arrested." The problem is not confined to New York—every big city has its share of child pornography and child brothels. Pimps will meet frightened girls and boys as they arrive at a bus terminal, offering them money, companionship, and shelter. Then they drug children, have them gang raped, and send them out onto the streets to work. It is a common conditioning process that is used quite effectively. If the child is ten or so, the pimps will give toys to keep him or her happy.[452] If the child is lucky, Father Ritter—the Mother Teresa of urban United States—will encounter him or her and put an end to the abuse. If the child is lucky, that is. Many are not.

The clamor for children's rights has led some enthusiasts to demand that children be entitled to do whatever adults do. It used to be that children's rights meant the right of children to be freed from abusive or neglectful parents. But no more. Educator John Holt says: "I propose that the rights, privileges, duties, responsibilities of adult citizens be made *available* to any young person, of whatever age, who wants to make use of them." From voting, to working for money, to directing and managing one's own education, to living away from home—in every conceivable respect—children should be free to do whatever adults do, unimpeded by restrictive laws.[453] It follows from Holt's logic that if adults may perform simulated sex acts in the live theater, children should be given an equal opportunity to do the same. Psychologist Richard Farson of the Esalen Institute is more explicit than Holt: "*Children should have the right to conduct their sexual lives with no more restriction than adults.*" "Sexual freedom for children," argues the psychologist, "must include . . . the right to all sexual activities that are legal among consenting adults. In fact, children will be best protected from sexual abuse when they have the right to refuse—but they are now trained *not* to refuse adults, to accept all forms of physical affection, and to mistrust their own reactions to people."[454]

Radicals in behalf of children's rights have surfaced in other countries as well. In the name of children's rights, Australian sociologist Paul Wilson has lobbied in defense of child molesters. The Queensland University scholar has also defended sexual relations between adults and children. Wilson became famous for his book, *The Man They Called a Monster*, a work dedicated to an understanding of the behavior of Clarence Osbourne. Osbourne, who committed suicide at the age of fifty-six, had had sexual relations with more than 2,500 boys over a twenty-year period, ending in 1979. Offering a compassionate picture of the child molester, Wilson discounted the harmful effects of adult-child relationships. He wrote, "A substantial number of relationships are initiated by the child, continued by the child, and often ended by the child or adolescent. While there are undoubtedly cruelly exploitative paedophile relationships, the vast majority are not of this type." It was due to such findings that Wilson argued that "children should have the right to conduct their sexual lives with no more restrictions than adults do."[455]

Although liberals take a much more tolerant or permissive position on sexual matters than conservatives, nearly all of them clearly draw the line where children are concerned. For example, Thomas Emerson, who generally opposes obscenity laws, sees no problem with laws that make exceptions for children.[456] The British Report on Obscenity also saw the need for laws protecting children. The Protection of Children Act 1978, which tightened laws against child pornography, was endorsed by the committee.[457] One would be hard pressed to find anyone who would object to laws banning child pornography in England, the United States, or anyplace else. But it would not be impossible: the ACLU objects.

Although the ACLU did not address the subject of child pornography before 1977, in a 1970 board meeting, an indication of its later policy was provided by some participants. When considering the Union's strong 1970 antiobscenity law policy, one member raised the question of whether the ACLU was extending itself so far that it would sanction the existence of a

Saturday afternoon movie showing "pornography for kiddies." One of the civil libertarians present said it was the parents' prerogative to define their own children's behavior and that the right of society to restrict children's activities was questionable. He said that the reason for the difficulty in dealing with this issue was that obscenity could not be discussed rationally; it involved a whole slew of emotional responses, based on confusion of our sexual identities and roles in society.[458] As it turned out, the board stated that as a practical matter there can be no legal substitute for parental responsibility.[459]

Under the ACLU constitution, the Board of Directors has the responsibility for making policy; however, the Executive Committee is empowered to make public policy statements in lieu of board action if a serious subject emerges between scheduled meetings. This happened in the spring of 1977 before the June meeting. The Union was being asked by the media and others what its position on child pornography was. It had none. The Executive Committee was pressured into action and delivered a statement that attempted to draw a distinction between the Union's defense of the dissemination of pornography and its opposition to child abuse. At the June board meeting, several members objected to the quick action taken by the Executive Committee and insisted that the entire board be included in the formulation of policy in this area. By a vote of 36-18 the members agreed to address the issue at the next meeting.[460]

At the September meeting of the Board of Directors, Jim Lawing moved that the following excerpt from the ACLU congressional testimony of Martin Guggenheim be adopted by the board as policy:

> The ACLU condemns the sexual exploitation of children for any purpose, and strongly urges that existing criminal laws prohibiting child abuse and contributing to the delinquency of minors be more vigorously enforced.

> To the extent that additional legislation is required, however, it is appropriate only to proscribe the conduct of persons who directly engage in illegal action, e.g., persons who act directly in the production of pornographic material in which children are used. It is inappropriate, unnecessary and unconstitutional to prohibit the publication, sale or distribution of such printed or visual materials. Distribution of such materials is protected by the First Amendment.[461]

The motion lost. It was criticized as being "overly general." Dick Feder moved the following substitute to serve as policy:

> While the ACLU may vigorously dislike and reject sexual exploitation of children for commercial purposes, activities in publishing and disseminating printed or visual materials are wholly protected by the First Amendment.[462]

The Feder motion was critized for "side-stepping" the issues, particularly the child abuse issue. Others said that the subject of child pornography was not a civil liberties concern! Feder's motion nonetheless carried and became official ACLU policy.[463] The original motion by Lawing, which would have put the ACLU on record as condemning the sexual exploitation of children, now gave way to the formula that the Union "may" vigorously "dislike" such perversions. The board could not bring itself to condemn child sexploitation without reservations.

ACLU activist Franklyn Haiman gives us a good idea as to how the Union reasons its policy on child pornography. The communication studies professor at Northwestern University begins by telling us that "we are strangely selective in our society about the kinds of things from which we try to shield children and those to which we casually expose them." Sex, he asserts, is one of those subjects about which we are "strangely selective." "On the other hand," he adds, "we rather unashamedly parade our treatment of others as objects-to-be-manipulated rather than as people-to-be-respected, although all of our religious and ethical teachings exhort to the contrary."[464] However, Haiman's own religious and ethical teachings, and his belief in treating human beings as persons—not objects—has not permitted him to oppose the distribution and sale of child pornography.[465] What is fascinating about Haiman's thinking is that although he strongly defends the sale of child pornography, he does not strenuously object to laws that make illegal the selling of firecrackers![466]

In 1977 New York State passed a law prohibiting the use of children in depictions of sexual activity. The law, which was defended by Covenant House lawyers in a court battle, defined such conduct as "actual or simulated sexual intercourse, deviate sexual intercourse, sexual bestiality, masturbation, sadomasochistic abuse or lewd exhibition of the genitals." The ACLU protested and joined in a test case. In 1981 the Union won in the Court of Appeals. The court said that the law would "prohibit the promotion of materials which are traditionally entitled to Constitutional protection from government interference under the First Amendment." The court left standing, however, the sections of the law permitting stiffer penalties against those who use children in materials what would be viewed (by the community) as legally obscene, or who promote or sell these materials.[467] An appeal was made to the U.S. Supreme Court.

On 2 July 1982, the U. S. Supreme Court upheld the constitutionality of the New York law. The unanimous decision, which overthrew the Court of Appeals ruling, was a victory for Father Ritter and a defeat for the ACLU. The court concluded that "the prevention of sexual exploitation and abuse of children constitutes a government objective of surpassing importance." Associate Justice Byron R. White said that "child pornography" was a "category of material outside the protection of the First Amendment" and could be regulated regardless of whether it met a test of obscenity. Justice Sandra Day O'Connor made it clear that it was of no importance whether the material allegedly had "literary, scientific or educational value": "For example, a 12-year-old child photographed while masturbating surely suffers the same psychological harm whether the community labels the photograph 'edifying' or 'tasteless.'"[468] The *New York Times* editorialized that "the decision is welcome for its attack on a disgusting business." It had nothing to say regarding the ACLU's role.[469]

In April 1983 Scott Hyman and Clemente D'Alessio were convicted under New York's child pornography law. They had been found guilty of distributing movies showing children aged seven to fourteen in sexually explicit activities. In a conversation with a New York undercover police officer, Hyman told of how young his actors were becoming:

> Hyman: Well what happens is with kiddie porn, you can get 7, 8, 9, 10 and 11-year-olds. Soon as you start trying to find 15, 16, 17-year-olds, you've got trouble. Eight, 9, 10, and 11 . . . . .
>
> Officer: They're easy.
>
> Hyman: No problem.
>
> Officer: That's fine. That's what I'm interested in.
>
> Hyman: Yeah, at that point (with older kids) you've got a kid that just came out of his childhood. He's in the middle (years), knows what you're doing, and can make the money himself.
>
> Officer: Is there a difference? If you want, like young kids, you have to ask for baby porn, is that it?
>
> Hyman: Yeah, baby porn.
>
> Officer: Now what ages is that?
>
> Hyman: That's babies.
>
> Officer: Like that's when you're talking about 7, 8, 9-year-olds . . .?
>
> Hyman: Five!
>
> Officer: Right!

Manhattan District Attorney Robert Morganthau asked for the maximum sentence. Marvyn Kornberg, who represented Hyman and D'Alessio was outraged: "It is almost inconceivable that the DA is requesting a *savage* seven-year consecutive sentence for such a minimal transaction. This would be the moral equivalent of asking for a 20-year sentence for a person selling a stick of marijuana. The request in unconscionable." His clients were sentenced for two to seven years.[470] If the ACLU had had things its way, they never would have been sentenced at all.

Freedom from Religion

According to British historian Owen Chadwick, morality and religion have been inextricably linked in practically every known human society.[471] Morality, grounded in religion, not only has been a near-universal feature of societies but rarely has been seen as a purely secular phenomenon. The need for a transcendental ethic, rooted in a system of spiritual beliefs and practices, has clearly been one of humankind's most perennial yearnings. The etiology of this need has been the subject of much discussion and disagreement, but no student of society will deny that morality qua religion has been one of humankind's most expressive, and most visible, qualities.

The Founding Fathers were sensitive to the relationship between church and state, due to the politicization of the church in medieval times. But they unquestionably saw the need for religion in society and fully understood the premium that the American people put on religion. George Washington was the first president to acknowledge the role of religion in society. In his First Inaugural Address he paid respect "to the Great Author of every public and private good," and beckoned the American people to "acknowledge and adore the Invisible Hand which conducts the affairs of men."[472] When he took his oath of office, Washington ad libbed the words "So help me God";[473] there was no mention of these words in the Constitution. In his Farewell Address, the first president said: "Of all the dispositions and habits which lead to political prosperity, religion and morality are indispensable supports. . . . Whatever may be conceded to the influence of refined education on minds of peculiar structure, reason and experience both forbid us to expect that national morality can prevail in exclusion of religious principle."[474] Thomas Jefferson, an anticleric who accepted the ethics of Jesus, also gave recognition to the significance of religion in daily life. When Jefferson was seen carrying a red prayer book, a skeptical citizen asked where he was going. "To church," he replied. "Why, Mr. President, you don't believe a word of it," the citizen said. "Sir, no nation has yet existed or been governed without religion," Jefferson replied. "I, as the chief magistrate of this nation, am bound to give it the sanction of my example."[475]

"Congress shall make no law respecting an establishment of religion, or prohibiting the free exercise thereof"—exactly what those words were intended to convey has been the subject of much controversy ever since the Bill of Rights was adopted. Although there are more than two views on the interpretation of the religion clause of the First Amendment, most observers either accept the language as meaning that there ought to be a strict separation between church and state or that the words basically mean that the Congress cannot establish a national religion. The former position was accepted by Justice Hugo Black: "The First Amendment has erected a wall between Church and State. That wall must be kept high and impregnable. We could not approve the slightest breach." This has also been the position of the ACLU since 1920.

Those who maintain that the interpretation of Black and the ACLU is erroneous point to James Madison's formulation of the "establishment clause." In Madison's first draft of the clause, he expressed his views clearly: "The Civil rights of none shall be abridged on account of religious belief or worship, nor shall any national religion be established." When Madison's draft was changed after congressional committee deliberations, he was asked what the new clause meant. He said he "apprehended the meaning of the words to be, that Congress should not establish a religion, and enforce the legal observation of it by law."[476] Repeatedly, Madison made the point that the Congress could not pass laws respecting *an* establishment of religion, meaning, as he said, that *a* national religion could not be countenanced, nor could one religious institution, sect, denomination, or tradition be favored over any other.[477] And although Madison's "Memorial and Remonstrance against Religious Assessments" is often cited as testimony to his aversion to breaching church and state lines, it was nothing more than an argument against the government's granting tax support for only one religion.[478] It should be noted too that at the time of the passage of the Bill of Rights, many states had established churches. Further proof that the strict separation of church and state interpretation is without historical validity can be seen by the readoption by Congress of the Northwest Ordinance of 1787. The same Congress that passed the First Amendment accepted the third article of the Ordinance without emendation: "Religion, morality, and knowledge, being necessary to good government and happiness of mankind, schools and the means of learning shall forever be encouraged." As Walter Berns has said, "It is not easy to see how Congress, or a territorial government acting under the authority of Congress, could promote religious and moral education under a Constitution that promoted 'the absolute separation of church and state' and forbade all forms of assistance to religion."[479]

Be that as it may, there is no confusion over which view has been the ascendant one in American history: the absolutist perspective has been favored. This is not to say that all the policies of the ACLU bearing on religion have been upheld by the courts. They have not. But the Union has managed to secure a more receptive ear in the judiciary than its adversaries have. From the beginning, the ACLU has looked askance at the role that religion plays, and, more importantly, might play, in society. It has not been hostile toward religion, but it has never accorded to religious institutions the same kind of vital contribution that the Founding Fathers did. The rationalism, secularism, and antitraditionalism of the ACLU's liberal politics does not allow it to practice the kind of tolerant attitude toward religion that it displays toward matters of sexuality. Quite simply, freedom of religion has not been given the same priority as freedom from religion. For example, the National Civil Liberties Bureau, the Union's forerunner, made a strong commitment to free speech and association but said nothing regarding religion.[480] Even when the ACLU was formed, it did not mention freedom of religion as one of its objectives, although it did include all the other components of the First Amendment as well as a commitment to racial equality.[481] That the ACLU ignored freedom of religion was no oversight: the politically driven liberal organization, dedicated to labor and in opposition to capitalism, had no reason to make religious freedom one of its objectives. A truly nonpartisan organization in service to civil liberties would have had to have made freedom of religion one of its primary goals. The ACLU was not, and is not, such an organization.

Although most of the Union's activities regarding religion have been directed toward the separation of church and state, it has, on a number of occasions, taken a strong stand on freedom of religious expression. One of the first such instances pitted the ACLU against the Klan. In 1922 the Klan was successful in lobbying for a bill in Oregon that forced every child to attend a public school. Aimed intentionally at Catholics, the law was passed by popular vote in an election.[482] The Union argued successfully in the courts that the law was an infringement on religious freedom.[483] The Klan persisted in an appeal until the U.S. Supreme Court rendered its efforts void.[484]

Does the government have the right to ask questions regarding religion or religious affiliation? The ACLU has found this to be a perplexing issue, as evidenced by its frequent reversals of previous decisions. In the summer of 1956 the Union declared that any questions about belief in God or attendance at church or synagogue were violative of the First Amendment. Shortly thereafter, it decided that if it is permissible for the government to ask whether one owned a refrigerator, it is fine to ask about one's religious affiliation as well. Then in another reversal in the fifties, the Board of Directors held that "factual inquiry, when made by a government official, might for some persons under some circumstances be an infringement upon the freedom (of religion)." The feeling at that time was that assembling information about religious beliefs would breach the "wall of separation" between church and state. This decision applied whether a reply was voluntary or compulsory.[485] Today the Union is still opposed to government collection and dissemination of religious information, although it does not object to special circumstances where the government must possess such data to fulfill its obligations to the individual (chaplains in military camps, hospitals, and prisons).[486] It is interesting to note that the Union's policy on the collection and dissemination of racial and gender information is more relaxed, having fewer reservations about government questioning than in the case of religion. This is partly due to the more private aspect of religion and partly to the fact that in the eyes of the ACLU (and the government) racial and gender information is necessary to accomplish goals of "social utility";[487] religious data serve no such purpose (affirmative action, etc.).

The private nature of religious beliefs and practices argues for restraint on those who would interfere with or challenge the religiosity of the faithful. A question arises, however, when there is reason to believe that the proponents of a cult seek to exploit the vulnerability of youths who, for whatever reason, are desperately looking for spiritual nourishment and belongingness. If the process is volitional, i.e., if the youths voluntarily seek to join a cult, the objections are relieved. There may be a fine line between espousal of a system of religious beliefs and the seductive misleading overtures of cult fanatics, but it is not impossible to distinguish between them. Moreover, once individuals join a cult or, for that matter, any established religion, the element of captivity may present itself, namely, to what degree are the new adherents allowed to gauge for themselves the truth and acceptability of the religious entity? This has become a more serious question in recent years as quasi-religious groups have emerged throughout the country. It is laced with civil liberties problems.

In the 1970s the ACLU considered this issue by examining the civil liberties implications presented by the alleged "brainwashing" techniques used by cult groups and by the subsequent "kidnapping" attempts by the parents of the youths involved. According to the Union, for those who had attained the age of majority there was no legal justification for the use of mental incompetency proceedings, conservatorships, or temporary guardianships. Unless physical coercion or threat of the same were being employed, those who belonged to such religious groups had every right to exercise their prerogative. This right must be protected, said the Union, in spite of the contention that "brainwashing" or "mind control" techniques were being used.[488] It regards as "essentially criminal in nature" the use of "deprogrammers" to kidnap cult members and "unbrainwash" them. The Union has fought bills legalizing deprogrammers wherever they have appeared, maintaining that "the government has no more authority to judge the validity of cults than of more established religions."[489]

Religion and the Schools

The first major trial in which the ACLU participated was the Scopes "Monkey Trial." On 21 March 1925, Austin Peay, the governor of Tennessee, signed into law the Butler Act, which made it illegal for any teacher in a state-supported school to teach that humans are descended from a lower order of animals. The author of the bill, J. Washington Butler, was a fundamentalist who feared the impact of science on religion. At issue were several overlapping concerns: academic freedom, freedom of religious expression, governmental authority, and parental rights. Lucille Milner of the ACLU spotted the case in a Tennessee newspaper and brought the issue to Baldwin's attention. According to Milner, he "saw its import in a flash" and decided to inform the board.[490] The board agreed to enter the controversy and placed an announcement in the Tennessee newspapers offering services to any teacher who would agree to challenge the law. George W. Rappleyea, a young engineer, read of the Union's offer in the 4 May 1925 edition of the Chattanooga *Times* and quickly sought a client for the ACLU; John T. Scopes, a high school teacher, agreed to challenge the law.

Although the trial was billed as "God Against Monkey" or religion versus science, the recent work of historian R. M. Cornelius indicates that the trial began as a public relations scheme to attract attention to the depressed economic conditions in Dayton, Tennessee.[491] That may have been the motive of Rappleyea, but it was not Baldwin's. In any event, the trial became a showdown between William Jennings Bryan, prosecutor and three-time presidential candidate, and Clarence Darrow, the noted criminal lawyer. Dudley Field Malone and ACLU attorney Arthur Garfield Hays assisted in the defense, and the Union marshaled the input of Felix Frankfurter, Norman Thomas, Elizabeth Gurley Flynn, Father John Augustine Ryan, and, of course, Baldwin. As Cornelius has observed, the trial became a "tour de farce" as eccentrics of every kind appeared: Joe Mendi—a trained chimpanzee—was there along with Deck "Bible Champion of the World" Carter and Louis Levi Johnson Marshall, "Absolute Ruler of the Entire World, Without Military, Naval or Other Physical Force." Throngs of journalists showed up, including H. L. Mencken, Joseph Wood Krutch, and Westbrook Pegler.[492]

Cornelius wrote, "A stranger trial there probably never was."[493] Members of the jury were caught up more in the drama of the event than in the proceedings themselves. Former colleagues and acquaintances were now adversaries; both Darrow and Malone had assisted the political ambitions of Bryan. Scopes had been in the graduating class at Salem High School when Bryan delivered the commencement address. Scientific experts came from all over to testify, but none of their statements was allowed as evidence. Darrow was cited for contempt and Bryan took the witness stand. Scopes was never called to testify. Moreover, Scopes was a math teacher who only periodically taught biology as a substitute. He later admitted, "To tell the truth, I wasn't sure I had taught evolution." No matter. If Scopes was found guilty (his defense counsel did not claim he was innocent but asked the jury to find him not guilty), Bryan would pay his fine, contending that the law should not have had a penalty.[494]

The outcome is well known. Scopes was found guilty and fined $100. When the ACLU appealed the case, the Tennessee Supreme Court upheld the law but reversed the conviction. The fine had been imposed by the presiding judge instead of by the jury, as it should have been. The intended effect was obvious: there could be no appeal to the U.S. Supreme Court because the lower court ruling had been reversed on a technicality.[495]

Fifty-five years after the Scopes trial was concluded, the Board of Directors of the ACLU was forced to issue a policy statement opposing the religious doctrine of creation in science classes.[496] The Scopes controversy was being replayed as fundamentalists once more sought to have their Biblical views taught in the schools. This time the issue was framed as a battle of "scientific creationism" against the evolutionary position. The names and places of the participants had changed, but the issue was the same. In 1981 in Arkansas, a bill was passed requiring equal time for creationism in classes studying evolution; Louisiana and Georgia followed suit. None of the attempts was successful, for ACLU legal briefs proved to be convincing. In the Arkansas case, the Union argued that creationism was a religion, not a science, and therefore the separation of church and state was at issue. Academic freedom arguments were also made. The Union contended that teachers "will either be forced to teach a doctrine which they . . . believe has no scientific merit, or they will refrain from teaching evolution science at all so that they need make no 'balanced' religious presentation to 'counter' evolution." The ACLU's formal complaint charged that the law was unconstitutionally vague because it "does not give teachers fair notice of what can or what cannot be taught, and it gives school officials virtually unfettered discretion arbitrarily to enforce its provision."[497] In 1982 a federal judge declared the Arkansas statute unconstitutional and dampened the aspirations of creationists elsewhere.[498]

It is clear that the teaching of religion in the public schools is unconstitutional, but what about the right of a member of a religious order who seeks to teach in the public schools? Should he or she be allowed to do so? This question became an issue in the early 1950s when the Free Schools Committee of Dixon, New Mexico, sought to have all members of the Roman Catholic religious orders barred from teaching in the public schools. The ACLU believed that although members of a religious order could not be categorically barred from teaching in the public schools, they could be prohibited from doing so if they insisted on wearing religious garb. If a nun were wearing a habit, declared the Union—even if she were teaching arithmetic—she would be actively demonstrating her religious belief. This, the ACLU held, was unconstitutional.[499]

Interestingly, if a nun were to trade in her habit for a turban, she would be assisted by the ACLU. In 1979 Marilyn "Rashidi" Pollard acquired the services of the Pittsburgh CLU after she was fired by the city school board for wearing a turban. The Islamic woman claimed that her turban was a symbol of her faith and that the school board's decision was a breach of her religious freedom. The school board's ruling voiced the identical logic that the ACLU followed with regard to nuns: the wearing of religious garb was prohibited so as to preserve church-state separation. However, in this case the affiliate said that the turban was not an obvious religious symbol; it was different from a crucifix or nun's habit, which have universal significance.[500]

Two related issues occurred in the 1960s when Congress was considering appropriations for (a) guidance counselors in private schools and (b) paying religious school representatives to supervise the administration of supplementary education centers. The Union lobbied against both pieces of legislation. It decided that because guidance counselors are concerned with students' "attitudes with philosophies of life," church-controlled schools did not qualify for financial support; these schools "naturally give a religious orientation to their counseling."[501] As for the other issue, the Union's basic fear was the influence of religious personnel in such government projects as Headstart.[502] Both of these positions, along with the statement against nuns in habits teaching in the public schools, demonstrate the Union's predisposition regarding religious personnel: all members of religious orders are, consciously or unconsciously, projecting their beliefs onto others.

The ACLU opposed the concepts of "shared time" and "release time." Typically, shared time means that students who attend sectarian schools are permitted to attend public schools on a part-time basis so as to fulfill certain state-mandated requirements. The Union has long argued, referencing the *Everson* case, that it makes no difference that the parents of these children are compelled to support public schools. It sees shared time as a device to confer substantial benefits upon sectarian schools.[503] Release time is a system whereby public school children are typically excused from class at the end of the day once a week so as to attend a nearby sectarian school for religious instruction. The ACLU sees this as a way of using the public schools "to secure enrollment and keep up attendance in class run by religious organizations." In practice, however, the teachers in Catholic schools release their own students early so as to teach, without charge, the public school students—students whose parents have freely chosen to place

their children in such classes. In the early fifties the Supreme Court, in the
Zorach case, upheld the constitutionality of New York's release time program. Justice William O. Douglas, in the majority opinion, disagreed with
the Union's position and declared that "when the state encourages religious
instruction or cooperates with religious authorities by adjusting the schedule of public events to sectarian needs, it follows the best of our traditions."
The ACLU, however, agreed with dissenting Justice Jackson's statement
that the school "serves as a temporary jail for a pupil who will not go to
church."[504]

Three out of four Americans are in favor of allowing public school
students to pray in the classroom.[505] It has been illegal to do so for over
twenty years. The ACLU has had something to do with that fact.

The ACLU did not address the issue of prayer in the schools before the
1950s. Although it was never sympathetic to the idea, it did not initially
condemn school prayer. In the early fifties it commented that prayers were
"probably" impermissible in the public schools.[506] Ten year later, when
Madlyn Murray and other atheists were seeking to abolish prayer in the
schools, the Union played an active role. The Supreme Court, in a 6-1
decision, declared that the "Regents' Prayer" in New York's public schools
was unconstitutional.[507] After seven years of attempting to ban prayer in
the schools, the Union had won.[508]

Shortly after this court case, the Union extended its policy to cover
voluntary prayers. Led by Senator Everett Dirksen, religious groups across
the country tried to undermine the high court's decision. The ACLU opposed voluntary prayers in the schools because "the naturally conformist
tendencies of children made the proviso a delusion."[509] I questioned Baldwin about the Union's policy.

W.D.: The ACLU has even gone so far as to deny the right of people to
voluntarily take the time during the day, as a schoolchild, to say a
prayer.

R.B.: Not on school time.

W.D.: Well whose rights are being infringed upon if there is a silent prayer
voluntarily said by a student?

R.B.: If they don't say anything? You mean if they don't—

W.D.: Right. Are you afraid they are going to proselytize the rest of the class?

R.B.: Well, they tried to get around it. They've tried to get around it even
further than you by calling it meditation.

W.D.: What's wrong with that?

R.B.: You don't say anything about God or religion or anything. I suppose
you can get by with that but it's a subterfuge, because the implication
is that you're meditating about the hereafter or God or something.

W.D.: Well what's wrong with that? Doesn't a person have the right to do that? Or to meditate about popcorn for that matter?

R.B.: I suppose that—it sounds very silly to me because it looks like an obvious evasion of the constitutional provision.[510]

The prayer issue, like the abortion issue, is one of those subjects that refuses to die. Given the conservative swing of the country since at least 1980, private pressure groups have sought to capitalize on the public's mood by lobbying for a return of prayer to the schools. Falwell's Moral Majority has led the way. The ACLU has led the opposition. Sensing that time was of the essence, the Union published an ad in the *New York Times* just after Reagan's election. The subject occasioned an ACLU jeremiad: "The Moral Majority—and other groups like them—think that children should pray in school. Not just their children. Your children." The title of the ACLU ad shows how worrisome the organization was: "If the Moral Majority Has Its Way You'd Better Start Praying."[511] Given the overwhelming support that prayer in the schools has with the public, it is no wonder the ACLU was alarmed. Something had to be done.

The Union had its work cut out for it. In one form or another, prayer in the schools had become an issue in many states by the end of 1980. It was not a regional issue. Attempts were being made to reintroduce prayers in Texas, California, Tennessee, Ohio, Louisiana, Massachusetts, New York, Connecticut, Arizona, Minnesota, Kentucky, and Oklahoma.[512] When the issue hit the U.S. Senate in September 1982, a filibuster was launched by opponents of a bill designed to officially sanction prayer in the schools. For the most part, liberals opposed the bill and conservatives approved. The liberals proved successful.[513] The ACLU, which is "unalterably opposed to the practice of filibustering,"[514] did not protest the strategy of Senate liberals.

On 24 May 1982, the New Jersey Assembly approved of legislation allowing one minute of silence in the public schools at the beginning of each day; the vote was 62-9. On 18 October the New Jersey Senate approved the bill by a vote of 30-5.[515] When Governor Kean vetoed the measure, the Senate overrode the veto by a vote of 27-8. Jeffrey E. Fogel of the ACLU said: "I expect that we will challenge it in the courts. If we feel that it will, in fact, not in theory, encourage prayer, we will move very quickly."[516] Fogel did just that: the New Jersey CLU filed suit in Federal District Court in Trenton challenging the bill. The legislation said nothing at all about prayer; it was designed to provide one minute of silence for "private contemplation or introspection"; it was voluntary.[517] But, like Baldwin, the New Jersey civil libertarians were concerned with the possibiliy that some of the children might actually be praying. Federal District Court Judge Dickinson R.

Debevoise agreed with the ACLU and enjoined the schools from continuing the minute of silence. Richard M. Altman of the ACLU commented that "if the purpose behind the law is not to reintroduce prayer, then what is its educational purpose or alleged benefit?"[518]

Separating Religion from Culture

In any introductory course in anthropology or sociology, students are taught that religion is an element of culture, a cultural expression that is universally recognized. It would be as difficult to separate religion from culture as it would be to isolate the family or community from the social. It should come as no surprise that when lawmakers attempt to dissect religion from culture, they are embarking on a surgical procedure that is fraught with difficulties. But removing religion from the womb of culture has become the practiced virtue of the ACLU over the past several decades.

When Pope John Paul II made his second trip to Poland in June 1983, he was greeted by millions of Catholics in his homeland. The Communist authorities provided the pope with an altar built atop a stadium in Warsaw and hung a towering cross beside it.[519] No one complained. When the pope visited six American cities in 1979, the authorities in each city made similar provisions to honor the pontiff. In Philadelphia, the city pledged to spend $75,000 to build a wooden platform from which the pope would say a mass. In Des Moines and Chicago, the closing of schools and office buildings was promised. Altogether, in five of the cities, the local Civil Liberties Union took action against the government for violating the First Amendment; the Chicago CLU did nothing,[520] perhaps in reaction to the heavy criticism that it endured during the Skokie incident. The local affiliates were following ACLU policy, which proscribes the use of public property or monies for religious purposes.[521] The Union did not accept the position of the authorities that extending honor to a foreign dignitary is an appropriate and established tradition. Similar steps have been accorded other leaders, such as the queen of England, who is both a secular and a religious figure.

The ACLU occasionally exercises pragmatism with regard to the use of religious organizations that serve public purposes. One of its policies that demonstrates its pragmatism concerns the status of federally funded, religiously owned child care facilities. Strict adherence to the "wall of separation" position would make it impossible to defend such an arrangement, but on this issue the social utility of day care outweighs rigid conformity to civil libertarian principles governing religion. Although the Union prefers that nonreligious facilities be utilized for providing federally funded day care, it does not object to the usage of religious facilities when there is no feasible alternative. The Union has made it clear that the facilities must be free from religiously oriented activities and symbols.[522] Its flexible approach to this subject is, of course, colored by its strong advocacy of day care; day care is good because it allows more women to enter the labor market.[523] In a similar vein, the ACLU defends the use of religious institutions when the government seeks to channel public aid for overseas relief programs, just so long as no proselytizing activities are taking place.[524]

Two policies that bear on the subject of cultural and religious expression concern the appointment of chaplains in military bases and prisons. Traditionally, the authorities have selected chaplains to serve Americans who were confined to government quarters. The ACLU objects to this arrangement on the grounds that there is pervasive control by government officials over the selection, compensation, and scope of duties of the chaplains.[525] Greater insight into the Union's rationale can be gleaned from a look at the board minutes on the military chaplaincy policy.

The Union believes that the military command plays such an integral role over chaplaincy that it is tantamount to the establishment of religion. When the board considered this issue in 1973, it was struck by Peter Bepler's assertion that because all chaplains are officers, there is a gulf between them and the bulk of service personnel. One suspects, however, that even if the chaplains were privates, it would not have mattered to the civil libertarians. Sociologist and board member Robert Bierstedt cited Article VI of the Constitution, which provides that "no religious test shall ever be required as qualificaton to any office or public trust under the United States." Bierstedt's reasoning for opposing military chaplaincy won unanimous board approval.[526] However, a religious test has never been a requirement for commissioned officers in the armed service. What the military has done is to assign a commissioned status to service personnel who are chaplains. The Air Force does the same for pilots and doctors: all members of these groups are officers because of their professional status.

When one examines the Union's history, "the record will show a lot of foolish statements and motions by somebody or other connected with the ACLU, like, for instance, taking 'In God We Trust' off coins or postage or denying Congress its chaplains." It was not a critic of the ACLU who said that—it was its founder, Roger Baldwin.[527] In its passion to stem religious influences, the ACLU has held, since 1954, that "the insertion of the words 'under God' into the pledge of allegiance is a violation of the constitutional principle of separation of church and state."[528] The Union exercises the same logic when it takes its stand against "blue law" legislation designed to curtail commercial activity on Sundays.[529] And when it comes to the display of religious symbolism on public property, the ACLU is steadfast in its conviction that arguments that address the cultural expressiveness of such symbolism are inadequate. Tradition aside, the Union opposes the display on public property of candelabra at Channukah,[530] the erection of a cross at Easter,[531] and the display of Nativity scenes at Christmas.[532] Most conspicuous of all, however, is the ACLU's annual ritual of filing suit in a federal court enjoining public school students from singing "Silent Night." It has also gone so far as to try and stop a city employees' Christmas pageant at the local zoo.[533] Such actions on the part of the Union have led law professor Basile J. Uddo to conclude, "The trivialization of the First Amendment becomes complete."[534] George Will has been more critical: "These people want to use state power to purge the social milieu of certain things offensive, but not at all harmful, to them. There is meanness, even bullying, in this—a disagreeable delight in using the community's law divisively, to abolish traditions enjoyed by neighbors."[535]

The ACLU has interpreted the First Amendment to mean that there ought to be more than a wall between church and state—there ought to be an iron curtain. As for religion itself, the Union does not believe what the courts and legislators have always believed, that churches and synagogues are of such great social utility that they are entitled to a tax-exempt status. The Union would like to strip church property of its tax-exempt status.[536] Baldwin branded this decision as "very foolish," and told me that "the courts will always sustain the principle that universities, educational institutions and churches are of such great social benefit that they should not be taxed."[537] Father Robert F. Drinan, the Boston liberal activist, summed up the ACLU's record on religion: "The Church-State positions taken by the ACLU are *not* nonpartisan; they are the result of one theory of the role of the state in a pluralistic society—a theory not subscribed to by a large body of eminent constitutional law experts in this country and not at all considered to be 'nonpartisan' by many religious groups."[538] Drinan wrote that in 1958, before the ACLU had taken most of its aggressive steps to delimit the role of religion in public life. If the image of nonpartisanship could not be sustained then, it surely cannot be sustained now.

Notes

1. Quoted, Sidney Hook, *The Paradoxes of Freedom* (Berkeley and Los Angeles: University of California Press, 1970), p. 14.
2. See Franklyn S. Haiman, *Speech and Law in a Free Society* (Chicago: University of Chicago Press, 1981), pp. 3-4, 431.
3. Quoted, Hook, *Paradoxes of Freedom,* p. 15.
4. Ibid., p. 39.
5. The case in question, *U.S. v. O'Brien,* has been treated by Haiman; see *Speech and Law in a Free Society,* pp. 27-30.
6. Irving Kristol, "Pornography, Obscenity and the Case for Censorship," *New York Times Magazine,* 28 March 1971, p. 113.

7. Thomas I. Emerson, *The System of Freedom of Expression* (New York: Random House, 1970).
8. Ibid., p. 17.
9. Ibid., p. 338.
10. Ibid., pp. 19-20.
11. Sidney Hook, *Philosophy and Public Policy* (Carbondale and Edwardsville: Southern Illinois University Press, 1980), pp. 125-26.
12. Haiman, *Speech and Law in a Free Society,* p. 25.
13. Ibid., p. 425.
14. Ibid., pp. 425-29.
15. Ibid., p. 181.
16. Ibid., pp. 178-80. *See F.C.C. v. Pacifica Foundation.*
17. Ibid., pp. 16-17. *See Cohen v. California.*
18. '81 PG, #3.
19. Nicholas Von Hoffman, "When Civil Liberties Become Liabilities," *Penthouse,* April 1982, p. 100.
20. "Rocker Osbourne Muzzled," *Civil Liberties Record of Pennsylvania,* March 1983, p. 1.
21. AR 1, p. 8.
22. AR 4, pp. 22-23.
23. AR 6, p. 19.
24. AR 7, p. 32.
25. AR 9, p. 28.
26. Hook, *Paradoxes of Freedom,* p. 10.
27. Diane Ravitch, "The Shameful Treatment of Mrs. Kirkpatrick," *Wall Street Journal,* 10 March 1983, p. 24.
28. James Q. Wilson, "Liberalism Versus Liberal Education," *Commentary,* June 1972, pp. 50-51.
29. Joseph W. Bishop, Jr., "Politics and ACLU," *Commentary,* December 1971, p. 57.
30. Only Barton Bean has even bothered to mention this scandal and from reading his "account," one gets no feel for what really happened. I stumbled on this information quite by accident while reading reels of microfilm on the ACLU in the New York Public Library. Bean makes a few curt references to the incident in "Pressure for Freedom: The American Civil Liberties Union," Ph.D. diss., Cornell University, 1955 pp. 158, 276, 279.
31. ACLU Papers, Vol. 1071, Reel 156. The article appeared in the December 1936 issue of the *American Mercury;* see pages 385, 395-96 for the cited information.
32. Ibid.; see p. 399 of the *Mercury* article.
33. Ibid.
34. *Material in Reply to Mr. Varney's Charges,* ACLU Papers, Vol. 1071, Reel 156.
35. Memorandum concerning the article on the American Civil Liberties Union by Harold Lord Varney in the *American Mercury,* December 1936. All of the subsequent citations on this incident can be found in the ACLU Papers, Vol. 1071, Reel 156.
36. American Civil Liberties Union, Inc. v. The American Mercury, Inc. and Harold Lord Varney.
37. Letter, Baldwin to Palmer, 12 January 1938.

38. Letter, Palmer to Baldwin, 18 January 1938.
39. Memorandum on "American Mercury" article, 20 January 1938.
40. Letter, Baldwin to Hays; copy to Palmer.
41. Letter, Hays to Baldwin, 27 January 1938.
42. Letter, Palmer to Baldwin, 4 February 1938.
43. Letter, Baldwin to Palmer, 8 February 1938.
44. Letter, Palmer to Baldwin, 4 March 1938. Palmer was hospitalized in the interim and could not reach Baldwin before March.
45. "The Civil Liberties Union: Political or Non-Partisan?" *Forum*, March 1938, pp. 207-11.
46. Baldwin's letter appeared in the 28 March issue of *Forum*.
47. Mencken's article is listed in the ACLU Papers along with the related material.
48. Letter, Baldwin to Mencken, 1 April 1938.
49. Letter, Baldwin to Palmer, 7 April 1938.
50. Letter, Baldwin to Ward, 6 April 1938.
51. Letter, Baldwin to Hays, 1 April 1938.
52. *Memorandum to Hays from Ward Regarding Mencken's Proposed Article,* 8 April 1938.
53. Letter, Hays to Mencken, 25 April 1938.
54. Letter, Mencken to Hays, 16 May 1938.
55. Letter, Hays to Baldwin, 17 May 1938.
56. Letter, Baldwin to Hays, 18 May 1938.
57. Letter, Baldwin to Ward, 19 May 1938.
58. *Article written by H.L. Mencken for publication in the American Mercury with the understanding that the American Civil Liberties Union will withdraw its libel suit.* This statement was sent to the Board on 27 May 1938.
59. All of the postcard replies are on file with the related material. The name of the third person whom I listed was illegible.
60. Letter, Baldwin to Mencken, 10 June 1938.
61. Bd. Min., 13 June 1938.
62. Letter from Baldwin to Board of Directors, 22 June 1938.
63. See ACLU Papers.
64. Postcard, Flynn to the board, 13 July 1938.
65. Letter, Mencken to Baldwin, 27 July 1938.
66. Western Union telegram, Baldwin to Palmer, 1 August 1938.
67. Letter, Palmer to Baldwin, 5 August 1938.
68. *Union's Libel Suit Against Mercury is Arbitrated,* 1 October 1938.
69. Quoted, William Gerber, *American Liberalism* (Boston: Twayne Publishers, 1975), p. 103. Nock wrote this in 1937.
70. See Gertrude Himmelfarb, *On Liberty and Liberalism* (New York: Knopf, 1974), pp. 49-50.
71. AR 3, p. 10; AR 4, p. 13; AR 5, p. 14.
72. Quoted, Fred W. Friendly, *Minnesota Rag* (New York: Random House, 1981), p. 96.
73. See ibid., ch. 4.
74. Quoted, ibid., pp. 61-62.
75. Ibid., pp. 62-65.
76. Ibid., pp. 78-83.
77. Ibid., p. 220.
78. AR 41, pp. 26-27.

79. AR 42, p. 28.
80. '81 PG, #7.
81. Douglas E. Kneeland, "Article on H-Bomb is Made Public by 'Progressive.'" *New York Times,* 2 October 1979, p. A17.
82. Memorandum, Ira Glasser to ACLU Affiliates and Board of Directors concerning the *Progressive* case, 9 April 1979.
83. Philip Taubman, "U.S. Drops Efforts to Bar Publication of H-Bomb Articles," *New York Times,* 18 September 1979, p. 1.
84. "Press, Bomb and Pistols," *New York Times,* 19 September 1979, p. A24.
85. Stuart Taylor, Jr., "Libel Law: A Puzzle Juries Have Trouble Solving," *New York Times,* 5 May 1983, p. 11.
86. '81 PG, #6.
87. '83 PG, #6.
88. See Nat Hentoff, "Throwing Libel Out of Court," *Inquiry,* December 1982, p. 13.
89. '81 PG, #313.
90. AR 18, p. 39.
91. '66 PG, #22.
92. '67 PG, #22.
93. '76 PG, #24.
94. AR 41, p. 23.
95. Ibid.
96. Interview with Reitman.
97. AR 41, p. 24.
98. AR 38, p. 12.
99. AR 39, p. 20.
100. AR 40, p. 24.
101. Ibid., p. 23.
102. '81 PG, #14.
103. Ibid., #20.
104. '66 PG, #17.
105. AR 40, p. 23.
106. '66 PG, #17.
107. '76 PG, #20.
108. '81 PG, #21.
109. AR 1, p. 15.
110. AR 2, p. 17.
111. AR 8, pp. 24-25.
112. Ibid., p. 25; AR 9, p. 14.
113. AR 10, p. 24.
114. AR 11, p. 32.
115. AR 13, p. 25.
116. AR 14, p. 6.
117. AR 11, pp. 31-32.
118. See AR 20, pp. 43 and 61; AR 18, p. 39; AR 26, pp. 53-54; AR 22, pp. 47 and 59.
119. AR 31, pp. 7-8.
120. '81 PG, #16.
121. Colin Campbell, "Book Banning in America," *New York Times Book Review,* 20 December 1981, pp. 1, 16-17.

122. '81 PG, #74.
123. Bd. Min., 6/18-19/77, pp. 7-8.
124. "Supreme Court Sends Island Trees to Trial," *Civil Liberties*, July 1982, p. 8.
125. Richard Levine and William C. Rhoden, "School Board Unbans Books," *New York Times*, 15 August 1982, p. E5.
126. Wayne King, "Kansans Protest Broadcasts of Hate," *New York Times*, 18 May 1983, p. A18.
127. "Spy Stories and Vile Racism," editorial, *New York Times*, 22 May 1983, p. 22.
128. Quoted, Peggy Lamson, *Roger Baldwin* (Boston: Houghton Mifflin, 1976), p. 215.
129. AR 22, p. 6.
130. "L.I. Woman Sentenced to Community-Service Work for Ethnic Slur," *New York Times,* 14 May 1982, p. B2.
131. Peter Kihss, "Survey Finds Sharp Rise in Anti-Semitic Incidents," *New York Times*, 30 December 1980, p. A9.
132. It did defend the free speech rights of William Randolph Hearst before this time, but not in relation to an employer-employee controversy over free speech rights.
133. Qouted by Lamson, *Baldwin*, pp. 218-19.
134. '81 PG, #50.
135. Interview with Baldwin.
136. Dennis Wrong, "Some Problems in Defining Social Power," *American Journal of Sociology*, May 1968, pp. 679-80.
137. AR 13, p. 27.
138. AR 14, p. 32.
139. AR 19, pp. 47-48.
140. AR 27, p. 72.
141. '81 PG, #98.
142. Ibid.
143. AR 31, pp. 67-68.
144. David Hamlin, "Swastikas and Survivors: Inside the Skokie-Nazi Free Speech Case," *Civil Liberties Review*, March/April 1978, p. 12.
145. AR 39, pp. 38-39.
146. AR 36, p. 35.
147. See Roger Baldwin, "Introduction," in AR 1, p. v.
148. AR 36, p. 13.
149. AR 39, p. 19.
150. '77 PG, #3.
151. '81 PG, #3.
152. AR 28, p. 39.
153. '81 PG, #42.
154. Bd. Min., 1/23-24/82, p. 1.
155. '81 PG, #301.
156. Joseph Sobran, "ACLU's Rules of the Game: Flexible," *New York Post*, 21 August 1981, p. 31.
157. Quoted, Himmelfarb, *On Liberty and Liberalism*, p. 35.
158. James Burnham, *Suicide of the West* (New York: Arlington House, 1964), p. 128.
159. Interview with John H. F. Shattuck, "The Defense of Liberty," *Center Magazine*, November/December 1979, p. 48.

160. Haiman, *Speech and Law in a Free Society*, p. 7.
161. David Hamlin, *The Nazi/Skokie Conflict* (Boston: Beacon Press, 1980), p. 126.
162. Haiman, *Speech and Law in a Free Society*, p. 98.
163. Aryeh Neier, *Defending My Enemy* (New York: Dutton, 1979), p. 4.
164. "Slander Charge Opposed," *Civil Liberties Record* (Pennsylvania), January 1983, p. 7.
165. Bean, "Pressure for Freedom," p. 297.
166. Biographical information was supplied by the Pittsburgh CLU to all members regarding the candidates for office in 1983.
167. AR 2, p. 24.
168. AR 4, p. 29.
169. AR 16A, p. 50.
170. '81 PG, #44.
171. Quoted, Haiman, *Speech and Law in a Free Society*, p. 275.
172. J. Anthony Lukas, "The ACLU Against Itself," *New York Times Magazine*, 9 July 1978, p. 11.
173. Ibid.
174. Ibid.; Everett Holles, "Suit Defending Klan Causing Dissension in Coast ACLU," *New York Times*, 27 February 1977, p. 20.
175. Holles, "Suit Defending Klan Causing Dissension in Coast ACLU."
176. Lukas, "The ACLU Against Itself," p. 11.
177. Bd. Min., 9/24-25/77, p. 12.
178. Bd. Min., 12/3-4/77, pp. 2-3.
179. Lukas, "The ACLU Against Itself," p. 11.
180. Hamlin, *The Nazi/Skokie Conflict*, pp. 5-7.
181. Ibid., p. 16.
182. Ibid., p. 28.
183. Ibid., p. 26.
184. William Safire, "Marching Through Skokie," *New York Times*, 27 March 1978, p. A19.
185. Hamlin, *The Nazi/Skokie Conflict*, pp. 27-32.
186. Ibid., pp. 62, 71.
187. Ibid., pp. 76-93.
188. Ibid., pp. 172-75.
189. Quoted, *New York Times*, 25 June 1978, "Week in Review" sec., p. 2.
190. Interview with Reitman.
191. Bd. Min., 6/18-19/77, p. 9.
192. AR '77, p. 3.
193. Joseph Tybor, "Jewish Lawyer Paying Heavy Price for Nazi Defense," *Pittsburgh Post-Gazette*, 9 May 1979, p. 33.
194. Ibid.
195. Bd. Min., 12/3-4/77, p. 37.
196. Jay Miller, "Members Rally to 'Save' ACLU," *Civil Liberties*, November 1978, p. 6.
197. Barbara Basler, "Mugger's Tale: He Prowled Without Fear Through a Fearful City," *New York Times*, 17 November 1980, p. B1.
198. Lee A. Daniels, "Queens Man Gets Probation in Fatal Attack at Garden," *New York Times*, 24 May 1980, p. 27.
199. "The Chief's Justice and Crime," editorial, *New York Times*, 11 February 1981, p. A26.

200. Linda Greenhouse, "Burger's Talk: Quick Dispute," *New York Times*, 10 February 1981, p. B9.
201. "The Chief's Justice and Crime," editorial, *New York Times*, 11 February 1981, p. A26.
202. Carl Rowan, "Why U.S. Is Hostage to Crime," *Pittsburgh Press*, 14 February 1981, p. B2.
203. Greenhouse, "Burger's Talk."
204. Ibid.
205. Quoted, Bean, "Pressure for Freedom," p. 271.
206. Interview with Neier.
207. Joyce Purnick, "Rise in Crime Against Teachers Is Termed a Chilling Fact of Life," *New York Times*, 15 December 1980, p. 1.
208. Interview with Neier.
209. Ibid. So angered was Neier with my line of questioning that he stopped the interview and requested that I leave his office. On the following day when I interviewed Reitman, 20 June 1978, I mentioned to him the way Neier treated me. Reitman, who was cordial and cooperative (as was Baldwin), told me that Neier had been under considerable pressure due to the Skokie incident and other events.
210. '76 PG, #43.
211. '81 PG, #45.
212. Bd. Min., 6/12-13/82.
213. Ibid.
214. "Law Requiring Firearms Challenged by A.C.L.U," *New York Times*, 2 June 1982, p. A18.
215. AR 37, p. 65.
216. AR 40, p. 77.
217. AR 42, p. 97.
218. AR 39, p. 63.
219. AR 43, p. 9; '76 PG, #217.
220. '81 PG, #202.
221. AR 31, p. 54.
222. AR 30, p. 56.
223. Jerry Berman, "The Lessons of Abscam: A Public Policy Report by the American Civil Liberties Union, October 10, 1982," pp. 3-4.
224. Ibid., p. 44.
225. Ibid., pp. 37-38.
226. Ibid., pp. 2-3.
227. AR 29, p. 16.
228. AR 30, p. 13.
229. AR 34, pp. 95-96.
230. AR 35, p. 98.
231. AR 36, p. 70.
232. AR 41, pp. 79-80.
233. Ibid.
234. AR 42, pp. 103-4.
235. AR 40, pp. 69-71.
236. '81 PG, #222.
237. Ibid., #120.
238. Ibid., #12.

239. AR '71-'72, p. 11.
240. '81 PG, #266.
241. George F. Will, "Is the ACLU Being Reasonable," *Newsweek*, 31 January 1983, p. 80.
242. Ibid.
243. Jackson Toby, "Children's Own Fault," *New York Times*, 28 July 1982, p. A23.
244. AR '71-'72, p. 17.
245. Arnold H. Lubasch, "Court Strikes Down Law on Detention of Juveniles," *New York Times*, 18 April 1981, p. 26.
246. AR '76, p. 30.
247. "9 P.M. Curfew Ordered for Children in Atlanta," *New York Times*, 28 January 1981, p. A6.
248. AR 37, p. 12.
249. '76 PG, #235.
250. Ibid.
251. Ibid.
252. '81 PG, #238.
253. Ibid.
254. Robert Martinson, "What Works?—Questions and Answers About Prison Reform," *Public Interest*, Spring 1974, p. 49.
255. James Q. Wilson, *Thinking About Crime* (New York: Vintage Books, 1977), p. 190.
256. '81 PG, #239.
257. Ernest van den Haag, *Punishing Criminals* (New York: Basic Books, 1975), pp. 24-62.
258. '81 PG, #239.
259. AR '72-'73, p. 15.
260. Interview with Neier.
261. AR '70-'71, p. 37.
262. "Court Upsets Death Penalty, Ruling Crime Not 'Heinous,'" *New York Times*, 12 November 1980, p. A16.
263. Himmelfarb, *On Liberty and Liberalism*, p. 307.
264. AR 29, pp. 84-85.
265. Interview with Reitman.
266. AR 29, pp. 84-85.
267. AR 35, pp. 96-97.
268. AR 36, p. 66; AR 41, p. 78.
269. AR 41, p. 78
270. Stuart Taylor, Jr., "Comeback of Death Penalty Revives Debate Ended in '72," *New York Times*, 14 June 1981, p. 28.
271. AR '76, p. 18.
272. Quoted, Aryeh Neier, "'Butting In' for the Utah Slayer," *New York Times*, 17 November 1976, p. A31.
273. Ibid.
274. "At Issue: Crime and Punishment," *Time*, 4 June 1979, p. 15.
275. ACLU, *Civil Liberties in Reagan's America*, October 1982, pp. 30-31.
276. Ibid.
277. Testimony of the American Civil Liberties Union on S.114, A Bill to Establish Rational Criteria for the Imposition of the Sentence of Death, before the Senate Committee on the Judiciary, 27 April 1981.

278. Ibid., p. 12.
279. Ibid., p. 4.
280. Ibid., p. 8 of Schwarzschild's testimony.
281. Taylor, "Comeback of Death Penalty Revives Debate Ended in '72."
282. Henry Schwarzschild, "Homicide by Injection," *New York Times*, 23 December 1982, p. 21.
283. Robert Reinhold, "Groups Race to Prevent Texas Execution," *New York Times*, 6 December 1982, p. 10. See also Reinhold; "Execution by Injection Stirs Fear and Sharpens Debate," ibid., 8 December 1982, p. 13.
284. Michael Norman, "Why Jersey Is Leaning to Executions by Injection," *New York Times*, 18 May 1983, p. B6.
285. Wallace Turner, "California Supreme Court Asked to Decide on Crime Bill's Legality," *New York Times*, 15 June 1982, p. A24.
286. "California's Backfire on Crime," editorial, *New York Times*, 21 June 1982, p. A18.
287. Wendell Rawls, Jr., "Pennsylvania Shapes Prison Law to Cut Crime," *New York Times*, 8 July 1982, pp. A1, B10.
288. Howell Raines, "Reagan Outlines Reforms in Laws to Combat Crime," *New York Times*, 29 September 1981, p. A1.
289. Ibid.; Peter B. Bensinger, "A Plan Calculated to Cut Crime," *New York Times*, 24 August 1981, p. A15.
290. Loren Siegel, "'Quick Fix' Solutions," *Civil Liberties*, February 1983, p. 5.
291. Ira Glasser, "The Coming Assault on Civil Liberties," in *What Reagan is Doing to Us*, ed. Alan Gartner, Colin Greer and Frank Riessman (New York: Harper and Row, 1982), p. 244.
292. Martin Garbus, "Excluding Justice," *New York Times*, 4 April 1983, p. A19.
293. Hook, *Philosophy and Public Policy*, pp. 133-34.
294. Himmelfarb, *On Liberty and Liberalism*, p. 312.
295. Daniel Bell, *The Cultural Contradictions of Capitalism* (New York: Basic Books, 1976), pp. 276-77.
296. Michael Oakeshott, *Rationalism in Politics* (London: Methuen, 1962), p. 1.
297. Edward Shils, *Tradition* (Chicago: University of Chicago Press, 1981), pp. 7-10.
298. See Peter Steinfels, *The Neoconservatives* (New York: Simon and Schuster, 1979), p. 124.
299. Hadley Arkes, *The Philosopher in the City* (Princeton: Princeton University Press, 1981), p. 427.
300. Michael Walzer, *Radical Principles* (New York: Basic Books, 1980), p. 6.
301. Henry Fairlie, "Who Speaks for Values?" *New Republic*, 31 January 1981, p. 17.
302. Tom Hayden, "The Future Politics of Liberalism," *Nation*, 21 February 1981, p. 209.
303. See N. R. Kleinfield, "TV Monitors Plan Sponsor Pressure," *New York Times*, 27 May 1981, p. D1; Tony Schwartz, "50 TV Shows Rejected by Proctor and Gamble," *New York Times*, 17 June 1981, p. C30.
304. Albert Shanker, "NEA Trying to Teach — or Indoctrinate," *New York Times*, 17 April 1983, p. E7.
305. David Shribman, "Poetry and Politics at Georgetown U.," *New York Times*, 22 October 1982, p. 10.
306. ACLU advertisement, "If the Moral Majority Has Its Way You'd Better Start Praying," *New York Times*, 23 November 1980, p. 22E.

307. See *Civil Liberties Alert, October/November 1982*, p. 4.
308. Christopher Lasch, *The Culture of Narcissism* (New York: Norton, 1978), p. 125.
309. '81 PG, #71A. The only concern that the ACLU has is that the religious liberties of parents not be unwarrantedly contravened. See Bd. Min., 4/3-4/82.
310. Edward B. Fiske, "A Third of High School Students Chronically Absent in New York," *New York Times*, 9 January 1983, p. 1.
311. Marcia Chambers, "High School Dropout Rate at 45%, Macchiarola Reports to City Board," *New York Times*, 17 October 1979, p. Al. See also Ronald Smothers, "City's Job Outlook is Worsening for 40 Percent Who Quit School," *New York Times*, 14 March 1981, p. Al. The estimated dropout rate for 1980 was approximately 50 percent.
312. Caren Marcus, "Discipline Heads City School Problems," *Pittsburgh Press*, 5 March 1981, p. Al.
313. Judith Cummings, "Non-Catholic Christian Schools Growing Fast," *New York Times*, 14 April 1983, p. 1.
314. Thomas A. Johnson, "Black-Run Private Schools Lure Growing Numbers in New York," *New York Times*, 5 April 1980, p. Al.
315. "N.A.A.C.P. Asserts Reagan Budget Profits the Rich at Expense of Poor," *New York Times*, 14 April 1981, p. A16.
316. "A Threat to Public Education," editorial, *New York Times*, 10 March 1981, p. A18.
317. '81 PG, #76.
318. Ibid.
319. '81 PG, #87.
320. Arnold H. Lubasch, "Judge Bars Federal Birth-Control Rule for Minors," *New York Times*, 14 February 1983, p. 1.
321. "Sue to Stop New Birth Control Rule," *Civil Liberties*, February 1983, p. 12.
322. AR 6, p. 22.
323. AR 7, p. 26.
324. '81 PG, #268.
325. Glenn Collins, "Courts, the Congress and Citizens are Redefining the Concept of Foster Care," *New York Times*, 22 July 1981, p. B4.
326. Gene I. Maeroff, "New Course in Schools: How a Citizen Behaves," *New York Times*, 4 May 1982, p. B1.
327. Edward B. Fiske, "Why a Reformer Changed His Mind," *New York Times*, 10 October 1979, pp. Cl, C4.
328. "U.S. Seeks to End Dress Code Role," *New York Times*, 18 April 1981, p. 8.
329. AR '75, p. 22.
330. See Joseph F. Sullivan, "Searches Limited in Jersey Schools," *New York Times*, 9 August 1983, p. Al.
331. Jerry E. Fogel, letter to the editor, *New York Times*, 25 June 1982, p. A30. Fogel made reference to the *Times's* support in his letter.
332. Ibid.
333. '76 PG, #66.
334. '81 PG, #72.
335. AR '70-'71, pp. 28-30.
336. Ibid., p. 28.
337. Tony Schwartz, "Students' Publishing Out of School Is Upheld by U.S. Court of Appeals," *New York Times*, 16 October 1979, p. B4.

338. ACLU, *Academic Freedom in the Secondary Schools* (New York: ACLU, 1968).
339. '81 PG, # 72.
340. Ibid.
341. Gerald Grant, "Children's Rights and Adult Confusions," *Public Interest*, Fall 1982, pp. 89-90.
342. '76 PG, #64; '81 PG, #69.
343. '81 PG, #73.
344. Ludmilla Thorne, "The Littlest Defector," *National Review*, 18 March 1983, pp. 314-20.
345. Angel Castillo, "A Ukrainian Family and a Question of Juvenile Law," *New York Times*, 9 September 1980, p. B8.
346. Thorne, "Littlest Defector," p. 316.
347. Georgia Dullea, "Custody and the Legal Clashes," *New York Times*, 23 July 1981, p. B4.
348. Richard Vigilante and Susan Vigilante, "Taking Liberties: The ACLU Strays from Its Mission," *Policy Review*, Fall 1984, p. 34.
349. Thorne, "Littlest Defector," pp. 314-20; "Ukrainian Boy's Sister, 19, Finds Love and Freedom in America," *New York Times*, 16 February 1982, p. A12; see also Nathaniel Sheppard, Jr., "Ukrainian Boy, in Letter, Contradicts Father on Family Life," *New York Times*, 1 May 1982, p. 10.
350. Quoted by Thorne, "Littlest Defector," pp. 320, 341.
351. Stuart Taylor, "Stalin's Kin," *New York Times*, 24 November 1984, p. 4.
352. Edwin M. Schur, *Crimes Without Victims* (Englewood Cliffs, N.J.: Prentice-Hall, 1965).
353. Gilbert Geis, *Not the Law's Business* (New York: Schocken Books, 1979).
354. Edwin M. Schur and Hugo Adam Bedau, *Victimless Crimes* (Englewood Cliffs, N.J.: Prentice-Hall, 1974), p. 7.
355. '81 PG, #209.
356. Ibid., #212.
357. Bd. Min., 12/6-7/75, p. 27.
358. Laurie Johnston, "Artist Ends Her Life After Ritual Citing," *New York Times*, 17 June 1979, pp. 1, 10.
359. '81 PG, #267.
360. Bd. Min., 12/4-5/76, p. 36.
361. Anna Quindlen, "Teen-Agers Call Illicit Drugs One of Life's Commonplaces," *New York Times*, 19 July 1981, p. 1.
362. Colin Campbell, "Federal Judge Strikes Down Law Banning Head Shops in New York," *New York Times*, 19 July 1981, p. 26.
363. Judd Burstein expressed this view in "Decriminalizing Heroin," *New York Times*, 6 October 1982, p. 27.
364. Peter Passell, "Make Grass Greener," *New York Times*, 29 November 1982, p. 18.
365. Robert M. Curvin, "What If Heroin Were Free," *New York Times*, 20 February 1981, p. A26.
366. Much of what follows is taken from the fine analysis of the ACLU's evolving position on drugs by Ronald Bayer, "Drug stores, liquor stores and heroin: an analysis of the libertarian debate," *Contemporary Drug Problem*, Winter 1975, pp. 459-82.
367. Ibid., pp. 461-62.

368. Ibid. See also '81 PG, #214.
369. '81 PG, #214.
370. Bayer, "Drug stores, liquor stores and heroin," p. 464-73; '81 PG, #209.
371. Himmelfarb, *On Liberty and Liberalism*, pp. 315-16.
372. Charles Tilly has nicely portrayed the differences between reactionary and modern forms of public disturbance in "Collective Violence in European Perspective," in *The History of Violence in America*, ed. Hugh Davis Graham and Ted Robert Gurr (New York: Bantam Books, 1969), pp. 16-37.
373. Quoted, Dennis Altman, *Homosexual* (New York: Avon Books, 1971), p. 122.
374. Ibid., pp. 83-84, 101-02.
375. *ACLU Position on Homosexuality*, 7 January 1957.
376. '66 PG, #246.
377. Bd. Min., 11/16/66, pp. 6-8.
378. '67 PG, #246.
379. AR '74, p. 6.
380. '81 PG, #261.
381. Bd. Min., 4/12-13/75, p. 30.
382. '81 PG, #261.
383. '76 PG, #81.
384. "ACLU Works for Gay Rights," *Civil Liberties*, November 1982, p. 7.
385. Quoted, Kate Millet, *The Prostitution Papers* (New York: Avon Books, 1973), p. 57.
386. Barbara Basler, "City's Prostitutes Invade Residential Communities," *New York Times*, 15 August 1981, p. 1.
387. Ronald Smothers, "Koch Taking Action Over Prostitution," *New York Times*, 18 October 1979, pp. 1, B20.
388. '81 PG, #210.
389. Interview with Baldwin.
390. '81 PG, #210. This policy was passed in April 1976.
391. Interview with Baldwin.
392. Richard Emery, letter to the editor, *New York Times,* 25 August 1981, p. A18.
393. David Margolick, "Prostitutes Not Entitled to Jury Trials, Top State Court Rules," *New York Times,* 8 June 1983, p. B22.
394. Eward Shils, "The Antinomies of Liberalism," in *The Relevance of Liberalism,* ed. Zbigniew Brzezinski (Boulder, Colo.: Westview Press, 1978), pp. 160-62.
395. Aryeh Neier, "Expurgating the First Amendment," *Nation,* 21 June 1980, pp. 737, 751-54.
396. *Winters v. New York.*
397. *Miller v. California.*
398. Emerson, *System of Freedom of Expression*, pp. 471-72; Warren Weaver, Jr., "Legal Efforts to Define 'Obscenity' Hinder Drive to Curb Pornography," *New York Times,* 16 February 1980, p. 26.
399. Haiman, *Speech and Law in a Free Society*, p. 166.
400. Warren Weaver, Jr., "Legal Efforts to Define 'Obscenity' Hinder Drive to Curb Pornography," *New York Times,* 16 February 1980, p. 26.
401. William Allan, "Public Access a Channel to 'Blue' TV," *Pittsburgh Press,* 13 October 1981, p. B-1.
402. William Allan, "Ugly George Stalks Women, Ratings," *Pittsburgh Press,* 12 October 1981, p. B-1.

403. William Allan, "Raw Sex Explodes Onto Home Screen," *Pittsburgh Press,* 11 October 1981, p. B-1.
404. Howard Polskin, "Sex on Pay Television—The Battle Lines Are Formed," *TV Guide,* 30 October 1982, p. 6.
405. Richard Meislin, "Bill to Limit 'Offensive' Cable TV Programs Is Introduced in Albany," *New York Times,* 28 May 1981, p. B1.
406. *Report of the Committee on Obscenity and Film Censorship,* (Chairman, Bernard Williams; London: Her Majesty's Stationery Office, 1979), p. 54.
407. Ibid., p. 56.
408. Ibid., p. 160.
409. Ibid., p. 122.
410. Ibid., pp. 160-62
411. Ibid., p. 163.
412. Haiman, *Speech and Law in a Free Society,* p. 22.
413. Ibid., p. 141.
414. Ibid., p. 164.
415. Ibid., p. 173.
416. AR 9, pp. 26-28.
417. AR 8, p. 8.
418. AR 29, p. 20.
419. AR 30, p. 12.
420. AR 33, p. 37.
421. AR 29, p. 23.
422. AR 33, p. 49.
423. Ibid., p. 40.
424. '66 PG, #4.
425. AR 40, p. 13.
426. AR 39, p. 9; AR 41, p. 13; AR 42, p. 18.
427. '66 PG, #4.
428. AR 36, p. 13.
429. AR 39, p. 15.
430. AR 40, p. 61.
431. AR 39, pp. 13-14.
432. Interview with Neier.
433. AR 39, p. 14.
434. Interview with Neier.
435. The term *secondary boycott* can be found, among other places, in '76 PG, #3.
436. Haiman, *Speech and Law in a Free Society,* p. 139.
437. AR 39, p. 12.
438. Interview with Reitman.
439. Haiman, *Speech and Law in a Free Society,* p. 144.
440. AR 40, p. 16.
441. AR 41, p. 14.
442. Haiman, *Speech and Law in a Free Society,* p. 140.
443. '77 PG, #4.
444. '81 PG, #20.
445. William Serrin, "Sex Is a Growing Multibillion Business," *New York Times,* 9 February 1981, p. B1.
446. Ibid., p. B6.
447. William Allan, "Sex Industry Victimizes Children," *Pittsburgh Press,* 17 January 1982, p. C1.

448. "Mother Called Child Porn Leader," *Pittsburgh Press,* 8 May 1982, p. A-1.
449. Ibid.
450. Arkes, *Philosopher in the City,* pp. 414-15.
451. Speech by Father Bruce Ritter, David Lawrence Convention Center, Pittsburgh, 16 September 1982.
452. Ibid.
453. John Holt, "Why Not a Bill of Rights for Children," in *The Children's Rights Movement,* ed. Beatrice Gross and Ronald Gross (New York: Anchor Books, 1977), pp. 319-25.
454. Richard Farson, "Birthrights," in *The Children's Rights Movement,* ed. Beatrice Gross and Ronald Gross (New York: Anchor Books, 1977), pp. 325-28.
455. Gary Sturgess, "Sociologist defends child molester," *Bulletin,* 17 November 1981, p. 46.
456. Emerson, *System of Freedom of Expression,* p. 497.
457. *Report Of The Committee On Obscenity and Film Censorship,* pp. 19, 159-66.
458. Bd. Min., 2/14-15/70, p. 15.
459. '71, '76 PGs, #4.
460. Bd. Min., 6/18-19/77, pp. 3-4.
461. Bd. Min., 9/24-25/77, p.10.
462. Ibid., p. 11.
463. Ibid.
464. Haiman, *Speech and Law in a Free Society,* p. 179.
465. Ibid., p. 165.
466. Ibid., p. 250.
467. Richard J. Meislin, "Using Children in Sexual Portrayals Legal Unless Obscene, Court Says," *New York Times,* 13 May 1981, p. A1.
468. Linda Greenhouse, "Justices Uphold Bar to Children in Pornography," *New York Times,* 3 July 1982, p. 1. O'Connor's statement appeared on p. 36.
469. "Cleaning Up Kidporn," editorial, *New York Times,* 7 July 1982, p. A18.
470. Covenant House Newsletter, April 1983.
471. Owen Chadwick, *The Secularization of the European Mind in the Nineteenth Century* (Cambridge: Cambridge University Press, 1975), p. 229.
472. Quoted, Walter Berns, *The First Amendment and the Future of American Democracy* (New York: Basic Books, 1976), p. 12.
473. Francis X. Clines, "Presidents and Churchgoing: A Sensitive Subject," *New York Times,* 23 March 1983, p. 12.
474. Berns, *First Amendment and the Future of American Democracy,* p. 13.
475. Clines, "Presidents and Churchgoing."
476. See Robert L. Cord, "Understanding the First Amendment," *National Review,* 22 January 1982, p. 26.
477. Ibid.; Berns, *First Amendment and the Future of American Democracy,* pp. 8-9.
478. Cord, "Understanding the First Amendment," p. 29.
479. Berns, *First Amendment and the Future of American Democracy,* pp. 7-8.
480. Bean, "Pressure for Freedom," p. 62.
481. AR 1, pp. 15-18.
482. AR 2, p. 19.
483. AR 4, p. 29.
484. AR 5, p. 13.
485. AR 33, p. 65.

486. '81 PG, #89.
487. '76 and '81 PGs, #310.
488. '81 PG, #97.
489. ACLU, *Civil Liberties in Reagan's America*, pp. 12-13.
490. Lamson, *Baldwin*, p. 164.
491. R.M. Cornelius, "Their Stage Drew All the World: A New Look at the Scopes Evolution Trial," *Tennessee Historical Quarterly*, Summer 1981, p. 130.
492. Ibid., p. 132.
493. Ibid., p. 133.
494. Ibid., pp. 133-34.
495. Roger Baldwin, "Dayton's First Issue," in *D-Days at Dayton*, ed. Jerry R. Tompkins (Baton Rouge: Louisiana State University Press, 1965), p. 57.
496. '81 PG, #77.
497. Roger Lewin, "Creationism Goes on Trial in Arkansas," *Science*, 4 December 1981, p. 1101.
498. ACLU, *Civil Liberties in Reagan's America*, pp. 10-12.
499. AR 29, p. 70.
500. Caren Marcus, "City School Aide Fired for Wearing Turban," *Pittsburgh Press*, 30 October 1979, p. A1.
501. AR 37. p. 26.
502. AR 41, p. 36.
503. '81 PG, #78.
504. AR 29, p. 69; '81 PG, #79.
505. There have been several polls on this issue; see *Public Opinion*, June/July 1982, p. 40.
506. AR 29, p. 70.
507. AR 38, pp. 20-21.
508. Gertrude Samuels, "The Fight for Civil Liberties Never Stays Won," *New York Times Magazine,* 19 June 1966, p. 58.
509. AR 42, p. 51.
510. Interview with Baldwin.
511. ACLU advertisement, "If the Moral Majority Has Its Way You'd Better Start Praying," *New York Times,* 23 November 1980, p. 22E.
512. Josh Barbanel, "Praying in Schools Still at Issue 17 Years After Ruling," *New York Times,* 26 December 1980, p. A20.
513. Steven V. Roberts, "Prayer Filibuster Is Sustained Again," *New York Times*, 22 September 1982, p. 10.
514. '81 PG, #35.
515. "A Moment of Silence in Schools Approved by Jersey Legislature," *New York Times,* 19 October 1982, p. 1.
516. Alfonso A. Narvaez, "Veto Upset in Jersey to Allow Moment of Silence in Schools," *New York Times,* 17 December 1982, p. 1.
517. Michael Norman, "Students Are Abuzz Over Moment of Silence," *New York Times,* 7 January 1983, p. 10.
518. Joseph F. Sullivan, "U.S. Judge Halts Jersey Schools' Silent Minute," *New York Times,* 11 January 1983, pp. 1, 45.
519. John Kifner, "Angry Chants and 'V' Signs Fill Warsaw," *New York Times,* 18 June 1983, p. 1.
520. Michael Knight, "Constitution and Crowds," *New York Times,* 17 September 1979, p. A18.

521. '81 PG, #95.
522. Ibid., #94.
523. AR '71-'72, p. 10.
524. '81 PG, #96.
525. Ibid., #s 84-85.
526. Bd. Min., 2/17-18/73, p. 20.
527. Quoted by Lamson, *Baldwin*, pp. 266-67.
528. '81 PG, #80.
529. '81 PG, #86.
530. AR 38, p. 22.
531. AR 38, p. 25.
532. AR 35, p. 39.
533. Basile Uddo, "The American Civil Liberites Union: One Step Too Far, Too Often," *America*, 19 May 1979, p. 414.
534. Ibid.
535. George F. Will, "Grinches Chop Away at Christmas to Strengthen Power of State," *Los Angeles Times*, 25 December 1979, p. 7.
536. '81 PG, #88.
537. Interview with Baldwin.
538. Robert F. Drinan, "Religion and the ACLU," *America*, 27 September 1958, p. 665.

5

Conclusion: The ACLU's Contribution to Freedom in the United States

Charles Lam Markmann concluded his 1965 book on the ACLU by commending the Union for adhering to a nonpartisan line and for contributing to the cause of freedom in the United States.[1] The evidence amassed here indicates that Markmann's first conclusion is unwarranted; the opposite case—that the ACLU is a decidedly partisan organization—has repeatedly been made. His second conclusion deserves to be qualified. It would be more accurate to affirm that the ACLU has selectively contributed to freedom in the United States.

Politics Makes Policy

The ACLU is a perfect example of what Irving Kristol calls the "new class." Members of the new class are well-educated activists who have an animus against business, are unmistakenly egalitarian, and can be found working in the public and nonprofit sectors of the economy, particularly in public-interest law firms, government, education, and the media. Although Dennis Wrong and others have raised legitimate questions over the extent to which this segment of the population actually constitutes a "class," it is nonetheless true that the members of the adversary culture are more strategically situated in the social structure today than they have been in the past. In a significant way, the history of the ACLU represents the emergence of the "new class" in the twentieth century.

Politically motivated from the start, the ACLU's first impulse was to enlist in the cause of militant labor by using civil liberties as a means toward that end. Its reluctance to defend capitalists, its initial opposition to the Wagner Act, its nonresponse to Prohibition, its disinterest in the First Amendment provision regarding freedom of religion, and its willingness to launch a libel suit and engage in the censorship of political discourse are evidence of its selective approach to civil liberties. Wedded to the politics of

327

liberalism in its radical form, the ACLU's initial preoccupation with equality and social justice precluded a purist approach to the subject of civil liberties. Nowhere was this more evident than in its attitude toward Soviet communism. To say that many high-ranking members of the ACLU were receptive to Stalinism would be an understatement. Like liberals elsewhere, they justified, rationalized, and understood repression in the Soviet Union as a temporary and expedient phenomenon in service to the making of the Good Society. Its selective perception of the evils of the totalitarian Left was perhaps the Union's most offensive exercise.

Present members of the ACLU recall the 1940 Resolution and the incestuous relationship that the board had with the FBI in the 1950s as its most shameful events. The latter incident was clearly inexcusable, but the 1940 Resolution was not at all inconsistent with the proclaimed purpose of the organization. An organization dedicated to civil liberties has every right to insist that its leadership commit itself without compromise to the defense of the Bill of Rights; supporters of the Gulag have no legitimate role to play in the ACLU. The real shame is that the Union finds it necessary to apologize for the 1940 Resolution. It should instead apologize for not having instituted it twenty years earlier.

As late as 1966 the ACLU was on record as approving of certain restrictions on the liberties of those who belonged to totalitarian parties;[2] it also disallowed anyone from serving on its governing boards who belonged to *or* publicly supported a totalitarian party.[3] It no longer holds to either of these positions. In 1966 it summoned the courage to say that the communist movement "is both a political agitational movement and a part of the Soviet conspiracy."[4] This statement cannot be found in its current policy guide.[5] What has changed? The nature of the communist movement or the thinking of the ACLU? As recent history indicates, it is surely not the former. The 1940 Resolution prescription barring from the governing bodies of the Union anyone who supports totalitarian principles has not been modified, as the ACLU would have it—it has been eliminated altogether for all practical purposes. To be sure, the Union's policy "Qualifications for Governing Boards and Staff" indicates that all personnel must be "unequivocally committed" to civil liberties,[6] but this is not enforced. As proof, consider Lillian Hellman's election to the National Advisory Council of the ACLU in 1982. The Board of Directors approved of Hellman's position after she was chosen by the Nominating Committee.[7] One would have to search high and low to find anyone in the United States who has offered more defenses to Stalinism than Lillian Hellman. Yet her civil libertarian friends have found her to be "unequivocally committed" to their cause.

As a "new-class" organization, the ACLU ascended to a position of considerable power and influence in the 1960s and 1970s. No longer sidetracked by McCarthyism, it redoubled its commitment to egalitarianism by advancing the cause of equal results. More than any other issue, it was the ACLU's affection for affirmative action that rendered its dedication to civil liberties a political exercise. There is absolutely no way that an organization dedicated to the rights of the individual could refuse to defend the rights of Bakke and others without departing from its proclaimed mission. That it did do so only verifies the charge being made here that the Union's commitment to civil liberties is selectively employed. Civil liberties and civil rights, individual liberty and social justice, are not identical. Attempts to squeeze social equality as freedom out of the Fourteenth Amendment is a political exercise—not a constitutional one.

Former board member and Harvard law professor Alan Dershowitz has argued that the ACLU should expand and contract like an accordion and not try to expand just to fill the vacuum.[8] True. But it does not. It does not because its objective is to actualize the agenda of contemporary liberalism. Indeed, the safest prediction that one could make about the future of the ACLU is that it will continue to expand its domain into non-civil liberties areas whenever its resources permit it to do so. From its support for unisex insurance to busing, the Union has consistently sought to justify its activities as a civil liberties crusade instead of as an egalitarian mission. Burt Neuborne, a bright and able addition to the ACLU leadership, is leading the way for the Union to enter headlong into non-civil liberties matters. Neuborne has been trying to persuade his colleagues to declare the poor as a victim group equally deserving of systematic legal protection. The Union's traditional approach to poverty has been to assert itself only when government entitlement programs were distributed unfairly. But Neuborne now wants the ACLU to declare food, medicine, and shelter as a liberty interest as well.[9] By fiat, quality-of-life issues have instantly been converted into the platform of the Bill of Rights.

Peter Steinfels has maintained that "one can have equality without liberty but not liberty without equality."[10] Agreed. But how much equality can be afforded without endangering liberty? For Michael Walzer, liberty and equality "stand best when they stand together."[11] To a degree there may by an optimal condition, but the maximization of one value will inevitably be done at the expense of the other. There is not a zero-sum relationship between liberty and equality, but neither is there a perfect correlation between them. To advance equality we need to advance the powers of the state. There's the rub. As Tocqueville noted, centralization and equality are inseparable. "Pluralist society is free society," explains Robert Nisbet, "exactly in proportion to its ability to protect as large a domain as possible that is governed by the informal, spontaneous, custom-derived, and tradition-sanctioned habits of the mind rather than by the dictates, however, rationalized, of government and judiciary."[12] But, as Michael Oakeshott has observed, the social engineers cannot resist the lure of the state to penetrate the recesses of society that Nisbet says are deserving of protection:

> To some people, "government" appears as a vast reservoir of power which inspires them to dream of what use might be made of it. They have favourite projects, of various dimensions, which they sincerely believe are for the benefit of mankind, and to capture this source of power, if necessary to increase it, and to use it for imposing their favourite projects upon their fellows is what they understand as the adventure of governing men. They are, thus, disposed to recognize government as an instrument of passion; the art of politics is to inflame and direct desire.[13]

Nothing in recent years symbolizes the ACLU's politics better than its relentless attack on the Reagan administration. Surely the ACLU should criticize any administration when it violates civil liberties. But when its statements are consistently one-sided and when its associations with liberal-Left organizations are so pronounced, public declarations of nonpartisanship read as propaganda. Let me be specific. Reagan was not in office two months when the Leadership Conference on Civil Rights, composed of liberal organizations, launched an attack on the administration for its alleged insensitivity to constitutional rights. The NAACP was there, as was the National Organization for Women, the Children's Defense Fund, the AFL-CIO, and over 140 other organizations. And, of course, the ACLU was there too. Union representative John Shattuck warned: "We all see a major threat that radical changes will be made unless massive support for constitutional rights is mounted."[14] When the year ended, Shattuck concluded: "1981 was a bad year for civil liberties. 1982 could be worse. In Washington, a mean-spirited Congress is dominated by a presidential administration whose hostility to individual rights is relentless."[15] At the end of 1982, Shattuck accused the Reagan administration of being an "implacable" foe of civil rights and liberties.[16] Ira Glasser, the executive director, told the members: "During the first two years of the Reagan Administration, we witnessed an unprecedented assault on civil liberties."[17] Henceforward, Glasser would be quick to charge "Reagan's America" with a general disrespect for freedom.[18] The Union was joined in its criticism of Reagan by Americans for Democratic Action and other liberal groups.[19]

The liberal march against Reagan made long strides in 1983 as the ACLU and its sister organizations took to the airwaves to criticize the administration. The Union hooked up with Common Cause, the Women's Legal

Defense Fund, the Sierra Club, and others by using the Vanguard Network on cable television to air its views. The new network allotted three and a half hours per week to liberal organizations,[20] and the "nonpartisan" ACLU could not pass up the opportunity to participate. In June 1983 the Union delivered a three-pronged attack on the Reagan administration. In an open letter to Ambassador Jeane J. Kirkpatrick, Ira Glasser said he was "disturbed" by recent attempts by college faculty and students to silence the ambassador on the campuses, but indicated that he was even more disturbed by her foreign policy positions and her alleged hypocrisy. "Do you honestly believe you can continue to limit the speech of those whose views you find abhorrent," Glasser wrote, "and still hope to persuade others to listen respectfully to your own?"[21] To which one might reply: Does the ACLU honestly believe that it can continue to write open letters such as this without undermining its credibility as a nonpartisan observer of civil liberties? Where was the open letter to Ambassador Andrew Young when he presided over the vote allowing Pol Pot's genocidal regime to become a member of the U.N.? And does Glasser honestly believe that "a primary goal" of the Reagan administration is to violate the Bill of Rights? That is exactly what he told ACLU members at the 1983 Biennial Conference.[22] And why does Glasser find it necessary to badger his constituents with demagogic letters like the one he sent out in June 1983 with "*CENSORED By Order of the President: Executive Order #12356*" printed in large red type on the envelope? The letter was a legitimate appeal for funds. Fine. But is it necessary to make alarmist gestures by stating that it is "ominous" that all members read the "emergency" letter "right now—before it is too late"?[23] Such irrationalism does not make for reasonable discourse and inhibits honest disagreement over the direction of freedom.

Section Two of the ACLU's constitution states that the organization's ends "shall be sought wholly without political partisanship."[24] In light of the ACLU's record, it is puzzling to know why it continues to manifest such pretentiousness. Aside from the 1940s and 1950s, the Union's activities have been decidedly consistent with liberal, and not infrequently liberal-Left, aspirations; even its departure from this line was politically motivated. People's perspectives on civil liberties are bound to reflect their political leanings. The same is true for the ACLU. All one has to do is to check the ACLU's score card on the congressional voting record. For example, for the 97th Congress, the Union signified its approval or disapproval of fourteen pieces of legislation affecting civil liberties voted on by the Congress. Not surprisingly, Gary Hart of Colorado received a 96 percent rating (favorable from the Union's position), Ted Kennedy garnered an 89 percent approval, while Paul Laxalt got a 7 percent rating, and Orrin Hatch earned a rating of 0.[25] Now, everyone knows that Hart and Kennedy are liberals and Laxalt and Hatch are conservatives.

Why does the ACLU not simply declare itself to be an organization in service to the objectives of liberal politics? There are two reasons that it continues to sell itself as a nonpartisan organization. Its reputation and status rest partly on the fact that it is perceived by many persons as being above politics; it does not have anything to gain if it is tagged as just another organization servicing the liberal agenda. The other reason is that if it is seen as a political action group, it would jeopardize its tax-exempt status.[26] It is interesting to note that the ACLU's lobbying efforts have not moved liberals to demand that its tax-exempt status be revoked, while Jerry Falwell's Moral Majority has come under severe pressure from groups like People for the American Way for doing the same thing.[27] There is literally no difference between the strategies of the two organizations: neither endorses candidates for political office directly, but both unquestionably seek to affect the political process in several ways.

Freedom and Order

The ACLU's finest contribution to freedom has been to assure the free circulation of ideas. Clearly the Union has had more to do with securing the right of political dissidents to express their views than any other organization in the country. A problem emerges, however, when paramilitary organizations are granted the same rights that individuals enjoy in expressing their political ideology. As we have seen, the Union fails to distinguish between freedom of expression and freedom of association. Tocqueville saw things differently by arguing that "*unlimited* freedom of association must not be entirely identified with freedom to write. The former is both less necessary and more dangerous than the latter. A nation may set limits there without ceasing to be its own master; indeed, in order to remain its own master, it is sometimes necessary to do so."[28] So convinced was Tocqueville of the necessity to put some limits on political association, that he repeated his position in the second volume of *Democracy in America,* adding, "I certainly do not think that a nation is always in a position to allow its citizens an absolute right of political association, and I even doubt whether there has ever been at any time a nation in which it was wise not to put any limits to the freedom of association."[29]

For over sixty years the ACLU has believed that it is wise not to put any limits on freedom of association. The result: Nazis are granted an equal opportunity to realize their goals. Unsettling as it may be for civil libertarians to acknowledge that a free society may have to choose between some freedom for everyone and total freedom for some, it nonetheless remains a realistic prospect; they prefer to believe that a free society means total freedom for everyone. What is particularly disconcerting about the ACLU's approach to freedom (on this issue as well as others) is its gnostic quality. Far too many ACLU notables have acted as though their perspective on freedom and the law were the only correct one. This is why they have occasionally become apoplectic when others have sharply disagreed with their positions. It is as though those who depart from its thinking not only do not understand the Constitution, but do not promote the cause of freedom either.

The First Amendment does not unconditionally give people the right to assembly. It specifically says that people have the right "peaceably" to assemble. Armed terrorists, with a history of violence, whose modus operandi is coercion unlimited, do not seek the right to peaceably assemble. They seek the right to create warfare. Examples are legion. Most recently, in 1979 in Greensboro, North Carolina, five people were killed and nine injured in a confrontation between Nazis, Klansmen, and Communists. The "Death to the Klan" march took place with the blessings of the local authorities. Before the "parade" began, two tactical squads of police (who were informed of the proceedings) were having lunch a half-hour from the scene of the demonstration; when the firings began, there were no police in sight. Police informant Edward Dawson commented, "You asked for the Klan, now you've got 'em."[30] But the ACLU was not listening. It elects to think that things might have been different had the police been on the scene.

Paramilitary organizations place a priority on the free flow of fusillade, not the free flow of ideas. Indeed, it is their goal to prohibit the free flow of ideas. Yet the ACLU has gone out of its way to see to it that such groups are given as many rights as the Boy Scouts. In defense of the Union, however, the civil libertarians have done a fine job in alerting the public to the dangers that await the implementation of laws that might be used as effectively against the Boy Scouts as they might be in stopping the Nazis. Before considering a rejoinder to the ACLU's position, it would be instructive to examine the Union's critique of such laws. The Skokie case offers many examples.

There was an attempt in Skokie to ban "symbols offensive to the community" and parades by political organizations in "military style" uniforms. David Hamlin of the ACLU is on solid ground when he says that such a law would necessarily ban parades by the Boy Scouts and the American Legion.[31] It is a weak argument to suggest that the First Amendment says nothing about marching in uniforms. It also says nothing about marching in sneakers. Lucky for Little Leaguers that no one takes such reasoning seriously.

Jerome Torshen, the primary lawyer for the Anti-Defamation League of B'nai B'rith in the Skokie case, filed suit against Frank Collin on a novel ground: the Nazis should be enjoined from marching because their march would create menticide. Torshen maintained that the Nazi march would be the "willful infliction of emotional harm" on the Jewish concentration camp survivors. This ADL litigation took the Union by surprise. Hamlin saw the irony in this argument: it assumed that those who would suffer menticide would want to see the Nazis march. The argument fails logically. It also failed in the courts.[32]

In a similar vein, invoking the obscene nature of the presence of Nazis in a community, Gary Wills has suggested, "The relevant body of law in this case is not the First Amendment but nuisance statutes." Wills likened the Nazis' expression to an obscene phone call: "The Nazis . . . are, in effect, broadcasting an obscene phone call to a whole neighborhood instead of a single house."[33] But there appears to be no legal precedent for entertaining such an open-ended proposal.

Many people have contended, with good reason, that the mere presence of Nazis marching in a Jewish community would provoke violence; it is on this basis that they argue against allowing the Nazis to march. Harry Kalven has called this position the "heckler's veto." It places the blame on those who intend to express themselves. Philosopher and ACLU member Carl Cohen has seen through this argument: "If that were granted, no truly controversial position on an incendiary topic could be freely presented. When it could be shown that the probable reaction would be intemperate or disorderly, the advocacy of an unpopular position would have to be forbidden."[34] That is exactly the problem with this position—only sterile debate would be permitted. Besides, the Supreme Court, in *Terminiello v. City of Chicago,* overthrew the conviction of a suspended Catholic priest to partake in an inflammatory racial speech; the riot that took place outside the hall in which Terminiello delivered his speech was not constitutional grounds for his arrest.[35]

The "clear-and-present-danger" argument represents one of the most popular ways with which to stop the Nazis. This position contends that Nazis marching in Skokie is akin to shouting "fire" in a theater falsely. Cohen found three reasons that this argument is deficient. "First, the theater audience is captive, subjected against its will to the shout and its sequel."[36] The Nazis do not command a captive audience. Aryeh Neier has written that "the analogy would be closer if, uninvited and without advance warning, the Nazis were to march into a Skokie synagogue during a service and to start chanting 'Heil Hitler.'"[37] Second, as Cohen points out, "the shouted warning is of such a nature that it permits no discussion." The Nazi march may be answered with a counterdemonstration. Third, the alarm in the theater is false. Nazi speech is false too, but, as Cohen suggests, "being right is not a condition on which permission to demonstrate may be premised."[38]

It appears that the only court-sanctioned way to thwart the success of the Nazis is to establish laws that address injurious speech. The Supreme Court has offered two precedents that have never been directly overruled: *Beauharnais* and *Chaplinsky*. In 1951 a White racist by the name of Joseph Beauharnais was convicted for distributing leaflets at a Chicago meeting urging the segregation of Blacks on the grounds that they all rape, rob, carry guns, and smoke marijuana. The concept employed in *Beauharnais* is group libel. The ACLU has opposed group libel laws consistently since the late 1930s.[39] Skokie lawyers succeeded in passing a group-libel ordinance, but it was struck down by the Illinois courts. The U.S. Court of Appeals for the Seventh Circuit maintained that *Beauharnais* required proof that that group libel would lead to some illicit action; somehow, the court was not convinced that it would.[40] The U.S. Supreme Court passed up the opportunity to settle the matter, i.e. to render judgment on the group libel law; it simply declined to order the requested stay. However, Justice Harry Blackmun noted that there was "some tension" between the Illinois ruling and *Beauharnais,* and conceded that *Beauharnais* was still precedent.[41]

When the Supreme Court decided *Beauharnais,* it was following the lead it had set ten years earlier in *Chaplinsky v. New Hampshire.* It was in *Chaplinsky* that the court acknowledged that there were certain "classes of speech" that were outside the protection of the First Amendment. Chaplinsky was arrested and convicted for shouting at a policemen: "You are a goddamned racketeer [and] a damned Fascist and the whole government of Rochester are Fascists or agents of Fascists."[42] The Supreme Court upheld the Jehovah's Witness's conviction in a unanimous decision. Judge Murphy, writing for the court, said that

> there are certain well-defined and narrowly limited classes of speech, the prevention and punishment of which have never been thought to cause any constitutional problem. These include the lewd and obscene, the profane, the libelous, and insulting or "fighting" words—those which by their utterance inflict injury or tend to incite an immediate breach of the peace. It has been well observed that such utterances are no essential part of any exposition of ideas, and are of such slight social value that any benefit that may be derived from them is clearly outweighed by the social interest in order and morality.[43]

The late Alexander Bickel once punctuated Judge Murphy's reasoning:

> Even speech which advocates no idea can have its consequences. It may inflict injury by its very utterance, as the Court said a generation ago in the

Chaplinsky case, of lewd or profane or fighting words. There is such a thing as verbal violence, a kind of cursing assaultive speech that amounts to almost physical aggression, bullying that is no less punishing because it is simulated.[44]

Although *Chaplinsky* was narrowed in 1972 in *Gooding v. Wilson* to apply to individuals—not to group encounters—the "fighting words" idea is extant. Bickel, one of the finest legal minds of the century, who might have been appointed to the Supreme Court had he not died prematurely, was able to do what ACLU lawyers refuse to do, i.e. recognize the reality of verbal violence. Certain words, in a heated confrontational context, are injurious and assaultive. The fact that even the ACLU does not charge that *Chaplinsky* has been abused by prosecutors and judges suggests that slippery-slope arguments carry little weight. The court properly seized on the intent of the First Amendment, namely, that at its core it provides for the free exposition of ideas; its decision in *Chaplinsky* did not do violence to that fundamental principle. The recognition that morality interests are a proper consideration for the court may not be persuasive to contemporary moral relativists, but it remains as cogent and defensible today as it did in the 1940s. The public weal is not an illusion—it is a social reality.

Amherst scholar Hadley Arkes reminds us that the Founding Fathers understood that a republican regime was "a regime of law before it was anything else. As a regime of law its first obligation was to render justice: to protect its citizens against harms that were inflicted on them unjustly, outside a process of law." Arkes holds that "the most the polity is obliged to do is to respect their [Nazis'] liberty to hold meetings, conduct discussion, and make themselves part of the public discourse."[45] I asked Alan Reitman what he thought of Arkes's suggestion that the Nazis could go speak in a civic arena if they wanted to, but they did not have the right to flaunt their swastikas in the face of Jews. He said, "It's a kind of cute position by saying—don't help them to speak—let them speak in an arena. But that would apply to the labor unions who tried to organize in certain places—so they can march in the streets."[46] That's one of the ACLU's favorite strategies—to compare Nazis to labor unions and other nonviolent groups. In the 1980s when the authorities in Mississippi were trying to stop the Klan, an ACLU lawyer took the complaint and "struck out KKK and wrote in NAACP."[47]

No society can exist without a degree of order, the exact measure of which is open to serious debate. A free society, which prizes civil liberties, must be prepared to accept the risks to order that are entailed in a commitment to the Bill of Rights. But a free society is not obliged to stand by passively while a destructive minority seeks to expand its ranks by exhorting others to enlist in its program of repression. Sidney Hook has argued that "democratic theory and practice would be self-stultifying if they admitted a right to revolution in a democracy because the *faith* of the democrat is that all morally legitimate demands can sooner or later be realized through democratic processes without recourse to revolutionary violence."[48] Similarly, Ernest van den Haag has maintained that "if freedom is to be inalienable . . . invitations to alienate it [cannot] be recognized as a legitimate part of the democratic process."[49] "Common sense, unlike ideology," wrote James Burnham, "understands that you can play a game only with those who accept the rules; and that the rules' protection does not cover anyone who does not admit their restrictions and penalties."[50] That Nazis fail to recognize the rules of democracy is self-evident. It is also evident that many liberals do not consider this to be of striking importance.

The ACLU cannot be persuaded. As Nat Hentoff noted, the Union had no choice but to defend the Nazis in Skokie.[51] The Union had no choice because it left itself with no choice. But the authorities are not tied to the ACLU's straightjacket. They are entrusted with the responsibility of maintaining the democratic process and that means that they have a right and a duty to protect that process from being undermined by those who profess an aversion to freedom. At the very least, the authorities should write and vigorously enforce laws that address the principles in *Beauharnais* and *Chaplinsky*. It may be necessary to do more. Other democracies have.

Marc Fredriksen is the leader of France's Federation of National European Action (FANE). It is the best-known neo-Nazi organization in the country. Responsible for murder, attacks on synagogues, and harassment of Jews, FANE prompted the authorities to respond: In 1980, it was outlawed.[52] Gundolf Köhler is the leader of West Germany's Defense Sport Group. It is the best-known neo-Nazi organization in the country. Responsible for murder, attacks on synagogues, and harassment of Jews, DSG prompted the authorities to respond: In 1978, it was outlawed.[53]

No one questions the fact that France and West Germany are democracies. And no one can maintain that the banning of neo-Nazi groups has led the authorities to extend their reach by outlawing nonterrorist organizations. The experience of these two European democracies renders dubious the ACLU contention that if the Klan or the National Socialist Party were outlawed, the authorities would vitiate the rights of other Americans as well. That position assumes that a slippery-slope condition would inevitably emerge; it also assumes that persons of law are incapable of discriminating between Nazis and those who seek to assemble peacefully. Sidney Hook's reply to the slippery-slope position is instructive:

> The risks and losses of abridgment, to be sure, are always there. So are the risks and losses of refusing to make the abridgment in moments of great

emergency. The abridgment is an incipient tendency which if unchecked *may* result in our hurtling down the slope. But our very *awareness* that we have stepped on a slope is a brake on our precipitous descent.[54]

The ACLU thinks the brakes will fail once we set foot on the slope. This all-or-nothing mentality is one of the most defining characteristics of contemporary liberal thought. The Union embraced this notion long before it became fashionable. Its opposition to the banning of Nazi books in Germany immediately after World War II was representative of the all-or-nothing cast of mind. ACLU claims that outlawing Nazi books would lead to further censorship in West Germany look rather feeble now; Nazi paraphernalia have been banned since the end of the war without endangering civil liberties for anyone save Nazis.

"The Constitution," as Justice Robert Jackson warned, "is not a suicide pact." If that means anything, it means that terrorists ought to be treated differently than democrats. But the ACLU refuses to make such distinctions. It insists that the free speech rights of democrats are jeopardized when we curb the free speech rights of terrorists. Irving Louis Horowitz and Victoria Curtis Bramson have seen through this collapse of intellect: "To argue that law must sanction lawlessness, or that the right to free speech can be proven only by defending the rights of those who would suppress speech, is to place a burden on a legal code that is objectively implausible and logically self-contradictory."[55] No one epitomized the Union's mindset on this issue better than Arthur Garfield Hays, one-time senior ACLU counsel. He once said that he would fight for Hitler's right to free speech and then hope for a riot.[56] His liberal optimism did not allow him to envision the possibility that Hitler would lead the riot against him and other law-abiding citizens. Lenin once said that the capitalist would sell the Communist the rope from which he would be hung. It can also be said that the ACLU would volunteer the platform from which the Bill of Rights would be hung. It would be a cruel irony if those who pervert and intend to subvert the meaning of freedom and democracy were to come to power (remote as this possibilty is) by exploiting the resources of the world's foremost civil liberties organization.

Professional terrorists are not the only threat to order that a democracy faces. Ordinary thugs are a menace too. Frank Carrington, executive director of Americans for Effective Law Enforcement, has labeled the ACLU as the dominant antivictim organization in the United States.[57] Whether Carrington is right or not may not be as important as the perception that many Americans have about the ACLU. The Union should be more sensitive to its image as an antivictim organization. It is certainly not antivictim to defend the rights of the accused, but it is inviting to think of the ACLU as antivictim when it presses hard for the rights of the accused and the convicted without offering the victims of crime an occasional genuflection. If it showed half as much sympathy for victims as it does for criminals, it would remove any stigma it currently carries. When people read about ACLU efforts to sue state prison officials in New York in behalf of inmates who rioted and were "brutalized" for their violence,[58] it raises the eyebrow of those who rarely read of ACLU empathy for crime victims.

The ACLU has done an excellent job in defending the rights of the accused. That is what it is supposed to do. The police are supposed to provide order. Both the agents of civil liberties and the agents of order are indispensable in a free society. Unfortunately, the ACLU often acts as though only its mission is essential to the production of a free society. More reasonable is Sidney Hook: "The potential victim has at least just as much a human right not to be violently molested, interfered with, and outraged as the person accused of such crimes has to a fair trial and skillful defense. As a citizen most of the rights guaranteed me under the Bill of Rights become nugatory if I am hopelessly crippled by violence, and all of them become extinguished if I am killed."[59]

When it comes to crime control, it is clear what remedies the ACLU opposes, but it is less than certain what strategies it recommends. It does not want to modify the exclusionary rule—a rule that the British, French, Swiss, Australians, and Canadians have learned to live without. And it surely does not favor incarceration. It prefers probation. Why? Because "probation maximizes the liberty of the individual, while at the same time vindicating the authority of the law and effectively protecting the public from further violations of the law."[60] Notice that the Union's first concern is to maximize the liberty of the convicted criminal. That priority does read as antivictim. The purpose of the criminal law is not to maximize the liberty of convicted criminals but to punish them and to maximize the liberty of the innocent. Furthermore, the law is hardly vindicated if molesters are simply ordered back into the community from which they came. The Union says that probation will allow the convicted to continue "normal community contact."[61] Considering the nature of the "normal community contacts" that repeat offenders experience, the ACLU's idea is patently oxymoronic.

Freedom and Morality

The Founding Fathers adopted the Bill of Rights as a series of provisions to protect the rights of the minority against the wishes of the majority, and to cordon off a sphere of liberty for the individual against the encroachments of the state. But the Founding Fathers were not myopic; they recognized certain responsibilities that the government had a right to exercise. Peace and domestic tranquility, among other values, were seen as fundamental to the ordering of the good society. Moreover, none of the members of the first Congress thought that liberty could be achieved without referencing the need for a modicum of social cohesiveness. Pluralism was essential, but it was never elevated to the status of an absolute. In short, restraints on the passions of the individual were as important as restraints on government. The pursuit of freedom in a democracy was not a directionless endeavor; it was done in service to the realization of a society wherein individual rights and the rights of the community could prosper without one endangering the other.

The writings of the Founding Fathers are laced with concern for moderation, checks and balances, and sobriety. Unfortunately, these qualities have often escaped the reasoning of the ACLU. In its seven decades of existence, the Union has exercised a monistic fixation on individual rights (except when social equality is involved). There is a direct line between the ACLU's perception of the individual and society and the position put forward by John Stuart Mill. The social consequences that inexorably flow from Mill's logic have been captured by sociologist Robert Nisbet: "From the Greenwich Village of the early twentieth century to the contemporary chaos of cultural anarchy, hedonism, narcissism, and generalized flouting of idols there is a straight line best defined as Mill's one very simple principle."[62]

In a trenchant analysis of Mill's thought, Gertrude Himmelfarb explains that Mill's position in *On Liberty* incorrectly equates individualism with liberty.[63] Defending Mill is Ronald Dworkin, who claims that Himmelfarb's argument "does not distinguish between the idea of liberty as license . . . and liberty as independence."[64] Dworkin complains that Himmelfarb wrongly assigns to Mill the former concept of liberty. He challenges the idea that the inner core of Mill's logic threatens anarchy: "In fact it promotes the more complex idea of liberty as independence."[65]

Himmelfarb has not misread Mill: the inner core of his logic does threaten anarchy (and by extrapolation, so does the ACLU's logic). Dworkin has misread Himmelfarb. She was careful to discriminate between the intent of Mill's doctrine (liberty as independence) and its effect (liberty as license). She admits that Mill did not foresee all the implications and consequences of his thought.[66] Her statement on Mill's purpose in writing *On Liberty* and its subsequent effect is cogently argued: "His only purpose there was to establish the practical principle of neutrality—the principle that society could no more intervene in matters of morality than in matters of truth. But in making this practical point as strongly as he did, he could not help weakening the status of morality and its hold upon the individual."[67]

"No society," contends Owen Chadwick, "could put into practice all the principles of [*On Liberty*] and remain a society."[68] What Mill did not emphasize was that man's capacity to function as a social being requires a substantial diet of social nourishment. "He did not fear the isolation of individuals or groups," said Isaiah Berlin, "the factors that make for the alienation and disintegration of individuals and societies."[69] Mill wanted the individual to be free from both state and society (as does the ACLU in matters of morality), but nowhere did he suggest where the individual ought to be anchored. As John Dewey noticed, Mill implied that individuals "have a full-blown psychological and moral nature, having its own set of laws, independently of their association with one another."[70]

Edmund Burke wrote that "men are qualified for civil liberty in exact proportion to their disposition to put moral chains upon their own appetites."[71] There are enough indications today to question whether some people are willing to put as much as a brace on their own appetites. Alexsandr Solzhenitsyn, as well as others, has drawn attention to the spiritual and moral vacuum in American society. Solzhenitsyn understands that moral pollution is as dangerous to the well-being of a society as air and water pollution may be. So do the Japanese. That is why the loss of social solidarity is seen by many Japanese leaders as the major threat to their democracy.[72] A "society" of depraved aggregates of individuals cannot appreciate civil liberties. They were meant to be enjoyed by whole human beings living and interacting in society.

The unremitting assault on norms, on community—in the name of individual liberty—is self-defeating. It will not make the individual free. On the contrary, the exposed, anomic, socially naked individual is likely to seek solidarity in some contemporary cult or total institution of one sort or the other. Despotism awaits the fully liberated individual, freed from custom, social convention, and tradition, as surely as it awaits those who seek communion with the state. We have learned that individuals are not free when they are totally in the grip of society, but we have yet to learn that they are equally unfree when society totally abandons its grip on individuals. Liberticide is a condition that emanates just as effectively from the enervation of societal control over the individual as it does from the eclipse of the individual by the state. Unbridled libertarianism yields libertinism—not liberty.

A free society, one that respects the individual and the social order, ought to write and enforce laws that censor hard-core pornography. The ACLU rejects any attempt to regulate or ban pornography because somehow it sees obscenity as vital a component of free speech as political discourse. It is fair to say that it comes to this conclusion by embracing the social vision of Gay Talese. Commenting on Talese's perspective and contrasting it with his own, is Ernest van den Haag:

> Gay's view—one that is widespread—is that society consists of individuals, each independent of each other, and that the task of the government is merely to protect the individual from interference by others. This is not my view. My view is that no society can survive unless there are bonds among its members, unless its members identify with each other, recognize each other as humans and do not think of each other simply as sources of pleasure or unpleasure. Human solidarity is based on our ability to think of each other not purely as means, but as ends in ourselves. Now the point of all pornography, in my opinion, is that it invites us to regard the other person purely as a subject of exploitation for sexual pleasure.[73]

James Fitzjames Stephens questioned the reasoning of those who opposed restraints on immorality. Why treat such efforts as if they were bad?[74] Similarly, Isaiah Berlin feels that those who oppose such efforts as "intolerable infringements of personal liberty" presuppose "a belief that the activities which such laws forbid are fundamental needs of men as men, in a good (or, indeed, any) society."[75] The ACLU, of course, is afraid that once we regulate or ban hard-core pornography, we will not stop until other arenas of freedom of expression are affected. Himmelfarb seizes on the irony of the liberal view: "It is ironic that liberals who hotly reject the 'domino theory' in foreign affairs implicitly hold to some such theory in the realm of civil liberties, the denial of any particular liberty presumably setting in motion a process that will result in the toppling of all liberties."[76]

Van den Haag has argued that "the main damage pornography does is not to the individual but to the social climate."[77] The ACLU is not unaware that there is some reality, what Durkheim called a social fact, that is the social climate. During the Vietnam war, it called attention to the "atmosphere" of violence that the war engendered at home by creating a "climate" of repression.[78] Even today it recognizes that "the First Amendment is not inconsistent with reasonable regulations designed to restrict sensory intrusions so intense as to be assaultive."[79] Well said. That position, which is derived from the Union's policy "Captive Audiences," is applicable to pornography as well. However, the ACLU continues to insist that nothing less than a direct cause-and-effect relationship be established between pornography and antisocial behavior before restraints can be employed. This is surely sociological subterfuge because, as any social scientist will confirm, unicausality is an oddity of the first order; human behavior is typically the product of multiple forces. But that is not to say that we are not affected by what we, and others, read and see. Alexander Bickel got it right when he said:

To grant this right [the right to view pornography] is to affect the world about the rest of us, and to impinge on other privacies and other interests as those concerned with the theater in New York have found, apparently to their surprise. Perhaps each of us can, if he wishes, effectively avert the eye and stop the ear. Still what is commonly read and seen and heard and done intrudes upon us all, wanted or not, for it constitutes our environment.[80]

Bickel wrote that before obscenity descended to new lows. One example of the "new obscenity" was featured on a public-access channel in New York: the show consisted of nothing but the killing of a dog.[81]

The ACLU maintains that obscenity is too difficult to define; what is obscene to one person may not be so to the next. But how credible is this popular assertion? A short walk from ACLU headquarters in New York City is Father Bruce Ritter's Covenant House. The children he and his underpaid staff try to help have frequently been used in pornographic movies—the kind of movies that the Supreme Court made illegal but the ACLU defended. If the ACLU cannot decide that child pornography ought to be outlawed, then there is virtually no form of pornography that it is not willing to defend as free speech. The Union, and many liberals, do not seem to recognize that obscenity is always partly but never always in the eyes of the beholder. To be sure, individual tastes differ. The same is true of wine tasting. The best bottle of wine, we are told, is that which best suits our taste. But no seasoned oenophile would admit that we are without standards, however subjective, for rating wines as excellent, good, fair, and poor. Standards do exist and that is why wine drinkers anxiously await the results of international wine-tasting contests. Standards exist with regard to obscenity too. We think it indecent if someone defecates in public. We think it indecent if children, and now infants ("bambino sex"), are used in pornographic movies. That some might find such examples okay, or even edifying, does not mean that culturally recognized standards of decency have not been violated.

Other democratic countries have not found it impossible to regulate or ban obscene material without impinging on free speech rights generally. For example, Britain, France, Germany, Italy, Sweden, Norway, Australia, New Zealand, and Canada have film censorship systems that control films intended even for adult viewing; Belgium, the Netherlands, and Denmark focus on protecting children only. The *Report of the Committee on Obscenity and Film Censorship* (United Kingdom) stated that no other country has a system "quite as relaxed as that of the United States, which is purely voluntary and aims solely at classifying films in order to provide advance information to help parents to judge whether their children should be allowed to see particular films."[82] Even this relaxed system is too restrictive for the ACLU: it wants no controls whatsoever. The Union's view is not widely accepted. For instance, when the British report was submitted to Parliament in 1979, it recommended that live sex performances be banned outright regardless of "any intrinsic merit [they] might possess."[83] Its proposals also discriminated between the print and pictorial media by suggesting restrictions on the latter.[84] Denmark, which is often regarded as having the most liberalized obscenity laws, outlawed the movie *Star Wars* for children under the age of thirteen.[85] In France, the minister of justice and culture may refuse a certificate altogether to films that are "offensive to human dignity"; approximately two dozen films are banned each year.[86] The Ontario Board of Censorship banned *Pretty Baby*, a story of a teenage prostitute in a New Orleans brothel, and cut portions of *The Tin Drum* before releasing it.[87]

The American people may or may not think it wise to follow the lead of other democracies by establishing a film censorship board. But if other free countries have not slipped on the censorship slope by washing away all civil liberties, there is no reason to believe that things would be any different in the United States.

The people in any community have a right, albeit not an absolute one, to maintain their way of life. The ACLU instantly recognizes this when it addresses issues concerning the Amish and the American Indian, but somehow fails to realize that their more modern brethren are entitled to the same sensitivity. On several occasions the Union has underscored the need for the courts to take into consideration the social and cultural needs of the Amish.[88] By allowing the Amish to educate their own children, the court was respectful of their customs and traditions. By the same token, the ACLU has exercised admirable sociological judgment by defending the right of American Indians to retain their "cultural and religious heritage."[89] It is a pity that the Union does not apply the same reasoning to the rest of us.

Nicholas Von Hoffman has said that "after ten years of increasingly crazy civil-liberties litigation, we as a society aren't free, but we are poorer." What led Von Hoffman to this conclusion was his observation that "the ACLU has so stretched and distorted the definition of our 'rights' that they are beginning to look to many people like wrongs. . . . The ironic triumph of the ACLU's activities has been to convince millions of people that civil liberties leave them naked and helpless against any and every sort of malefactor."[90] A strong statement, coming as it does from a person not known to harbor ill feelings against liberals. Von Hoffman has caught onto something real: in involving itself in many frivolous lawsuits and having driven civil liberties directly into the face of other worthy values, the ACLU has assaulted the sensibilities of many Americans. "The dedicated, tunnel-visioned enthusiast at the local ACLU office," charges Von Hoffman, "re-

mains a committed and disinterested believer for sure; he remains dedicated and pure of heart as he trivializes the Bill of Rights."[91] Yes, when
ACLU lawyers declare that tattooing is an "art form" deserving of First
Amendment protection,[92] they are trivializing the meaning of civil liberties. Or when they seek to ban the singing of "Silent Night" in the schools.
It is sad but true that civil libertarians are more concerned about the right
of a fourteen-year-old girl to buy a dildo from the corner drugstore than
they are in the quality of her religious training. Not to sell her the dildo
would be to discriminate—may even be "sexist"—and the ACLU will have
none of that! Whether she suffers from spiritual poverty, however, lies
outside the corrective hand of the quality-of-life civil libertarian.

The Future of Liberalism

Charles Frankel sees as "liberalism's great task" the need to balance the
rights of the individual and the rights of the community.[93] The ACLU,
being a strong force in the liberal community could help to bring about a
renaissance of liberalism. As a point of departure, it could begin to examine the relationship between civil liberties and other competing and noble
values. By doing so, it would divert the Union away from its hypercon-
centration on individualism. It might come to accept Madison's challenge
to those who professed an interest in democracy: "A good government
implies two things: first, fidelity to the object of government, which is the
happiness of the people; secondly, a knowledge of the means by which that
object can be best attained."[94] Achieving the happiness of the people is a
tall order. But it surely cannot be achieved by sacrificing standards of
civility in exchange for civil liberties.

"Liberals have learned, at fearful cost," notes Himmelfarb, "the lesson
that absolute power corrupts absolutely. They have yet to learn that absolute liberty may also corrupt absolutely."[95] Henry Fairlie was thinking
along the same lines when he told liberals that they have "perverted every
good truth they have held in their trust into a trivial rhetorical posture.
They have all but stripped society of any redeeming social value. They have
left themselves with barely an argument to defend the decencies of which
they were once the jealous guardians."[96] Liberals need to recognize, as
Madison did, that "liberty may be endangered by the abuses of liberty as
well as by the abuses of power."[97] Accepting Madison's advice suggests that
it would be wise to reassess the relationship between freedom and order.

Freedom and order are not direct opposites. It is true that a society can
have order without freedom, but it is also true that a society cannot have
freedom without order. Order, when taken to extremes, descends into authoritarianism. That much is acknowledged by everyone. What is not com-

monly recognized is that freedom, taken to extremes, descends into
anarchy *that abets* the likelihood of authoritarianism. The surest way to
prevent order from descending into authoritarianism is to safeguard a large
area wherein civil liberties can thrive. The surest way to prevent freedom
from descending into anarchy, and the specter of authoritarianism that
awaits its unfolding, is to take restrictive steps that insure peace and
tranquility.

Rationalists from Plato to contemporary Marxists have believed in the
final harmony of ideas.[98] But rational harmony and ultimate agreement of
values has never been achieved.[99] Liberty, equality, justice, peace, happiness, security, order, social solidarity—all are virtuous goals. At some
point, however, decisions must be made as to which value, in a given
circumstance, ought to be honored more than any other. What is critical is
not to emasculate other values while elevating one above the other. As
Samuel Huntington has suggested, "A value which is normally good in
itself is not necessarily optimized when it maximized."[100] Surely liberals
understand this when they criticize business people for relentlessly pursuing profits to the exclusion of other values. The same is true when liberals,
or conservatives, relentlessly pursue only one value; the effect is to dissipate
and enervate other values. The ACLU has yet to learn this lesson. Having
made some vital contributions to freedom in the United States, and being
in a position to make many more, the ACLU would make us all better off if
it would practice more moderation and restraint in its decision-making.
Ideally, an organization dedicated to the Bill of Rights should never be put
on the defensive. That the ACLU has is largely its own fault.

Notes

1. Charles Lam Markmann, *The Noblest Cry* (New York: St. Martin's Press, 1965), pp. 426-28.
2. '66 PG, #85.
3. The 1940 Resolution was still policy in 1966.
4. '66 PG, #85.
5. '81 PG, #99.
6. Ibid., #520.
7. Bd. Min., 6/12-13/82.
8. J. Anthony Lukas, "The ACLU Against Itself," *New York Times Magazine*, 9 July 1978, p. 26.
9. Burt Neuborne, "The ACLU and Poverty," *Civil Liberties*, June 1983, p. 5.
10. Peter Steinfels, *The Neo-Conservatives* (New York: Simon and Schuster, 1979), p. 231.
11. Michael Walzer, *Radical Principles* (New York: Basic Books, 1980), p. 256.
12. Robert Nisbet, *Twilight of Authority* (New York: Oxford University Press, 1975), p. 240.

13. Michael Oakeshott, *Rationalism in Politics* (London: Methuen, 1962), p. 191.
14. Bernard Weinraub, "Liberal Groups are Joining Forces to Defend Their Goals and Gains," *New York Times*, 9 March 1981, p. B6.
15. John Shattuck, "State of Siege: The Bill of Rights in Congress 1981-82, "*Civil Liberties Alert*, February 1982, p.1.
16. John Shattuck, "Victories in Congress Offset by Defeats in Administration," *Civil Liberties*, November 1982, p. 1.
17. Memo, Ira Glasser to ACLU members, 6 December 1982.
18. See ACLU, *Civil Liberties in Reagan's America*, October 1982, for several examples.
19. Adam Clymer, "Liberal Study Finds Reagan Lacking," *New York Times*, 3 June 1982, p. B10.
20. Lynn Rosellini and Phil Gailey, "Liberals on the Air," *New York Times*, 3 January 1983, p. 9.
21. Ira Glasser, "An Open Letter to Ambassador Jeane J. Kirkpatrick," *Civil Liberties*, June 1983, p. 12.
22. "Civil Liberties Leader Assails Administration," *New York Times*, 20 June 1983, p. A10.
23. Letter, Ira Glasser to ACLU members, June 1983.
24. '81 PG, #501.
25. *Civil Liberties Alert*, October/November 1982, pp. 11-12.
26. Robert Pear, "Administration Drafts Rules to Limit Lobbying by Nonprofit Groups," *New York Times*, 1 July 1983, p. A7.
27. "Falwell's Letter Raises Tax Dispute," *New York Times*, 13 October 1982, p. 16.
28. Alexis de Tocqueville, *Democracy in America*, ed. J. P. Mayer, (Garden City, N.Y.: Doubleday, 1969), p. 191.
29. Ibid., p. 524.
30. PBS's "Frontline" aired a documentary on the Greensboro violence on 24 January 1983; Jessica Savitch presided over the film and offered commentary.
31. David Hamlin, *The Nazi/Skokie Conflict* (Boston: Beacon Press, 1980), pp. 77-79.
32. Ibid., pp. 99-117.
33. Quoted, Franklyn Haiman, *Speech and Law in a Free Society* (Chicago: University of Chicago Press, 1981), pp. 137-38.
34. Carl Cohen, "The Right to Be Offensive—Skokie: The Extreme Test of Our Faith in Free Speech," *Nation*, 15 April 1978, pp. 3-4, (reprint).
35. Ibid.
36. Ibid.
37. Aryeh Neier, *Defending My Enemy* (New York: Dutton, 1979), p. 141.
38. Cohen, "Right to Be Offensive," pp. 3-4.
39. See AR 17, p. 55; AR 29, p. 21; AR 41, p. 27; '81 PG, #6.
40. Hamlin, *Nazi/Skokie Conflict*, p. 160.
41. Hadley Arkes, *The Philosopher in the City* (Princeton: Princeton University Press, 1981), p. 31.
42. Quoted, Cohen, "Right to Be Offensive," p. 4.
43. Quoted, Hadley Arkes, "Marching Through Skokie," *National Review*, 12 May 1978, p. 590.
44. Alexander Bickel, *The Morality of Consent* (New Haven: Yale University Press, 1975), p. 72.

The Politics of the ACLU

45. Arkes, "Marching Through Skokie," p. 591.
46. Interview with Reitman.
47. ACLU, *Civil Liberties in Reagan's America*, p. 24.
48. Sidney Hook, *The Paradoxes of Freedom* (Berkeley and Los Angeles: University of California Press, 1970), p. 113.
49. Quoted, Neier, *Defending My Enemy*, p. 145.
50. James Burnham, *Suicide of the West* (New York: Arlington House, 1964), p. 229.
51. Nat Hentoff, "The ACLU's Trial by Swastika," *Social Policy*, January/February 1978, p. 52.
52. "French Jew Says He Infiltrated Neo-Nazi Group," *Pittsburgh Press*, 30 November 1980, p. B6.
53. "Neo-Nazi Group Suspected in Blast That Killed 12 at Munich Festival," *New York Times*, 29 September 1980, p. A4.
54. Hook, *Paradoxes of Freedom*, pp. 47-48.
55. Irving Louis Horowitz and Victoria Curtis Bramson, "Skokie, the ACLU and the Endurance of Democratic Theory," *Law and Contemporary Problems*, Spring 1979, p. 343.
56. Barton Bean, "Pressure for Freedom: The American Civil Liberties Union," Ph.D. diss., Cornell University, 1955, p. 389.
57. Frank G. Carrington, *The Victims* (New York: Arlington House, 1975), p. 205.
58. "Inmates Win Right to Sue the State," *New York Times*, 18 June 1983, p. 26.
59. Sidney Hook, *Philosophy and Public Policy* (Carbondale and Edwardsville: Southern Illinois University Press, 1980), p. 132.
60. '81 PG, #239.
61. Ibid.
62. Robert Nisbet, *Prejudices* (Cambridge: Harvard University Press, 1982), p. 214.
63. Gertrude Himmelfarb, *On Liberty and Liberalism* (New York: Knopf, 1974), p. 310.
64. Ronald Dworkin, *Taking Rights Seriously* (Cambridge: Harvard University Press, 1978), p. 262.
65. Ibid., p. 263.
66. Himmelfarb, *On Liberty and Liberalism*, p. 309.
67. Ibid., p. 312.
68. Owen Chadwick, *The Secularization of the European Mind in the Nineteenth Century* (Cambridge: Cambridge University Press, 1975), p. 30.
69. Isaiah Berlin, *Four Essays on Liberty* (Oxford: Oxford University Press, 1969), p. 183.
70. John Dewey, *Liberalism and Social Action* (New York: Capricorn Books, 1935), p. 40.
71. Quoted, Robert Nisbet, *The Twilight of Authority* (New York: Oxford University Press, 1975), p. 72.
72. Ezra F. Vogel, *Japan as Number 1* (New York: Harper Colophon Books, 1979), pp. 128-29.
73. The exchange between van den Haag and Talese was moderated by Walter Goodman, "What Is a Civil Libertarian to Do When Pornography Becomes So Bold," *New York Times*, 21 November 1976, sec. 2, pp. 1, 26.
74. James Fitzjames Stephens, *Liberty, Equality, Fraternity* (London: Smith, Elder, 1874), p. 60.

75. Berlin, *Four Essays on Liberty*, pp. 169-70.
76. Himmelfarb, *On Liberty and Liberalism*, p. 323.
77. Goodman, "What Is a Civil Libertarian to Do," exchange between van den Haag and Talese, p. 26.
78. '76 PG, #108.
79. '81 PG, #42.
80. Bickel, *Morality of Consent*, p. 74.
81. William Allan, "Sex Industry Victimizes Children," *Pittsburgh Press*, 17 January 1982, p. C1.
82. *Report of the Committee on Obscenity and Film Censorship* (London: Her Majesty's Stationery Office, 1979), p. 142.
83. Ibid., p. 162.
84. Ibid., p. 160.
85. Ibid., p. 225.
86. ibid., p. 226.
87. Andrew H. Malcolm, "Ontario Censors Cut 'The Tin Drum,'" *New York Times*, 3 June 1980, p. C7.
88. Bd. Min., 5/23/66; '76 PG, #75; AR 36, p. 29; AR 42, pp. 51-52.
89. '81 PG, #313.
90. Nicholas Von Hoffman, "When Civil Liberties Become Liabilities," *Penthouse*, April 1982, pp. 100-1.
91. Ibid., p. 101.
92. George Will, *Statecraft as Soulcraft* (New York: Simon and Schuster, 1983), p. 89.
93. Charles Frankel, "Does Liberalism Have a Future?" in *The Relevance of Liberalism*, ed. Zbigniew Brzezinski (Boulder, Colo.: Westview Press, 1978), p. 119.
94. James Madison, Federalist Paper 62 in *The Federalist Papers*, Mentor Book ed. (New York: New American Library, 1961), p. 380.
95. Himmelfarb, *On Liberty and Liberalism*, p. 335.
96. Henry Fairlie, "Who Speaks for Values?" *New Republic*, 31 January 1981, p. 18.
97. Madison, Federalist Paper 63, in *The Federalist Papers*, Mentor Book ed. (New York: New American Library, 1961), p. 387.
98. Berlin, *Four Essays on Liberty*, p. 168.
99. Kenneth Minogue, *The Liberal Mind* (London: Methuen, 1963), p. 200.
100. Samuel P. Huntington, "The Democratic Distemper," *Public Interest*, Fall 1975, p. 37.

Name Index

358   The Politics of the ACLU

Subject Index

employees, 61; hospital patients, 61; juveniles, 263-64; lawyers/clients, 61; mental patients, 61; mentally ill, 88, 89, 92; mentally retarded, 61, 88, 89; migrant farm workers, 92; minorities, 61-81; old people, 61; policemen, 61, 62; poor, 61, 81-88, 92, 329; pornographers, 92; prisoners, 61, 92, 264-65; property, 45; servicemen, 61, 173, 193, 199, 200; students, 61, 92, 274-77; tenants, 61; veterans, 61, 94; victims, 258, 259, 264, 338, 339; young people, 61. *See also* Bill of Rights; Economic rights
Rockefeller Foundation, 19
Roe v. Wade, 95, 100-02, 279
Roosevelt administration (FDR), 156
Roth v. U.S., 287, 291
Rowan v. U.S. Post Office, 292
Russian Revolution, 132-34, 144

Sacco and Vanzetti, trial of, 129-31, 165
San Antonio School District v. Rodriguez, 85, 108
San Diego CLU, 252, 253
Scatter-site housing, 71, 72
Schenck v. U.S., 8, 127
Scopes "Monkey" Trial, 16, 302-4
Scottsboro case, 65
Scranton CLU, 228
Security tests, 158, 168, 169, 174
Sedition Act (1918), 127
Sedition, 156, 157
Segregation, 67-69
Senate Committee on Government Operations, 172
Senate Committee on the Judiciary, 268
Senate Subcommittee on Immigration and Refugee Policy, 205
Senate Subcommittee on Internal Security, 165
Sex Side of Life, The, 244
Sexual assault, 95
Sierra Club, 331
"Sixty Minutes," 241
Skokie, xi, 3, 19, 48, 251-57, 308, 333, 334, 337
Smith-Connally Act, 53
Smith Act, 156, 173, 176, 185
Social justice, meaning of, 57

Socialist Party, 39, 140, 145
Society for Cutting Up Men (SCUM), 91
Solidarity (Poland), 207
South African Rugby team, 228
Southern California CLU, 43, 157, 190, 194, 201, 252, 253, 267
Soviet Russia Today, 138
Soviet Union, 132-38, 144, 145, 147, 149, 151, 161, 163, 164, 168, 172, 173, 175, 230, 234-36, 267, 328
Spanish Relief Campaign, 150
Sputniks, 172
Star Wars, 344
Strange Interlude, 290
State Department, 193
Students for a Democratic Society (SDS), 57, 193, 195
Stuyvesant Town, 69
Subversive Activities Control Act, 192
Subversive Activities Control Board, 67
Suicide, 279
Survey, 28
Symbolic speech, 226-28

Taft-Hartley Act, 53
Teachers, 61, 153, 165, 169, 173, 174, 191
Teamsters Union, 156
Terminiello v. City of Chicago, 334
Terrorism, 206
Times (Chattanooga), 303
Tin Drum, 344
Tinker v. Community School District, 225, 276
Totalitarianism, 191, 328
Trial of Elizabeth Gurley Flynn, 190
Tribune (Chicago), 239
Tropic of Cancer, 290
Tropic of Capricorn, 290
Truancy, 275, 276
Truman administration, 172
Tuition tax credits, 69
Twentieth-Century Fund, 273

Ugly George Hour, 288
Ulysses, 176, 245
Union of Russian Workers, 127
Union shop, 46, 55
Unions, *See* Labor
U.S. Civil Service Commission, 153
Unisex insurance, 329